The German Empire
1871–1918

Hans-Ulrich Wehler was born on 11 September 1931. He studied History and Sociology at the Universities of Cologne, Bonn and Athens/Ohio, USA. He received his PhD in 1960 and completed his habilitation thesis in 1968. He taught at the University of Cologne from 1968 to 1970 and at the Free University of Berlin during 1970 to 1971, before moving to a Chair of History at the University of Bielefeld in 1971. He has held several guest professorships: at Harvard University (1972), Princeton (1976) and Stanford University (1983/4).

His publications include: *Sozialdemokratie u. Nationalstaat, 1840–1914* (1962, 1971²); *Bismarck u. der Imperialismus* (1969, 1984⁵); *Krisenherde des Kaiserreichs 1871–1918* (1970, 1979²); *Geschichte als Historische Sozialwissenschaft* (1973, 1980³); *Das deutsche Kaiserreich 1871–1918* (1973, 1985⁶); *Der Aufstig des amerikanischen Imperialismus 1865–1900* (1974); *Modernisierungstheorie u. Geschichte* (1975); *Historische Sozialwissenschaft u. Geschichtsschreibung* (1980); *Nationalitätenpolitik in Jugoslawien* (1980); *Preußer is wieder chic . . . Politik und Polemik in 20 Essays* (1983); *Grundzüge der amerikanischen Außenpolitik* (1983). He has also edited anthologies such as: 'Historische Reihe' of the *Neue Wissenschaftiche Bibliothek*, 39 vols. (1966–80); *Deutsche Historiker*, 9 vols. (1971–82); *Arbeitsbücher zur modernen Geschichte*, 10 vols. (1976–81); *Neue Historische Bibliothek*, 18 vols. to date (1983/4); co-editor of *Kritische Studien zur Geschichtswissenschaft*, 64 vols. to date (1972–84) and of *Geschichte und Gessellschaft. Zeitschrift für Historische Sozialwissenschaft* (1975ff.).

HANS-ULRICH WEHLER

The German Empire
1871–1918

Translated from the German by
KIM TRAYNOR

Berg Publishers

LEAMINGTON SPA/DOVER, NEW HAMPSHIRE
1985

Berg Publishers Ltd
24, Binswood Avenue, Leamington Spa,
Warwickshire CV32 5SQ, UK
51 Washington Street, Dover,
New Hampshire 03820, USA

First published 1985
© Berg Publishers 1985
Translated from the German by permission of
Verlages Vandenhoeck & Ruprecht, Göttingen
© Vandenhoeck & Ruprecht, Göttingen, 1973

British Library Cataloguing in Publication Data

Wehler, Hans-Ulrich
   The German empire 1871–1918.
   1. Germany—Politics and government—1871–1918
   I. Title II. Das Deutsche Kaiserreich 1871–1918
   English
   320.943   JN3388

   ISBN 0-907582-22-2
   ISBN 0-907582-32-X Pbk

Library of Congress Catalog Card Number 84-73484

Printed in Great Britain by Billings of Worcester

Contents

Translator's Preface

The purpose behind this translation is to bring the work of Professor Hans-Ulrich Wehler to the attention of a wider readership outside Germany, where this book was first published in 1973.[1] It may also serve as a valuable introduction to some of the main concerns of West German scholarship in the field of modern German history since the publication in 1961 of Professor Fritz Fischer's study of German war aims in the First World War.[2]

The questions raised by Fischer's work concerned the role of continuity in German history and the influence of social and economic factors on the political decisions of her statesmen in the period before 1914; they led a new generation of younger German historians to call, in the early 1960s, for a more systematic re-interpretation of the recent German past together with the development of an appropriate theoretical framework which would adequately explain the socio-economic processes behind these decisions.

Much of the ensuing discussion questioned the validity of the central tenets and methods of the classical German historicist tradition.[3] Upheld by the majority of university historians (in their role as German civil servants) this tradition, with its emphasis on the state, the crucial importance of foreign policy and the decisive role of statesmen exercising their free will, had dominated German historical thinking throughout the nineteenth century. Early attempts to widen the scope of academic enquiry beyond the purely political sphere into the realms of social and economic history were largely ignored. Those social scientists, like Max Weber, who did not share the ideological presuppositions of the historical profession remained suspect in the eyes of a socially and politically conservative body, for their critical analyses involving a demystification of the social process and its power relationships were seen as too closely related to oppositional Socialist views on the social problems created at the time by the new forces of capitalism and industrialisation.

1

Through a combination of political, social and, not least, institutional factors the influence of historicist assumptions persisted relatively unbroken down to and even beyond the demise of the German nation state in 1945.[4] It was not until the challenge posed by Fischer, who himself followed conventional methods in arguing his case from official diplomatic archive material, that a new orientation began to appear in the published works of German historians.[5] A growing number looked increasingly towards the modern social sciences for suitable methodologies to investigate the historical phenomena under discussion. It was argued that historicism's strict dependence on the philological method, its belief in the individuality of historical reality through intuitive understanding while judging an historical period on its own terms, had led in the past to conservative judgements favouring the status quo, together with an avoidance of moral issues and a failure to raise the main questions to which answers were necessary for an understanding of German historical development.

Taking as a starting point the concept of structure from the *Annales* school in France, historians began to apply economic cyclical theories and to some extent re-imported the Weberian tradition of sociology from American and British universities, where it had flourished after its eclipse in Germany under the National Socialists. Through the use of concepts and models possessing general validity, a new emphasis was placed on examining the role of impersonal forces governing the actions of historical subjects.

Foremost among the advocates of this approach, Hans-Ulrich Wehler has called for the integration of theoretical analysis and empirical research.[6] History's new role is to perform the task of a critical social science which rejects the positivist pretence of value-free and objective research and seeks to make sense of the past by the use of explicitly developed theories in order to increase future chances for a more rational orientation of society. Drawing upon his own earlier research on Bismarck and the roots of German imperialism,[7] while also incorporating insights from other monographs on the period, Wehler's structural analysis of the German Empire provides the English reader with a synthesis of over a decade's research on the subject by German historians: without doubt it constitutes the most substantial contribution so far to a development which has since been described as an historiographical revolution.[8]

While the translator has aimed to remain as faithful as possible to the original text, where it has been felt necessary to add an explanation to assist comprehension, an appropriate paraphrase or description has been incorporated into the text after consultation with the author. Dates have been added occasionally, especially in the section dealing with the Workers' and Soldiers' Councils, in order to make the historical background to the issue under discussion more readily intelligible to the reader to whom the period may be unfamiliar.

An attempt has been made to avoid the unnecessary intrusion of German into the text, the only significant exceptions to this being the names of organisations or political parties and the key concept of *Sammlungspolitik*. In the former case, the German version has been included on its first appearance only, in order to enable the reader to recognise references in other works where the name may appear in its original form or where the translation of the term may differ. Where the English version is already familiar from the existing literature, conventional usage has been followed. In the case of *Sammlungspolitik*, the term is explained initially in English and retained thereafter in its German form for the sake of brevity. Finally, for the same reason, the two main German employers' organisations, following their initial appearance, are subsequently referred to by their customary German abbreviations.

Introduction

This book was written in the autumn of 1972 on the basis of notes for
a lecture course at the University of Cologne in the late 1960s. At
that time only a number of older surveys were available on the
history of the German Empire of 1871, apart from a textbook by
Hans Herzfeld, a more essayistic account by Golo Mann and a
number of articles in reference books. There was no modern study
which took on board changing scholarly and political perspectives
and which was concise enough to be used in seminars and classes.
Nor, curiously enough, are we in a better position in this respect in
1984, despite the intensive debate on the history of the German
Empire which has taken place during the past decade.

My lectures were written against the general background of the
so-called rebellion of students and junior staff in West Germany, and
this intellectual climate favoured the presentation of sharply formulated hypotheses. Indeed, even in relatively peaceful Cologne the
atmosphere of lively argument and intense curiosity contrasted
pleasantly with the apolitical 1950s or the general atmosphere of
phlegmatism and passivity of the mid-1980s. Academic teaching
meant not to evade critical questions and to stimulate further critical
reflection of problems. It appeared preferable to advance hypotheses
which were not meticulously substantiated rather than to ignore
completely areas which had not received much attention before.
Everything was geared to discussion, to the pointed exchange of
arguments and to a questioning of outdated interpretations. Given
that I had to confine the text to some 240 pages, the primary focus of
this book is on political history. In this respect, too, it bears, like
most studies, the marks of the period in which it was conceived.

My text attempts to take a thematic approach to the history of the
German Empire. But there were also didactic considerations behind
structuring this book according to themes. The divisions are designed to identify objectives and stages of learning which are intel-

5

ligible. It is also hoped that individual sections or chapters may be used in preparation for a seminar or a class discussion. It is for this reason that these parts are fairly self-contained, even if this made a few repetitions unavoidable.

It is not difficult to discover considerable gaps in my analysis, and reviewers have been quite explicit about these. Thus the focus is very much on Prussia. Other German states and regions — the Ruhr, upper Silesia, Lower Bavaria — merely appear in the margins although their divergent histories and traditions do help us to gain a better understanding of the institutional, political and cultural fragmentation of the German Empire. However, apart from the fact that our knowledge of these regions was then more limited, both lack of space and the central role of the Prussian 'Empire State' appeared to demand that the hegemonic power in Central Europe be placed at the centre of the analysis. This has resulted in certain imbalances which had to be accepted.

The whole area of cultural life is also missing — that is, culture in the broad sense of modern social anthropology rather than 'high' culture. I felt that at that time I was least in a position to provide an outline of these aspects. But the most serious weakness, in my view, is that I did not incorporate the chapter on 'Social Structure and Societal Development', as originally envisaged. I found my draft of this chapter too problematical in view of the many questions on which the state of research was far from satisfactory. On the one hand, this was due to the difficulties with which an analysis of social stratification and class structure in the nineteenth and early twentieth centuries is confronted; on the other hand, empirical work on these questions was totally inadequate. I was also of the opinion that, in line with the real-historical context, social and economic problems should be closely linked. To some extent this has been attempted; but it is, of course, no substitute for the desirable and detailed analysis of Germany society.

I cannot emphasise too strongly, that many sentences and judgments have deliberately been put very pointedly. They are intended to shake the reader up, to stimulate reflection and, above all, to provoke objections; they are not supposed to confirm received views or even to become orthodoxies in themselves! This means that some judgments lack a firm foundation; they are hypotheses which further research will have to either verify or refute. More generally, the discursive examination of problems has taken precedence over the provision of factual information. There are advantages in this approach, but also disadvantages which I am only too well aware of.

On this positive side, I hope that I have given an impression of the German Empire as a totality and of the interconnections of its politics with its economy and society, however inadequately. Nevertheless, and its many gaps notwithstanding, my analysis ought to offer a clearer picture of how irregular economic growth, the polarisation of classes, the divisions of the educational system, the special position of the military, the processes of political decision-making, and so on, were interlocked, thereby enhancing at the same time our chances of learning something from this period of German history in a paradigmatic fashion.

There are two further aspects to which I should like to draw special attention. The guiding question underlying this book has been to investigate why Hitler's National Socialist regime came to power some dozen years after the end of the monarchy; why this regime succeeded in establishing a system of unprecedented terror and barbaric mass extermination; and why it proved capable of conducting a second total war. These questions will remain forever an acute thorn in the flesh of the generation to which I belong. The thread which is running through this book is the basic assumption that we cannot adequately grasp the history of the Third Reich without recourse to the history of the German Empire of 1871.

The second point relates to my conviction which I have also followed in this book that as historians we are all participants in a long-drawn-out discourse in the process of which some hypotheses will be confirmed, others will be accepted as a stimulus to further discussion and some will finally be rejected as unproductive. In this sense, this volume represents an intermediate state and today I would, of course, express and view many things differently. My analysis has unleashed a lively controversy in recent years. I have accepted some of the criticisms; at the same time I have continued to defend its central arguments. The fact that the German edition has run through six impressions may be taken as an indication that there are still readers who find it interesting and that it has not yet been replaced by superior competitors of similar length. I am currently working on a *Grundriss der deutschen Gesellschaftsgeschichte* from the nineteenth century to the present, and in this context I hope to return to old questions as well as to new ones relating to the history of the German Empire. This will also provide me with an opportunity to take up the many constructive criticisms which reviewers of the present book have made. It will also be the occasion to refute various neo-conservative and dogmatic attacks.

The select bibliography has been updated for the English language edition. As far as possible, I have also incorporated the recent Anglo-Saxon literature in order to make it easier for the reader to inform himself further on individual points and controversies. The text as such has been left unchanged on the whole so that the reader can easily find the controversial passages.

I would like to thank Marion and Volker Berghahn for their continued interest in the translation of this volume into English. I would also like to thank Kim Traynor, the translator, who had to face the extremely difficult and thankless task of translating the complex teutonic language of the original, which so clearly betrays its origins in the debate that was then taking place in Germany. In my view he has been successful.

It is thanks to them all that this volume has at last been made accessible to English-speaking readers.

H.-U. W.

I

The Configuration of 1871: the Agrarian Revolution, the Industrial Revolution and the Founding of the State

The German Empire of 1871 was a unique creation among the nation states of Europe. It not only emerged from a series of three wars within the space of six years as a result of a 'revolution from above' carried out by the Prussian military, but was, moreover, founded at a time when the completion of an agrarian revolution coincided with the breakthrough of the industrial revolution in Germany. Socio-economic upheavals of profound significance coincided with the diverse ramifications at home and abroad of the appearance of a new political structure in Central Europe. It was this that was responsible for the problematical nature of this state, and not primarily the crisis of a 'latecoming' nation state which was never fully realised. Each of these developments would in itself have created major problems. Together, however, they produced extraordinary complications. Over seventy years ago the American sociologist Thorstein Veblen gave a penetrating analysis of the configuration of factors at this time: in a largely traditional society, only partially adapted institutionally between 1866 and 1871 and still ruled over by pre-industrial élites, the most advanced Western technology forced itself through with unprecedented speed and accelerated social change. How the representatives of that traditional society reacted to the socio-economic and political structural changes during the following fifty years forms a central theme in the history of the German Empire. Accordingly, we may proceed from Alexander Gerschenkron's general explanatory model, which postulates that the more rapid and complete the 'great spurt' forward of an industrial revolution (from an agrarian to an industrial society),

9

the more complicated will be its effects and resultant problems. While, on the one hand, Germany certainly enjoyed some 'advantages of backwardness', being able to adopt certain features from the more advanced societies of Britain and Western Europe, on the other hand, the very success of its economic revolution involved apparently unavoidable costs in terms of uncommonly acute social problems.[1] What attempts were made to solve these problems? On whom did the costs of change fall in the long and short terms? Who profited from change? What was the significance of these problems in terms of their consequences? And how are they to be judged in retrospect?

Proceeding from this outline of the German Empire's problematical origins, we must first enquire into the most important influences at work in this period: namely, the development of the agrarian economy, of industry and of domestic politics in the new Germany under the leadership of Prussia.

1. The agrarian revolution and the land-owning aristocracy

The agrarian revolution, which in Germany is usually concealed behind the misleading term 'the emancipation of the peasants' began.in the latter part of the eighteenth century. It was accelerated by the legal reforms of 1807–21, and entered its final phase in the long period of economic prosperity between 1840 and 1876. It resulted in a structural transformation of the agrarian economy which, legally formalised and promoted, and encouraged by modernisation and rationalisation measures, led to an immense increase in productive efficiency. Riding on the crest of a wave at a peak in the business cycle, the self-confidence and sense of power of the land-owning aristocracy, accustomed as it was to its exercise, was revived. Enjoying the outwardly stable economic base of a flourishing agricultural sector, it took part in the internal conflicts surrounding the German Empire's founding and thus reasserted its historical role and claim to leadership over its rival bourgeois exponents of the other revolution of this period: the industrial revolution.

Since the turn of the nineteenth century countless legal changes were made in the area of seigneurial rights from the period of a feudal power structure in the areas of land rights (for example, ownership, labour services, and taxes in kind), personal rights (serfdom and its attenuated form binding the peasant to the soil) and the arbitration of disputes (that is, judicial powers). Indeed, in some cases they were completely removed, though not to the extent that the rural population became less dependent in an informal and, hence, less oppressive sense. This prolonged process of change was determined by several aims. The immediate impetus behind the speed of these changes came from the state of emergency which resulted from the Napoleonic Wars. Reparations payments and the costs of the war made an increase in state revenue imperative. This could be achieved only by modernising the economy 'from above', which meant, in the first instance, the agricultural sector. In order to stimulate maximum output and maximise profit, agriculture was reorganised along competitive lines. The state's economic policies hoped to reap maximum benefit by releasing work energies, providing new incentives and encouraging productive efficiency. At the same time the idea gained ground that modernisation was the *sine qua non* if the German states, in particular Prussia, were to hold their own with any prospect of success in competition with other nations. From the standpoint of the most influential interest group, the land-owning aristocracy, against whose wishes the agrarian laws could never have been drawn up, the new legislation promised several benefits: the abolition of seigneurial duties concerning the legal protection of peasants, the removal of burdensome obligations and improved efficiency by the use of wage labour, but, above all, an increase in directly disposable land. Here the late-absolutist state came to the aid of its main pillar of political support on a massive scale by providing subsidised credit banks and tax benefits. The peasants, on the other hand, received no support before 1850 and had to purchase their freedom dearly. It was only through cash payments or by ceding land that they could free themselves from the legal claims of the ruling landlords, and many of them were too poor to do this. The system of large-scale agricultural enterprises which gradually arose at the expense of peasant ownership, especially east of the river Elbe (between 1811 and 1890 the area occupied by the great estates here increased by two-thirds!), and which also drew most benefit from the new methods of cultivation and rationalisation, proved able not only to provide tolerably well for a rapidly growing population, but was also increasingly capable of channelling agricultural produce into the far more lucrative export trade, particularly to England after the abolition of the Corn Laws in 1846. These export-orientated large-scale agricultural producers viewed Free Trade as the most desirable foreign trade policy. In contrast, 'protective tariffs were seen in feudal circles as a mistaken policy of the urban bourgeoisie against whom they were struggling'.[2] The prosperity which emerged in the early 1840s can be gauged not only from the pricing of agricultural produce. Land prices also rose threefold in the five decades before 1875. The quantitative effect of the changes which had taken place is also evidenced by the fact that Prussian arable land under cultivation doubled in the fifty years between 1816 and 1866 (from 26.5 per cent to 51.4 per cent of the entire land surface area). Uncultivated land shrank in the same period from 40.3 per cent to 7.1 per cent; and while the yield from increased agricultural land rose from 100 index points to 194, the population grew 'merely' from 100 to 173.[3] A surge of productivity lay behind this visible achievement in the supply and export of produce which, according to Hans Rosenberg, brought the land-owners to 'the historical peak of their economic power' between 1840 and 1876. This was accompanied by an increase in their purchasing power. The agrarian market became more capable of absorbing commercial and industrial products and increased its capacity for capital saving. The accumulation of capital from export earnings directly benefited agriculture with its continual need for capital. At the same time, the agrarian sector, chiefly no doubt through its accumulation of private wealth, earnings from international trade and increased tax yields, contributed indirectly to the formation of capital for Germany's early industrial enterprises. It required only the ingenious legal device of the joint-stock company to channel these capital resources into industrial investments.

Finally, to single out one final important consequence: the quali-tative changes in legal relationships (for example, the transition from rents paid in labour to individual land-ownership, from servi-tude or even hereditary serfdom to formal legal independence, from labour services to wage labour, from the inherited legal status of tied labour to the abolition in particular of the *Junker* right to sanction peasant marriages) liberated an enormous demographic growth in those strata of small tenant farmers no longer bound to the soil. This was especially true of the north-east of Germany. Prussia's popula-tion, for example, grew by 37 per cent between 1815 and 1840, and by 26 per cent, from 25 to 38 million, between 1840 and 1860. Because of the negligible increase in the number of vacancies avail-able in the traditional occupations, together with their diminished value caused by surplus labour, hundreds of thousands of Germans emigrated in the years before 1850. As many as 2 million left in the years between 1850 and 1870. As well as this, many more poured

into the new industrial centres and conurbations where they formed
a reservoir of a mobile and initially unskilled labour force which the
factory system increasingly needed alongside its skilled craftsmen.
Population growth, increased consumption, capital accumulation,
urbanisation and internal migration were thus closely linked functionally with the agrarian revolution. For this reason the success of
this revolution was one of the essential preconditions of the German
industrial revolution.

The loosening of the old feudal ties reached its culmination only
after the shock of the 1848 revolution. Between 1811 and 1848 some
70,000 Prussian peasants had achieved emancipation by ceding land
and a further 170,000 by cash payments. But between 1850 and 1865
as many as 640,000 bought their freedom from 6.3 million days of
service at the plough and 23.4 million days of manual work. Whereas
previously only the land-owners had been able to rely on financial help
(from their own credit institutes established for the nobility by
Frederick II), new state-owned mortgage banks now provided assistance for the peasants. However, these also increased the mobile
capital at the disposal of the great land-owners, as did the peasants'
mortgage redemption payments. Since 1807 the land-owners had
been transformed as a result of the legal changes from 'an hereditary
nobility to an aristocracy based on the ownership of land which
could be disposed of at will, a mobile economic class of owners of
capital, estate managers and employers'. Yet the nucleus of the old
nobility within this group continued to form 'at the same time, an
exclusive feudal professional estate' which after 1849 continued to
enjoy the privilege of assistance from the state. A new law on
entailed estates was introduced in 1852. In the following year the
Prussian Upper House became an aristocratic preserve, and the first
steps towards regional administrative autonomy were shelved for
what was to be the next forty years. In 1856 the land-owners had
their police powers renewed. Of the 12,339 estates in that year,
whose owners were eligible to sit in local and district assemblies,
7,023 latifundia of over 5,000 hectares still belonged entirely to the
nobility.

However slowly the 'transformation of the landed aristocracy into
a modern entrepreneurial class of agricultural businessmen' may
have crept along — by 1885 only 13 per cent of East Prussian estates
had been in the same family for over fifty years — the traditional
ruling élite of the land-owning aristocracy, which was prominently
represented in the army officer corps and the civil service, still
defended its social and political privileges as vehemently and effec-

tively as it did its economic interests. *Junker* estates remained completely exempt from basic land taxes up until 1861, and Free Trade was kept for agricultural exports up until 1879.[4] The aristocracy also enjoyed direct access to the Court as one of the formal centres of decision-making. Thanks to its unthreatened predominance in the upper echelons of the ministerial bureaucracy, the diplomatic service and the army, it controlled the three main pillars of the post-1848 German state, and thus the levers of power together with the essential instruments for its defence. Without the economic base provided by the agrarian revolution this reassertion of their old position as political masters would have been scarcely conceivable. Economically successful, despite the revolutionary upheaval of 1848, and once again socially and politically relatively secure in the saddle, the ruling nobility went forward into the 1860s. The successes and achievements of the Prussian military state and Bismarck's policies were, therefore, to benefit a prospering pre-industrial élite. Accustomed to prestige and the exercise of power, and with the doubts raised by the 1848 revolution now suppressed, it acceded first place to the bourgeoisie only in the sphere of the industrial economy.

2. The industrial revolution and the urban bourgeoisie

As in the agrarian sector, the early stages of Germany's industrialisation to some extent followed a course of natural, unchecked development. However, it was also partly a result of deliberately planned measures aimed at modernisation. These were, moreover, designed to serve the self-assertion and pursuit of success of those ruling groups which controlled the state after the hiatus of 1807–15 From the very beginning model workshops under the state's direction, together with state-aided enterprises, were to provide an important impetus, since these possessed modern machinery and received long-term commissions, underwriting guarantees and other benefits. They formed isolated islands of economic planning in a gradually expanding sea of emergent private industry. In the early 1840s industrial growth rates climbed sharply, but because of the crisis in agriculture and commerce between 1845 and 1847, the revolution of 1848–9 and the post-war depression up to 1850, the breakthrough of Germany's industrial revolution can only be dated with any degree of certainty to the beginning of the 1850s. By 'revolution' is meant, following conventional usage, a rapid, hectic and short-lived process. It does not mean a development spanning more than a hundred years, which is how the term 'industrial revolution' is often misleadingly used in popular media jargon, rather than the more precise 'industrialisation'. The question, therefore, of arriving at some form of periodisation to define an important phase in the overall development of this process becomes especially urgent. Which criteria can one employ to justify singling out 'the specific compression of industrialisation processes into periods of rapid growth' (Gerschenkron)[5] from the undeniably continuous development of the whole?

The economy is a process of social interaction. It follows therefore that social criteria determine whether the means of production are deployed and utilised in such a way as to result in the emergence of the historically specific example of industrial capitalism. The social structure and social norms of behaviour permit modern technology and factory production methods to assert themselves. Fundamental technical advances, the replacement of human skills and manpower by machinery, improvements in the manufacture of materials by machine-made tools, and so forth, possess a latent revolutionary potential which is released only when certain social conditions prevail. These decide whether the system of political authority is reproduced in the work-place, whether unenlightened despotism may be imitated with the government's blessing and whether firms may become places purely for the pursuit of profit. They also decide whether the willingness exists to transform innovations resulting from empirical craftsmanship and scientific invention into lasting technological advances, and whether the industrial work-force can be recruited and disciplined to suit new industrial work-methods. This crucial process of creating a reservoir of trained labour, together with expanding foreign and domestic markets and encouraging capital accumulation, has never occurred anywhere without the assistance of the state functioning as part of the social structure. We can indicate these fundamental advance decisions only in passing and need not concern ourselves with details of other important, though as yet partly undefined, factors governing the pace of rapid industrialisation, for example, changes in cultural norms and the social prestige of the entrepreneur, the growth of innovation, changes in the technical processes themselves, legal privileges conferred on capital and its owners (whereas labour for a long time was not deemed a property worthy of legal protection) and the idea of risk-taking (with its reward of material gain) applied solely to capital and not to the work-place or the erosion of workers' energies. Regarding such preconditions, let it only be said here that they appear to have been sufficiently realised in Germany by the middle of the nineteenth century. Favourable social, institutional and psychological conditions were, therefore, either already in existence or were soon created to speed up decisively the process of modernisation.

If we concentrate solely on specifically economic criteria, we can take as our starting-point the existing consensus of research into economic growth and economic history. According to this, at least three phenomena lie at the core of the industrial economy (leaving aside the agrarian sector). Firstly, an abrupt increase in GNP leading to a rise in per capita income. Secondly, an extraordinary rise in the growth rates of key, or 'strategic' industries (represented in graph form as Gerschenkron's 'kink in the curve'). Thirdly, an increase in net investment in the national economy of approximately 10 to 12 per cent of the net national product.

On the basis of these preliminary factors we may conclude in the case of Germany's development that up until 1850 social changes, legal reforms, institutional changes — both natural and deliberately planned — economic growth imitating foreign models, half-hearted encouragement by the state and long-term political aims all worked together to build up the conditions which enabled the onset of the industrial revolution. The first prosperity period of this revolution asserted itself with considerable force in the years before 1857. The growth rates for industry and the economy as a whole shot upwards. The level of investment and consumer goods production doubled. Foreign trade expanded by 130 per cent. The estimated annual net rate of investment climbed to 8, then 10, and even reached 12 per cent, before levelling off in 1873. The key industries of iron, mining and engineering also showed a marked advance. The value of pig-iron production in the Prussian-led Customs Union (*Zollverein*), which grew by 250 per cent, increased from 24 million marks in 1848 to 66 million in 1857; that of coal production, which grew by 138 per cent, from 25 to 62 million, and that of iron-ore and coal-mining together went up from 45 to 135 million marks. Railway construction, too, proved to be a crucially important leading sector in Germany's industrialisation. Between 1850 and 1860 the network doubled in size from 6,000 to 11,500 kilometres. German engineering firms were already able to gain the lion's share (more than two-thirds) of contracts to supply locomotives and rolling stock. In 1858 the Berlin firm of Borsig delivered its thousandth locomotive. The knock-on effect from this leading sector pulled iron and coal production, engineering and countless other supply industries along with it. Freight traffic on the Prussian railways increased sevenfold.

From 1857 to 1859 this economic development was, however, interrupted by the first world economic crisis, which affected Germany as it did other countries. Thereafter her economy recovered and the revival continued until the brief recession of 1866. It underwent further expansion between 1866 and 1873, entering into an unprecedented prosperity period which was to end with the onset of the second world-wide economic crisis. In 1866 a million tons of pig-iron were produced. In 1870 the figure was 1.5 million, and by 1873 it had risen to 2.2 million tons. Coal production climbed between 1860 and 1870 by 114 per cent to 26 million tons, or double the volume of French output. During this decade the railway network almost doubled in size to 19,500 kilometres, then between 1870 and 1875 by as much again to 28,000 kilometres. Between 1850 and 1870 the volume of rail freight traffic increased twenty-one times over, as measured by tonnage per kilometre. This branch of the transport industry remained the most important industrial 'leading sector' and forged ahead for three decades, pulling along the development of other branches of industry by its 'backward' and 'forward linkages'.

Annual productivity measured in man-hours increased between 1850 and 1860 by 8.5 per cent, and from 1860 to 1870, owing to improved technology, by as much as 42 per cent. The increase in nominal wages in the 1850s did not, however, lead as yet to a lasting improvement in real wages. This was because of a sharp rise in the price of essential consumer items. Potatoes went up in price by 125 per cent between 1850 and 1855, rye by 150 per cent and wheat by 100 per cent! Between 1866 and 1873, however, the cost of living failed to catch up with wages, so that in terms of real wages workers' incomes eventually did show an appreciable increase.[6]

During the 1860s the new industrial labour force, continuing its older tradition of combining in associations, began to organise itself into political parties and early forms of trade unions. After a short period of rivalry Lassalle's Workers' Associations merged with Bebel's and Liebknecht's Eisenach Party to form in 1875 at Gotha the Socialist Workers' Party (*Sozialistische Arbeiterpartei*) in which Marx's theories of the class struggle and the emancipation of the working class eventually came to dominate. By the end of the industrial revolution in Germany, therefore, the workers had a political mouthpiece which sought to unite all members of the same social class for the political and social conflicts to come. A break with bourgeois liberalism had already taken place as a result of irreconcilable conflicts of interest. Helped by the upswing of the

business cycle, industrial workers successfully influenced the outcome of industrial conflicts in their favour by the increasing use of
the strike weapon. Between 1864 and 1873 there were 903 strikes;
188 took place in 1871, followed by 215 in 1872 and as many as 255
in 1873, that is, a total of 631 in the first three years of the German
Empire's existence. Here, too, the pattern for modern conflicts over
the distribution of the national product and efforts to realise greater
equality became visible. The propertied and educated middle classes, among whom there had been talk of a 'red menace' since the
period before 1848, viewed these conflicts, in the main, as the
harbinger of an impending social revolution.

If one takes the British industrial revolution as the classic pioneer
model, the German variant was forced to find its own home-grown
solutions to emulate England's original achievements, since these
could not be brought about in the same form in Germany. The large
German banks which emerged in the 1850s and 1860s took on the
function in Germany of supplying the wealth of capital that had
been available to British industry from the City of London. From the
outset they combined two activities usually separated in England:
commercial banking and long-term industrial financing. As all-
purpose banks (*Universalbanken*) they became, according to Gerschenkron, 'a strategic factor in Germany's industrialisation'; they
mobilised investment capital by issuing stocks and channelling it
into industry. They also coordinated the founding of new heavy
industry and soon controlled important sectors of the economy by
acting as a substitute for private economic planning. In this way
they contributed to Germany overcoming its relative economic
backwardness; at the same time they came together in the early
phase of bank concentration to form a powerful oligarchy of high-
finance. By regulating government loans via the 'Prussian consortium' of large banks, they were able to determine the general course
of Germany's economic development to a considerable extent. From
the early 1870s the so-called D-banks (the Disconto Gesellschaft,
Deutsche Bank, Dresdener Bank and Darmstädter Bank) set the
tone. These are the historical facts behind the development which
gave rise to the concept of 'finance capital'.

One further factor which enabled Germany to catch up on the
prolific technological development in England was created in the
long term by the determined expansion of the education system.
This placed human capital at the disposal of the economy on an
astonishing scale. True, the German grammar schools and universities remained committed to the principles of the humanist-educated

élite, a fact which scarcely prepared their *alumni* for the economic struggle of everyday life. But there soon existed a close connection between cameralist studies (i.e. economics and jurisprudence) or political science and the industrial economy. Here one need think only of names like Unruh, Hammacher, Miquel and Bamberger among others. Moreover, the larger German states had also founded educational institutes for the technical and engineering sciences as well as commercial colleges from the early 1820s onwards. Beuth's Technical Institute in Berlin dated from 1821. Following the French example, the polytechnics of Karlsruhe, Munich and Stuttgart were founded in 1825, 1827 and 1832 respectively. These were followed by the Technical College in Dresden in 1828. To these can be added the professional and vocational schools set up to transmit craft skills. Viewed *in toto*, these were the establishments that produced the experts, the technical cadres which gave further impetus to the process of industrialisation after the 1850s. Although little is known in detail about the way scientific knowledge develops to the point where it becomes an economically productive resource, or about educational investment and its effects, the systematic exploitation of scientific knowledge became so evident that, up to the watershed of the 1890s, the process of industrial economic growth, which depended on technological innovation, relied to a steadily increasing extent upon the practical application of scientific research. The lack of a national domestic market prior to 1871, which might compare with Great Britain's opportunities for foreign trade, was overcome in 1834 with the creation of the Prussian-inspired Customs Union. The significance of this 'package' of 130 bilateral and multilateral treaties, in force during the century between 1819 and 1918, has admittedly been overrated. On the other hand, it should not be regarded as unimportant, for it was an essential precondition of Germany's successful industrialisation. For its member states the Customs Union was, thanks to its rising revenue and shrinking administrative costs, a financially lucrative venture. It promoted a standardisation of law and a uniform currency by means of monetary conventions and a new commercial code. It concluded advantageous trade treaties, provided tariff protection against external competition, as well as duty-free river traffic and a low tariff area in the home market. All of these measures provided strong stimuli for long-term economic development. Prussia, as its leading member, remained undeniably the main beneficiary of this Customs Union and its policies from the 1820s onwards. As early as 1829 a French diplomat in Munich described it in grandiose terms as 'one of the most significant events since the Reformation'. In this 'gigantic system', Prussia would achieve unprecedented power. Metternich was also in no doubt that 'its decisive result' would be 'Prussia's predominance'; he added that a new 'second, smaller confederation' was emerging within the German Confederation 'which was a state within the state in the fullest sense of the term, and which would become accustomed only too soon to pursuing its own aims with its own methods'.[7] This remark hit the nail on the head. Vienna made no serious attempt to destroy this rival. Twice, however, Austria attempted to force her way in, once under Bruck and Schwarzenberg after the 1848 revolution, but with no greater result than the trade treaty of 1853 which it took a quarter of a century to achieve. Negotiations on joining dragged on until 1860. By and large, this successful stroke of Berlin's economic policy made up in full for Prussia's diplomatic reverse at Olmütz in 1850. The Franco-Prussian Treaty of 1862 confirmed Prussian supremacy before Austria's renewed approach under Rechberg between 1862 and 1865 failed once again. The Habsburg Empire lost out in this competition, and not only in terms of its trade. Since the breakthrough of the industrial revolution in Prussia had already taken place, this state also possessed an incomparable dynamism and enjoyed a superior lead over Austria in terms of industrial growth. It was not without good reason that, ten years after their failure, anti-Prussian liberals who had favoured the inclusion of Austria in a unified Germany now looked upon Prussia as the genuinely modern state of the Confederation's two rivals. One must beware, however, of drawing an inevitable and straight line between the Customs Union and the German Empire of 1871. The scope for new political and military trials of strength was still very limited. The lead that Prussia had gained as an industrial state was still precarious and not universally acknowledged. With hindsight, however, it can be seen that the industrial revolution had enabled her to make the decisive leap forward towards the continuous development of a permanently expanding economic system whose secular, long-term trend was one of sustained, albeit uneven, economic growth.

3. Domestic politics: reactionaries, liberalism and the constitutional conflict

Of the two social classes that promoted this development, the bourgeoisie and the working class, the bourgeoisie had suffered defeat in its attempt in 1848 to gain a joint share of political power. Nowhere in Germany had it tried to gain complete power and its defeat had the effect of a lasting shock. Marx's 'third fundamental class',[8] that is, the land-owners, particularly the aristocracy, re-asserted itself. Since, however, the masses were also on the move — cases of unrest among journeymen revealed the demands of the newly-created proletariat — the major conservative laws of the 1850s, designed to stabilise the political system, clearly bore 'the stamp of victorious reactionary politics'; this is how the conservative writer, Hermann Wagener, put it when he triumphantly commented on the consolidation of *Junker* rule.[9] These laws combined with a paternalistic policy to compensate the subordinate sections of society. Driven by a sense of necessity, those social groups performing a leadership role adopted a series of social welfare measures to benefit the peasantry, artisans, industrial workers and their children. Another thirty years were to pass before they would again be forced to make comparable concessions. A policy of internal political repression and efforts by the authorities to redress several serious social ills were the peculiarly contrasting accompaniments to a rapid liberalisation in the economy which released a good deal of those energies that flowed into industry and the advancement of the bourgeoisie. Following the abortive revolution of 1848, the transition to a 'New Era' of liberal government under King William of Prussia was proclaimed. It was, therefore, only to be expected that the economically successful, albeit politically heterogenous, industrial bourgeoisie would once more voice its political aspirations in concert with 'progressive' businessmen, civic leaders, artisans and civil servants — in short, middle-class groups. Although it was not brought about by design, the quarrel which began over the Prussian army reforms grew into a conflict revolving around the constitution. It led eventually to a new trial of strength between bourgeois parliamentarianism and the absolutist military state. And once again the bourgeoisie was defeated. That is why the 'Constitutional Conflict' marks the second great turning-point in Prussia's domestic politics and, consequently, in German history as a whole, since almost two-thirds of the German Empire was later absorbed by her. The outcome of this conflict was to seal the political impotence of the bourgeoisie up until 1918.

The confrontation took shape in 1860 when a new law was laid before the Diet to enable the already approved plans of von Roon's War Ministry to be implemented. These involved a technical reorganisation of the army; but they also contained more than this.

While an increase in the strength of the peacetime army went uncontested, the proposed legal provision for a three-year term of compulsory military service for an annual intake of 63,000 recruits, as against 40,000 previously, proved to be a stumbling block. The proposal was seen as an issue involving internal social control, since it was a step towards the further militarisation of society. Secondly, the national militia (*Landwehr*) was to be weakened radically in favour of the regular army; this was tantamount to destroying the genuine citizen army of the Scharnhorst–Boyen reforms. While the Prussian Diet approved the additional expenditure involved, differences of opinion between the War Ministry and the majority faction of so-called 'Old Liberals' proved irreconcilable on the questions of length of military service and the fate of the national militia. Using skilful tactics, the military *camarilla* played up the conflict into the alternatives of an army under the control of the monarch or of the Diet. It brought about a situation in which the Crown declared the reform subject to the absolutist executive power of the 'Supreme War-lord'. Based on constitutional feudal rights and beyond the control of representative institutions, this denied the need for any form of legal control. In a quite undisguised fashion the military was to be kept free of any middle-class parliamentary influence. Henceforth, the fundamental issue of defence and, therefore, the position of the army in the state, involving the political constitution in the widest sense, stood at the centre of the debate. The military realised at an early stage the conflict of principles involved. Given the mentality of the professional soldier at the apex of the state hierarchy, they made maximum capital out of it. In the course of the controversy the 'Old Liberal' majority in the Diet collapsed. The new Prussian Progressive Party (Deutsche Fortschrittspartei), which now emerged, was returned in the December elections of 1861 as the largest political grouping and included in its ranks a large number of liberal civil servants. In March 1862 liberal ministers were removed from the government, which was now completely dominated by von Roon. New compromise proposals put forward by the Diet, which was anything but belligerent in its approach, failed because of the monarch's opposition, whereupon it withheld its approval of the 1863 budget. The King seriously considered abdicating at this point. His son was widely regarded as a liberal and so, for a short time, it seemed that a victory for the parliamentary majority might be possible. Now the choice suddenly appeared to be between a constitutional monarchy, on the one hand, and a quasi-dictatorship based on plebiscitary approval, on the other. In point of fact the attempt to achieve parliamentary control was prevented and the monarchy itself was to be eroded in the course of the next few decades. But the legacy of recourse to a charismatic dictator legitimised by plebiscitary approval was to remain.

In 1862 the representatives of the military state thought neither of abandoning nor of partially conceding their position. In the autumn of 1862, amid a situation of acute crisis which they had quite clearly engineered, they put forward the only candidate of the extreme conservative, ultra-royalist and outright absolutist clique for the office of Prussian Prime Minister. This was Otto von Bismarck, of whom the Prussian King had prophesied in 1848 that he was to be used only once the bayonet freely reigned. Against this background of the Constitutional Conflict, the defence of the threatened military state and the preservation of its social and political power structure, Bismarck stepped into the centre of the decision-making process of German politics as, in the words of Manfred Messerschmidt, 'the stabiliser of monarchical power'. For the next thirty years he was to fight vehemently and with staggering success on behalf of the groups that lent him support, groups representing the old Prussia and its ruling élites against the forces of social and political progress. But the consequences were to prove completely disastrous in the long run for the majority of Germany's population.

So far as an electorate, which could be mobilised for an election turn-out of at most 50 per cent, articulated political views at all, a clear majority of voters favoured liberal policies. In 1862 the Conservatives formed a small minority, but a powerful one. Above all, their government controlled 'all the instruments of organised power'.[10] Bismarck, finding himself at last in the most important position in the political apparatus, was not a man who was averse to applying these in domestic and foreign policy. It is sometimes forgotten that he carried out a harsh policy of repression against the liberals in domestic politics. Imprisonment, deportation, press censorship and intimidation by the courts were all devices he made good use of as the new head of government. He never underestimated his main opponents, the liberals. He would even have joined hands with Lassalle's Workers' Associations against the progressive liberals had the former been a real power factor. These genuine liberals were still his arch-enemies a quarter of a century later. Since they believed it was impossible to govern a state based on the rule of law without a budget approved by parliament, Bismarck's government now resorted to the 'gap' theory of the Prussian constitution. This meant, in the government's view, that in the event of failure to reach agreement on legislation, the traditional prerogative of the Crown to make the final decision allowed the government to continue to rule in accordance with the terms of the last regular budget. The ample flow of tax revenue, brought about by the rise in economic prosperity, would even permit a generous management of the economy; and while the dispute over the constitution continued with unremitting bitterness, the representatives of the bourgeoisie displayed their schizophrenia in pursuing their own interests. Often in the self-same parliamentary sitting the economic policy of Bismarck's government, which was one of outright liberal Free Trade, was as unreservedly approved and sanctioned in law as its approach to domestic affairs was roundly, though ineffectually, condemned. Yet it is not certain how this conflict in internal politics would have ended had not Bismarck, while observing his maxim that 'as long as we gain respect abroad, we can get away with a great deal at home', shown also his equally dubious 'skill for running internal politics on the steam-power of foreign affairs' (Oncken). The prophecy of the conservative *Kreuzzeitung* newspaper on Bismarck's assumption to office, to the effect that he would 'overcome domestic difficulties by a bold foreign policy',[11] was soon fulfilled.

4. Wars for hegemony and 'revolution from above'

After skilful diplomatic preparations, which if viewed as a technical masterpiece can still be admired, Bismarck in 1864 involved Prussia's Habsburg rival in a combined war against Denmark over the Schleswig-Holstein question. Since 1848 the acquisition of these duchies had been an agreed aim of German nationalists from the liberals' programme right through to the political left. During the discussions concerning the only serious military engagement in the war, the storming of the fortifications at Düppel by Prussian units, Bismarck's strategy revealed itself quite clearly. For weeks the attack was the subject of argument; the commanders in the field could see no necessity for taking the fort. But Bismarck, along with von Roon, the War Minister, insisted stubbornly and in the end successfully on the attack in order to gain from the prestige which a favourable outcome would bring in the country at large. Indeed, 'the announcement of victory electrified Prussia' and inflamed nationalism to the point where it undermined 'liberal opposition to absolutism on the home front'. Even before Berlin and Vienna had established their brief condominium over the duchies, the constitutional principles of the progressive liberals began to melt away. This confirmed Lassalle's suspicion that the liberals had used the Schleswig-Holstein issue 'to divert attention from the internal situation and, under the guise of patriotism, to avoid having to solve a conflict for which they were no match'.[12]

The outcome of the bloody civil war in which Bismarck's Prussia expelled Austria from the German Confederation in 1866 at Sadowa, or Königgrätz, was by no means a foregone conclusion. Despite the meticulous planning of the General Staff under Moltke, victory for Prussia emerged only during the course of the battle itself. Bismarck was able to say without exaggeration that a defeat would have made his fall from power inevitable. Instead, this second successful war brought about the moral collapse of the progressive liberals in North Germany. Apart from those few of their number around Eugen Richter, who saw the need for a liberal-constitutional state as more necessary than ever, continued liberal insistence on its realisation was soon regarded as intransigence. A swing-round to the victorious government camp became the order of the day. This is not hard to understand of a movement unaccustomed to power and responsibility, which had been defeated in 1848. But the hollow triumph of a sheer unprincipled pragmatism (*Realpolitik*), which often degenerated into an unprincipled accommodation with the power of a formerly detested opponent, broke the moral backbone of many liberals, or unsettled them to the point where they began to question the best beliefs that had guided them in the past.

Bismarck, who was shrewder than short-sighted right-wing conservatives, now agreed to make a sham concession to the liberals. He introduced an Indemnity Bill which retrospectively approved government policy since 1862. Did this, as some believed at the time and long after, solve the Constitutional Conflict? The answer must be no. Bismarck achieved only a 'procrastinatory compromise formula'[13] which concealed basic conflicts of interest for a time but did not settle the crucial issue of a modernisation of the constitution. Instead, a solution to this problem was postponed for almost sixty years. This tactically brilliant manoeuvre represented, therefore, a barely-veiled victory for the old regime. The nucleus of the authoritarian state in which the military enjoyed autonomy remained essentially intact. The newly created North German Confederation with its pseudo-parliamentary trimmings was formed around this core as the distinctly recognisable prelude to the formation of a German national state along the lines of a 'Greater Prussia'.

For a third time Bismarck succeeded 'in engineering a war at a precise juncture which suited his plans'.[14] The nervous suspicion that had been harboured in Paris for years towards the rise of Prussia was well known, especially to Bismarck, and so were the conceivable consequences. It was roused to a clumsy declaration of war by the provocative Hohenzollern candidature for the Spanish throne and Bismarck's exploitation of French mistakes of protocol. The victory over France in 1871 relieved the Chancellor of all anxieties concerning the affiliation of the South German states and, hence, the expansion of the North German Confederation into a unified Germany excluding Austria. It also removed his anxieties over a prolongation of the 'iron' army law. This law, which accounted for 95 per cent of the Confederation's expenditure and virtually paralysed parliamentary control, was due for renewal in December 1871. One need have no doubt that in its final phase the short-lived liberal Empire of Napoleon III diverted attention away from its own internal difficulties towards foreign policy by means of Bonapartist policies. But these ran up against the equally Bonapartist and coolly-calculated long-term policies of his Berlin counterpart. Certainly, Bismarck held several irons in the fire. He never aimed for war as the only possible course open to him; but only a peaceful solution to the problem of German unification in 1870 would have testified to 'genuine statesmanship' on his part, and no-one has ever maintained that Bismarck 'applied his ingenuity to avoid war'.[15] The German Empire of 1871 emerged from this new gamble; a Prussian policy of calculated risk had paid off again. To invoke the generally accepted formula that at this time war was still a legitimate, or at least generally acceptable, means of resolving conflicts between states, and that Bismarck had merely carried out three such 'duels' in an astonishingly short space of time, does nothing to explain the crucial function of this continuation of an aggressive diplomacy by 'other means'. Quite apart from the question of whether Prussia's aims in Germany could ever have been realised without exchanging blows with its rival, two main motives have to be considered because of their effect on decisions taken within the *arcana imperii* of Berlin's policies:

(1) There is no evidence at all that these three wars for Prussian hegemony were determined strictly by economic interests. What cannot be denied easily, however, is that they were used as devices to legitimise the prevailing political system against the striving for social and political emancipation of the middle classes, or even the proletariat, a process which was partly determined by economic developments. Certainly, so far as their initiators were concerned these wars produced

their desired effect. Jacob Burckhardt, whose sceptical judgement on other matters was highly regarded in Germany, recognised quite clearly, as early as 1871, that 'the three wars were waged for internal political reasons. For seven years we enjoyed and took advantage of the fact that the whole world believed that only Louis Napoleon fought wars for reasons of internal politics. Purely from the point of view of self-preservation, it was high time to wage these three wars in order to deal with internal problems'.[16] As initially proclaimed in glaring terms by the 1848 revolution, confirmed by the constitutional conflict and underlined by the organisational success of labour, the industrial revolution had not only set society irrevocably in motion by stimulating political demands, but had begun to destroy the late-feudal power structure based on estates. It had given rise to irrepressible doubts about the system of inherited privilege and brought about a 'revolution of rising expectations'. In view of the strength of these developments the traditional strategy of 'taming' the forces in question could no longer be achieved successfully. The immediate and, even more so, the indirect consequences of the industrial revolution required the use of extraordinary methods by the groups which had traditionally held power in society. Since they possessed in Bismarck a political potential *sui generis* — and anyone who does not hold the view that 'men make history' will have to concede this — they were prepared to risk three wars as an almost desperate therapy for stabilising the monarchical system. The victorious outcome of these wars produced the desired effect. The authoritarian social and political system was once more legitimised. From then on one was able to feed on the massively prestigious success of Bismarck's diplomacy and the Prussian military. The internal crisis appeared defused. The main opponents, the National Liberals, succumbed, as desired, to the effects of this pacification carried out by the militant methods.

(2) The men of central government in Berlin, with an eye to the future, were fully aware that an expansion of Greater Prussia would fulfil the liberal bourgeoisie's desire for a unified nation state. It would also provide the best possible solution to the problem of uniting Germany while excluding Austria. The Austrian defeat in the German 'civil war' and the creation of the North German Confederation confirmed these calculations. The opinion was often enough expressed that a war fought in a common cause would soon overcome any resistance by the South German states to a Prussian-dominated Germany. It was also bound to have the effect of uniting the nation. 'To unite Germany by using force against France' was a

goal which Moltke envisaged as attainable in 1866. And this is precisely what happened when during the Franco–Prussian War national passions supplied the powerful driving force behind the policy which culminated in the Empire's founding. Just as the liberals had been brought to heel in the wars of 1864 and 1866, so too were the South German states by the war of 1870–71. This war, therefore, served a dual function. It was intended not only as 'a war of unification to round off the process begun by the Prussian war of secession in 1866'. It was intended, too, to cut short the fundamental political and social crisis of the Prussian military monarchy as 'a preventive war to achieve integration in internal politics'. This unification of Germany 'by the sword' and the overcoming of her internal problems by means of war had already been forecast as Prussia's mission by Clausewitz.[17] It cannot be denied that 'Bismarck's use of military force to solve the problem' of German unification was 'no less revolutionary than the liberal attempt of 1848. He broke once and for all with the old Empire's federalist tradition which had included Austria, and replaced it with a more limited nation state under Prussian hegemony and excluding Austria'.[18]

The conservative 'white revolutionary' in charge of Prussian policy was in this respect following the tradition of 'revolution from above'. He himself termed it a 'reform from above' and put it into practice using radical methods in its military phase. Shortly after the French Revolution the Prussian minister von Struensee had informed the French ambassador that 'the salutary revolution' which in France had proceeded 'from below upwards' would 'gradually develop from above downwards in Prussia'. By a policy of limited concessions the explosive revolutionary potential would be defused and a salutary transformation brought about by peaceful means. This 'revolution from above' had also been advocated in outline relatively early by Clausewitz. 'Europe cannot avoid a great general revolution', he wrote in 1809. 'Only those kings who know how to enter into the spirit of this great reformation and keep ahead of it will be able to survive.' Or, as his contemporary Gneisenau put it: 'Wise laws designed to forestall the outbreak of revolution are like detonating a mine laid under our feet from which we have removed the explosive bit by bit'. Long before Lorenz von Stein or Gustav von Schmoller had popularised the idea of a 'social monarchy' the intervention of the Crown determined practice in Prussian politics. That is why Bismarck, with a self-confidence that came from many years of practising 'revolution from above', took the view that 'in Prussia only kings make revolutions'.[19] After the bureaucratic variant of this tactic had failed to defuse the mine in 1848 and the principle of compensating the bourgeoisie for its lack of political power with economic concessions had been continued during the period of reaction, the only permanently reliable guarantor of this policy in German national politics, internally and externally, was the army. In the early 1860s bourgeois liberalism again showed itself to be too weak, even if the dynamic of social developments had not lost its momentum, all traditional strategies to unify Germany without Austria had failed. It was at this point that the army, in its role of executor of Bismarck's plans and those of the traditional élites, cut through the Gordian knot of domestic and foreign affairs by unleashing three wars. Even if, in the absence of a long overdue examination of the Confederation's capacity for reform and its federalist plans, one holds to the view that Bismarck's 'blood and iron' solution was inevitable given the circumstances of the time, one can scarcely deny that, in the end, this conservative revolutionary's successes only served to exacerbate the permanent crisis of German society and politics.

After 1870 keen observers from quite diverse political camps recognised the facts of the situation only too clearly. Gustav Freytag, respected spokesman for the educated middle class of National Liberal persuasion, voiced his suspicion that 'we have achieved greatness. Now the means by which we acquired it are casting a shadow over our future. We shall all pay a price for it'. The underlying problem of whether the Greater Prussian imperial state could keep the peace better, or at least as well as, the destroyed German Confederation (for long regarded wrongly as being of secondary importance once national unity had been achieved), was also recognised by the Saxon diplomat, Alexander von Villers. Perhaps too much in the style of Metternich's intransigent attitude towards the liberals, and taking too little account of new social currents and driving forces within Prussia, he noted that

the German Confederation, the last expression of statecraft in European diplomacy . . . had a defensive character. Within it Prussia was the aggressive yeast which set the well-kneaded dough in ferment. Germany not only lived at peace with her neighbours. She also acted as a brake upon every other European state that desired to break the peace internationally. The only, albeit unavoidable, fault in this organism was the assumption that

all its members possessed moral grandeur. . . . Prussia had long
let it be known that she would not let herself be outvoted by the
others. On the day this was said, the Confederation should have
stifled her for ever. But consideration was shown and, as a result,
the Confederation broke up.

In an impressive appeal to the Prussian Crown, the liberal academic
and publicist, G.C. Gervinus, who had democratic leanings, argued
movingly that

> the break-up of the German Confederation in 1866 has trans-
> formed two-thirds of the Empire into a state based on policies of
> war which is capable of aggression at any time. Without being an
> enemy of either Prussia or Germany, one can see in this a threat to
> peace in this part of the world and to the security of neighbouring
> states. . . . It is not a clever move to blind ourselves with patriot-
> ism to the fact that the events of 1866 have revived and magnified
> to an unreasonable extent the danger to this part of the world and
> the entire epoch from a social and political order one had believed
> was dying out. After five centuries of desiring, striving, and
> hoping to outgrow the military system of earlier times . . . a power
> based on the permanent use of war has emerged with a frightening
> superiority of which the military states of previous centuries, bent
> on conquest and expansion, could never remotely have con-
> ceived. . . . This judgement on the situation would have been greatly
> scoffed at had it been expressed formerly. But after the experiences of
> 1870 one would not wish to question it. These events have rejuven-
> ated this warrior state and have led inevitably to a rise in its
> self-esteem.

Was Karl Marx not also right when, after a similar analysis, he
sarcastically characterised the German Empire as 'a military despotism cloaked in parliamentary forms with a feudal ingredient and
at the same time influenced by the bourgeoisie, decked out by
bureaucrats, and safeguarded by the police'?[20]

We shall return to this in more detail in connection with our
analysis of the political system after 1871. What remains certain at
any rate is that the policies of Bismarck's Prussia 'fled' forward in
response to socio-economic and political pressures in order to stabilise and legitimise the state. As a result of three wars the Germans
were given an Empire in the shape of a Greater Prussia which
excluded Austria. It had been brought about by an extension of the
'revolution from above' using military means. The republican ideal
of a 'people's state' appeared finally discredited. Perhaps the crea-

tion of a nation state by the liberal bourgeoisie could in fact have come about after a successful 'revolution from below'. This had been the view in the spring of 1848, not only in Germany but in England. Later, however, it became increasingly clear that the 'small leap' forward by the 'enlightened monarchical state' had led the nation without a revolution up a blind alley. In fact the administrative practice of this state, in conjunction with the idea of 'revolution from above', had for a long time 'proved sufficiently strong to compete with the avowal of human rights'. Just as 'the poison of an unresolved and protracted crisis' had circulated since 1848 in 'the body of the German people', so no original act of emancipation by Germany's political sections of the population stood at the outset of the new state. Instead, the authoritarian Prussian state expanded on the strength of its dazzling successes into the German Empire of 1871.[21] Bourgeois industrial society was expected to accommodate itself within this structure. The aristocratic forces of the military and the landowners celebrated the triumph of their aggressively waged defensive struggle against powerful contemporary trends. The history of the new German Empire began in this light. In 1914 an even more hazardous leap forward, carried out by the self-same social groups, was to lead to its downfall.

II

Towards an Industrial State

1. The first phase of advanced industrialisation: uneven industrial growth and the structural crisis in agriculture, 1873–1895

During the period between 1850 and 1873 the German industrial revolution experienced an upswing in the business cycle. Germany was able to reap economic benefits at this time as a result of the 'advantages of backwardness'. In a relatively short space of time it reduced the economic and technological lead enjoyed by the industrialised countries of Western Europe, both through the practical adaptation of tried and tested methods and the introduction of deliberate training programmes. The German states, in their role as developing countries, borrowed whatever appeared useful to them from the more advanced nations, whether by imitating industrial processes, purchasing patents or by industrial espionage. In the early 1870s industrial capitalism, as 'the first method of production to institutionalise self-sustaining economic growth', showed a decisive spurt of development in the German Empire.[1] The global term 'Empire' can be misleading, however, since industry became dominant only in certain regions, e.g. in the Ruhr, the Saar, Upper Silesia and Saxony. Elsewhere relatively traditional conditions continued to prevail for a long time; or they changed only gradually as a result of the effects of industry. The process of economic growth in Germany continued, therefore, in a characteristically uneven manner.

The breakthrough of the industrial revolution was followed by the first decades of advanced industrialisation which transformed Germany into an industrial state within the span of a single generation. This transformation came about chiefly during the economic trend-period between 1873 and 1895. Beyond the overall trend, however, the historically significant characteristic of these years was the persistent recurrence of interruptions to economic growth in both the industrial and agrarian sectors. These had important consequences in causing and determining changes within the period itself as well as in their long-term effects lasting up until 1918. The decline in growth rates, the pessimistic economic climate and difficulties of readjustment were all the more oppressive for contemporaries because the twenty years of economic expansion culminating in an unprecedented boom between 1867 and 1873 established the level of expectations for the 1870s. The decade began with great promise, but the psychic reaction of society to the upswing made the real problems more acute; for the experience of the depression was to make the necessary readjustment to market conditions extremely difficult, even when the economic indicators began to point to a revival.

The industrial trend-period which lasted until 1895 was ushered in by the second world-wide economic crisis in the autumn of 1873. In the space of a few weeks, following a sharp fall on the stock exchange and bank failures, the crisis turned into a serious depression which continued without improvement until February 1879. The downturn in the economy halved the growth rates over a six-year period and led temporarily even to stagnation and a fall in production in some sectors. This was accompanied by a generally constant price deflation. The depression thus constituted the longest and most sudden interruption to German industrial growth up to that point. The important index of iron consumption fell over a short period of time by 50 per cent, and by 1879 miners' wages had been halved. The depression affected virtually every area of social life. In the same year the Berlin Chief of Police judged that its 'effect on earnings, together with pronounced social distress', was 'spreading doubts about the appropriateness of the social order and dissatisfaction at existing conditions among more and more otherwise calm and moderate sections of the population'. In Engels' view, it was one of those 'earthquakes that cause bourgeois society to shake at its foundations'.[2]

A short-lived recovery between the spring of 1879 and January 1882 failed to stimulate either the economy or the consciousness of contemporaries before a second, albeit considerably weaker, depression set in, which was to last until August 1886. Although the economy was not so hard hit as in the period between 1873 and 1879, the main significance of this downturn lay in the fact that it made the shock experienced during the 1870s even more traumatic and acute. People's apparent defencelessness in the face of the business cycle's drastic fluctuations seemed to underline once more how three fundamental and desired aims of capitalist activity could fall apart at any time: stable growth, the rational calculation of anticipated returns and the prospect of the regular maximisation of profit. Some even believed there was a danger of a breakdown in the social order because of the lack of permanent, if uneven, growth. And if the experience of industrial development had not been as novel as it still was at the time, the unspecified long-term trend of the second recession still offered little concrete consolation in view of the failure of all the benevolent market mechanisms of liberal economic theory. Now, at last, Marx's apt prognosis, made earlier in connection with the approaching crisis, appeared confirmed. This crisis, he said, will, 'because of its ubiquity and intensity, drum the lesson of the dialectic even into those blessed by success in the new holy Prusso–German Empire'.[3]

Between the autumn of 1886 and the beginning of 1890 the economy experienced a powerful upturn. The year 1889 could even be regarded as one of pronounced prosperity. But it was followed by a moderate downturn which dominated the period between January 1890 and February 1895. Thereafter a new trend-period of international and national prosperity was established on a wide front and continued from 1895 to 1913. In the twenty-odd years of Bismarck's chancellorship there were, therefore, only four years of economic boom. In Caprivi's period as Chancellor there was not even one! No realistic analysis can overlook this fact. The reason for the long interruptions to growth was a steadily increasing excess capacity resulting in over-production. This was a phenomenon typical of liberal capitalist production in the period of industrialisation. Because of the business cycle, the unpredictability of the market, the immobility of fixed capital and the uncertain prospects of long-term demand, it tended permanently to a condition of over-investment and susceptibility to crisis. In addition to this, the general problems of this trend-period were rendered even more acute by three further factors:

(1) The classic leading sectors of the German industrial revolution (iron, mining and railways) gradually lost their initial dynamism. Railway construction in particular fell from its leading position. Between 1870 and 1879 it had attracted 25 per cent of annual net investment in the German economy. By 1885 this figure had dropped to 13.5 per cent and by 1889 to 5.7 per cent. These figures, which reveal a contraction by four-fifths, concealed massive

movements of capital with profound effects on the metallurgical industry and a negative knock-on effect upon countless supply firms. Only the new leading sectors of the 1890s, that is, electrical engineering, the motor construction industry and chemicals, along with the expanding sector of service industries, managed to keep the upturn moving forward in their new role as cycle leaders.

(2) The unprecedented nature of the experience of industrial growth being hampered for years on end heightened problems of readjustment. At the same time that German industry was having to adapt itself to the gradually emerging world market and all its variables, it also had to come to terms with a domestic market that was becoming increasingly involved in the former, but which had not yet undergone expansion by a deliberate economic policy, to say nothing of an energetic policy to increase individual earnings or expand consumer demand.

(3) At the same time, the population of the German Empire grew dramatically during this very period of industrial and agricultural depression. Between 1873 and 1895 it jumped from 41.6 million to 52 million, an increase of 10.4 million, even discounting the fact that some 2 million Germans emigrated during these decades. This population rise produced enormous problems regarding the creation of employment and the value of available jobs. If, however, a situation of acute poverty comparable to the pre-1848 period did not arise, this was primarily because industry continued to expand despite all set-backs. Caught in the grip of a structural crisis, agriculture could absorb only a negligible amount of the labour force; growth industries managed to do so only from the mid-1880s onwards. Although bad living conditions did arise in the new conurbations, it was only thanks to industry itself that the process of urbanisation did not turn into a deadly danger to society. While the total population increased by 4.1 million each decade between 1871 and 1890, the urban population (statistically defined as communities of 2,000 or more inhabitants) climbed by approximately 3.5 million. In other words, the residential and industrial areas of the towns had to cope with over three-quarters of the increase in the German Empire's population. In the view of the traditional ruling élites and the bourgeoisie, these were the two decades during which the threshold was crossed from a predominantly agrarian to a predominantly industrial state, even though this was still argued over and by no means settled as an issue.

There can be no doubt that the three depressions in the industrial economy created sufficiently serious problems. But the fact that a structural crisis in agriculture coincided with a sharp decline in trade, both crises thus overlapping, reinforced the gloom which continued to spread and accounts for the contemporary notion of a 'Great Depression' which people spoke of in all Western industrial countries at the time. Ever since 1852 Germany had produced a small import surplus in rye. By the end of the 1870s, however, this continually exceeded 1 million tons and by 1879 had reached 1.3 million. Even more important was the fact that from 1876 onwards she changed from being a net exporter of wheat to being a net importer — and her imports were climbing rapidly. The same was true of oats and barley. Suddenly, in the second half of the 1870s, Germany realised how dependent she was upon grain imports. At the same time, a sharp fall in the price of her produce heralded the emergence of a competitive world market and the painful beginnings of a structural crisis in German agriculture which has lasted to the present day. By 1885 agricultural prices in Germany had fallen by approximately 20 per cent and the price levels of the 1870s were not reached again until 1912. In 1879 the average annual income in the agricultural sector fell below that of 1872.

This crisis in agriculture was mainly the result of powerful overseas competition, especially from the virgin territories of North America. After 1879, in particular, cheap American wheat, benefiting from a steady fall in production and transport costs, had the effect of depressing the entire price structure of the Central European agricultural market. At the same time, Russia, pursuing her own need to modernise — which depended mainly upon export profits for its financing — increased her grain exports appreciably. Canadian and Argentinian wheat, too, soon made their appearance on the market, and German grain producers, saddled with high production costs, heavy mortgages and exorbitant transport costs, proved no match for the competition. They immediately lost their main export customer, Great Britain, to the USA. The price of Prussian wheat, politically the most sensitive, sank from 221 marks per ton in 1880 to 157 marks per ton in 1886. For five years in all, the slump in the fortunes of the East German grain producers ran parallel with the second industrial depression. The old ruling élite of Prussian estate-owners, a class for whom Free Trade had been a dogma since the mid-1840s and whose profits were now directly hit, reacted to the international excess in production less in terms of a willingness to adapt and re-adjust economically. Rather they resorted to political action in order to defend the economic base of their superior social and political position. In an astonishingly short space of time they swung round behind a policy of agricultural protectionism. Although a brief recovery in the economy as a whole brought them some relief between 1887 and 1890, depressions in both the agricultural and industrial sectors coincided once again during the period of Caprivi's chancellorship.

If one considers the remarkable strains of the 1870s, 1880s and early 1890s, one gains some idea of what uneven industrial growth and the crisis in agriculture meant for those living at the time. Certainly, the crises had different effects upon different groups in German society. Producers were hard hit by the fall in prices and the need to find a sales market for their produce. Those on fixed salaries, on the other hand, were materially better off. For the vast numbers of wage-earners in the industrial working class, wage reductions, dismissals and short-time working throughout the 1870s created an all-pervading atmosphere of bleak hopelessness which without doubt aided the rise of the Social Democrats in Germany. To quote the Berlin Chief of Police again, even calm sections of the population were led by the conditions of distress into considering 'whether, indeed, an improvement in conditions could be brought about through the realisation of socialist theories'. As early as 1877 the Social Democrats won the fourth highest number of votes of all the parties in the elections to the new imperial parliament, the *Reichstag*.[4] When real wages began to show a gradual improvement in some sectors of industry, and at the same time the cost of living index fell, the grain sector still experienced no improvement. Both influential interest groups and broad sections of the population felt themselves constantly exposed, either directly or indirectly, to the violent fluctuations of industrial capitalism and the agricultural sector. For this reason a profound and momentous change in German economic policy is linked to this period of crisis. After the initial shock of the crisis in Central European agriculture and the six years of industrial depression, which resulted in the complete discrediting of the liberal economy and its associated theories, ideas and values, Free Trade gave way to a system of protective tariffs. It was the agrarian and industrial entrepreneurs who argued the loudest for protection against foreign competition, and the government soon legitimised their complaints with its thinly veiled slogan: 'Protection of the nation's work'; it was a sentiment at once economically chauvinistic and inimical to the best interests of the consumer. However, in view of the prevailing economic instability these groups held it as an urgent priority to stabilise prices in the home market while following a policy of dumping produce abroad. They also desired the undisturbed exploitation of a domestic market protected by higher tariff walls, a policy which withheld the advantages of falling prices on the world market from German wage- and salary-earners. The protective tariffs on agricultural produce, with which Germany led the way in Europe in 1879, were entirely in keeping with these interests. Between 1885 and 1887 the original tariff increased fivefold. By pursuing this policy Bismarck's government attempted to freeze 'the *status quo* in the class structure of land ownership and its distribution', in order to defend the 'collective position of ownership', especially of the great land-owners east of the river Elbe, and thus maintain their position of privilege at the expense of the less influential urban population. Even at a cursory glance, the Empire's agrarian policy based on tariffs revealed itself as a 'superficially camouflaged piece of class legislation'.[5]

At the same time, industrial tariffs singularly benefited heavy industry and strongly discriminated against the more export-orientated light industries producing manufactured goods. They placed difficult obstacles in the way of firms upon whose efficiency and success not only foreign trade and the balance of payments depended, but virtually the entire *modus operandi* of an economic system that was constantly outdistancing the strength of consumer demand in the home market. Judged from a purely economic standpoint, the whole policy of tariff protection appeared dubious. It proved completely ineffective when faced with new downturns in the economy after 1882 and 1890. In fact, as the highly-recommended panacea of earlier policies intended to combat the effects of the business cycle, it failed completely. But as a means of stabilising the political system, which was where its real significance lay, it did perform a vitally important function. If, as Gerschenkron has suggested, there was a 'great democratic opportunity'[6] after 1876 to wrest political power from the pre-industrial *Junker* élite because of the agrarian crisis, this chance was lost on account of an entire package of government-inspired protectionist measures and subsidies, of which the customs tariffs of 1879, 1885 and 1887 were only the most obvious. These tariffs won the support of industry, which was itself seeking protection, and were agreed to by the representatives of the bourgeoisie from their own motives of self-interest.

If all this succeeded in prolonging the predominance of the land-owning aristocracy, at the same time the victorious onward march of industry continued with all the strength of a natural force.

All the decisive economic statistics show an industrial predominance by 1890. The subsequent lively debate on whether or not Germany was 'an industrial or an agrarian state' was no longer, in fact, an open question but already an economic *fait accompli*. Industry finally overtook agriculture in the 1880s. In 1873 the latter's share of the net national product, based on 1913 prices in billions of marks, was 37.9 as compared with 31.7 for industry. By 1889 industry had caught up. In 1895 it overtook agriculture by 36.8 to 32.2, and the value of industrial output exceeded that of agriculture by 6.5 to 5.1. Of net investment, again based on 1913 prices, 22 billion marks flowed into agriculture in 1870, but by the mid-1870s it was down to 10 billion marks compared to 33 billion marks industry and commerce. The hiatus of the first economic depression brought about an almost equal level of 10.8 to 10.6 billion around 1879. This single figure, which shows a two-thirds contraction, makes the severity of the recession quite obvious. Industry then pulled away for good. In 1885 industrial investment rose by 11.5 to 37.5 and in 1890 by 13.8 to 45.3. In other words, industry's share of net investment rose from 14 billion to 45 billion marks over two decades!

These net investment figures concealed a critical redirection of the economy. The share of 45.3 billion marks claimed by industry decided the future course of the country's general development far earlier than most contemporary observers realised. Even the most superficial indicator of employment figures (which conveys nothing of varying levels of productivity, volume of production etc.), revealed that the die was cast in 1890. Although in 1871 the comparable figures for those employed in agriculture and in industry, transport, trade, banking and insurance was still 8.5 to 5.3 million, and 9.6 to 7.5 million in 1880, by 1890 the figures stood at 9.6 to 10 million. Thereafter, the trend accelerated to the disadvantage of agriculture. Wherever one looks, be it at wealth-creation, labour productivity, or its share of foreign trade and total production output, industry was everywhere triumphant, even though this development was not yet statistically apparent to contemporaries. That it had succeeded in becoming predominant despite obstacles to growth over the years and despite the long-term trend of price deflation with its resultant problems, merely underlines the tremendous dynamism developed by the unfettered process of industrialisation following its revolutionary breakthrough.

2. Industrial prosperity and the subsidised agrarian sector: the rise of 'organised capitalism' and state interventionism, 1895–1914

This powerful development of industry completely dominated the trend-period which followed between 1895 and 1913. The total output of industry and handicrafts, which had increased from 26.6 billion in 1873 to 45.4 in 1894, jumped from 48.9 in 1895 to 100 billion in 1913. In 1890 the share of net investment between industry and agriculture stood at 34 to 11.5 billion respectively. By 1900 it was 54.9 to 9 billion, and in 1910, 43 to 10 billion marks. The difference in the value of production was similarly striking. The German Empire's population grew from 49.2 million inhabitants in 1890 to 67 million in 1913. The overwhelming majority lived in towns, a sign of the urbanisation caused by the process of industrialisation. It was the urban population which would have benefited most from the unrestricted export of industrial products and importation of agricultural produce. Whereas 64 per cent of the population in 1871 still lived on the land in communities of less than 2,000 inhabitants, with only 5 per cent living in cities of over 100,000, a balance between the urban and rural populations in the early 1890s gave way to a situation in which by 1910 barely 40 per cent lived on the land (a 24 per cent decrease within 40 years), 21.3 per cent in the big cities (an increase of 16 per cent) and 27.4 per cent in medium-sized towns of between 5,000 to 100,000 inhabitants (an increase of 8.5 per cent over the 1871 figure of 18.9 per cent). The figure for those employed in agriculture, who numbered 9.8 million in 1900, increased to 10.5 million by 1910. In industry, transport, trade, banking and insurance, however, there were 10.3 million employed in 1900, rising to 13 million by 1910. The figure for those employed by large-scale concerns showed a similar increase. In 1875 firms employing up to 5 workers accounted for 64 per cent of the 18.6 million total employed. In the 30 years before 1907 this share dropped by half to 31.9 per cent of a total of 28 million employed. Firms in the category of between 5 and 50 employees grew to 26 per cent; those with between 50 and 1,000 employees grew to 37 per cent and those with over 1,000 employees increased to 5 per cent. The share of the total work-force grew fastest among large-scale industrial firms, from 1.9 per cent in 1882 to 5.7 per cent in 1907. The average hours worked decreased from 72 hours per week in 1872 to 62 in 1900 and 57 in 1914. Despite all the doom-ridden predictions of the impending decline that shorter hours would bring, productivity constantly rose. The same was true of the average life expectancy of the German population. In 1871 it was a mere 37 years, or, rather, 35.6 for men and 38.3 for women. By 1910 this had already risen to 47 years, i.e. 44.8 for men and 48.3 for women.[7] (In West Germany in 1980 it was 72 years.) This increase caused new problems with regard to the housing supply, the care of old people and the creation of employment. Only the further expansion of industry itself proved capable providing a measure of relief in the long term.

The year 1895 is an important base year for the economic historian, not only because it marked the onset of a boom period, but because the mid-1890s constituted a formal 'watershed between two distinct epochs in the social development of capitalism'.[8] Up until that time a system of modern large-scale industrial enterprises had been developing which henceforth dominated the economic landscape. Beyond this, large firms, whether family businesses, joint-stock companies dependent upon banks or massive trusts, pointed to a new qualitative stage of development and form of organisation in the industrial economy. After decades during which small and medium firms had been the norm and in which the liberal theory of competition might still have had relevance, big business came to dominate industrial activity. For years its oligopolistic form of competition, social significance and political importance could not be accounted for by bourgeois economic theory. Marx's theory of industrial concentration and centralisation, on the other hand, had predicted this development early on and integrated it into an analysis of the entire social structure. Marxist social scientists like Hilferding, Bauer, Kautsky and others, drew attention to this phenomenon; but scholars like Max Weber, Schumpeter and Schulze-Gävernitz also clearly identified this new economic structure at the same time as American observers were noting the rise of 'corporation capitalism'. This new form of 'cartel capitalism' of big business, which emerged from the end of the 1870s onwards, strove to ensure, to an unprecedented degree, economic stability, the rational calculation of commercial opportunities and prosperity by means of secure profits for the individual firm or, on a larger scale, through cooperation between members of the oligopoly. Not least as a result of this, scientific research was brought into company activities so that the regular flow of technological innovations — the life-blood of industrial expansion — could be controlled from within. The effects of irregular growth, inherent in the economic system with all its consequences, were to be ameliorated by forms of short-term substitute planning worked out by the interested parties. There remained less and less room in this 'organised capitalism' for liberal competition, which acted as a price regulator, for the autonomy of industrial enterprises, or for the acquisition of profit as a reward for individual risk-taking. In many ways this new brand of capitalist organisation was influenced by the general view that modern industrial development could no longer be left to the self-regulation of the market in the sense of Adam Smith's 'Invisible Hand'. At the same time, however, the camouflage of a liberal market economy was retained.

'Organised capitalism' was inseparably connected with the process of concentration in other areas of economic organisation. While horizontal and vertical concentration increased their permanent assets by leaps and bounds, companies expanded according to the law of productive efficiency, rationalisation and the maximisation of profits into large concerns or trusts controlling a major slice of the market. Factories in the same branch of industry combined to form cartels or monopolist syndicates. These cartels often arose as short-lived 'children of necessity',[9] especially during the depressions of both trend-periods, but became a general feature in an economy increasingly structured by such combines. For a long time they were seen as a typically German form of concentration, but in Anglo-Saxon countries this merely expressed itself in other legal forms. The process of concentration among individual companies and branches of industry can be traced also on the level of the national economy. Protective tariffs intended to shield a close-knit domestic market, alongside numerous examples of state interventionism in foreign trade which treated the national economy as a unit, belong in this context. We can also see the plans which existed for supranational combines in a 'Central Europe' (*Mitteleuropa*) cartel of states and customs union, together with certain features of imperialism and its tendency towards monopoly markets, as extensions of internal national economic concentration. What this process of concentration meant for the influential groups in industry and banking, for pressure groups and, hence, for politics in general, is a problem which has not yet been explained by the social or political historian. At any rate, it was one of the earliest and most typical signs of the emergence of an advanced industrial-capitalist economy in the German Empire.

The world economic recovery, the three new leading sectors of German industry and the unprecedented new investment opportunities for major firms and banks pulled the German economy into a whirlwind boom period after March 1895. It would, however, be quite misleading to describe the trend-period from 1895 to 1913 as one of high prosperity throughout. It was twice interrupted by severe, though relatively brief, depressions between March 1900 to March 1902 and July 1907 to December 1908. Towards the end of this trend-period, from April 1913 onwards, the onset of a further depression cast its shadow over the last months before the outbreak of the First World War. There was certainly no levelling-out of the business cycle. The fluctuations of crisis followed by downturn, depression, upturn, boom and crisis, inherent in the capitalist system, continued to occur. But the phases of the cycle in the strictest sense (1895–1900, 1902–1907, 1909–1913, during which net investment ran at 15 per cent of the GNP) testify to an explosive expansion of industrial production which, because it overcame slumps considerably more quickly than previously, gave rise to a widespread sense of boom. Between 1895 and 1900 production increased by exactly a third, as estimated by a well-informed economist of the time. His study of the economy as a whole noted, however, that domestic consumption in the same period increased by only a fifth.[10] The enormous increase in production did not maintain its level during the second boom beginning in early 1902, since some sectors experienced a mild recession between April 1903 and February 1905. But after the crisis of 1907 and 1908 the boom became so impressive as to exceed output levels for the last five years before the turn of the century. Indeed, output again attained the levels reached between 1867 and 1873. The net national product of the German Empire rose by 10 billion marks from 42.44 in 1908 to 52.44 billion in 1913.

Between 1907 and 1913 production in the classic sector of coal-mining increased by a third, from 143 to 191 million tons. Iron production increased by as much as a half, from 13 to 19.3 million tons. The German Empire's rail freight traffic also increased by a third. But above all, the electrical industry, represented by Siemens and AEG (whose advances led to a one-third increase in lignite production from 62.5 to 87 million tons), the chemicals industry and the motor construction industry (whose electrical motors stimulated growth in small and medium firms) all achieved unprecedented growth rates. The greatly increased need for new sales markets, caused by inevitable over-production, provided a further stimulus to German exports in the world market. Imports rose by 2.2 billion marks, exports by 3.3 billion, and the total volume of foreign trade by a third from 15.6 to 20.9 billion marks.[11] German industry's success in the world economy has remained a much-discussed phenomenon ever since the 1880s and 1890s. The growth of European and American protectionism spurred it on to increased efforts and a remarkable achievement of high export figures. Both this and the general effects of continued growth contributed to a relaxation of tensions within German society.

Here was the economically brilliant exterior that Wilhelmine Germany presented to the world. However, capital formation experienced increasing difficulty in keeping pace. Once reserves had been exhausted, the incessant strain on credit brought closer a politically dangerous limit in both her internal and external politics. In addition, differences in the distribution of income and private wealth grew ever greater. The wage-earning mass of the industrial work-force were hardest hit by a rise in unemployment. The previous all-time high of 319,000 in 1908 was overtaken by a figure of 348,000 in 1913. At the same time, many white-collar workers, artisans and civil servants benefited little from the economic upswing. If, for example, we compare the growth in real wages between 1890 and 1914 in Great Britain, France, Sweden and the USA, where they rose on average by an annual 4 per cent, with those in the German Empire, which showed only a 1 per cent rate of annual increase, the conclusion that real wages in Germany lagged far behind is completely justified.[12] This imbalance in a rapidly growing GNP has to be contrasted soberly with fine-sounding phrases on 'the rising prosperity of the German population' before 1914. The slow rise in real wages was one of the reasons behind an increase in the number of women in employment. It rose by one and a half times between 1905 and 1913. Countless families were able to make ends meet only if the wife was in full-time employment. The almost constant and steep rise in the cost of living — by a third between 1900 and 1913 — was a result of the rise in food prices which followed Bülow's 1902 tariff, itself a direct consequence of the nature of imperial Germany's power structure.

The tariffs which came into force after 1879 were determined to a large extent by the land-owning aristocracy in the provinces east of the river Elbe. A well-informed observer, the liberal politican Friedrich Naumann, estimated the size of this 'old ruling class' around 1900 at about 24,000 in a population of some 56 million. Yet this small power-élite ruled the countryside, initially without restriction, from their isolated feudal estates and posts as district governors entirely in accordance with their own interests. Not until 1891 did it prove possible to introduce a law to permit the central authorities to govern the Prussian rural communities. For decades *Junker* resistance to a codification or revision of the traditional legal system had brought them nothing but advantages. In practice the old system had amounted to a 'legal anarchy' which favoured the authority of the land-owner. Yet even after 1891 little changed in everyday practice. For agricultural labourers, farmhands and others who lacked legal rights, the refuge of internal migration to the industrial regions and their rising prosperity became an attractive prospect during this period. The resultant exodus from the land represented, therefore, a kind of 'covert strike'.[13] Furthermore, the aristocracy's interests were as much looked after by the district and provincial administrations as by the army and by government policy. Thanks to the successful wars of the 1860s, Bismarck's rule and Prussian hegemony, the Chancellor's reliable majorities in the Diet, Prussian civil servants and the Court, together with direct and informal control over numerous key political positions, the German Empire's policies were strongly influenced by aristocratic interests. The liberal deputy, Ludwig Bamberger, spoke of a 'reign by *Junker* such as had never been seen before'. This was the situation which lay behind the criticism of 'agrarian party rule over Germany' right up to the last years before the war.[14]

The aristocracy's claim to leadership in the state was so deeply rooted historically and so tenaciously defended that the bourgeoisie, disorientated by the events of 1848, the Constitutional Conflict and Bonapartism, succumbed to a process of feudalisation, or to be more exact, of 'aristocratisation'. In other words, it began to imitate the nobility's modes of behaviour and life-style, accommodating itself in the process to aristocratic values and aspirations. To own a feudal estate, to have one's son serving in the Garde du Corps or practising a neo-feudal code of honour in the university duelling fraternities, became the new bourgeois ideals which were perfectly in harmony with a renunciation of the struggle for political predominance. This aping of an alien life-style suited the 'spirit of pompous obsequiousness' expressed by the German middle classes in their relations with their 'hereditary rulers', the nobility. The owners and directors of companies sought to legitimise their entrepreneurial power by exercising paternalism and adopting a posture of 'master in one's own house', thus transferring the land-owner model of authority and the related mentality of a military command structure to industry.[15]

One can view these developments as evidence of the effects of the aristocracy's historical role and its success as a class. Its insistence on a position of dominance was, however, challenged by the transition to an industrialised society in which social groups pursued divergent interests and by the impersonal effects of a world market in agriculture which exposed the economic base of the East Elbian land-owners to rapid erosion. In 1895 Max Weber thought he could already discern the 'economic death throes' of the *Junker* class. Moreover, it was 'incompatible with the national interest in the long run . . . that an economically declining class should exert political authority'.[16] The old ruling élite tried to arrest the decline by a ruthlessly defiant struggle and by mobilising government support and subsidies in its favour. But since the processes at work lay outside its effective control, this defensive struggle, waged by the agrarians against their powerful opponents of foreign competition and industry, was conducted with an increasingly bitter, even desperate, intransigence. Following the last tariff increase under Bismarck in 1887, the trade agreements of Caprivi's period as Chancellor after 1891 favoured industry at a time when agricultural prices reached their lowest level since the 1870s. The duties on produce were lowered by about a third. It was in response to continuing pressure from the great land-owners that the 1902 tariff was increased. It came into force after March 1906 and considerably exceeded the levels set in 1887. Within the framework of a new 'policy for rallying collective interests' (*Sammlung*), to be discussed below, a bargain was struck which was first analysed in a classic study by Eckart Kehr: the agrarians tolerated the building of the German battle fleet for the industrial bourgeoisie, and in return the latter supported increased agricultural tariffs for the Prussian grain producers. Once more they profited from increased protectionism; but in all no more than 25 per cent of agricultural undertakings and about 18 per cent of the rural population actually benefited from the higher grain prices. In contrast, according to the economist Lujo Brentano's careful calculations, a worker had to work 13 to 18 days more to make up for the higher food prices caused by the new duties.[17] This piece of undisguised class legislation was carried over until well into the new century. The Bülow tariff was in fact renewed in 1925 and remained in force until 1945 — yet another example of historical continuity in the policies of vested interests which pushed through enormous privileges for a *Junker* class that was neither capable of economic competition nor of any attempt to adjust to new conditions. The great land-owners were to find their ideal finally realised in the framework of the 'Reich Food Estate' market organisation of the Hitler era.

In 1894 a motion was introduced by the Conservative deputy, Count Kanitz, which sought to establish an import monopoly for the imperial government and authorise it to sell in the domestic

market at the average price calculated from the years 1850–90,
provided that this remained higher than the price on the world
market. It was defeated in the German parliament, to the great
chagrin of the agrarian lobby. In addition to Germany's bill for
annual total food consumption, amounting to 7.5 billion marks, the
acceptance of this motion would, as Schmoller estimated in the
mid-1890s, have burdened the German consumer once again with
the expense of an outright gift of 500 million marks to the grain
producers. The 'estate responsible for upholding the monarchical
state' succeeded, however, in obtaining a system of import coupons
which had the effect of indirect export premiums. It meant that rye
could be exported once more at the expense of the German taxpayer.
After 1908 the German Empire became the 'second biggest rye-
exporting country in the world' and the entire economy was burdened artificially not only with the maintenance but also with the
expansion of grain production.[18] The success of pig breeding in the
north-west of Germany clearly showed how well her farmers were
capable of adjusting to the new conditions of a world market.
Conversely, the rise in rye production, by 33 per cent between 1900
and 1913 (from 14.4 to 19.1 million metric hundredweight), which
directly benefited the exporting grain producers on account of the
system of import coupons, accelerated growth in animal husbandry
and milk sales in the importing countries. This in turn made it more
difficult for German agriculture to change over to alternative crops.
It was a vicious circle, caused by the fact that the Prussian land-
owning aristocracy's defensive campaign proved only too successful
politically and economically. What was true of it in general was also
true in this particular case. This reactionary class prolonged its
existence and political predominance at the expense of the majority
of the population. It did so by only partially adjusting to the process
of modernisation, increasing the efficiency of its agricultural methods
but also skilfully exploiting its capacity for influencing legislation on
foreign trade.

The irregularities of industrial growth affected not only specific
interest groups to an unprecedented degree after 1873, but the entire
population. Because of its wide-ranging effects on the economy,
society and politics, already evident before 1879, the 'organised
capitalism' of big business also asserted itself rapidly in an attempt,
so to speak, at self-help. But alongside this, early forms of modern
state interventionism were being developed, at first hesitantly and
tentatively but more deliberately and on a massive scale later.
'Organised capitalism' and state interventionism were in fact two

sides of the same coin; two aspects of uneven industrial development
under the aegis of big business and the process of industrial concentration. Vested interests called for 'the private mobilisation of state
power' as necessary to their continued success, and this resulted in
'a much greater degree of government intervention in economic
affairs'.[19] The political leadership, power-élites and the bureaucracy,
in short the 'state', became increasingly involved in the management of the economy and in economic policy-making. These
groups possessed their own motives, which were dictated by the
need to stabilise and legitimise the existing political system. The
interventionist state cannot be reduced simply to the notion that it
acted as a mere agent of the economy itself. For a long time past,
even in the era of Free Trade, the state had, of course, assisted
economic interest groups with commercial treaties, consulates, gunboats, guaranteed interest rates, subsidies and diplomatic ma-
nouevrings. But it was only after the fast tempo of industrialisation
following the industrial revolution's breakthrough and the problems
caused by uneven growth that the need for social controls grew
really urgent. The fluctuations of economic development had produced incalculable effects on society as a whole. Here, too, the
experience of the 1873–79 depression proved crucially important; for
the trying out of policies designed to control the economy effectively
was widely regarded as imperative after that time. In 1879 the
Secretary of State at the Imperial Ministry of Justice, Heinrich von
Friedberg, commented that for years, 'all our thoughts, whether
optimistic or pessimistic, were exclusively involved with and dominated by economic policy'. Now, however, they had 'achieved
complete predominance'. In keeping with this development the state
began to intervene even more directly than before; or it interfered
covertly, whether by means of protective tariffs or import coupons,
reduced freight rates for export goods by rail and canal, preferential
rates on goods imported for processing before re-export, or tax
benefits. It also provided government subsidies, for brandy distil-
leries and shipping lines, or gave help in potentially large markets, in
the acquisition of colonies and in the use of consular services. In
short, there was a whole range of measures designed to help the
government realise its own economic and socio-political aims. From
all this it follows that, contrary to what neo-liberal economic theories have maintained, state interventionism was not something 'alien,
grafted on to the system' but 'immanent to it and an embodiment of
its urge for self-preservation'. 'Nothing illustrates the concept of the
dialectic more clearly.' State interventionism confirmed the system's

capacity to learn from experience, its powers of resilience and, indirectly, its tendency to break down, if left entirely to market forces.[20]

Here we can detect the birth of a phenomenon of our own times. Under the prevailing system of state-regulated capitalism political authority is chiefly legitimised by the government's concern to correct disturbances to economic growth so as to preserve the continuing stability of the economy and society. The 'need for legitimacy' which governs modern societies leads to the adoption of 'an economic programme' to replace the liberal ideology of a capitalist market economy discredited since 1929 at the latest. This 'economic programme' puts an obligation upon the ruling élites and their allied interests, whose main priority is to maintain the system, to preserve the conditions necessary to stabilise the entire system and forestall any risks to continued growth. Consequently, they require 'a policy to secure the loyalty of the wage-earning masses by compensating them in order to avoid conflict'. Constant and, whenever possible, balanced economic growth assumes, therefore, a critical 'function in legitimising political authority'.[21] The initial phase of this policy, which cannot be deduced from purely economic motives, coincided in Germany with the Bismarck era. Numerous moves carried out in connection with the growth in state interventionism can be seen in this light as attempts by the state and its supportive social groups to create improved conditions in order to stabilise the economic and social system. These were intended not only to improve opportunities for further economic growth, but also to defuse internal conflicts over the distribution of national wealth and access to power. They were designed to shore up the political rule of an authoritarian state and its privileged classes in the face of growing criticisms of traditional and charismatic authority. The post-1879 system of protective tariffs and the economic and social imperialism dating from this period, together with government plans to create monopolies, its nationalisation of the railways and various new measures in foreign trade, taxation and fiscal policy, begin to reveal their rationale only if one takes into account their function in legitimising the existing system.

It should be borne in mind that, theoretically in accordance with the economic theories at the time and, practically, within the scope permitted by the law and the political interests involved, the government's freedom of action was severely limited. Its actions often appear as tentative and pragmatic, suffering many set-backs and requiring countless experiments before a specific instrument at its disposal could be used with any prospect of success. The initial priority given to foreign trade policy in terms of protectionism and imperialism begins to make sense only when we realise that of the three modern tools of government attempts to steer the economy (monetary, fiscal and foreign trade policies) neither of the first two could be used to prop up the government in Germany. Since the Imperial Treasury operated according to rules imposed by the gold standard and, moreover, was unable to pursue policies of the kind associated with a modern central bank, the government had no suitable lever at its disposal for an anti-cyclical monetary policy. There were, likewise, no central institutions through which Berlin's fiscal policy could be made to influence the economy. Within the theoretical and institutional possibilities of the time, therefore, the only field left for early attempts to manage the economy was foreign trade.[22] As a result, the first lever to be applied was protective tariffs. When, in spite of rising tariffs, a protectionist policy failed to provide shelter from the fluctuations of the world economy, measures to encourage exports again increased. 'Organised capitalism' and state interventionism set out on the same road which held out the prospect of a bright future. Parliamentary struggles, press feuds and the confusing variety of contemporary disagreements should not obscure the reasons behind growing state interventionism.

At no point did this development take place unopposed. Nor did it proceed rapidly and without friction. But viewed from an historical perspective it would seem that state interventionism in Germany revealed its Janus-faced character early on and in clear outline. It can hardly be denied that a country's economic dynamism with its enormously far-reaching social and political effects requires some form of direction, however much the actual extent of this has remained a subject for debate. In the case of imperial Germany, however, the future belonged to state interventionism as an accompaniment to her ongoing advanced industrialisation. Only social controls could guarantee a gradual defusing of serious conflicts of interest in a modern industrial society; and only orthodox liberals of the Manchester school, or those pursuing a group egoism, could deceive themselves on this point. At the same time, everything depended upon who benefited from the state's intervention, the social costs it entailed and the specific aims it pursued. Imperial Germany's social power structure entirely ruled out a socially egalitarian economic policy which would have promoted the well-being of the majority of her population. This has to be stated without hesitation, for it is empirically irrefutable. It was the pre-industrial élites, such as the great land-owners, the new barons of heavy industry and, in particular, the political leaders of Germany's authoritarian government, who derived the greatest benefit from state interventionism in the long and short terms. At the same time, it was also the case that the 'artificial increase in the cost of living caused by tariffs' was one of the 'most effective means of creating massive unrest' which in turn increased 'the breeding ground of Social Democracy'.[23] Right up until 1918 German state interventionism retained its decidedly illiberal, anti-democratic features. The social and economic effects of the stabilisation that it regularly achieved were decidedly conservative. They worked not only to the advantage of narrow economic interests, but always benefited those social groups which harboured a hostility towards democracy. The successes of state interventionism continued, therefore, to legitimise authoritarian rule still further in Imperial Germany.

III

The Ruling System and Politics

1. The political system

1.1 *Constitutional monarchy or pseudo-constitutional semi-absolutism?*

Four and a half years after victory in the Austro-Prussian war, but before the end of Bismarck's third war, Greater Prussia, which had been expanding since 1866, was rechristened 'the German Empire' in a ceremony at Versailles which anachronistically imitated the ancient Germanic custom of electing a warrior chieftain. What was this German Empire, founded as it was by contractual agreement on 1 January 1871? How might its political system be defined, while at the same time observing the traditional distinction between constitutional law and constitutional reality?

The German Empire's basis in institutional and corporate law was rooted in the Imperial Constitution of 4 May 1871 which was closely modelled on the North German Confederation's constitution of 1867. In accordance with this statute of association, twenty-two sovereign German principalities and three Free Hanseatic towns combined to form a 'perpetual union'. The principle behind its formation was the setting up of a two-tier system comprising a chief state in the shape of the Empire, to which the affiliated subordinate states, while assuming certain responsibilities, surrendered specific sovereign rights. Only in one area did this federal, though not confederate, main state exercise direct unitary sovereignty from the outset and that was in the case of the so-called 'imperial province' of Alsace–Lorraine. This province was not accorded any form of autonomy or independent sovereignty within the Empire's structure until 1918, even though this was originally a basic principle in the Imperial Constitution and applied to all member states. Formal sovereignty was vested in the Federal Council (*Bundesrat*) on which the various states were represented. At the same time, this formed a

52

part of the legislature, its delegates being appointed by the executives of the member states. Prussia's special position in this scheme was recognised both in law and in fact. In the words of Arthur Rosenberg, the Federal Council merely acted as 'the constitutional fig-leaf of Prussian rule over the Empire'. Bismarck saw its sittings primarily as 'meetings of Prussian ministers at a national level, augmented by the participation of ministers from the other states'.[1] Symbolically, however, the German Emperor came to be increasingly regarded, especially in the popular consciousness, as the actual sovereign of the German Empire. The Imperial Chancellor chaired the meetings of the Federal Council and assumed ultimate responsibility by the countersigning of all laws. This was certainly not responsibility in the parliamentary sense of the word, but in the limited sense of a counter-signature secured by the bureaucracy of the absolutist state as proof that it based itself upon the rule of law (*Rechtsstaat*). The Imperial Chancellor, in particular, represented the full weight of this Prussian 'Empire State' by virtue of his dual role as Prussian Prime Minister and Minister for Foreign Affairs. This powerful combination of offices created an extremely important key position; either of whose props could be given up only at the risk of a considerable erosion of power.

Beside the monarch, the Federal Council, and the Imperial Chancellor, the parliament (*Reichstag*) with its 400 deputies elected by direct and secret male suffrage counted as the fourth power factor. Bismarck had introduced this parliamentary suffrage earlier at the time of the North German Confederation. He had done this for, 'as was well known, exclusively demagogic reasons' and, as Max Weber put it, 'as part of his Caesaristic struggle against the obstinate bourgeoisie of the time'. The Chancellor had openly built his hopes entirely upon the vast numbers of reliable conservative voters in the countryside, in order, with the aid of this pseudo-parliamentary tactic, 'to overthrow', as he himself put it, 'parliamentarism by parliamentary means'.[2] For a long time he succeeded in obstructing the development of parliamentary influence but, on the whole, his conservative scheming was often frustrated by the *Reichstag*'s political composition, or else was satisfied only by the use of additional pressure tactics. He was obliged to oppose the gradual spread of 'democratic and parliamentary sentiment for a unified Germany' within the *Reichstag* by means of an 'entirely federalist ideology and rhetoric' which was intended to gloss over rival plans for 'Prussian hegemony in a united Germany'. This tactic succeeded in obscuring constitutional reality to a considerable extent. But even if one leaves

aside the constitution and the many inhibiting factors in the German
political tradition, the *Reichstag*, despite its right to approve the
budget, could not become an independent power factor; the right of
dissolution lay beyond its control — with the Emperor and the
Federal Council. As Thomas Hobbes had said centuries before of
such political bodies: 'For if there be a right in any else to dissolve
them, there is a right also to controule them, and consequently to
controule their controulings.'[3]

Can this hybrid of Prussian hegemony and imperial federation,
which combined ancient authority with modern suffrage, be accurately and adequately described as a 'constitutional monarchy'?
Should one see in this monarchy, limited as it was by a constitution,
a political form in its own right, or merely a transitional phenomenon — a procrastinatory compromise, a sham peace, a truce between the monarchy and a bourgeoisie of liberal–parliamentary
persuasions? Did it embody an astonishing victory of feudal forces?
Or was it merely the first step on the road to a parliamentary form of
government based on popular sovereignty? Until recently many
people, including the overwhelming majority of German historians,
have seen in this state 'an appropriate solution to the German
constitutional problem' of a hundred years ago.[4] But what does
'appropriate' mean in this context? Given the historical options
available before 1871, should one, in the absence of any new critical
research, conclude that Bismarck's solution was, in the light of the
facts, the only possible one? Should one continue to label this
monarchy 'satisfactory', even from the historical perspective of the
present? The nostalgia for the 'sane' world of the pre-1914 authoritarian state in Germany wants to do both. A sober critique, however, no longer falls for either.

In the expression 'constitutional monarchy' the main emphasis
was placed on the noun and not the adjective. It was certainly a case
of rule by the King. The Prussian monarch controlled not just the
three pillars of absolutism in the dominant Prussian state that
comprised two-thirds of the German Empire — the army, the
bureaucracy and diplomacy. In his role as Emperor he also controlled the new imperial administration together with its army and
foreign policy. The German parliament never succeeded in penetrating these *arcana imperii* with its influence. The power structure of
the absolutist state remained constitutionally safeguarded and essentially unchanged. If provision for the exercise of the monarch's
executive power is the essential criterion of constitutional monarchy,
the Prussian King and German Emperor possessed 'decisive and,

hence, crucial' influence within the Imperial Constitution by virtue of his control over the three pillars of the state. In other words, the forces of absolutism remained 'a power which determined the nature of the constitution'. And since the levers of power from the old authoritarian state were still under the control of the monarch (and his advisers!), any important decisions depended upon the authoritarian head of state.

Secondly, although the constitution was an unavoidable concession to the liberal demands of the bourgeois era, the hardcore of the traditional ruling system remained. Marx underestimated this firm nucleus in his polemic against Germany's constitutional monarchy, describing it as 'a thoroughly self-contradictory and self-nullifying hermaphrodite' — although his prognosis turned out to have been realistic in the long run.[5] The political system was, in fact, an autocratic, semi-absolutist sham constitutionalism, because the real power relationships had not undergone any decisive alteration. This was all the more true if one, as here, uses the term 'power' in a wider sense than that implied by constitutional law. The controversial formulation of 'a monarchical, semi-absolutism running counter to the times' is certainly on the right lines.[6] But it should not be seen as a form of neo-absolutism, since the continuity of the old absolutist regime remained preserved behind its constitutional facade. Even so, to describe Germany as a pseudo-constitutional authoritarian monarchy still does not adequately account for the true nature of the German Empire's constitutional reality after 1871. This can be discerned only, as Lassalle put it, 'in the actual power relationships which exist within a country'.[7] If one wishes to define the German Empire's form of government in proper historical terms, it is necessary to distinguish between the two phases of 1871 to 1890 and 1890 to 1918. With regard to the first of these periods, it is also vital to take full account of Bismarck's role as well as the social function of the political authority which he chiefly embodied.

1.2   *The Bonapartist dictatorship up to 1890*

The liberals, who had finally succumbed to *Realpolitik* between the time of the Constitutional Conflict and the founding of the Empire at Versailles, were willing to put up with 'Bismarck's bold tyranny . . . in the interest of creating the Empire'. But after a few years of National Liberal influence on legislation and an equally pronounced self-deception as to their own worth, critical thinkers in their midst began to speak of the 'brutal rule of an omnipotent *Junker*'s frivolous and whimsical notions' as a 'chancellor dictatorship'.[8] This concept was not understood in an exact constitutional sense in the 1870s and 1880s, of course. As all its critics were aware, the subordinate position occupied by the Imperial Chancellor was laid down un-equivocally in the constitution. But as a description of constitutional reality, the term readily suggested itself, with the result that even the historian Friedrich Meinecke viewed the German Empire's first chancellor as exercising 'a kind of dictatorship'.[9] In fact, there can be little doubt as to this dictatorial element. Whether from the left or right of the political spectrum, well-informed contemporaries who knew those involved agreed on this point. 'Everything depends entirely on Bismarck' was the judgement of the ultra-conservative German ambassador in St Petersburg, General von Schweinitz: 'There has never been a more complete autocracy'. He saw the guiding motto of 'Bismarck's dictatorship' as being *Moi, je suis l'état.* That 'everything hinges on Bismarck', was also the view, based on close observation, of the later Secretary of State and Minister of Education, Bosse: 'He has the ministers completely on a leash'. 'Under the rule of this Jupiter', complained the Mecklenburg del-egate to the Federal Council, Oldenburg, 'everything carried on in the correct rhythm and proffered dumb obedience . . . everyone placed himself without fuss under the yoke.' 'Old Liberals' like the Rhenish entrepreneur Mevissen regarded Bismarck as having been 'omnipotent for some time'. The 'Prince's absolutism stood at the zenith of its power and presumption'; and the liberal Friedrich Kapp mocked bitterly that 'Bismarck acknowledges only one form of government: himself'. He needed only 'a majority of eunuchs' in the *Reichstag* 'who would not be allowed to open their mouths'. Foreign observers like the English ambassador, Lord Ampthill, spoke in equally clear terms of a 'German dictator whose power is at its height'. The American minister John A. Kasson, spoke of 'an effectively all-powerful dictator' whose 'prestige at present is without parallel in European history'. These judgements were echoed sev-eral times over by the French diplomats St Vallier and de Courcel.[10] As if further proof was required even Kaiser Wilhelm I confessed: 'It isn't easy to be an emperor under a chancellor like this one'. Against the entire spirit of the constitution, but in a revealing Freudian slip, his remark that 'Your subjects [i.e., ministers and imperial secretaries of state] must possess your confidence', revealed the true hierarchy in Berlin. 'I am master of Germany in all but name', was how Bismarck with reputed candour described in exact terms his skilfully feigned role as a 'vassal of Prussia'.[11]

Nevertheless, the concept of a 'chancellor dictatorship' is still not enough. It is too narrow and personalistic. For a comparative typology of forms of political rule, which can accommodate the constitutional reality of imperial Germany, the concept of Bonapartism is particularly useful. Its explanatory value in illuminating the social function of political authority is to be found in its peculiar combination of charismatic, plebiscitary and traditionalist elements, all of which were also clearly in evidence in Germany. Deriving from the regime of Napoleon III, and classically analysed in Marx's *Eighteenth Brumaire*,[12] Bonapartism is best understood as an authoritarian form of government which first appeared in a relatively early phase of industrialisation when the pre-industrial élites were still able to demonstrate their strength; the bourgeoisie was making rapid advances. while simultaneously threatened from below by the workers' movement — foreshadowed by the 'red spectre' of the revolutionary years of 1848 to 1849. It would be quite misleading, however, to speak of an equilibrium existing between the major social classes. The traditional power structure, hitherto based on estates, was being challenged at this time. The bourgeoisie was being strongly moved by the fear of social upheaval into accommodating itself with the forces of tradition. It renounced its claim to the direct exercise of political power at time when the workers were arousing fears as a force for modernisation, or at least as a symbol for change. In the light of such a specific constellation of forces, often viewed as an open-ended state of 'suspension', extraordinary opportunities could open up for a charismatic politician to carry out a policy of stabilisation on behalf of the ruling classes by the use of certain devices appropriate to the times. Historical examples show that these always involved a mixture of limited compromises, including surprising concessions to progressive demands (suffrage, welfare measures, commercial legislation) on the one hand, and blatantly harsh repression and persecution of opponents (the anti-Socialist laws, press gagging, deportations) on the other. It also meant diverting pressures for emancipation at home into the sphere of foreign affairs by means of either a militant political adventurism abroad or a policy of imperialism. The threat of revolutionary measures (*coup d'état*, mobilising of national minorities) or their actual implementation (suffrage, territorial annexations) was also ever-present. It was this last characteristic that distinguished Bonapartism from traditional conservatism, as Bismarck's conservative mentor, Ludwig von Gerlach, was to discover. With the help of this combined strategy, sanctioned at the polls by plebiscitary approval, the traditional and the industrial élites strengthened their position of predominance once more (although the latter had to accept certain political limitations). Moreover, the position of the pre-industrial élites was prolonged beyond its appropriate life-span in a society in which powerful social changes were at work. The dictatorial rule which emerged in this situation was widely accepted, indeed demanded, by the ruling class on the grounds of its need for protection. For a time it was able to achieve a relative balance between the various powerful social forces at work; it even attained a certain degree of independence in the face of the existing configuration of power relationships. In many ways it was fighting a desperate defensive campaign against the social and political consequences of Germany's industrialisation. In terms of its social effects, this rearguard action meant — in the short term in other countries, but in Germany in the long term — a socially conservative, anti-emancipatory obstruction of modernisation throughout German society, allowing for no more than partial change.

Bismarck fitted into this scheme as the representative of the traditional ruling élites and the 'saviour' of the 'law-abiding middle class'. Engels was thinking of the latter in particular when, after the coup of Bismarck's electoral law in April 1866, he drew a general conclusion in his perceptive analysis of conditions in France:

> Bonapartism is indeed the true religion of the modern bourgeoisie. It is becoming increasingly clear to me that the bourgeoisie does not have the will to rule directly, and so . . . a Bonapartist semi-dictatorship is the normal form. The great material interests of the bourgeoisie carry this through, even against the bourgeoisie's own wishes, but it does not let them have any share of political power. At the same time, this dictatorship is itself forced in turn to adopt the bourgeoisie's material interests against its will. So now we have Monsieur Bismarck adopting the programme of the National Union (*Nationalverein*). Putting this into practice is another thing, of course, but Bismarck is scarcely likely to fail with the German bourgeois.[13]

Indeed, Bismarck did not fail. He not only fulfilled the German bourgeoisie's economic aspirations and protected it from the restive proletariat, but consolidated the position of the traditional ruling élites which, in the light of history, proved to be no less successful. His cooperation with the National Liberals who advocated Free Trade may have temporarily deceived them as to the true nature of his 'semi-dictatorship'; but his regime revealed itself blatantly after the onset of the second world economic crisis in 1873. From 1879 onwards it became even more obvious than ever. Up until that point Bismarck's regime had been favoured by the social and political framework in which it operated: a rising economy, relatively low political participation and weakness in the political parties *vis-à-vis* the bureaucracy. We should not, therefore, make too much of Bismarck's undisputed skill as a politician. From 1879 onwards, however, as a result of changing circumstances whose effects caused him to turn his thoughts increasingly towards a *coup d'état (Staatsstreich)*, he found that his management of the system was becoming increasingly difficult.

Bismarck balanced traditional and modern elements in a combination that was typical of Bonapartism. For example, he combined an absolutist-style military policy with state interventionism on behalf of vested interests and underpinned it by plebiscitary approval. Through a policy of war up to 1871 and later, in the 1880s, of social and economic imperialism, he sought to stifle internal problems by diverting attention to the sphere of external affairs. Through it all he lived off an undeniable and heightened charisma derived from his role in the founding of the German Empire, his foreign policy and his successful mediation over a long period between the two dominant social classes. Ludwig Bamberger, one of the major liberal figures, concluded with grudging admiration after thirty years' proximity to Bismarck: 'One had to have been there to be able to testify to the power this man exerted over all those around him at the height of his influence. There was a time when no one in Germany could say how far his will extended . . . when his power was so rock-solid that everything trembled before him'. Not everyone possessed the ironic detachment which caused Burckhardt to remark that 'in Germany . . . Bismarck was practically the reference point and yardstick for that mysterious thing we call authority'. But even this conservative, who saw Bismarck's mistakes and weaknesses clearly, had to admit after the shock of the three revolutions of 1789, 1830 and 1848 'that there was no alternative in sight, wherever one cared to look, for carrying out the supreme task of stemming the tide of revolution'.[14] A clear-headed judgement will therefore conclude that 'after 1862 Prussian-dominated Germany had found its Caesar'. As the historian Heinz Gollwitzer put it:

> The 'Bonapartist' character of Bismarck's policies was hidden beneath the cloak of monarchical tradition, which he wore as the King's servant and Imperial Chancellor with considerable de-

corum and skill. What distinguished him from earlier masters of monarchical government was the 'modern' element in his political game, the 'Bonapartist' ingredient. It was discernible in his recurring policies of risk-taking at home and abroad, in his manipulation of universal suffrage, his skills as an agitator, contempt for legitimacy, and the ambivalence of the conservative revolution.[15]

In order, however, not to stress the personal element too much but, instead, slightly to modify Marx's analysis of the German Empire, it might be best described, for the period before 1890, as a Bonapartist dictatorship based on plebiscitary support and operating within the framework of a semi-absolutist, pseudo-constitutional military monarchy. It favoured the traditional élites, but was at the same time subject to a rapid industrialisation process with its effect of partial modernisation; it was thus to some degree influenced by the bourgeoisie and the bureaucracy. This definition accounts in full measure for Bismarck's position at the head of an informal pyramid of power and for the socially conservative function of his Bonapartist methods of rule.

Two further considerations arise. This Bonapartist phase derives its importance from the fact that it overlapped with the period in which the German Empire was founded. The turning-point of 1879 is of crucial importance in this connection. Although Bismarck cooperated up to this point with the liberals in domestic affairs, economic legislation and foreign trade policy, after 1873 the depression undermined first the economic, then the political foundation of this unstable alliance of forces. And yet it did not simply represent a *societas leonina* as far as the National Liberals were concerned. In tackling the problem of interruptions to industrial and agricultural growth the imperial government changed course after 1876. It began to pursue an anti-liberal, conservative regrouping of forces whose main support came from the major interests in industry and agriculture. This 'cartel of the productive estates', as it was called, first emerged in spectacular fashion with the adoption of the protective tariffs of 1879. From then on, until 1918, variations of this type of conservative *Sammlung*, designed to rally major interests, were to form the basis of government policy. Parallel to this ran a policy of carrying out de-liberalisation measures in many different areas of political and social life. Since these developments were encouraged by Bismarck, and their consequences given the stamp of legitimacy by this enormous authority, a disastrous course was set prior to 1890 for the entire direction taken by the German Empire's subsequent historical development. For this reason, Bamberger, whose worldly-wise scepticism rejected any personality cult, concluded that 'Bismarck has determined the course which institutions, the laws and — more important — which minds will follow'.[16] The first crucial dozen years of this *Sammlung* policy, which rallied agrarian and industrial interests, coincided with the era of Bismarck's Bonapartist semi-dictatorship and the supporting policies it adopted. These ranged from Puttkamer's policy for the civil service, as discussed below, to state social insurance schemes, from experiments with professional advisory bodies to advise the government on the national economy to overseas expansion. And all these policies paved the way, as early as the Bismarck era, for the emergence of an anti-liberal, authoritarian German state. Hans Rothfels, in writing on the subject of the continued 'obstruction to the development of civic responsibility' and 'the glorification of excuses' in German politics, rightly concluded that, after 1945, 'no matter how long and tortuous the road from Bismarck to Hitler', the first Imperial Chancellor seemed 'to be the one responsible for the change in course, or at least its legitimisation, and one whose unfortunate progress towards its culmination in our own time has been only too apparent'.[17]

Bismarck's road to the twentieth century was in fact paid for by the immediate imposition of a massive burden on Germany's internal social and political development. This problem will be dealt with later in more detail, as will the equally heavy burden he imposed on foreign policy. So far as the German Empire's social constitution is concerned, however, the impression was already widespread by 1890 that 'the great man has produced a downright fiasco'. Burckhardt noted that 'he can no longer heal the Empire's internal wounds', and as famous an historian as Theodor Mommsen was even of the opinion that 'Bismarck has broken the nation's backbone. The damage done by Bismarck's period in office is infinitely greater than the benefits it has brought. The gains in power will be wiped out in the next great upheaval of world history. But the oppression wrought [by the German variant of Bonapartism] was a disaster which can never be put right'.[18] Certainly, there is still much that will have to be said about this undeniable damage, but it should not obscure one fact: the new power structure, built up by the dominant classes and their *Sammlung* policy, began to function well enough in Bismarck's time and continued to do so without him, regardless of any frictions which might have existed. This became clear after 1890 when Bismarck's dismissal led to the disappearance of the 'pilot' from Berlin and, hence, the symbol of Bonapartist rule.

1.3 *The permanent crisis of the state after 1890: polycratic, but uncoordinated authoritarianism*

After Bismarck's dismissal the Prusso-German pyramid of power no longer had a peak. In other words, the constitution that was tailored to his abilities and the constitutional practice arranged around him no longer had a focal point of coordination. A power vacuum was created and subsequently a climate arose in which various personalities and social forces appeared in an attempt to fill it. Since, in the long run, neither they nor Parliament succeeded, there existed in Germany a permanent crisis of the state behind its façade of high-handed leadership. This in turn resulted in a polycracy of rival centres of power. It was this system which caused the zig-zag course so often followed by German politics from that time on. First the young King tried to be both Emperor and Chancellor in one, attempting to replace a system based, in form at least, on two centres with — in Bismarck's mocking phrase — a brand of 'popular absolutism'.[19] This experiment was the springboard for the setting up of his so-called 'personal regime'. But this never received constitutional sanction; nor did Wilhelm II succeed in changing constitutional reality for any length of time, however much the Byzantine sycophancy of his clique of advisers tried to surround the decision-making process with the illusion of monarchical power. Both his personal abilities and institutional pressures for the linking of imperial policy to military authority and its representation showed that the last Hohenzollern monarch was incapable of governing the German Empire alone. Even before the new century dawned he had failed with his anachronistic game. To be sure, his exaggerated pretensions remained. He repeatedly transgressed the limits laid down for him by the constitution while exploiting the legally sanctioned prerogative granted to the executive power in a constitutional monarchy. In emotional rhetoric he stressed his bizarre view of the Emperor's role until the world war revealed completely that in terms of his share of political power he had, in the judgement of Hans Delbrück, merely played the part of a 'shadow emperor'.

On the other hand, the chancellors who, without exception, had risen to high office by dint of effort via the bureaucratic and diplomatic hierarchy — regarded by Bismarck as an undesirable path, but in Max Weber's view a fateful one — were as little able to fill the

vacuum as was the Emperor. The honourable Caprivi, much under-
rated because he lacked a power-seeking instinct, even managed to
destroy a good part of the very institutional support on which
chancellors had previously depended. The short-lived Caprivi era
saw an attempt to satisfy the needs of an industrial state by means of
a foreign trade policy which favoured industry. For a time this
secured the necessary political support. But the period gave the
conservative agrarians such a shock when they discerned the combination of forces so clearly ranged against them that they immediately ousted the Chancellor. Their conduct in the ensuing years was,
without doubt, deeply influenced by those experiences of 1890 to
1894 in which they had perceived a threat to their position. After
this the aged Prince Hohenlohe-Schillingsfürst took over as the
figure-head of a period of transition. Bülow after 1900 was supposed
to become Wilhelm's 'Bismarck', but he merely embodied the
malleable manipulator. Bethmann Hollweg, as the prototype of the
'cultured', hard-working, conciliatory bureaucrat, failed in the bureaucracy's management of problems. His 'policy of the diagonal'
was applied to a system which could, in reality, no longer be
governed in this way. Michaelis, Hertling and Prince Max von
Baden were but pale figures on a stage which from 1916 onwards was
dominated by the military dictatorship of the Third Supreme Army
Command. What classical political theory had described, since time
immemorial, as 'the commonweal' could be coordinated only in
isolated areas or achieved in a fragmentary fashion by German's
imperial chancellors.

Alongside them, however, appeared secretive key figures, like
Admiral von Tirpitz, who profoundly influenced the social, financial
and military aspects of domestic and foreign policy by the building
of the German battle-fleet. Between 1898 and the shattering disillusionment which set in, at the latest, in the summer of 1914, when
he saw his entire concept wrecked, he probably possessed a greater
influence on the decision-making process than all three chancellors
of the period. For a time, as Secretary of State for the Navy, he filled
the vacuum in Berlin's politics to a considerable extent. Other key
figures among the Wilhelmine power-élite, who were now incom-
parably stronger than in the period before 1887–90, were the managers of the large organisations representing industrial interests, the
leaders of organised pressure groups and the planners of the General
Staff. The industrial pressure groups, in particular, alongside the
Prussian bureaucracy and the imperial administration, became,
next to the army and the navy, centres of power which were largely

responsible for the decisions taken by government policy. Behind the outward show of a constitutional monarchy, which many compared in a self-congratulatory manner to parliamentary England or republican France as a superior German political form of the state, lay concealed a high degree of weakness and lack of coordination at the centre. At the root of all the major problems of imperial policy lay the central dilemma of a tension that could not be overcome: a tension between a rapid economic and social development towards an industrial society on the one hand, and its inherited, petrified political structure on the other. The crucial obstacle to modernisation was posed by the economic and political interests of the traditional élites who, though few in number, remained passionately interested in maintaining this state of affairs at a time when the interests of the bourgeoisie could have found their expression only in a parliamentary system. Faced with these contradictions in domestic affairs which, irreconcilable in peacetime, were sustained by the pre-industrial élites until 1918, the German Empire could not be moved into making a political accommodation with the social conditions of the time. It could be manouevred only through short-lived compromises between rival centres of power into an increasing ossification. The political forces in German society were contained in an inert system which hardened in the face of increasingly discernible tendencies which pointed to a liberal society, i.e. the growing counterweight of parliamentary forces. This reduced to impotence the liberal 'movement against the preservation and consolidation' of the system, as Bismarck put it in terms reminiscent of Metternich's defensive strategy.[20] 'Wilhelminism', a term often used quite inappropriately to sum up this era, was a label which effectively concealed the interplay of pressure groups, quasi-autonomous institutions and politicians who lacked formal political responsibility. It can be seen as 'the half-conscious and half-unconscious attempt to resolve the contradictions which existed between the political structure and social developments by means of a personal and symbolic concentration of constitutional power, using the national *Imperator* as an integrating factor'. But this dream of 'a German Caesar who would suppress class conflict with a rule of iron and offer a latecoming nation its place in the sun' revolved in reality around a weak figure atop a clay pedestal.[21] It was not Wilhelm II who imposed his will on government policy during this period, but the traditional oligarchies in conjunction with the anonymous forces of an authoritarian polycracy. Their power sufficed, even without a semi-dictatorship, through the use of a Bonapartist strategy in defence of their political rule — but with what disastrous consequences!

1.4 *The bureaucracy as an element in political rule and an organisational model*

Behind the rapid political scene-changes during Bismarck's period in office and within the polycratic system of Wilhelmine Germany the bureaucracy provided a high degree of continuity in the state. It constituted the hard core of the state apparatus, and both chancellors and ministers had to take account of its political weight. Higher civil servants considered themselves superior to party politicians at any rate. Yet neither the Prussian nor the imperial bureaucracy represented exclusively an executive organ of the political leadership. Rather, they were in a position to prepare and formulate decisions in advance, taking them directly or — what was equally significant — delaying, obstructing or rejecting them. In this process they cooperated closely with the ruling élites, particularly the aristocracy, and exerted influence as an obedient executive. This influence was built upon accumulated expertise, experience and a traditional sense of their own importance. During the period when modern states first emerged the German bureaucracy had provided the territorial princes with a useful tool in their clash with the old feudal estates and their assemblies, in the building up of a centralised financial, fiscal and military system, and in the establishment of the monarch's direct political rule over his subjects. It had expanded alongside the growth of the modern absolutist territorial state, had continually acquired opportunities to influence decisions and exercise power; and finally in Prussia, where it functioned as a prominent élite, it even achieved the position of joint ruler for some twenty years following the Napoleonic Wars. It was toppled from this height of influence and power during the 1815–48 period which culminated in revolution as a result of social processes increasingly developing outside its control. Nevertheless, it remained a power factor that could not be ignored, although, like the political parties, its importance was not adequately, acknowledged in the constitutions of the German states. Because of Germany's comparative economic backwardness, it was able, however, to exert a considerable influence on the process of industrialisation.

After 1849, and again after the Constitutional Conflict, life was made difficult for civil servants of liberal persuasions. Bismarck repeatedly demanded that 'civil servants taking sides with revolutionary tendencies hostile to the government' should be 'removed from their posts through compulsory early retirement'. It was a threat which he carried out.[22] A thoroughly prosecuted conservative policy, aimed at creating an administration which was politically entirely homogenous, was put into practice from the late 1870s onwards by Bismarck and the Prussian Minister of the Interior, von Puttkamer (see below, III.6.1). One can discern the methods employed by looking at what happened in the Ministry of Justice. A great many liberal jurists found themselves forced into early retirement, a freeze on promotions was announced, and the period of service at the rank of administrative trainee (*Assessor*) was extended from eight to ten years. From this time on a preliminary vetting procedure based on fraternity student connections and the reserve officer's commission was adopted. This could be carefully followed up during the candidate's four-year period of training as a junior administrator (*Referendar*). The so-called 'certificate of means', supplied by the candidate's parents, had to guarantee in advance that their son would be provided with adequate finance to enable him to live in keeping with his 'station', both during this period and the subsequent years he might spend as a government administrator (*Assessor*). Those who could demonstrate their unswerving loyalty to the state could, given also the respect commanded by considerable private wealth, be regarded as politically reliable. Whereas liberal lawyers were forced into private practice, the selected favourites of Puttkamer's system rose to become public prosecutors who subsequently spent years as civil servants tightly bound by the Ministry's leash. From the ranks of this extremely conservative group, which worked its way up the system under Puttkamer and which represented a completely new type of extremely conservative bureaucrat subservient to authority, were also drawn, after several rounds of promotion, the new presiding judges and executive grade administrators.

It cannot be denied that these Bismarck–Puttkamer reforms, which were applied to the whole civil service, were entirely in keeping with the rationale of the system. Contrary to the persistent legend of an apolitical German civil service, the bureaucracy in Prussia and the Empire was now more politically homogeneous than ever. It was trained into a 'reliable mentality' in accordance with conservative and authoritarian maxims, though for obvious reasons 'the fraudulent gospel of an objective and neutral executive' continued to be 'eagerly preached'.[23] Civil servants also continued to be relatively highly paid. Even the lower grades earned more than skilled workers. At the same time, their long-established partisan representation of specific interests became even more corrupt. After 1879 the policy of state interventionism persistently strengthened the bureaucracy's influence as state subsidies and government planning gained in importance. An effective liberalisation of the Empire's policies was made extraordinarily difficult even by the mere existence of this caste-like conservative civil service. It was regarded by the Imperial Chancellor Hohenlohe-Schillingsfürst as being 'more powerful than Emperor and Chancellor'. Given its iron grip, liberal policies appeared well-nigh impossible, and if a chancellor ever ventured to run 'affairs in Prussia or the Empire according to strictly liberal views', he would, as the Bavarian envoy to Berlin, Count Lerchenfeld, put it in 1903, have had to start by changing the 'entire bureaucratic organism'. That would have meant an uphill struggle; but, in any case, the idea of carrying out domestic policy in accordance with a 'strictly liberal' outlook never occurred to any imperial chancellor.[24]

The cartel of dominant conservative forces could therefore rely on the administrative apparatus, the size of which grew considerably before the war. Taking the results of the 1907 census on occupations and professions, Germany, according to Otto Hintze's estimate, had at this time around 1.2 million civil servants with 2.4 million dependents, making up about 4 per cent of the population. For every 10,000 of the population there were 126 government employees, as compared with 176 in France, 113 in the USA, and 73 in Great Britain. If one ignores services like the post office and the railways, there were 390,000 government civil servants directly in the administration and the judiciary, of which some 55,000 occupied the upper grades, 257,000 the middle and 77,000 the lower grades. Whether the proportion of these figures was much changed towards the end of the imperial era, it is difficult to estimate.[25]

The remarkable administrative efficiency of this army of civil servants was the result, among other things, of the long evolution of typically bureaucratic methods of organisation, patterns of behaviour, recruitment and career structures throughout its history. These were conceptualised in Max Weber's theory of bureaucracy, which to some extent reflects the historical experience of the German civil service stretching back over four centuries.[26] The growth and training of a professional body of specialists reflected the differentiation which had developed in its functions and tasks. The formalisation and impersonal regularisation of its procedures, its house style of written documentation and continuity in conducting its affairs, its filing systems and use of forms, were all designed with the aim of

carrying out directives and decisions and of simplifying their super-
vision, amendment and planning. The idea was to achieve as fully as
possible the calculability and rationalisation of administrative procedures. Regulated channels of jurisdiction, clear lines of demarca-
tion between different areas of competence, the institutionalisation
of vertical channels and set hierarchies of functionaries and agencies
fitted into this overall tendency of regulating organisational functions into a rational scheme. Uniform criteria on standards of
education, examinations and certification were linked to an automatic system of graded promotion based on experience and senior-
ity. This, however, could be circumvented by the use of political
'connections'. The 'servant of the state' enjoyed various financial
and legal privileges. His receipt of a salary for life afforded him
security during times of economic crisis. The state provided him
with financial help and a pension. In return for being thus looked
after, he was expected to serve the state with absolute loyalty. He
enjoyed its special protection in legal disputes and privileged legal
treatment accorded only to the administration. All this raised him
above other social groups and helped foster an *ésprit de corps*. A
uniform, sabre and decorations were the visible trappings of his
social status up until 1918. Even the humble position of junior postal
clerk enjoyed some of the self-esteem based on the portion of state
power that it represented. But this institutional structure and its
work methods had a particular tendency to ossification, procrasti-
nation and pettifogging. A maximum of bureaucratic organisation
by no means guaranteed maximum efficiency, since, as Weber also
thought, spontaneity, inventiveness, an ability to respond quickly
and an unconventional approach were not exactly rewarded when
civil servants attempted to master difficult jobs. The time spent at
the green baize table in the Ministry, obstacles in the way of career
progress, career ambition, aloofness towards the public, an outward
appearance of inscrutability and an insider's obsequiousness towards superiors resulted in serious and, moreover, irremediable
faults. To be sure, the Prusso-German bureaucracy was in no way
unique at this time, as its carefully cultivated image was wont to
imply. For example, the professional civil service in England and the
senior civil service in France also worked admirably. But the German civil service did perform a whole variety of tasks quite effectively, kept firm control over its areas of influence and, above all,
proved invaluable as an element ensuring political stability.

The organisational structure of the hierarchical pyramid of authority gave the highest posts in the civil service an enormous potential

for the exercise of power. All the decisions to be made fell upon them, and the impulses behind these decisions were sent further down the line, often in the form of confidential instructions. Because of this the ruling élites demanded absolute reliability and an identification with the system from its members. Consequently, the proportion of aristocrats working in this area and other senior decision-making positions remained extremely high until 1918 — and beyond. After 1871, it is true, the time was past when, as in 1858, 42 per cent of all Prussian civil servants in the middle and upper grades had been drawn from the nobility. Even so, around 1910, 9 out of 11 members of the Prussian State Ministry, 38 out of 65 privy councillors, 11 out of 12 senior presidents, 25 out of 36 district presidents, and 271 out of 467 district administrators came from the nobility. In the senior posts of the Foreign Service in 1914 there were 8 princes, 29 counts, 54 nobles without a title and only 11 officials recruited from the middle class. At the same time, 55.5 per cent of all the administrative trainees (*Referendare*) in the Prussian government were nobles; in 1890 it had been 40.4 per cent and in 1900 the figure was 44.6 per cent. In 1918, 55 per cent of *Assessoren* were still recruited from the nobility. Nobles made up a third of all officials at the Prussian Ministry of the Interior, which controlled an important pillar of traditional government in the shape of the provincial administrations.[27] From these figures it becomes clear how the social origins of officials in key positions must have predetermined the political attitudes of the civil service in general. The reputed monopoly of posts enjoyed by the jurists helped to reinforce a politically inflexible outlook, since legal studies and courses in methods of administration fostered a typically inflexible approach. The influence of the Laband school's legal positivism, which tended to legitimise the governmental *status quo* of 1871 by investing it with 'the sanctity of a pure and apolitical rectitude', together with a training programme in accordance with Puttkamer's ideas, guaranteed the authoritarian state a steady supply of obedient experts. Not least, the filter of religious denomination accounted for even greater homogeneity. Between 1888 and 1914, out of 90 chancellors, secretaries of state and Prussian ministers, only 7 were Catholics. In 1904, 16 per cent of junior government *Referendare* and 7 per cent of government *Assessoren* were Catholic. In the Prussian Ministry of the Interior there was, typically enough, one messenger boy who was Catholic.[28] These figures need to be borne in mind if one is to appreciate the policy adopted by the Catholic Centre Party towards the civil service. Similarly, it is only by knowing something of the history of the Prusso-German bureaucracy in the Empire that we can begin to appreciate the burden imposed on the Weimar Republic when it inherited a long-established civil service of this complexion.

The model role of the state bureaucracy also profoundly influenced the general process of bureaucratisation in German society. This extended far beyond its original public sphere. Only now in the twentieth century can we discern this process as having affected all societies which show a high degree of specialisation and division of labour. Because of Germany's administrative history, however, bureaucratisation asserted itself comprehensively at an early juncture. In the history of the German Empire it can even be treated as a process distinct from other social, economic and political developments, since in addition to national, provincial and local government, throughout these decades it made great strides in Germany's political parties and pressure groups, in trade and industry, banking and transport. This is confirmed by taking a closer look at the Agrarian League, the Social Democratic Party, or the firms of Siemens and Krupp, to name but a few examples. Not only were the civil service's organisational methods copied, but the privileges, influence and security of its members were increasingly regarded as highly desirable goals, worthy of emulation. This can be seen clearly in the case of industry's white-collar workers. The model character of the state bureaucracy was imitated early on in industry, probably even before a specialisation of functions in administrative and work practices had developed its own momentum. This somewhat premature bureaucratisation gave advanced industrialisation in Germany its particular character, just as the bureaucracy's influence had done previously in the early stages of industrialisation and the industrial revolution. It had clearly visible advantages for upward mobility within firms, just as, by the same token, it definitely promoted the organisational efficiency of 'organised capitalism'. For the rapidly growing stratum of white-collar workers the 'industrial official', based entirely on the example of the civil servant, remained the role model. The social and psychic complement to this role, which at an early stage received the legal support of the employers, was a group mentality which was averse to disputes, inclined to identify with management in their role as 'masters' and to distance itself from the manual workers. This mentality was to have a long-lasting effect on general attitudes. Efforts towards achieving a form of political integration favouring social inequality and the functionally unnecessary growth of hierarchies at the expense of egalitarian reforms (for example, the insurance law of 1911 for white-collar workers) helped bind this 'new' middle class to the old ruling political system.[29]

The pros and cons of bureaucratic organisation can be traced in similar fashion in other areas of social reality, from residents' registration offices to the free trade unions. At any rate, a process of bureaucratisation which began early, became widespread, and was often more determined by the bureaucracy's pre-industrial traditions than the material requirements of specialised administrative needs, helped to shape Imperial Germany's social structure, collective consciousness and political and social life to an extraordinary degree. For this reason it was possible to speak in general terms of a 'bureaucratic state'. This also helps explain why, as became obvious in 1918, so much resentment built up against the eternal bullying regulation of life of the bureaucrats. Attempts to liberalise and democratise society were certainly not made any easier by the fact that the process of bureaucratisation was modelled on the historical example of the conservative Prusso-German civil service.

2. Central problems: the defence of the status quo against political mobilisation

If the dilemma of the German Empire is correctly diagnosed as one of the defence of the social and political *status quo* against 'fundamental democratisation' (Karl Mannheim), as implied by industrialisation, and the gradual mobilisation of a still largely unpolitical citizenry, one can identify a fundamental weakness in the written and unwritten constitutions. Before 1918 political opposition was in certain respects illegal. The policies of the state were kept free of pressures for reform. Such pressures have to be seen as expressions of a legitimate desire for changes, if in a time of incessant social change the risk of paralysis in the system was to be avoided. Industrial societies with their historically unprecedented dynamism can escape institutional petrification only if they do not suppress impulses for reform, but instead sanction opposition to the prevailing system. At the same time, it is imperative that they recognise the absolute necessity of gradual adaption to change and the need to maintain institutional flexibility. In wise anticipation of the problems which will otherwise arise, they have to incorporate healthy and inevitable pressures for reform into the system and acquiesce in reformist efforts. If not, they will build up a potential for revolution or a collapse of the system. Constant discrimination of political opposition was, however, a characteristic of the German Empire and thus one of the causes of its downfall. This can be verified by examining the position occupied by the political parties, which were deliberately confined to the periphery of power.[1]

2.1 *The impotence of the parties*

The five-party system in Central Europe took shape as early as the revolutionary period of 1848–49 and survived into the 1920s, until its future was placed in doubt by the political extremes of Left and Right in the shape of the German Communist Party and the National Socialists. The Conservatives occupied the Right, the Catholic Centre Party the middle ground between them and the Liberals, while on the Left stood the Socialists, who were joined eventually by the originally independent middle-class Radicals. This system contained within itself many different shades of opinions and factions, witnessing the repeated formation of new splinter groups and the absorption of others. The one thing that was missing was a clearly drawn line between traditionalists and progressives, a polarisation which would have come about only if there had been a successful bourgeois revolution. However, in the 'land without a revolution' a peculiarly blurred texture of inter-party relationships came into being.[2] All the political parties in Germany were characterised by a mixture of, on the one hand, a loyalty to principles which ranged through to doctrinaire rigidity, and, on the other, by a readiness to adapt, even to the extent of sheer opportunism. Originating ideologically from philosophical schools and a background of theological disputes, they were committed to debating ideal ends, the pursuit of ideological purity and teleological programmes. But, regardless of all their philosophical orthodoxies, they displayed in their practical use of tactics a high degree of cringing conformity towards the existing structures of power. Even the notion of *liberté*, as derived from earlier political philosophy, was understood either as something conceded by the power of the state or something which complemented it. Rarely was it justified as being based on natural law. Early liberal party theory, a doctrine of the radical bourgeois Left, was faced with the claim of official ideology that only the state could represent the whole, in contrast to the particularism of the parties. Energetically promoted by influential popularisers like the historian Heinrich von Treitschke, this view repeatedly bolstered the prestige of the authoritarian state, nurtured an antipathy to party politics and forced the parties to impose their own limits. In addition to this came historical effects of far-reaching significance resulting from a multiplicity of social structures and divergent political ideals, regional factors and denominational ties. What was there to prevent division between East Elbian *Junker* and Protestant conservatives in the south-west, democrats in Baden and free-traders in Hamburg, and between those in turn and Catholic magnates in Silesia, factory workers in Saxony and farmers in the Rhineland? Countless divisions, overlappings and contradictions split the Liberals, were laboriously and temporarily bridged among political Catholics and kept the Conservatives well apart from the rest. A clean division of groups based on their pursuit of ideological or material aims is always a naive proposition. Both elements were linked inextricably from the outset, and it was above all the material interests which were responsible for subdividing party groupings from within. What is remarkable, however, is the length of time, from the 1860s to 1929, that Germany's political parties stuck to their original ideological platforms and early conflicts and how long they indulged in ritualised discussions, on account of their exclusion from the 'corridors of power' and the need for compromise. Both these factors impeded the process towards a greater democratisation of German society. This major task of all parties of the Centre or the Left, as seen in their efforts to encourage steps towards emancipation, miscarried. By 'democratisation' is meant the slow realisation of legal, political and social equality achieved in stages. T.H. Marshall's theoretical scheme, which assigns moves towards an egalitarian society to sequential periods in time, approximates to the British experience only.[3] In Imperial Germany, however, the situation was complicated to an extent which can scarcely be overestimated. For, whereas each of these three levels of equality would have been difficult to achieve independently in Central Europe, all three began to overlap. The cumulative effects of this had to be tackled, if not at national level then at least in Prussia , if not among the urban population then at least for the rural labourers. But the political parties, representing perhaps the most important motivating forces behind this movement towards greater democratic participation, were curbed in their ability to act both by Bismarck's Imperial Constitution and by those of the major federal states, because these constantly encouraged conformity to the traditional order.

The Liberals As early as the 1860s bourgeois liberalism lost its power to unite divergent interests. Committees composed of civic dignitaries (*Honoratioren*) proved incapable of winning over the masses and social liberalism remained a fringe phenomenon. The critical hiatus came with the abrupt 'separation of bourgeois and proletarian democracy', which remained submerged until 1869. On account of irreconcilable differences of interest and aims, the left-wing liberal 'Progressives' (*Fortschrittliche*), representing the new workers' movement, broke away under the leadership of intellectuals and politicians from the journeymen's associations, such as Wilhelm Liebknecht and August Bebel.[4] German liberalism thus lost the only pool of voters which could have turned it into a mass party. With the perspicacity of a political opponent, the conservative political philosopher, Friedrich Julius Stahl, noted the weakness of the Liberals when he analysed their notions of bourgeois equality and antipathy to the nobility and the old order:

> Just let them obtain equality and then let the have-nots have the same rights as themselves. They'll soon abandon the idea and start making political and legal distinctions in favour of the haves. They'll want a property qualification for the vote, financial securities in return for a press licence; they'll reserve their drawing-rooms for the fashionable set, and not even grant the poor the same respect and courtesy they show the rich. Taking their revolutionary principles only so far and no further is what typifies the posture of the Liberal Party.[5]

Liberalism not only went against one of its own ultimate objectives, that of a levelled-out society based on one class, the middle class (thus contradicting its own notion of an exclusive society based on property and education); from now on it also underwent a constant process of disintegration, helped along by its retention of a loose style of organisation based on local dignitaries and accompanied by short-lived absorptions of dwindling liberal splinter groups. The tension which came to the fore after 1871, between a middle-class electorate and an industrial–capitalist élite, constituted one of German liberalism's fundamental problems.

The Constitutional Conflict led in 1866 to the defection of the National Liberals from the Progressive Party (*Fortschrittspartei*). For about ten years they rode on the crest of a boom period in party growth. In 1871 and 1874 it was the 'done thing' for the middle-class to vote National Liberal; but in 1879–80 this heterogeneous collection of interests broke up after the discrediting of liberal economics and policies during the six-year-long depression after 1873. 'The disintegration of the old parties', as observed from 1875 onwards by

Kapp, a National Liberal left-winger, led first to the destruction of the party's 'jumble of every possible, and sometimes contradictory, action, opinion and goal'. Similarly, Friedrich Hammacher on the right of the party considered 'the collapse of the National Liberal Party' as 'inevitable', since a party 'with its head in the clouds, that does not bother about the country's economic ills, or treats class differences with a theological aloofness, must go under'.[6]

That point had been reached by 1880. The so-called 'Secession' of Manchester liberals took place, and with them went the best liberal minds: Bamberger, Mommsen, Barth, Stauffenberg and Kapp. What remained was 'the Hanoverian line of Bennigsen and Miquel' which helped 'instil a sense of demoralisation which the Bismarck regime was spreading in order to place Germany finally under *Junker* domination as never before'.[7] The right-wing liberalism of the industrial *haute bourgeoisie* consolidated itself in 1884 on the basis of its conservative Heidelberg Programme and in the wake of the sensational and last left-liberal election success of 1881 (in which they won 115 out of 397 *Reichstag* seats and 23 per cent of the vote). Meanwhile, the so-called 'Secessionists' joined forces with Eugen Richter's old 'Progressives' to form the hapless new Progressive Party (*Deutschfreisinnige Partei*) in 1884. The fortunes of this liberal party, which deserved its name, were, however, rapidly declining in the socially conservative and authoritarian atmosphere of the Bismarckian state. By 1887 its number of seats had fallen to thirty-seven, a defeat from which it never recovered. Whereas the National Liberals survived with dwindling numbers up until 1918, left-wing liberalism split in 1893 into the Liberal Union (*Freisinnige Vereinigung*) and the Liberal People's Party (*Freisinnige Volkspartei*). Friedrich Naumann's National Social Union (*National-Sozialer Verein*), which was intended to act as a new rallying-point, failed lamentably. Not until 1910 did these different groupings join forces again, this time in the Progressive People's Party (*Fortschrittliche Volkspartei*). After the German Empire's initial years, during which, despite all criticisms of their weaknesses, the liberals, as in previous decades, had constituted a 'party of movement', there was now no united liberal party to represent the bourgeoisie in internal politics. With the new shift to the Right in 1879, the advent of 'organised capitalism' and state interventionism and, above all, the rise of the Social Democrats, unity would never be achieved again.

Yet another development within bourgeois liberalism, beginning directly after 1873, was to have important consequences. A radical right-wing protest began to make itself heard on the fringes of this movement. Part of the liberal electorate switched allegiance and, in reaction to modern industrialism, joined protest parties whose politics were based on antisemitism. By the end of the German Empire these parties had won over half of the some 600,000 dissident voters hostile to the system, not counting the SPD (*Sozialdemokratische Partei*). Although still of no great importance before 1914, it was the start of a development which was to make rapid strides after 1918 and which will be dealt with later. Antisemitism involved right-wing liberalism; the left-wing Liberals, like all parties left of centre, suffered disadvantages resulting from the redrawing of *Reichstag* constituency boundaries in 1874 and upheld until 1918. This gerrymandering favoured rural areas and ignored the enormous demographic shift towards the great urban centres with their large numbers of voters.

The Centre Party   The 'party of the constitution', the Catholic Centre Party (*Zentrum*), stood mainly to the right of the Liberals in the political spectrum. As a minority party based on religious denomination in a country heavily influenced by the Protestant north of Germany, it was very tightly organised and can be seen virtually as the political arm of the numerous occupational Catholic organisations upon which it was based. It was led mainly by clerics, and in predominantly Catholic areas it pursued uncompromising policies. In areas of mixed denomination it helped to form a firm base for scattered Catholic communities. Intent on defending its autonomy as a minority, the Centre remained authoritarian in its internal affairs. It followed the Church's teachings and the social philosophy of neo-scholasticism, while shutting itself off from the outside world and encouraging a strict isolation from social developments by a constant defensive campaign against its 'hostile' environment of industrial capitalism, socialism, urbanisation and a modern technological society based on science. It encouraged the formation of a Catholic 'subculture' within German society, a clearly separate social milieu which in many places came to resemble a ghetto. Despite this, it lost votes from the mid-1880s onwards. Its share of the total vote dropped from 23 per cent to only 16 per cent by 1912. Three reasons can be advanced to explain this. During the *Kulturkampf* of the 1870s, in the direct confrontation between a traditionalist Church and the secular State, the dividing line between it and its Protestant opponents remained clearly marked. Every enlightened liberal must have found the dogma of the Immaculate Conception promulgated in 1854, the anti-liberal Syllabus of Errors of 1864, and the declaration of Papal Infallibility in 1870 simply to have been signs of the Vatican's backwardness and irrationality. Although deep scars left over from this time still affect political Catholicism in Germany to this day, the state of open conflict did subside. The earlier untempered attitude of enmity gradually lost the aggressive posture which had successfully swung 80 per cent of enfranchised Catholics behind the Centre, and from then on the party's attractiveness waned. It became noticeable that church-going among the urban population was falling off, and a diminishing commitment to Christian principles of social morality was connected with the decline in the Centre's vote. Although it succeeded in uniting diverse groups over an astonishingly long period of time under the banner of a common religious denomination, the growth of conflicts of interest in a developing industrial society militated against its attempt to unite Catholic interests. Farmers drifted off to the Conservatives, white-collar workers to the Liberals and workers to the SPD — to wherever they felt their specific interests were more effectively represented. Even so, the system of majority suffrage and the distribution of constituencies in favour of rural areas gave the Centre a quarter more seats in the *Reichstag* than that to which its proportional share of the total vote would have strictly entitled it. Yet, by looking at one key aspect, one can see how the Centre's policies backfired. The party supported the clergy's efforts to monopolise primary socialisation in the parental home and the elementary school. However, urbanisation, internal migration, differences within the school system and a host of other factors allowed a whole range of uncontrollable influences to affect young Catholics, who were growing up in fewer numbers in the village schools of relatively static rural areas. Traditional rural animosity towards urban living, mobility and secularised higher education, alongside a passionate desire to provide children with a Catholic education and the dogged, backward-looking fight against mixed marriages, led to a weakening of the Centre Party's influence at a time when problems were shifting to other areas. This traditional hostility towards modernity has exacted its price in the 'educational deficit' suffered by Catholics down to the present day.

Because of its dwindling vote, which declined by a third over two decades, the embattled Centre continued to fight tenaciously for retrograde aims often set by the Church. It never fought for change in the direction of greater democracy in a society it viewed as hostile. By appearing ultra-patriotic and displaying an exaggerated loyalty to the German Empire, it tried to compensate for the discrimination and inferiority felt at the time of the *Kulturkampf*; this, however, only brought it closer to Conservatives of all shades of opinion. We can follow this development in, for example, parliamentary votes on armaments, the building of the battle-fleet and imperialist policies. At the same time, we should not underrate the left wing of the party or the out-and-out anti-socialist Christian trade unions. The blatant tactical wheeling and dealing of the party, and its comparatively greater political scope for doing this, resulted mainly from the fact that it was accountable to Catholic organisations rather than its voters — and there was not much talk of internal party democracy among the local priests who controlled these bodies. The policies adopted by local Catholic associations and the party itself could therefore be determined by a small oligarchy of party and association leaders. Where its own vital interests were at stake, the Centre actively supported clearly reactionary policies such as the Three-Class voting system for the Prussian Diet. This made it easier for the Centre to pursue its policy on schools. On the other hand, it would just as readily engage in the defence of religious or ethnic minorities when it came to deciding important issues in this area.

The Conservatives   The strength of the Prussian 'Old Conservatives', as the largest party representing the traditional ruling élite of the landed aristocracy, army, Protestant clergy and bureaucracy, was based traditionally on their inherited and successfully maintained positions of political dominance. After 1871 they still retained access in many places to the levers of power and a focus of loyalty in the person of the Emperor as King of Prussia, Supreme War-lord, and *Summus Episcopus* of the established Protestant Church. But disagreements with Bismarck and adjustment to the new policies of the government brought about a regrouping of forces from which the new German Conservative Party (*Deutschkonservative Partei*) emerged in 1876. The Free Conservatives (*Freikonservativen*) had already broken away from the Old Conservatives in 1866. They sat in the *Reichstag* as the German Empire Party (*Deutsche Reichspartei*) and represented a small, but powerful merger of large-scale agrarian and industrial interests with the higher ministerial civil service. The first Imperial Chancellor was able to build confidently upon this party of 'Bismarck *sans phrase*', thus lending it a great deal of influence which, though not always readily visible, was nevertheless tenaciously defended up to 1918. For twenty years the German Conservatives relied on their position of importance east of the Elbe, on the intermediate positions of power of their district administrators, the

Landräte, and a small hierarchy of professional politicians who, like
their liberal counterparts, were responsible for the work of the party.
They succeeded in making inroads among the new electorate and
transformed the party into a modern, broadly-based organisation at
the same time as the most powerful agrarian pressure group in the
German Empire, the Agrarian League (*Bund der Landwirte*) was
becoming, after 1893, the basis and recruiting ground for the party.
This alliance proved extremely useful to the German Conservatives.
Although the League primarily pursued the aims of large-scale
agrarian interests, it succeeded in organising small- and middling-
scale farmers, leading them into the fold of the Conservative Party.
Without this recruiting service, which operated in the same way as
the People's Union (*Volksverein*) served the Centre Party for Catholic
Germany, it would scarcely have held on to its share of the vote at
around 14 per cent until 1912.

The organisational success of the Agrarian League created a
strong institutional structure for the Conservatives with their aristocratic consciousness and defence of sacrosanct privileges, monarchist loyalties and right-wing opposition to the government, large
agrarian interests and peasant resentment of modernisation. Coming after the old-fashioned style of associations representing specific
interests and the first pressure groups of the 1870s, the League
represented a new type of organisation, that of an effective and
well-organised lobby prepared for action.

This success was largely due to the creation of an effective ideology which at an early stage included elements of extreme nationalist
'blood and soil' mythology and antisemitism as its essential
ingredients.[8] Modern political antisemitism penetrated the German
Conservative Party not only via the 'Christian-social' conservative
followers of the Imperial Court Chaplain Stöcker, who pursued an
anti-Jewish line after 1878, but also via the League. Here it merged
with the old antipathies among the nobility and with middle-class
and peasant passions directed against 'money and cattle Jews', and
could be channelled easily into party politics. While antisemitism
pervaded the campaigning and electioneering propaganda of the
Conservatives, it was simultaneously made 'respectable' by its inclusion. It would therefore be misleading to take the election figures
for the various antisemitic parties, which on the whole are
unimpressive, and conclude that as an organised political force
antisemitism was after all only an insignificant fringe phenomenon.
In fact, in the long term it gained a disproportionately large influence through the German Conservative Party which made political

antisemitism respectable.

In view of the Conservatives' numerical strength in parliament it should not be forgotten that, quite apart from their informal strength and institutional power in the administration, they had a firm hold in the Prussian Diet by virtue of the Three-Class voting system. This Diet, which in the early 1860s had appeared to them as a frightening 'bastion of progressive liberalism', had been transformed after the successes of Bismarck's wars into 'an instrument of the Conservatives' persisting political domination', not only in Prussia, of course, but in the Empire as well. Imperial chancellors in their role as Prussian ministers after 1890 had to bow often enough to the wishes of this conservative assembly.[9] Yet at this time only a mere 4 per cent of those eligible to vote belonged in the first class compared with 84 per cent in the third! Among the conservative National Liberals and in the ranks of the Centre Party no one wished to stand up to the German Conservatives and Free Conservatives. That is why the Prussian power élite had very good reason to acclaim von Puttkamer's Three-Class voting system 'as a precious commodity which the government is not inclined to give up'.[10]

The Social Democrats   Whatever one's assessment of the strengths and weaknesses of German Social Democracy before 1918, it cannot be denied that here was a movement organised during the 1860s which strove for emancipation and stood up for every democratic right based on the principle of equality. At Gotha in 1875 Lassalle's Workers' Associations joined with the Eisenach group around Bebel and Liebknecht to form the Socialist Workers' Party (*Sozialistische Arbeiterpartei*). There soon followed a twelve-year period of persecution under the anti-Socialist laws, from 1878 to 1890, but the state was unable to prevent the party gaining in strength despite deportations, press censorship and innumerable harassments. As early as 1878 this party, which differed from all others in its new style of organisation and embodiment of principles based on a critique of the system, became the fourth largest in the *Reichstag*. From then on 'the red spectre haunted every last beer-parlour'.[11] Bismarck's government, as unscrupulous as it was resolute, attempted to exploit fears which had been growing since the pre-1848 period and even tried to pin the blame for the continuing economic depression on the Social Democrats. 'As long as we fail to stamp on this communist ant-hill with domestic legislation', the Chancellor pointedly remarked, 'we shall not see any revival in the economy.'[12] The anti-Socialist laws were intended to do the 'stamping', but they neither influenced the business cycle nor did they prevent the political advance of the industrial work-force. Despite all the official proscription and informal ostracism Social Democracy was able to consolidate its strength.

When the anti-Socialist laws lapsed in 1890, the party emerged from a time of persecution into a period of broad expansion with a strong sense of solidarity and a greatly increased membership. By 1912 it rivalled all other parties in strength. The long interruptions to economic growth during the 1870s and 1880s unquestionably strengthened the credibility of its Marxist theories. The reality of conditions in Germany appeared to confirm its analysis and forecast of the inevitable collapse of the capitalist system.[13] At the same time, disappointment that the ideal of a republican people's state had succumbed to a victorious military monarchy between 1866 and 1871 was soon overcome as the period of struggle under anti-Socialist laws bearing the naked 'stamp of brutal class rule' (Schmoller)[14] encouraged the onward march of Marxist class theory. A problem which still requires further explanation is why the workers' movement in Germany became increasingly Marxist towards the turn of the century, formulating all its problems and aims in its struggle for emancipation in the language of Marxism, whereas this did not occur at all in the USA, and in England and the rest of Western Europe only in a much more limited form. One explanation for the German development lies in the persisting residue of traditions which, because of the failure of the bourgeois revolution, were carried over from the late-feudal era. These traditions gave rise to a sharp division between the social classes and social strata which were at first understood as being modern. It was in Prussia, in particular, that this modern class differentiation was so pronounced, and up until 1918 the political struggle of the Social Democrats was mainly directed against surviving feudal institutions. This marked division of classes appeared, however, to confirm socialist class theory even before the class structure of an industrial society had fully developed. Since it became the dominant formation, after a smooth transitional period, the actual course of historical development was taken by the Social Democrats as proof of the analytical power of Marxist theory — as if it had been eternally valid — even though the theory had in fact anticipated the German development and was applied by them at first to divisions based on the traditional feudal estates. Conversely, American industrial workers were probably unreceptive to Marxism because the American Revolution made possible the institutional realisation of equal rights, thus robbing socialism of a good deal of the ideological appeal it had in Germany by holding out the promise of an egalitarian society.

In Imperial Germany's class society Social Democrats were everywhere discriminated against, even after 1890 when they were still accused of un-German behaviour (*vaterlandslose Gesellen*). The world-wide economic recovery was accompanied by a growth in revisionist ideas. Rising wages and successes at the polls were a reflection of the legalistic practice of a party of reform which not only increasingly represented the workers, but was becoming, especially in South Germany, a left-wing liberal party 'continuing the work of the old-style bourgeois radicalism'.[15] Yet the quasi-revolutionary rhetoric, to which the integrationist ideology of Kautsky's followers clung, was exploited by opponents to discredit further a party which at this time was tolerated constitutionally on account of its actual moderation in practice. Since its policy of attaining equal rights within bourgeois society and its loyalty to the nation (after joining the International in 1869) were both challenged, it gradually began to isolate itself. Social Democracy began to form its own 'subculture' within German society. Trade unions, schools to educate party members, countless social and sports clubs, newspapers and workers' libraries, all showed, on the one hand, how seriously the Social Democrats took their ideal of emancipation; on the other hand, these reinforced a tendency to isolate themselves further from the rest of society. Rather than persist in attempts to change society completely, they were often sufficiently content to build up a self-enclosed 'subculture' in place of a political programme — not least on account of the opportunities for advancement it allowed. This was first taken up again by the Independent Socialists (*Unabhängige Sozialdemokratische Partei Deutschlands*) after 1917 when they demanded measures to change the system and break down the social structure. It was possibly the low rate of social mobility in Germany, at least compared with the situation in the USA, that enabled the workers to hold on to their able leaders during this period.

Because of this 'outsider' position with its manifold consequences, the growth of the SPD and the Free Trade Unions (*Freie Gewerkschaften*) did not contribute as effectively as one might expect to the democratisation of German society. This is not to devalue the undeniable achievements within this 'subculture'. Nor should one overestimate the available alternatives, given the bitter enmity it faced and the painful experiences of the past which encouraged an obsession with organisational matters. Secondly, the unerring growth in the SPD's development intensified the sense of threat felt by all the other political groups and so contributed indirectly to the stengthening of their efforts to counter it. Every attempt at progressive reform was stubbornly resisted so as not to give the impression of any willingness to compromise with the 'reds'. The way in which constituencies were distributed resulted not least from this fear of the SPD. It enabled Conservative deputies with a tenth of the votes cast for a Berlin SPD deputy to be elected to the *Reichstag* or, with even fewer votes, to the Prussian Diet. Because of this callous arrangement, together with the tactical advantages to be gained with the middle-class vote from accusations of anti-patriotic feeling, a political alliance between the Liberals and the Social Democrats in the shape of a united socialist-liberal front 'from Bassermann to Bebel' could not be created. Theodor Mommsen from the left-wing liberals advocated this in vain. Everyone in Germany surely knew, he argued, 'that with an intellect like Bebel's you could equip a dozen East Elbian *Junker* to shine among their peers'.[16] August Bebel himself, the impressive leader of the Social Democrats for more than forty years and a fearless parliamentarian in the *Reichstag*, felt by way of example the kind of persecution to which his party was subject. Shortly before the death of the 'red Emperor' in 1913, he met Gustav Mayer, the early historian of the German labour movement, in the corridors of parliament and was greeted there by Chancellor Bethmann Hollweg with the remark that he hoped his health had recovered. 'I've been a member of this House since its creation, that is since 1868', said Bebel turning to Mayer, but 'that was the first time a member of the government has said anything to me outside of proceedings.'[17] The leaders of the middle-class parties fared little better. This was the reality of the 'united nation' of the German Empire.

2.2 *The incorporation of pressure groups into the state: anti-democratic pluralism and its opponents*

Large pressure groups have often been seen as elements of a modern pluralism and, therefore, somewhat naively as a factor which contributes *per se* to democratisation. The German experience of a society moulded by these groups at an early stage shows rather the opposite. Those associations representing economic interests preferred authoritarian policies and supported a political system which continued to be distinguished by its more or less anti-democratic pluralism. This is certainly true in the case of the large right-wing organisations such as the Navy, Army and Colonial Leagues, which were based on mass membership and devoted themselves to political agitation. To adopt a high-sounding moral tone on this subject will not, however, help to provide a sound historical analysis. The organising of interest groups into associations performing a mediating role between the political leadership and the bureaucracy, and the parties and Parliament, was undoubtedly an inevitable process. But the social effects of this certainly deserve to be criticised harshly, as indeed they were by contemporaries. The real problem was not the naked pursuit of self-interest by the different groups concerned but the length of time during which there was an absence of any counterweight to the powerful blocs of producer interests. Until the trade unions and the Social Democrats became power factors, upholding consumer interests and backed by a broad section of public opinion to the point where they could not be ignored, the cartel of owners of the means of production, together with the political auxiliaries and lobbies of the monarchical system, created a bastion that was well nigh invincible. This accounts for the fact that a blatant form of class legislation could be maintained for so long. We need only look at the examples of foreign trade, taxation, armaments and agricultural policy. To expect democratisation to be furthered, even indirectly, by this authoritarian 'syndicalism' of pressure groups, would be a very mistaken notion. The contribution made by the Agrarian League, for example, was confined to 'a show of democracy and the use of undemocratic methods for undemocratic ends by an anti-democratic mentality'.[18]

In many respects the pressure groups were a symptom of the process of industrial concentration, of the transition to 'organised capitalism' and of the need to control, to some extent, the process of economic growth. The new interest groups of the 1870s were able to link up everywhere with traditional institutions. The Association for Economic and Tax Reform (*Vereinigung der Steuer- und Wirtschaftsreformer*) (1876–1928), representing large-scale agrarian interests, continued the work of agricultural bodies like the National Economic Collegium (*Landesökonomiekollegium*) (1842), the Union for the Protection of Landed Interests (*Verein zur Wahrung der Interessen des Grundbesitzes*) (1848–52) and the Congress of North German Farmers (*Kongress Norddeutscher Landwirte*) (1868), just as the Agrarian League did after 1893, only more effectively. The Central Association of German Manufacturers (*Centralverband deutscher Industrieller* — CdI) (1876–1919), as the corporate body representing in particular heavy industry, including coal, iron and steel, built upon the experiences of the Union of German Iron and Steel Industrialists

(*Verein Deutscher Eisen- und Stahlindustrieller*) (1874) and the Union of Mining Interests (*Verein für die Bergbaulichen Interessen*) (1858), or the so-called Long Name (*Langnam*) Union — more accurately known as the Union for the Protection of Common Interests in the Rhineland and Westphalia (*Verein für die Wahrung der gemeinschaftlichen Interessen in Rheinland und Westfalen*). In keeping with a successful *Sammlung* policy to unite collective interests, the CdI and the Agrarian League worked directly together in 1913 in the 'cartel of the productive estates' which critics dubbed appropriately the 'cartel of snatching hands'. The late rival of the CdI, the Federation of Industrialists (*Bund der Industriellen* — BdI) (1895–1912), which represented the export-orientated light and manufactured goods side of industry (Stresemann's political springboard), decided to join forces with the CdI in 1906. In 1913 it cooperated in the formation of a Union of German Employers' Associations (*Vereinigung Deutscher Arbeitgeberverbände*) (1913–33), and in 1914 figured in the War Committee for German Industry (*Kriegsausschuss der deutschen Industrie*), until the two main organisations merged in 1919 under the name of the National Association of German Industry (*Reichsverband der deutschen Industrie*).

The chambers of commerce stood at the disposal of trading interests such as the Congress of German Economists (*Kongress Deutscher Volkswirte*) of 1858 and the German Trade Council (*Deutscher Handelstag*) of 1861. Their liberal free-trading inclinations were, however, heeded less and less after 1876 as heavy industry, strongly backing protectionist policies, gained a clear supremacy which even the Union for Trade Agreements (*Handelsvertragsverein*) (1900–18) and the Hanseatic Federation of Commerce, Trade and Industry (*Hansabund für Gewerbe, Handel und Industrie*) (1909–34), representing commerce, could no longer match. Small-scale craftsmen (*Handwerker*), whose importance is frequently underestimated, received backing from the *Innungen* (guilds), which returned to their status as corporations under public law between 1881 and 1897. Like the chambers of commerce and industry, they were assigned their own rights of jurisdiction. The craftsmen were also supported after 1833 by the General German Artisans' Federation (*Allgemeiner Deutscher Handwerkerbund*), which despite being extremely successful has remained relatively unknown. Until the Artisan Law of 1897 it avoided *laissez-faire* and came near to creating a corporatist system, though it did not succeed completely in realising the ideal of a closed shop.

From the 1870s onwards, when economic crises encouraged a crystallisation of interests, these various associations combined everywhere to form influential representative organs. They soon found a direct route to high-level government, as well as to the political parties and the civil service. Just as the district administrators helped the Conservatives, the pressure-group associations built up an intermediate power structure within the economy. Bismarck's anti-parliamentary and unconstitutional plans for a corporatism based on the professions (a substitute parliament of interests in the event of a government-inspired *coup*) even aimed at formally incorporating interest groups into the political system. Although the Prussian National Economic Council (*Preussischer Volkswirtschaftsrat*) of 1881 survived for only a short time and an Imperial Council (*Reichsrat*) failed to get off the ground, these large associations, acting as pressure groups, were gradually integrated on an informal basis because of their influence in practice and their *de facto* participation in decision-making.

The change-over to protective tariffs provided the first striking example of this development. The draft proposal for the 1878 tariff was shaped to a great extent by the CdI. Both before the *Reichstag* and the Federal Council's Commission of Inquiry its passage remained under the protection of the CdI's members. The minutes of the hearings were edited by its chief manager, Henry Axel Bueck. After its approval in July 1879, this tariff represented the first modern piece of legislation in Germany to bear the stamp of a top-level business organisation all over it. This development can be traced through the different stages of tariff legislation in 1879, 1887 and 1902, and a similar story can be told of legislation in other areas. From here there led a straight path to the Joint Standing Orders of the Federal Ministries (*Gemeinsame Geschäftsordnung der Bundesministerien*) in present-day West Germany, in which cooperation between the civil service and the business federations has been formalised.[19] In a country where the use of the strike weapon in industrial disputes has long been regarded as reprehensible, and where the ideal of a society free of conflict has long prevailed, it was to take decades — far beyond the German Empire's demise — before the dominance of these pressure groups could be challenged and, in some cases, broken.

Those organisations devoted to political agitation and the mobilisation of mass support were from the beginning closely connected with associations representing economic interests, both in terms of common personnel, and institutionally via corporate membership. Their main emphasis lay upon the achievement of political aims, that is, the mobilisation of popular sentiment in favour of certain decisions in government policy, and not only at election time. The German Navy League (*Deutscher Flottenverein*) (1898–1934) supported the building of Tirpitz's battle-fleet. It grew to have 80,000 individual and corporate members and, thanks to its activities as 'a centre for political lobbying on behalf of heavy industry', as Kehr saw it, had a budget of millions of marks at its disposal for propaganda.[20] The German Army League (*Deutscher Wehrverein*) (1912–1935), with its 36,000 members, involved itself no less successfully in debates over armaments, particularly those of 1912 and 1913. Its promoter, a retired general, August Keim, represented, like Bueck, Heinrich Class and Alfred Hugenberg, a modern type of manipulator of public opinion. The German Association of the Eastern Marches (*Deutscher Ostmarkenverein*) (1894–1935) — also called the HKT-Union (*Hakatisten*), after its founders Hansemann, Kennemann and Tiedemann — organised a campaign against the Polish minority. This campaign went as far as supporting the expropriation law of 1908 and the demand for a reallocation of land on an ethnic basis, which as a political programme anticipated National Socialist practice after 1939. Following the merger of the German Colonial Association (*Deutscher Kolonialverein*) of 1882 with Carl Peter's Society for German Colonisation (*Gesellschaft für Deutsche Kolonisation*) of 1884, the German Colonial Society (*Deutsche Kolonialgesellschaft*) (1887–1936) rose to prominence as one of the great propaganda associations whose significance in terms of influence cannot be judged properly on the basis of its fluctuating membership figures. In the Pan-German League (*Alldeutscher Verband*) (1891–1939), to name another important example, right-wing radical ideas of extreme nationalism combined with an abstruse, yet portentous conglomeration of racialist, pan-German, expansionist ideologies. This explosive mixture cannot be accurately defined as the wishful dream of a misguided minority, the lunatic fringe with which every society has to contend. As a depository of pre-war militant nationalism the Pan-Germans were able to influence the bureaucracy and government policy to an increasing extent, although their final self-destructive success came — after the ominous interlude of the German Fatherland Party (*Deutsche Vaterlandspartei*) of 1917–18 — only with the election breakthrough of the National Socialists in 1929. They loudly demanded the goals of 'living space', recognition of Germany as a 'world power' and rearmament programmes, along with a 'national dictatorship' as the violent solution to internal class conflict. It was precisely among the influential academic middle class, the 'opinion-makers' of the German Empire, that such ideas spread. No historian can describe this development as penetratingly as Heinrich Mann was able to in his novel *Der Untertan*. As early as 1866 the banker Karl von der Heydt, one of the founders of the Pan-German League, described colonialism as 'merely a means of attaining economic and political world domination for Germany. It was simply, therefore, a factor in pan-Germanism'. The rather more moderate historian Karl Lamprecht, who died in 1915, himself a member of the Navy League, Union of the Eastern Marches and a Pan-German, demanded on several occasions prior to the outbreak of war in 1914, 'the greatest possible expansion of the state or, put another way, the concentration of all the nation's energies for a united effort abroad to be carried out by a hero and master. These are the initial requirements for a state in need of expansion'.[21] The military dictatorship of 1916 saw itself as the executor of such desires in its bid for world power. Here the ground was prepared at an early stage for the Nazi dictator's claim after 1933 for world domination.

The contention that the authoritarian German state was able to control the self-interest of the pressure groups from above and bring about general good for society owing to its superior position, is revealed on closer inspection to be the exact opposite of the truth. It was precisely in the authoritarian Empire that these groups were able to proliferate and fill the gaps which existed in its constitutional structure. It was the emasculation of the political parties in Germany that invited the predominance of interest groups. However much the associations persisted in trying to influence important legislation, it was Parliament's incapacity to coordinate its activities that encouraged their pursuit of self-interest. Since Germany's constitutional structure meant that aims could not be formulated via the *Reichstag* and the political parties with the involvement of organised interests, pressures were all the more directly exerted by vested interests in cooperation with the bureaucracy and the political leadership. In view of these realities, the illusion of 'above party' government increasingly appeared to be the bare-faced 'life-lie of the authoritarian state'.[22]

The opponents of the employers' interest groups and nationalist lobbies experienced little of the 'above party' nature of government. Apart from the SPD, these were the organised trade unions representing the workers. Having developed from the artisans' and workers' associations, especially during the 1860s, their initial weakness in the face of their overwhelmingly superior opponents was all too evident. The split that existed between trade unions pursuing a

Social Democratic line, liberal unions following Hirsch and Dunker and, later, the Christian trade unions, could certainly not be overcome during the life-time of the German Empire. However, the General German Workers' Association (*Allgemeiner Deutscher Arbeiterschaftsverband*), following Lassalle's line, and the International Trades Union Cooperatives (*Internationale Gewerkschaftsgenossenschaften*), founded by Bebel and Liebknecht, though originally separate, merged like the two socialist parties in Gotha after 1875. This move created the organisational nucleus of the strongest and most powerful of all the unions, the Free Trade Unions (*Freie Gewerkschaften*). In 1877 they had 50,000 members in 1,266 local branches. The anti-Socialist laws then hit the Social Democratic unions. Between 1881 and 1886 they were able to rally their forces again in the so-called Central Associations, before the strike ordinance of 1886 issued by von Puttkamer, Prussian Minister of the Interior, initiated a new wave of repression. Nevertheless, some 395,000 workers took part in over 1,100 strikes in 1889 and 1890. After the end of the Bismarck regime there were still 58 Central Associations in existence with 300,000 members in 3,860 local branches. From 1890 onwards their growth became unstoppable. Appointed by the Trades Union Congress, a General Commission led by Carl Legien attempted up until 1918 to coordinate expansion and activities on a national level through a steering committee, hindered though it was in this task by the Prussian law governing associations. The following figures demonstrate its success: in 1900 the Free Trade Unions had a membership of 680,000 workers; in 1904 this passed the million mark and in 1910 exceeded 2 million. By 1913 there were 2.5 million members (compared with 343,000 in the Christian trade unions, 280,000 in the 'yellow', or pro-employer, unions, and 107,000 in the liberal unions). Members had 130 workers' secretariats at their disposal for free advice and legal assistance, while nearly 3,000 full-time workers maintained the running of the whole organisation from its head offices. In numerous industrial disputes (1,433 in 1900, 2,113 in 1910 and 2,127 in 1913, in which 100,000, 156,000 and 254,000 strikers took part respectively) the trade unions fought determinedly for an improvement in wages and conditions. Along with the SPD they gradually built up a position as a power factor to be reckoned with.

Running parallel to this came a decline in political militancy. Within a system whose principles were by now rarely questioned, the Free Trade Unions concentrated before 1914 on obtaining a greater share of the national product for organised labour. It can be assumed that a majority of Free Trade Union members voted SPD, but these union men were by no means straightforward auxiliaries for the party. On the contrary, they helped the spread of a quietist, reformist mentality throughout it. This was also partly disseminated by the growing number of *Reichstag* deputies drawn from the ranks of trade union officials. However one may judge the General Commission's desire to play safe, or whatever one may think of the bread-and-butter policies of the unions, one should not belittle their organisational achievements in the most adverse circumstances. Nor should one belittle their efforts to strengthen the sense of solidarity among the workers, the discernible progress they made in creating a counterweight to the power of the employers and the bureaucracy, or their courage and self-sacrifice in holding out during strikes.

2.3　*The 'negative integration' technique of political rule: 'enemies of the Empire' against 'friends of the Empire'*

The leadership of the 'princely insurance institute against democracy',[23] created in 1871, was immediately faced with a dilemma once the economic and political euphoria surrounding the Empire's founding had subsided. Since German political life lacked the two focal points, for and against a bourgeois revolution, artificial positions for the rallying of political forces had to be found both during and after the Bonapartist regime. The elation felt in 1870–71, which, measured at the polls, had produced *in toto* a truly pro-government National Liberal majority, did not last long. To be exact, it lasted until the world-wide economic crisis of 1873 turned into a depression. With a sense of foreboding, the right-wing liberal, Heinrich von Sybel, summed up the general feeling of satisfaction among the bourgeoisie at the fulfilment of their nationalist and political aspirations in 1871: 'How have we deserved the grace of God in being allowed to experience such great and mighty things?' However, he added the anxious question: 'And how are we to live hereafter?' Bismarck himself is said to have posed a similar question at this time: 'What is left for us? What will seem worth experiencing after such great successes and great and mighty events?'[24] This scepticism, indeed almost a fear of everyday life in the affairs of national politics, proved to be only too justified after 1873. Under the pressure of not only the economic crisis but political and social crises, the heterogeneous character of the German Empire, whose constituent parts had been shaped by basically differing historical traditions, began to reveal itself quite clearly. The absence of a common system of values and norms became very evident as the experience of the war faded. In its place a depression hung over the country. Prussia's ideological justification of her special position in the Empire had not yet succeeded in acquiring a popular basis; indeed, south of the river Main it never did. Those who had been defeated in 1866 and 1871 showed as little enthusiasm for Prussia as the supporters of a republic and a democratic 'people's state' had before them. The bridge which led over to an 'imperial nation' had to be crossed at varying speeds by Germany's different social classes and groups. In view of this situation, Bismarck developed a technique of political rule which has been described as one of 'negative integration'.[25] He made use of the primeval socio-psychic opposition between 'in-groups' and 'out-groups' and thus stylised internal conflicts so as to lead a majority of elements 'loyal to the Empire' against a minority of 'enemies of the Empire'. The latter had to be made to appear a 'serious danger' without ever posing any real threat to the system. The various coalitions of groups loyal to the Empire were held together primarily by their enmity towards a common foe — in other words, on a negative basis. Supporters of the Papacy, advocates of a Germany that included Austria, citizens of Alsace-Lorraine and Danes and Poles, were immediately predestined for the category of the 'Empire's enemies', but could hardly fulfil the requirement of appearing to pose a grave threat to the system. Thus political Catholicism, parliamentary liberalism, Social Democracy and liberal Judaism were built up as the true 'enemies of the Empire'. During the *Kulturkampf*, which was not, in fact, exclusively a conflict over the competing claims of Church and State in a society undergoing modernisation and secularisation, it was the Catholics who were made the target group. By branding the Centre a Catholic party of the 'Empire's enemies', Bismarck not only ruled out any possibility of parliamentary cooperation with the Liberals, but could in government propaganda associate Catholics within the German Empire with Polish and Habsburg Catholics on the basis that 'some mud will always stick'. In this way he was able to identify them with external political threats as well. Shrewd Catholic observers like Bishop von Ketteler saw in this unscrupulous branding of a minority as criminals a principally anti-constitutional and anti-social move aimed at restoring the 'old monarchist, absolutist, militarist Prussia . . . in its entirety'.[26]

Scarcely had a new understanding with the Vatican begun to take shape when a fresh government campaign began to bear down upon the current danger of the left-wing Liberals, described variously as 'crypto-republicans', 'electoral cattle from Richter's cowshed, blink-

ered by the idea of progress', or the 'nihilistic *Progress* faction'. Yet
another target was the ultimately more dangerous Socialist Workers' Party, described as 'a symbol for the cancer of social revolution
gnawing away at the innards of nations and states'. Here, too,
Germany's political parties were associated with foreign powers
such as Liberal England or the Socialist International in order to
cast doubt on their loyalty to the Empire.[27] Since power relationships in Germany made the liberalism of middle-class politicians
initially appear a greater threat than the democratic ideas of the
Socialists — for Bismarck overestimated liberalism just as he underestimated Social Democracy — the Chancellor did not shy away
from the use of antisemitism as a way of fending off liberal Jews.[28]
Ever since the emancipation decrees of the early nineteenth century,
politically active Jews, even in Prussia, had been pressing for the
realisation of complete civic equality. For this reason, quite a few of
their number were to be found among the Liberals and, later, the
Social Democrats, with whom they could pursue their aims. The
Jew as the 'progressive' 'enemy of the Empire' became, with Bismarck's express approval, the scapegoat of German domestic politics long before the cliché of the 'Marxist Jew' gained currency. It
goes without saying that the Poles and Alsatians both remained
'enemies of the Empire'. Since Liberals and Social Democrats often
joined with them in their fight for minority and constitutional rights,
and because of the Poles' traditional adherence to the ideal of Polish
independence, or Alsatian feelings towards the French motherland,
the general insinuation of treachery could be levelled at the various
opposition parties. As soon as 'foreign support appeared useful to
their party interests', the Chancellor concluded, 'they would leave
their own fatherland in the lurch' and run to meet a victorious
France with 'no less an obliging subservience than that which
Napoleon encountered in the Rhenish Federation'.[29]

When, however, the 'hostile gang' of the 'Empire's enemies' could
not provide sufficient fuel to achieve the aim of 'negative integration', Bismarck could always threaten to use his secret weapon of a
coup by the state. This hung over parliamentary politics in the 1870s
and 1880s like the sword of Damocles. Bismarck declared that the
growth of opposition in the *Reichstag* would lead 'all the quicker to
the ruin of the parliamentary system and prepare the way for rule by
the sabre. Germany would not be able to carry on. The treaties
binding the member states would have to be abrogated . . . and this
would overturn the constitution'.[30] Many an objection by the member states, the Federal Council and parliamentarians was silenced in

this way. People obviously thought that the man who had attempted to organise the counter-revolution in 1848 and had survived the Constitutional Conflict was quite capable of such a wrecking tactic, right up to the crisis of his dismissal in 1890. It was an opinion which did not exactly weaken the Bonapartist constitutional monarchy in the short term. Furthermore, the exceptional position occupied by Alsace–Lorraine and the situation in Prussia's Polish eastern provinces provided the opportunity over a number of years to bring pressure to bear upon the *Reichstag* and the parties. Marx was not the only one who had predicted in 1870 an ossification of Germany's 'military despotism' in internal politics as a result of this annexation in the west. Burckhardt had also realised immediately that 'even outside of war' Alsace–Lorraine 'constantly provided at least the din of war, the possibility of mobilisation and the like', 'that is, a quiet state of siege in Germany itself, on account of which constitutionalism and other such relics would cease to be spoken of'.[31] Even much later, in 1913, the Zabern Affair confirmed this forecast. Up until then French thoughts of *revanche*, kept alive by protests against the annexation of the provinces, helped to shape both domestic and foreign policy in the Greater Prussian military state. Once Bismarck had established the technique of 'negative integration' in party politics, his successors continued to make use of the strategy. The tensions which existed in Germany's class-ridden society appeared to necessitate the creation of a bloc against the 'Empire's enemies', a term now applied chiefly to the Social Democrats. Additional methods to achieve integration were to be employed on an increasingly larger scale and involved greater risks, as will be shown later.

Against the background of long-term influences from the period of the German Empire's creation the ingenious technique of 'negative integration' was in itself a highly ominous development. Yet there are three further aspects of politics at this time which deserve to be highlighted. Firstly, Bismarck stirred up an existing widespread resentment against the parties, intending to transcend them with his own dualism of 'enemies' and 'friends', thus replacing them with two antagonistic groupings of a very mixed composition. When Bismarck caustically remarked that 'the present degree of incapacity and megalomania in Germany is disproportionately represented among professional parliamentarians' he was not only encouraging the antipathies of bar-room politicians towards the parties and parliament, but lending such sentiments an authority upon which they were to rely, not just up to 1918 but well beyond.[32] Secondly, the rigorous transformation of some of the parties into his mere instruments further weakened their will to become involved in helping to shape the direction taken by the state. That Bismarck viewed them simply as 'post-horses' to 'take him to the next stage of his journey' was recognised by those around him very early on, and later the view was often expressed that Bismarck treated the parties 'as if they were states'. He 'manoeuvred them from one position to another, made alliances and broke them'.[33] This left a legacy of deep scars, however, and at the same time increased the party politicians' sense of impotence.

Above all, German domestic politics, along with broad sections of public opinion, became accustomed to the notion that a deep division existed among the citizens of the state. The 'Empire's enemies' were discriminated against as second-class citizens by means of formal legal distinctions aimed at the Social Democrats and national minorities, or through informal mechanisms which affected Jews and Catholics. This was the case not only in the army and the civil service but in other areas as well. These groups were excluded from the sphere of legality based on general legal norms which should have been applied irrespective of person. As people became accustomed to this development the level of tolerance towards such illiberal tendencies before they appeared offensive was gradually increased. That one had some neighbours who were inferior became part and parcel of everyday life during the fifty years of the German Empire's existence and helped to foster a mentality which polarised citizens on a 'friend' and 'foe' basis. This helps explain why the psychological barriers against the physical liquidation of minorities could be broken down so quickly in, of all people, the nation of 'poets and thinkers'. Viewed from an historical perspective, it is possible to trace a line from the 'enemies of the Empire' both to the attacks on Jewish synagogues in 1938 (*Reichskristallnacht*) as well as to the Nazi ideal of a 'folk community' (*Volksgemeinschaft*) with its necessary corollary of 'parasites on the nation' which had to be exterminated.

2.4 Sammlungspolitik: *a policy to rally collective interests in a 'cartel of the productive estates upholding the Empire', 1876–1918*

One of the lasting products of the period of the 'great conservative counter-revolution' between 1848 and 1879 was produced in its final phase. This was the development of a policy designed to rally big business and large-scale agriculture behind it.[34] Despite occasional rifts between the two, this idea was to form the basis of government policy right up until 1918. The conservative economist, Schmoller, was to conclude that 'under Bismarck's patronage an alliance between big business and landed property came into being which ruled Germany from the late 1870s onwards', a judgement which concurred with that of his opponents on the Left. This anti-progressive alliance was anti-liberal by design at first, virtually embodying the deliberalising policies carried out from that time on. Subsequently, however, the anti-Socialist element, which was also present from the start, became more and more evident. Bismarck's attitude was one of ambivalence. On the one hand, he tried to make credible his claim that the fight against the Social Democrats was a case of 'saving society from murderers and arsonists, in fact, from what took place under the Paris Commune'. This meant that a 'war of annihilation' was necessary against the Socialist Workers' Party. He had no desire continually to carry the constitution tucked under his arm. Instead, he wanted 'to brush aside the barriers erected by the constitution's excessive doctrinaire concern for protecting the individual and the political parties in its so-called fundamental rights. Where Social Democracy was concerned the state had to act in self-defence' and 'could not be squeamish in the methods it employed. *A corsaire corsaire et demi!*'. As the effects of this threatening policy became clear to the terrified 'German Philistines', as Radowitz at the Foreign Office rejoiced, the Socialist Workers' Party nevertheless continued to grow in size. Consequently, the tone became shriller: 'menacing robber-bands', 'criminal theories of subversion', 'treat them in accordance with martial law', even to extermination of 'the country's rats'. These were the watchwords as attacks were intensified through the use of the biological metaphors of a policy of liquidation whose realisation still lay in the future.[35]

On the other hand, Bismarck clearly recognised that the problems caused by uneven industrial growth, 'the symptoms of which are the socialist threats to our society' (!), stimulated the growth of Social Democracy. Consequently, a policy of providing compensations was adopted which would help counter the effects of these 'threats' and secure loyalty. Bismarck certainly did not share the naive fear of revolution felt by the average middle-class citizen who desired order, even though he often remarked, when taking the long view, on the prospects for his social conservative 'building of dykes' that 'those who go hungry . . . will devour us'. Yet it is quite misleading to speak of a *cauchemar de révolution*; he simply had pessimistic expectations of the future. 'Papa says', reported Herbert von Bismarck when passing on details of an election briefing, 'that we can either move tactically against the Socialists or smash them, but they can never be a danger to the present government.' It was not permissible to admit that, generally speaking, 'Social Democrats were preferable to the Progressives'; but 'personal views' were free. At any rate, Bismarck made it known to the Prussian Ministry of State that, precisely because of the Utopian nature of their aims, he did not 'regard the growth of the Social Democrats as particularly disquieting'. He believed that with Prussian troops he was still a match for German democrats in the event of conflict.[36]

The Chancellor's self-confidence began to flag, however, as the Social Democrats gradually gained the support of millions at the polls. At the same time, increased economic prosperity, the spread of revisionism, parliamentary reform and trade union successes were all signs that their radicalism based on revolutionary rhetoric was being 'tamed'. What remained, therefore, was the idea of manipulation. It would be possible to launch a policy aimed at rallying certain interests, using the 'red menace' at every possible turn to give it impetus. Alongside this, a general feeling spread inexorably among the ruling classes that they were being forced increasingly into a corner by the rising tide of the Left. Not that this produced any incentive to carry out social reforms in peacetime. To resist such impulses had, after all, been an aim of the *Sammlung* policy from the very beginning.

The 'cartel of productive estates upholding the state' opposed any trend towards the emancipation. It had formed the hub of Bismarck's policies during the period of 1876–79. The 'cartel *Reichstag*' of 1887 appeared to confirm this once more, and even after his dismissal the Chancellor regarded the determined calls to continue a 'conservative *Sammlung*' as his own 'legacy to domestic politics' (Stegmann). It seemed necessary to remind people of this in view of the abrupt change which Caprivi's pro-industrial foreign trade policy had meant for the agrarians. Although this attack on their long-defended 'rights' gave them only a short-lived fright, it was still necessary to win over the industrialists to a new compromise by means of a well-worn anti-socialism, intended to plaster over divergent interests through its ideological appeal. Certain social and historical factors remained constant throughout. The policy of *Sammlung* was financially backed by a majority of the interests it served, and buttressed the monopoly of power enjoyed by these privileged minorities. But, however justified one is in stressing this continuity, it would be misleading to give the impression of a monolithic bloc

barring the way to all forms of social and political modernisation
between 1879 and 1918. It underwent change, experienced rifts,
shifting alliances and new arrangements involving compromise. On
closer scrutiny, however, we can see it as forming two concentric
circles. These emerged after the mid-1890s and lasted for twelve years.
The Prussian Minister of Finance, Johannes von Miquel, with
Prussia's internal power relationships clearly in mind, attempted to
fill the smaller, inner circle with a renewed alliance between heavy
industry and major agrarian interests. However, this proved to be
too narrow a basis for imperial policy. Since he wanted at all costs to
avoid linking up with the conservative Centre Party, Tirpitz and
Bülow developed an overall strategy. They proposed using the
German battle-fleet as a political rallying-point, hoping to involve
the bourgeoisie as a whole and ultimately also to win over the
Catholic Centre, as a 'party of the constitution', to the conservative
line in domestic politics (see III.5.2). It was made additionally
palatable to the more traditional middle classes through social
welfare measures like the Artisan Law of 1897. The hard core of
Miquel's *Sammlung* was held together by the Bülow tariff of 1902 and
a whole series of Navy Bills. By these means, and with the support of
the commercial middle class, the 'agrarian-industrial condominium
directed against the proletariat' could continue in its prime social
and political function of 'securing and strengthening the socially
threatened position of the ruling élites'.[37] Through a whole range of
measures in keeping with the interests of its protagonists, the Imperial German 'cartel based on fear' safeguarded their positions of
privilege on repeated occasions.

This strategy was helped along by a noticeable decline of intellectual and constitutional energies among the political parties after the
mid-1870s. The only obvious exception was the Social Democrats.
As the parties accommodated themselves to the decisions of 1871
and 1879, an out-and-out conflict of socio-economic interests gradually replaced constitutional ideals among the Liberals and the
Conservatives. Bismarck analysed this accurately in stating 'that in
internal affairs the predominance of economic issues is making
inexorable progress'. Yet he himself encouraged this process
whereby 'learned types who, without a business, property, trade or
industry, live off a salary, fees and dividends' would have to 'submit
to the economic demands of a producing nation or else vacate their
parliamentary seats'. Bismarck's designs in domestic policy could
expect more tangible success from satisfying the material interests
represented by the *syndici* of the pressure groups than from wrestling

with the political aspirations of full-time politicians. He did all in his power to encourage the long-term trend whereby 'the parties could emerge as sharply defined communities of social and economic interests, on which one can count and pursue tit-for-tat policies'. As Otto Hintze put it in 1911, this trend pre-dominated 'to an unprecedented degree' from the 1870s to the immediate pre-war period. The policy of *Sammlung*, based on finding a new way of balancing major interests against each other at different intervals, was both a consequence of this development and a cause of its further encouragement. This, as Hintze put it, visibly favoured the 'monarchy's leadership of the state' at the expense of greater 'parliamentary infuence'[38] in Germany's authoritarian Empire.

In 1907, as a substitute for the Centre, the so-called Left-Liberals joined the pressure groups and parties which represented the broadly-based *Sammlung*. Not long before, one of their number, Friedrich Naumann, had aptly described the device which in fact held the alliance of 'iron and rye' together: 'They are feigning fear in order to further their own interests'.[39] From 1907 onwards the Bülow Bloc once more demonstrated the effectiveness of the appeal of *Sammlung*: but in 1909 the customary, over-acted minor quarrels among the groups represented gave way to a genuine distintegration. The agrarians pushed through their own sacrosanct self-interest so flagrantly during the ratification of the imperial finance reform that for a time their alliance with industry was on the verge of collapse. That the BdI found its way to cooperate from 1909 to 1911 with the relatively liberal *Hansabund*, in which the trade and export industries pursued a quite different economic policy from heavy industry (only to pull out again because of the latter's supposedly soft line on Social Democracy), reveals more clearly than many other signs the depth of the division which had been created. True, a small-scale *Sammlung* was re-formed, made up from heavy industry, major agrarian interests and the middle classes. But the link with the Centre, with trade and the Agrarian League did not work at first, even though anti-Socialist and antisemitic sentiments were vigorously stirred up. This was due not least to the fact that the navy lost its power to bind diverse elements together as well as to the costly dreadnought construction programme in 1908. Contrary to earlier calculations, this programme created problems which proved explosive in terms of fiscal policy. Bethmann Hollweg's rallying-cry for a '*nationale Sammlung*' in the 1912 election campaign could not prevent a victory for the parties of the Left. This in turn led to an acceleration of the shift to the Right by the traditional partners of the *Sammlung*. True, the 'cartel of the productive estates' now materialised. But all organised attempts to stem the tide of the Left with a bloc formed by all the right-wing parties failed on account of their own irreconcilable differences. Instead of the intended 'peaceful change in the constitution' towards greater parliamentary influence in imperial policy — for which Bülow, overthrown by right-wing anti-parliamentary groups, was the worst example imaginable — a polarisation of forces occurred. This did not lead, however, to organised clashes between them on a grand scale. Rather, they remained in a strange state of paralysis amid an atmosphere of gloomy fear and complete mutual mistrust. The abortive right-wing cartel demonstrates this, as do the two successful *Reichstag* votes of no confidence in Bethmann Hollweg. These led nowhere, except to show that the government could not be harmed by the constitutionally impotent Left. The quasi-paralysis was brought on by a crisis in a deeply divided nation, to which there appeared to be no solution; this was without doubt one of the main factors which led to the policy of high-risk diplomacy in the summer of 1914.

The desire for an impressive right-wing cartel was not met until the founding of the German Fatherland Party in 1917. It represented an updated continuation of earlier right-wing alliances, this time in the shape of the first German proto-fascist mass movement.[40] While it is true that political antisemitism had existed as proto-fascist element from the 1870s onwards, it was not until 1917 that it was able to acquire a basis of mass support. The National Socialist German Workers' Party (NSDAP) can in fact be considered the legitimate offspring of the Fatherland Party. In the history of its members, its social background, ideology and programme the various connecting threads are clearly visible. It ultimately represented a large *Sammlung* movement which appeared to be a necessity to German conservatives; but one they could 'tame' for their own purposes. Whatever enormous burdens the imperial policy of *Sammlung* stored up for the Weimar Republic, in the years before 1918 it consistently served the political ends of the traditional and the recently emerged ruling élites in German society as they pursued their increasingly selfish interests. As Walther Rathenau put it in a memorable formula, it was the product of a 'state in which for centuries no one has ruled who was not a member of, or convert to, military feudalism, the feudalised bureaucracy, or the feudalised, militarised and bureaucratised plutocracy'.[41]

3. Integrating devices and structural hostility towards democracy

In addition to authoritarian constitutional norms and the Bonapart-ist constitutional reality, the impotence of the parties and the self-interest of the pressure groups, the various techniques of politi-cal rule and the conservative long-term alliances, there were devices intended to promote integration which were tightly locked into these elements to ensure that the entire framework of the social order could serve the purposes of the ruling élites for as long as possible. It is important to distinguish between, on the one hand, ideological influences and motive forces and, on the other, institutional arrange-ments and mechanisms intended to stabilise the system. Here we shall select only a few examples from the many available on the grounds that they were typical. A discussion which confines itself to several ideological factors alone cannot provide an adequate analy-sis. It is institutions which in the long run guarantee the internalis-ation and acceptance of political authority. Herein lies the crucial signifiance of the educational system in reinforcing social relation-ships based on political authority: through primary socialisation (effected in the immediate family) to secondary socialisation (by peers, schools and universities). Because of the fundamental import-ance of this type of institutionalised control of behaviour, which, to put it briefly, preferred control by others to the encouragement of personal responsibility, we can also discern a structural antipathy to democracy as being one of its most important consequences. This antipathy was certainly one more feature of Germany's social his-tory during the time of the Empire.

3.1 *The ideology of the state and emergency laws*

The traditional German ideology of the state, which hung over the Empire of 1871 like an all-embracing cloud, was derived in the main from three sources:

(1) The practice of absolutism in the German states, particularly after the end of the Thirty Years' War, led to the population becoming accustomed to a steadily increasing degree of guidance from above. Whereas elsewhere the process of modern state building did not rule out various forms of decentralised self-government, in German-speaking Central Europe a relatively uninterrupted prog-ress towards centralising power based on the bureaucracy and army

came to prevail. It should not be forgotten that this variant of 'enlightened' absolutism gave the larger German states a comparatively high degree of administrative efficiency. This had the effect of immunising the population against revolutionary unrest and 'contamination' by the West, while at the same time enhancing the aura surrounding the leaders of the state. As a result, an enormously powerful set of influences — which carried the authority of centuries — acted continuously, not only on the everyday administrative and legal practices of government, but also on areas of social change and economic policies produced by the action of the state.

(2) The specific influence of a vulgarised Lutheran belief in authority provided an ideological support for this development in the same way as its counterpart of counter-Reformation Catholicism did in Catholic states. However one cares to interpret Luther's political thought, this much is certain: in its everyday effects the established Lutheran Church transformed whoever ruled the state into a divinely ordained figure of authority. Since one owed the ruler obedience and was not entitled to oppose him by any appeal to a right of resistance, he was effectively placed above criticism. This development can be traced in particular in Prussia, the largest of the German Empire's constituent states; it was especially significant because of her position of hegemony within Germany.

(3) The same was true of Hegel's idealist notion of the state which was disseminated by the Prussian universities from the 1820s onwards. From the university lectern, as part of the surge of idealist philosophy, the state was given temporal sanctification as the embodiment of morality, transcending even divine right. But this in the end merely degenerated into a blind worship of the state which, after sinking into the sediment of received opinion, continued so much the longer in its effects. Two important social groups became the main vehicles of this idealism: the bureaucracy, as Hegel's 'general estate', claimed that it was virtually the state incarnate; and the educated bourgeoisie, which in time provided no-less-influential 'opinion-makers' and also subscribed to Hegelianism. Both these groups were responsible for feeding it into the discussions of the élites, into public opinion and the education system. In the 1880s Franz von Roggenbach, the Liberal, commented: 'The state sophists of Berlin have been singing for so long the song that the state is the most perfect creation the human spirit is capable of constructing, that it has become a matter of indifference to them whether or not

individuals are reduced to the level of trained machines'. Along with others who criticised this development this aristocrat from Baden recognised that the authoritarian ideology of the state stood in the way of any political modernisation of Germany and directly favoured the structure of political power in the German Empire. 'Whether the spirit of the times which works so powerfully to confirm the state's absolutism with its parliamentary trimmings and naive playing about with a semblance of constitutionalism, would ever change', he could not say.[1] In fact, the ideology of the German state, and in particular its myth of the above-party nature of government, continued to dominate until 1918 and beyond.

Whenever politically active minorities or emancipatory movements challenged the *status quo* and, hence, the claims of official ideology, special laws were passed to bring them round to the state's reasoning. The Catholics were the first to experience this at the time of the *Kulturkampf*, to be followed by the Social Democrats between 1878 and 1890. Legislation directed against national minorities began to assume an increasingly harsher character, culminating in special measures which made a mockery of the notion of the equality of the citizen before the law. In addition, the German 'bureaucratic state' practised discrimination internally by means of ordinances and decrees directed against Social Democrats, Catholics, Jews and liberals in the administration, army, judiciary and imperial civil service. Together with the more informal mechanisms of prejudice and resentment, which are even more difficult to identify, these exercised as enduring an influence in the long run as the temporary definitions of legal discrimination. Whereas the state's ideology provided the fiction of a united society of unanimous citizens, the social consensus was in fact engineered by the use of legal and administrative immunities and privileges. The reverse side of this seemingly monolithic exterior of the authoritarian state was the coercion of those holding contrary opinions, against whom it regularly exercised its monopoly of power.

3.2 *Nationalism and enemy stereotypes*

Nationalism originally began its victorious advance during the closing years of the eighteenth century, appearing as an anti-aristocratic, liberal and emancipatory ideology of the advancing bourgeoisie. In contrast to the war-plagued world of the *ancien régime*, it offered the ideal of reconciliation and friendship which would spring into being between all peoples, regardless of frontiers, once they were organised into nation states built on representative institutions for the propertied and educated bourgeoisie. A hundred years later there was little talk of this basic liberal principle or of harmonious international cooperation. This was a general European trend, but it was particularly prominent in Germany. After the abortive revolution of 1848, which again formed a marked break, German nationalism lost, indeed jettisoned, its liberal elements in favour of those originally inimical to it. Contrary images and opposite attitudes came to dominate it completely. From the very beginning, this transformed, modern style of nationalism moved in two directions. It was aimed at both external and internal opponents. For this reason it is wrong to emphasise exclusively its impact on foreign policy, bearing in mind that the nationalism which directed itself against France and later England resulted from nationalist phobias rooted in internal conditions. For it lay in the Janus-faced character of nationalism in Imperial Germany that it was not only militant towards foreign nations but aggressive towards its internal enemies. It was capable of being mobilised against either. And indeed it was mobilised, whether in the case of Catholics who were rejected by the Empire's predominantly Protestant society, or in the case of Social Democrats, who were denounced as 'un-patriotic' because of their membership of the International. There were many citizens in the 'national community' not deemed fit to belong to the nation; 'parasites on the nation' who had to be combated. Towards the end of the Bismarck period, a deeply concerned Bamberger was able to comment that 'a generation has grown up to whom patriotism has always appeared in terms of hate; hatred for everything that does not blindly submit to them, here or abroad'.[2] The dual function of this aggressive nationalism can be clearly observed in the *Reichstag* election campaigns. What before the first two elections of 1871 and 1874 might still appear to have been an echo of wartime patriotism, now emerged visibly as a strategy for the retention of power. At the right moment tensions in foreign affairs were fabricated or the possibilities of dangerous international threats conjured up. The resultant fear of external enemies could be translated into electoral ammunition for those 'loyal to the Empire', while the camp of those 'enemies of the Empire', who were likeliest to criticise this strategy, would be denounced as politically unreliable on account of their very criticism and tarred with the brush of collaboration with foreign powers. Catholics were easily associated with the Roman curia, as were Social Democrats with the International, Poles with the entire Polish opposition to the partitions, Liberals with parliamentary England, and every force left of centre with the international 'solidarity of revolutionary and republican interests'.[3] The poisoning of the country's political atmosphere, which resulted from abusing nationalism and foreign policy for electoral purposes, did not particularly trouble the leaders in Berlin as long as it was their parliamentary supporters who benefited at the polls, enabling them to drape their legislative proposals in the colours of national necessity. Bismarck knew very well how to galvanise an 'inert and apathetic electorate' which, faced with difficult social and economic problems after 1873, could be accused of a 'certain national languor', by using the 'heat' generated by international affairs at election time. This can be demonstrated in all the *Reichstag* elections from 1887 onwards, but especially those of 1884 and 1887.[4]

His successors copied this technique. As late as 1912, anti-French, -English and -Russian nationalist sentiment was still accompanied by a refusal on principle to acknowledge 'loyalty to the Empire' in any of the government's opponents. This feeling was fanned by deliberate manipulation in order to achieve 'negative integration'. However, rather than picture this nationalism as a force in its own right, it would make more sense to enquire at the outset what Germany's rulers actually stood to gain from allying themselves with it. This does not mean pursuing a conspiracy theory. Nor does it mean denying that influences derived from nationalism itself through its propagation in education, the army, press and literature to some extent gave it an independence of its own which could also have affected the ruling élites. But, quite apart from the crucial question of the rulers' own motives, one can detect that, no matter how much the power-élites had themselves assimilated certain aspects of nationalism, they also made a completely rational and calculated use of it. They employed to a considerable degree their various techniques of political rule in order to exploit its dynamism. We can follow the methods employed, as, for example, when Bismarck engineered unity in the 'cartel *Reichstag*' in 1887 under the threat of a 'danger', first from Russia and then from France; when Bülow fought his way through the 'Hottentot' elections in 1907 under the banner of imperialist power struggles; or when Bethmann Hollweg played up disagreements over armaments policy in 1912. We can recognise here the same basic pattern of artificially whipped-up conflict which was fuelled even further by bringing nationalism into play.

In search of an explanation for this growing, passionate, xeno-
phobic, vulgarised nationalism one encounters not only the influence of national beliefs, received perceptions and clichés, as
transmitted in the various processes of political socialisation, but
sees in the objects of nationalist animosity a reflection of the antagonisms of the societies involved and the competitive international
situation in which they were bound up. It is these resilient basic
structures which help explain the powerful appeal of a nationalism
based on 'friend–foe' categories. Put a different way, the contradictions within bourgeois society and an international system based on
competing states found their expression in nationalism. They nourished it and encouraged a specific scale of priorities in national
values. The interplay of the social structure, the economy, politics
and ideology enables us to show clearly how nationalism was rapidly
penetrated by the spread of racialist beliefs. The oligopolistic nature
of political power relationships within German society and between
the members of the system of competing states encouraged the view
that it fell to a few racially privileged 'superior' nations to carve up
the world and dominate it. In place of the liberal goal of self-
determination and the democratic ideal of equality, 'organised
capitalism' gave rise to an 'ideal of political rule based on oligarchies'. In the domestic sphere this ideology defended the 'position of
the rulers *vis-à-vis* the working class'. In external affairs it justified
the notion of a permanent competitive struggle by using racialist
ideology.[5] Without taking into account the continuing oligopolism of
large-scale concerns, cartels and employers' associations in domestic
politics, the spread of German racialism through imperialist expansion cannot be adequately understood; although it can be made to
appear innocuous if analysed solely in terms of intellectual history.

3.3 *Antisemitism and policies towards minorities*

From the mid-1870s onwards racialist views sprouted in German
domestic politics like so many poisonous fungi. Alongside traditional
forms of antisemitism of the religious, cultural and economic varie-
ties, biological forms of organised political antisemitism now appeared. Its rapid rise must be seen in the first instance as a
phenomenon related to the crises of the trend-period which followed
the second world-wide economic crisis. From that time on it can be
closely correlated with the fluctuations of the economy. Here was a
crisis ideology which concentrated the emotional tensions, concrete
disappointments, hysteria and insecurity caused by the slumps, and

directed them against a minority which had long suffered discrimination. As a form of psychic escapism from the painful experiences of uneven economic growth and deteriorating social status, antisemitism provided a focal point for discontented elements which saw in the figure of the Jew a scapegoat for all the ills of the period. In antisemitic grievances, expressed, for example, in no fewer than 500 publications on 'the Jewish question' between 1873 and 1890 alone, and containing all the commonplaces of the twentieth century's virulent antisemitism, the mood caused by the depression sought and found a safety-valve, as did the general malaise felt by the 'old' middle classes faced with the anonymous pressures of industrial capitalism.

Outbursts of antisemitism, evident in Berlin after the autumn of 1879 and Court Chaplain Stöcker's anti-Jewish agitation and excesses against Jews in Pomerania in 1881, suddenly alerted German liberalism to the new danger. Even before this time, there had been 'in the younger days of every German Jew . . . a painful moment which', according to Walther Rathenau, 'he would remember for the rest of his days'. It was the point when he 'realised completely for the first time that he had come into this world as a second-class citizen and that no amount of ability and merit could ever free him from this condition'.[6] From this period on dark resentments were stirred up even more, won the approval of a wider society and were translated into political or even direct action. As early as December 1880, after a large antisemitic gathering in the Friedrichstadt district of Berlin, 'organised gangs stood outside the busier cafés and roared . . . repeatedly in unison, "Jews out!"'. They prevented Jews or anyone who looked Jewish from entering. By these means they provoked brawls, the smashing of windows and other kinds of wild behaviour. All this was done, of course, in the name of defending German idealism against Jewish materialism'.[7] It was no wonder then that Theodor Mommsen, who organised the liberal resistance to the antisemitic professors around Treitschke at the University of Berlin, asked himself, 'where is our shameful barbarism leading us?' Bamberger too 'felt sick' at this so-called antisemitism and 'its awful, boundless release of base feelings which take pleasure in hatred and the oppression of those who are their equals or their betters. The vital organs of the nation: the army, the schools, learned society, are full to the brim with it . . . it has become an obsession which won't leave one alone'. And after the first outbreaks of anti-Jewish violence, the great Berlin banker, Gerson von Bleichröder, lamented with considerable foresight that they were 'only the start of the catastrophe of a terrible social revolution'.[8]

But neither von Bleichröder's personal approach to the Emperor, nor the petitions of the left-wing Liberals could halt antisemitism. The socio-economic structures which created it were far more powerful than any such noble protestations. Quite unabashed, the Conservatives called upon their voters as early as 1884 to renounce the 'service of Jewry'. The fact that 'Jewry' was a tool of 'international and un-German powers' as it was put in typical jargon, 'must bring every true German finally to the realisation' that 'it would never put the interests of the German fatherland first'.[9] In the Centre Party too, the antisemitic features which had long been part of its propaganda since the 1870s came increasingly to the fore. The antisemitic organisations of the 1880s, the Christian-Social Party (*Christlich-Soziale Partei*), the Antisemitic League (*Antisemitenliga*), the Social Empire Party (*Soziale Reichspartei*), the German People's Union (*Deutscher Volksverein*), the German Reform Party (*Deutsche Reformpartei*) and the German Antisemite Union (*Deutsche Antisemitische Vereinigung*) came together in 1889 to form the Antisemitic German Social Party (*Antisemitische Deutschsoziale Partei*). From its merger with the Antisemitic People's Party (*Antisemitische Volkspartei*) of 1890 (known as the German Reform Party [*Deutsche Reformpartei*] after 1893) there emerged the German Social Reform Party (*Deutschsoziale Reformpartei*) of 1894. This grouping split again in 1900 into its original two parties. Though their vote never exceeded 300,000, the Hamburg programme of the United Association of Antisemitic Parties (*Vereinigte Antisemitenparteien*) envisaged, as early as 1899, 'the final solution'. 'Since the Jewish problem will reach world proportions in the course of the twentieth century', it explained, it would have to be 'solved in the end by the complete exclusion and . . . finally, annihilation of the Jewish people.'[10] That, despite its excesses, antisemitism became socially respectable and acceptable at Court after its sudden emergence in the 1870s was no doubt partly due to the encouragement it was given by the first Imperial Chancellor. Bismarck had no scruples about using the antisemitic movement for his own electoral purposes. True, he never parted with his Jewish banker, his Jewish lawyer or his Jewish family doctor, and the fact that he called the *Reichstag* deputy, Lasker, a 'stupid Jewboy' and coarsely referred to Minister Friedenthal as a 'Semitic pants-shitter' can be put down to the typical prejudices of an aristocrat.[11] Yet shortly before the 1884 *Reichstag* elections, he allowed a newspaper — without any later denial — to quote him as saying, 'the Jews do whatever they can to turn me into an antisemite'. And later, he said he wished 'that articles on the election results would stress that the Jews and the Poles had collaborated at every turn', and furthermore that 'Jewish money has been behind the progressive republicans'.[12]

In a directive to the Prussian Minister of the Interior, von Puttkamer, before the impending elections in 1884, he wrote that 'the great mass of the people would be offended' if the government were openly to oppose antisemitism. If, on the other hand, they were to approve of it too openly, 'we would make a lot of Jewish money flow into the Progress Party's election funds', for 'the Jews have always been behind the Progressives'. Furthermore, they were 'ridiculously sensitive; . . . why should one prevent people who feel driven to curse the Jews from doing so?'[13] If behind such cynical comments the great manipulator still felt confident of his ability to keep antisemitism in its place, such utterances nevertheless directly sanctioned the rowdy antisemitism of the gutter. It was also in evidence among his closest associates; not only in his violently antisemitic press secretary and lackey, Moritz Busch, but in his eldest son Herbert von Bismarck. The latter would have liked 'to have boxed the upstart Bleichröder round his Jewish ears'. As Secretary of State at the German Foreign Office, he established the rule that no 'Jewish fool' should be recruited, and sneered at the 'Jewish-minded' British Under-Secretary of State, Meade.[14] Antisemitism also played a significant part when Bismarck ordered the deportation of some 30,000 Poles from Prussia's eastern provinces in 1885. A third of those expelled were Jews.

Full of foreboding, Bamberger described early on the effect of Bismarck's position, adopted for expediency, in these impressive words:

> What is peculiar to our present situation is that this truly great man, who now rules us, delegates anything which he does not control himself to the power of the mob. That is the only collaboration he will put up with. Perhaps it has always been like that. But it is twice as bad when a people with barbaric tendencies hear the praises of brutality sung as if it were a kind of idealism based on strength, manliness and morality. That is what it amounts to; and out of this is growing a vile spirit which is now . . . trying to grab the reins.

In view of the frightening scale of antisemitism, Mommsen's highly sceptical tone is understandable:

You are deceived if you believe that I can do anything about it. You are deceived if you believe that one can do anything at all with reason. It is all in vain. What I could give you . . . would still be just reasons — logical and moral arguments. But no antisemite would listen to them. They listen only to their own hate, and their own envy, to their worst instincts; . . . there can be no protection against the mob — whether it's a mob on the streets or a mob in the drawing-room it makes no difference. A rabble is a rabble, and antisemitism is the outlook of a rabble. It is like a horrible epidemic, like cholera. It can neither be explained nor cured. One has to be patient until the poison dissipates and loses its strength.[15]

But what proved significant in the long run was that, although the openly antisemitic parties could attract only a very small number of protest votes right up to the last pre-war elections of 1912, anti-semitism, with Bismarck's approval, became widespread among the Conservatives, at first via the Agrarian League, as already noted. By this route it found its way into the old power-élites, where its slogans became respectable in the drawing-rooms and a mere commonplace in right-wing publications. As industrialisation progressed the social basis of antisemitism was broadened, owing to the almost chronic insecurity felt by the petty bourgeoisie (the 'old' *Mittelstand*), who clung to their ideal of the small independent business man in spite of economic cycles and the formation of concentrations of capital. Antisemitism became a constant feature of a syndrome opposed to capitalism in its advanced form. And it remained so until, after 1929, in the wake of further profound economic crises, German fascism was able to exploit this radical right-wing protest against modernity.

However, it is not only antisemitism which affords insights into Germany's internal condition at the time, but also the policy adopted towards national minorities. Like the Poles (before 1918 every tenth Prussian was Polish!) or the French in Alsace-Lorraine, the Danes of North Schleswig, the Lithuanians and Masurians, these national minorities had been incorporated into the state by the decisions taken in 1871. After a short time the imperial government began to assert its ideals of national and cultural homogeneity at their expense. As far as language was concerned, the law gave absolute precedence to German. Its use as the official language was enforced in education, public assemblies, judicial proceedings and commercial and military law — in short, in all spheres of public and legal life. Alsace-Lorraine was treated relatively generously. Apart from the fact that the number of native French speakers was in any case small, the respect shown for French culture probably made it difficult to pursue a rigorous campaign against the French language. In contrast to the position in the east the Germans could find consolation in the fact that their numbers in the population were steadily rising. The Danes were certainly worse affected, but here German policy has to be seen as a reaction to the Danes' own similar policy on language after 1848. The greatest measure of harshness was, however, reserved for the campaign against the Polish minority. Constantly influenced by ideas of an East–West cultural divide and Germanic superiority over the Slavs, this struggle was conducted not only against the linguistic and cultural identity of Prussia's Poles but against their material landholdings by means of agrarian laws. This is where German policy encountered its fiercest opposition in a defiance which, broadly speaking, came to an end only with the Poles' successful attainment of self-determination in 1918. Generally speaking, two different nationalisms clashed so violently with one another in the east, that it is difficult to imagine how, given the historical circumstances, their entanglement could ever have been avoided. Even so, it need not have been so unacceptable in the form it actually took.

In this area, too, decisions of fundamental importance were taken during the Bismarck period. Certainly, the Imperial Chancellor was prepared to stick to the arrangements of the old multinational Prussian state as long as the Poles saw themselves as subjects of the German Empire and submitted to its authority. But behind the façade of *raison d'état* there lurked a passionate hatred for the Poles which erupted from time to time: 'Thrash the Poles so they despair of living', Bismarck wrote as far back as 1861. 'I have every sympathy for their situation', he added, 'but if we want to survive we can do nothing else but exterminate them. The wolf cannot help it if he is as God made them, but because of it we shoot him dead if we can.'[16] In the 1870s the penetration of the German language into all the areas inhabited by minorities was given legal and administrative backing. Only the Lithuanians, Masurians and Sorbs were exempted for a while longer. In 1871, and again in 1878, the minimum hours of German taught in schools in North Schleswig was increased. In 1872 German was made the official language of Alsace-Lorraine, the common language of instruction in 1873, and the procedural language in the Assembly of Notables of the Provincial Committee in 1881. While numerous exceptions to the regulations were made for the French, and remained in force until 1914, in

Prussia's partitioned Polish territories a decree made German the only language to be used in elementary schools after 1873. The precedence of German was reinforced and more thoroughly implemented by the law of 1876 on its use in commerce, and that of 1877 on its use in the courts — though the latter did not apply to Alsace–Lorraine until 1889. It was during the 1880s, however, that its use as an official language was implemented even more forcefully. In 1888 a decree made German the sole language of instruction in North Schleswig. As a result, tensions increased considerably, reaching a climax in the deportations ordered by the Chief President von Köller and the treatment between 1897 and 1901 of those who had opted for Danish citizenship under the terms of the 1866 Treaty of Prague.

After the expulsion of the Poles in 1885 the anti-Polish Settlement Law of 1886 formed a prelude to irreconcilable conflict. This law enabled a state commission, with growing funds at its disposal, to purchase land in the eastern provinces for the benefit of German peasants. It was intended to cut the ground away from under the Polish landed aristocracy, viewed as an important source of the Poles' defiant national will. In a similar manner, the *Kulturkampf* had been directed against the influence of the Polish clergy in this zone of conflict. As Bismarck explained to his circle of intimates, 'in all this legislation on [internal] colonisation the idea was to rid the country of the trichinosis of the Polish nobility.' In this vicious metaphor he revealed not only what Holstein called 'his boundless contempt for humanity' but a frightening affinity with the biological vocabulary of antisemitism and its talk of 'Jewish parasites'.[17] The intentions of Berlin's legislators came to nothing, however. They were resisted by the Polish community as it isolated itself further, assisted by the demographic factor of an increasing Polish birth rate. Far more property was soon finding its way into Polish rather than German hands, and the settlement commission found that it was mainly German land that fell under its powers of disposal. Since it spent almost a billion gold marks before 1914 on its programme of 'Germanising the soil', it appeared less an anti-Polish institution defending German interests than a financial operation to bale out German *Junker* who were heavily in debt by enabling them to sell off their estates at favourable prices. For this 'lucrative patriotism' of the agrarians, camouflaged as German self-assertion, the commission's funds represented a 'reserve bank' which, with the aid of large sums, succeeded 'also in Germanising them', as the socialist writer Franz Mehring sarcastically commented.[18] Because of the failure of this policy for the eastern provinces, the Prussian Diet eventually passed an expropriation law against the Poles in 1908. It was implemented by the Prussian government in 1912. This flagrant violation of the Constitution showed how the guarantees of a 'state based on the rule of law' could be shelved when it came to campaigning against national minorities. As early as 1904 'new settlements' in the disputed areas were made dependent on permission being obtained from the district presidents. This arrangement delivered the Poles to the chicanery of the authorities' discretionary powers. They were instructed in 1898 by the Imperial Chancellor, Prince Hohenlohe-Schillingsfürst, to 'promote German interests' both on and off duty. Similarly, the government's language policy gradually came to a head. In 1901 it led to open resistance by Polish parents and in 1906 to school strikes by Polish children. The 1908 Imperial Law on Associations finally contained a notorious paragraph 12 on language. This laid down that only areas with over 60 per cent of their population comprising traditionally settled groups could retain their own language for a transitional period alongside German. This meant that basic rights guaranteed by the Constitution were being made dependent on the result of a political head-count of citizens' nationality. It meant, to use Schieder's formulation, that the 'stage of an ideological state nationalism' had been reached which finally overstepped the limits of the Constitution. Not until April 1917, six months after the Central Powers announced the setting up of a Polish kingdom, was paragraph 12 reluctantly rescinded.

During the war the point was almost reached where the Poles were expelled on a grand scale. Previously, in 1887, the later Imperial Chancellor, von Bülow, had revealingly expressed the hope that a future conflict would allow 'the Poles to be evicted *en masse* from the Polish parts of the country'.[19] The fact that he himself did nothing after 1900 to prevent the annual influx of some 300,000 Polish seasonal workers from Russian Poland and the Austrian Galicia could well be connected with the fact that so many East Elbian estates were dependent on the physical manpower supplied by these workers. The aggressive Union of the Eastern Marches had insisted on 'resettlement' and 'expulsion' from the 1890s onwards. After 1914 ideas like this came together in a plan for a 'Polish border strip' along Germany's eastern frontier to be annexed for strategic reasons and for the purpose of settlement. It was to create space for German settlers who would form a 'bulwark against the tide of Slavism' following an 'ethnic reallocation of land'. It meant an expulsion of the Poles on a massive scale. Yet even a liberal historian like Friedrich Meinecke was able to view this prospect with equanimity.[20] The content of government memoranda on the subject prefigured the radical policy of Germanisation after 1939 every bit as clearly as the embryonic forms of barbaric oppression which manifested themselves in the German Empire's morally corrupt language policy. As regards the eastern provinces, one can scarcely avoid detecting the genesis of later ideologies and policies, including the need for 'living-space', Germany's 'civilising' mission, and its imperialism in the east. Yet the contradictions within this policy could be seen in the way that the Poles were treated as 'enemies of the Empire'. The laws which operated to the detriment of those citizens of the state who spoke a different language had a double-edge to them. They helped prepare the way for dismantling the 'state based on the rule of law' and its constitutional principles by the use of legal methods sanctioned by the state itself. They also encouraged a situation in which discrimination against minorities came to be accepted. Expulsion and expropriation, social ostracism and a 'germanising' repression, all played a part in the Wilhelmine Empire. Had it not been for the acceptance of such public injustices, the path towards the violent events of a latter period could never have been made so smooth so soon.

3.4 *Religion as an ideology of legitimation*

In the conflict between the different nationalities on the eastern frontier religion played a considerable part. A romanticised Polish national Catholicism saw its arch-enemy in a Germanising Protestantism. Conversely, on the German side the struggle against a Catholic Polish nationalism was coloured by a militant Protestantism. In view of the dominance of nationalism and socio-economic factors, these influences were admittedly relegated to a subordinate position. Yet in the internal politics of the German Empire of 1871 the two major denominations of the Christian religion remained important for a number of reasons in the classic land of religious division.

The Lutheran state church: 'throne and altar' One of the most important consequences of the sixteenth-century Reformation was the creation of an established Lutheran Church. This was accompanied by the transformation of territorial princes into petty Protestant popes in their role as heads of the Church in their respective states. No matter how strongly influenced the Prussian dynasty and many of its leading élites were by Calvinism in their ambitions and pursuit of success, this did not succeed in loosening the authoritarian hold of Lutheran ideology at a popular level. Neither did it succeed in instilling its belief in the right to resist tyranny or in a more liberal relationship with government, viewed as an agency of social control devoid of divine sanction. Lutheran religiosity induced in the Germans a 'metaphysical view of the state based on a purely emotional sensibility'. This was an outlook which was to have far-reaching political consequences. At the same time, Pietism, which was influential among the more important social groups, stressed a 'retreat into the inner self' which often led to an orthodox and sanctimonious hypocrisy. Its call for the world to be reformed first through a reform of the self deliberately forwent any attempts to change the political structure of the state. After the 1870s the anti-liberal bias of a Protestantism reacting to the thrust of modernisation since the 1850s had the effect of reinforcing such attitudes. The established Lutheran Church, especially after the union between Lutherans and Calvinists in 1817, was allowed as an institution under public law to raise taxes with the help of the state and shape the curriculum of the state elementary schools. Religious instruction was made subject to its approval — as, indeed, it still is today. At the head of the clerical hierarchy stood the King, enthroned as the *Summus Episcopus*. Because legal and spiritual authority were both vested in him, his rule clearly possessed a 'Caesaro-papist' character which reinforced an anachronistic belief in divine right. In Prusso-Germany the state placed at the disposal of the spiritual powers 'the outward means of coercion' to 'maintain its position of power' and enforce its collection of revenue. In return, the Church assured the State 'recognition of its legitimacy and the compliance of its subjects by means of religion'.[21]

After 1871 the combination of kingship and emperorship with the office of *Summus Episcopus* created a powerful instance of authority, at least in the North German 'Empire State' of Prussia. For the pastor at parish level — especially in the countryside where patronage depended on royalist feudal land-owners — the traditional alliance of 'throne and altar' acquired new lustre. The functional significance of the Lutheran sermon, Lutheran religious instruction and Lutheran army chaplains should not be underestimated. They contributed to the stabilisation and legitimation of Hohenzollern Caesaro-papism, especially in the countryside and the small towns where 'compliance' was easiest to achieve. The other side of this almost complete identification of interests between Church and

State could be seen in the industrial towns and regions. Here it was patently clear that the Lutheran Church had become a church for the propertied and powerful; it thus, in a manner of speaking, contributed to the 'precipitation' of the proletarian worker. By means of missionary work, doss-houses, Pastor Bodelschwingh's workers' colonies and similar institutions, attempts were made at least to bring about improvements in selected areas. But while the noble motives behind these efforts deserve recognition, they could not dispel the overall impression that the Church preferred the company of the satisfied bourgeoisie or the noble on his feudal estate to that of the farm labourers and the exploited urban masses. The rapid extinction of Church life and Christianity in the industrial cities was closely bound up with the Church's refusal to take a stand on the issues of the day. To give an example: in Berlin as early as 1874 a mere 20 per cent of married couples went through Lutheran services and no more than 62 per cent of newly-born babies were baptised.[22] Because of the Church's identification with the old aristocracy and the new plutocracy there was a certain straightforward logic in the SPD's overwhelmingly anti-clerical attitude. This was also shared by the trade unions of the organised labour movement. Marx's ideological criticism of religion as the opium of the people was more than obvious, given the experiences of everyday life in the German Empire. Germany also confirmed de Tocqueville's analysis, made after his journey through America in the 1830s: 'Religion cannot partake of the secular power of rulers without drawing some of the hatred they provoke on to itself. The more democratic a nation becomes, and the more republican its society, the more dangerous is the association of religion with the power of the state.' If this was not yet generally the case in Germany, it was certainly true for the democratically minded workers who for some time had inclined towards a republic. It was also true for the diagnosis that the alliance of 'throne and altar' was misleading religion into 'sacrificing the future for the sake of the present'.[23] The problem was made worse by the lack of any free churches, or 'sects' as they were pejoratively described by some, which could have stood up for the underprivileged. They had done this with undeniable success in Great Britain where they managed to impart a sense of class identity even before the advent of trade unions and political organisations. In Germany it was left to the Social Democrats to fill this gap. It might even be said that the workers' movement contained elements of a substitute religion and an inner doctrine of salvation. Given the spiritual alienation of the urban workers, the 'future state' envisaged by Social Democrats meant far more than simply an ideal constitutional framework. It was no accident that in 1911 Eduard Bernstein entitled a retrospective analysis of the SPD's historical development *From Sect to Party*. On the other hand, the Social Democrats soon began to pursue their aims by resorting purely to revolutionary rhetoric. In this way they contained the workers' potential for protest and contributed indirectly to the stabilisation of the political and social system as a whole.

Roman Catholicism: estate-based ideology and its claim to monopoly   For the Catholic Church, whose symbiosis with the former Holy Roman Empire had been in many respects as close as could be imagined, the new Protestant Greater Prussian Empire was viewed primarily as a hostile threat. Although the oft-quoted *'casca il mondo'* of a Vatican dignitary enormously exaggerated the effect of Prussia's rise and the German Empire's creation, the *Kulturkampf* which followed was not calculated to lessen this initial animosity. Instead, it brought the interests of the Church and its secular institutions, including the Centre, much closer together — closer at any rate than its leader, Ludwig Windhorst, sometimes thought desirable. Castigated as a sinister ultramontane power behind the Catholic 'enemies of the Empire', yet itself intent on the rigid assertion of its traditional views, the Catholic Church did not find itself in an easy position up to the mid-1880s. Thereafter the continuing religious conflict in Germany's domestic politics relaxed somewhat; but anti-Catholic discrimination remained in all its possible forms. Political Catholicism for its part became more tolerant in the management of its own internal affairs. It was not only the dogma of the Immaculate Conception and the declaration of Papal Infallibility that shocked enlightened public opinion of the time. In the 1864 Syllabus of Errors, an index of eighty 'errors of the times', orthodox Catholicism ranged itself implacably against liberalism, socialism and modern science. The call for increased ecclesiastical control of education and research reached totalitarian proportions. In a fit of radical conservative blindness some of the most dynamic forces of the nineteenth century were put under the ban. In terms of canon law the Syllabus remained binding for the faithful until a revision, at least in part, was forced upon subsequent popes many decades later.

Having manoeuvred itself into a corner, the Roman Catholic Church, under the halo of its supreme functionary's infallibility atop a hierarchy of equally self-assured professional dispensers of salvation, could extricate itself only with some difficulty. The contempt it felt for the deeply held Protestant principle of toleration made any coexistence with rival organisations or educational claims very difficult. Without doubt, Thomist neo-scholasticism, encouraged in its development by several popes since the mid-nineteenth century, also reinforced the anti-modernist character of Roman Catholicism at this time. This batch of theorems was opposed to the social mobility of the modern age and its notions of parliamentary representation and democratic equality. It cemented the backward-looking traditions of Catholicism, and turned the values of a vanished world based on estates into an ideology. It sought to tie the nineteenth century into the strait-jacket of the medieval order while the tide of history moved in the opposite direction. The Catholic minority's relationship to the *Reichstag* and the federal assemblies, as the only places where it could put forward its legitimate claims and possibly push through their acceptance, was frequently crippled by the overbearing influence of neo-Thomist ideas. Catholicism was even less likely than Protestantism to make an active and lasting contribution to the spread of parliamentary influence in Germany, to say nothing of its eventual democratisation. It gradually came to terms with the Protestant-dominated German Empire. Indeed, an exaggerated patriotism attempted to refute the charge that Catholics were less reliable citizens. It hoped to break down the distrust, built up over many years, that was shown towards it by its 'hostile' Protestant environment. The results of this should not be ignored. So as not to be outdone on the issue of loyalty, a Catholic German became just as compliant and prudent a subject of the dynastic state power as his Lutheran neighbour. Although outside of Germany's Catholic states ·Catholicism did not confer any exclusive religious sanction on the head of the state in the way the Lutheran State Church did, like the Social Democrats, it, too, contributed indirectly to strengthening the German Empire once the *Kulturkampf* had evaporated. This was especially true of the whole web of Catholic associations which were in keeping with the doctrine of estates, flourished relatively unhindered and absorbed many social energies. At any rate, no devout Catholic seriously questioned either the authoritarian structure of the Constitution or the state's authoritarian policies. Wherever the state gave it a free hand, Catholicism tried to push through its claim to a monopoly in Catholic affairs, as it has done in various countries in the twentieth century. Since the *Kulturkampf* had resulted in a greater secularisation of Germany society — wherein lay its true significance — Catholicism concentrated on the family, education and its own associations, where it took a line no less authoritarian than the monarchical state. Its arguments against mixed marriages, claims to a monopoly of socialisation in the elementary schools, or the notion of Christian trade unions as an alternative to the more powerful Free Trade Unions have already been mentioned above (III.2.1). Thus Catholicism continued to be perceived as a threat, albeit a latent one, by Prussia's ruling élites and the Protestant bourgeoisie; while for its part it did not relinquish its justified distrust of Protestant Prussia. These tensions, to be sure, did not make impossible a rapprochement on tactical grounds. And beyond this, there existed a basic affinity between these opposing parties in terms of their authoritarian hold over society — already achieved in some areas and hoped for in others. There were also wide areas of common interest where neither was prepared to give way to the other. It was precisely for this reason that no reconciliation could ever come about.

3.5 *The matrix of the authoritarian society: socialisation processes and their control*

The individual is trained in social behaviour through various socialising processes at different stages in his or her life. Norms and values which govern subsequent behaviour are internalised and impulses channelled into modes of behaviour which are approved of by cultural tradition and convention. Whether termed super-ego, conscience or a code of honour, society equips the individual with certain controls throughout the socialisation process, providing a catalogue of prescriptive behaviour patterns, rewarding certain kinds of social conduct and establishing certain expectations as an individual fulfils particular social roles. In accordance with this 'enmeshing' (Theodor Litt) of the individual with society, history manifests itself not merely as an external force operating *upon* the individual, but also always as an internalised force *within* him or her. In short, deep down in a person's psyche there are certain forces at work, however mediated or distorted they may appear. A 'given social structure' selects 'specific psychic tendencies', whether or not these are made explicit.[24]

Families It falls to the family to play a fundamental role in the task of socialisation, going as far as the transmission of class-based language codes which to some extent determine a child's future. In Germany's rural areas during this period the extended family was still frequently encountered. It comprised the nucleus of the married couple and their children, together with the grandparents and several relatives. But even here, the transition to the nuclear family was already under way (though it was not as abrupt a development as in the large cities), and this meant a considerable reduction in the complexity of transmitted experience. The *pater familias* represented the normative model of the nuclear family. He made the decisions, with the mother subject to him in law and the children dependent on both until the age of majority was reached. There can be little doubt that the internal authoritarian structure of families was largely viewed as binding. Yet it also gave rise to quite specific forms of generational conflict, especially in father-and-son relationships. At the same time, it is also true that a relaxation of these norms occurred in certain strata, particularly after the 1890s. It appears that there also existed a connection between liberality and a generous upbringing on the one hand, and a rising level of education and material security on the other. Here is a wide field of study for the social historian of education. Emanating from those social strata whose children passed through the new Youth Movement (*Jugendbewegung*), new ideas and practices of child-rearing percolated through to other social groups.

As regards primary socialisation in the family, the view is often expressed that a direct relationship exists between the authoritarian family and authoritarianism in politics. Whether, in fact, 'paternalism in the family leads to the formation of authoritarian ideas of behaviour which then establish an authoritarian political disposition' is still an open question.[25] Certainly, comparisons hardly bear this out. The New England Puritan, the Victorian Englishman and the Republican Frenchman were scarcely outdone in terms of severity by the Wilhelmine father-figure. An authoritarian family structure would thus appear to be quite compatible with very different kinds of 'political culture'. On its own it can hardly establish political authoritarianism for a society as a whole. If, on the other hand, it is embedded in a society which uses authoritarian models and codes of conduct in general, it may well act as a kind of multiplier. In this case a line can be established which leads from an anthropomorphic 'God the Father' through the prince as a father-figure of his people and paternalistic employers to the father of the family. The most plausible definition of the consequences of the family as it existed in Imperial Germany would be to see it as an 'amplifier' of prevalent historical tendencies, while avoiding a monocausal approach and holding it responsible for too much.

The elementary schools   With regard to secondary socialisation in the schools between the ages of six and nineteen, the main focus of interest should not be on education as such, or even the type of instruction. One should concentrate instead on how the education system perpetuated the social structure and social power relationships. In this respect it formed part of the dominant political system. Max Weber was perhaps too soon in claiming that 'the differences in education . . . today, as distinct from the class determining factors of property and division according to economic function', are 'without doubt the most important criteria in class differentiation; especially in Germany where almost all positions of privilege inside and outside government are not just dependent on a qualification of specialised knowledge, but "general culture", at whose service the entire school and university system is placed'.[26] This was not entirely true. In Germany, as elsewhere, there existed other more dominant privileges based on birth and property. These tended to count for more than expertise. Similarly, upward mobility on the strength of professional training was anything but a general phenomenon, and varied instead between the different social strata. The German Empire's school system did not become a 'central clearing-house' for future security, status and affluence. Nor was it a basic 'determining factor in the class structure' in the sense of 'class membership' ceasing 'to determine the level of education' in favour of 'the level of education determining class membership'.[27] It still required many decades before the state made any serious attempt to work towards equality of opportunity for its citizens in this area. It can be established that before 1918 the consequences of decisions, which were everywhere evident in the elementary schools, grammar schools and universities, made access to educational institutions forever dependent on the place a pupil and his or her parents occupied in the class system. These decisions in turn perpetuated that system. Exceptions provided by examples of individual success stories — in 1890 there was one son of a worker in every thousand students — cannot do away with the unequivocal statistics on this question. Having said this, it is also true that the figures reflect a gradual upward mobility by separate stages over two to three generations.

Before the 1848 Revolution some 82 per cent of children in compulsory education had learnt to read and write. After 1870 it was practically 100 per cent, even if children in the countryside often acquired only scanty knowledge. After the Revolution the state tried, in its role as patron of the schools, to act upon a statement by Hegel. 'If the realm of ideas is revolutionised,' he wrote in 1808, 'reality cannot hold out.'[28] The representatives of the old regime saw one of the causes of the revolutionary movement in the expansion which the education system underwent. As a new kind of authority it subjected inherited standards to serious reflection and tended to encourage a critical attitude to social arrangements never before questioned. Given its politicising effect, their view was well justified. In 1849 the Prussian King went so far as to put 'all the misery' down to 'pseudo-education', 'irreligious mob wisdom' and 'the ostentatious show of fake learning'. As a result, any instruction likely to lead to the forming of opinions was placed under strict control.[29] In Prussia, for example, Stiehl's regulations and Raumer's directives of the autumn of 1854 prescribed the reinforcement of patriotic feeling and loyalty to the monarchy as prime teaching objectives. In a very elementary way, faith in received truths was to be sustained and, moreover, strengthened by the Church exercising a greater influence on teaching. In this way the teaching of history was used as an anti-revolutionary mind-drug for the inculcation of a patriotic mentality.

When, despite this, the Social Democrats emerged and proceeded to grow in strength, teaching was given the additional function of developing powers of resistance against the 'red menace'. In several directives on the auxiliary role of schools in 'combating socialist ideas' (in 1889, 1901 and 1908), the task of immunising 7.8 million elementary schoolchildren was prescribed in the kind of language Wilhelm II liked to use in his sensation-seeking speeches. After many decades of being exposed to enormous pressures, and having already been purged of liberal influences to some extent, school-teaching was not embarrassed to take up this new duty of 'political education', as it came to be called at the time. It obeyed the various directives on imparting attitudes and translated them into a code of virtues such as diligence, fear of God, obedience and loyalty. These could be contrasted in slogans with the godless, riotous subversion of the 'unpatriotic fellows'. This black-and-white imagery, to which more than 10 million elementary schoolchildren were exposed before 1914, can be traced with precision in history textbooks. Their content and style of presentation were meant, like the teachers' manuals, to foster the 'predisposition of the will' which revealed itself in school speeches and the celebrating of national occasions like the anniversary of the Battle of Sedan. A directive on 'the care of youth', issued in January 1911, even tried to ensure patriotism among young workers in limbo between leaving school and enlisting in the 'school of the nation', the army. The social and psychic effects of these influences are by their very nature difficult to measure, but we may assume their importance was great, bearing in mind how nationalism spread through the SPD and caused its shift to a nationalist position between 1914 and 1918. Here one can clearly recognise the manipulative use of nationalism to stabilise the social power structure, as well as the internationalisation of sublimated relationships based on social control.

The grammar schools   For the vast majority of German schoolchildren at the time formal education ended with the elementary school. A system of vocational schools made it possible for them to continue with their education, but only in certain areas, and the training was poor. Only a small percentage succeeded in passing through the needle's eye of admission to grammar schools and from there on to higher education. In 1885, for example, out of a population of 47 million, of whom 7.5 million were in elementary schools, only 238,000 attended the secondary schools. Of these, Prussia accounted for 133,000. This figure broke down into 84,300 children in grammar schools, 24,700 in schools specialising in modern languages and 5,100 in schools specialising in science.[30] Grammar-school pupils came predominantly from the families of the professional middle class and the civil service. In this way, the educated class continually reproduced itself. The spread of a narrow neo-humanism had given rise to the ideal of an educated élite which dominated the entire system of higher education after the 1820s. It took firm root after the setback suffered by the bourgeoisie in 1848–49, and developed into an arrogant, vulgarised idealism every bit as one-sided as the materialism it violently criticised. In political terms it was responsible for another aspect of *Realpolitik* in that it hastened the retreat into what Thomas Mann later called an 'inwardness protected by power'. It gave rise to a socially defensive attitude towards the lower classes which consciously upheld class barriers and reserved for a relatively narrow social stratum the advantages of higher education, defined here as the sum total of enhanced material and intellectual opportunities in life.

The aim of the grammar school was to prepare future scholars for study at university. The other types of secondary school, long opposed by the grammar schools, prepared their pupils for the technical universities which emerged between 1860 and 1890. A fairly high number of pupils left after six years of secondary schooling with the 'one-year certificate', as it was known. This opened up the prospect for them of only one year's military service and a career in the middle ranks of the civil service. The drop-out rate from the grammar schools was probably not insignificant, although no exact statistics on this are available. After 1834 the *Abitur*, the school-leaving certificate, became the required entrance qualification for university admission, and up to 1902 the grammar schools enjoyed a monopoly of training university candidates. Of those who gained the *Abitur* by no means all went on to university. In 1885 the total student population of the universities was a mere 27,000, or one-tenth of the secondary school population. But whoever managed to get this far had already climbed on to the first rung of a ladder which led to a varied and distinguished career.

While grammar-school pupils, still identifiable from the rest of the population by their school uniform, continued to provide the main source of recruits for the ruling élites, there also arose from their ranks a significant protest movement. This was the *Wandervogel* or Movement of Free German Youth. In terms of social composition it consisted mainly of grammar-school pupils and some university students up until 1914. Originating in the period between 1897 and 1900, formally founded in the Berlin district of Steglitz in 1901 and reaching its apogee shortly before the war at their gathering on the Hohe Meissner mountain, the groups involved were predominantly school pupils from the Protestant upper and middle bourgeoisie from the smaller and middle-sized towns or big-city suburbs. Along-side its revolt against the drudgery of the school, its call for a return to nature and 'a natural way of life', its release of creative energies and positive influences on the teaching of youth, a balanced appraisal must also recognise the existence of certain negative aspects which outweighed its positive side. The anti-liberal, anti-democratic, anti-urban and anti-industrial *Wandervogel* groups re-treated all too often into a Germanic social romanticism. Jews were denied membership, as were girls in most cases. The writings of Paul de Lagarde and Julius Langbehn's *Rembrandt as an Educator* were preferred reading; and an exaggerated élitist self-esteem, giving rise to an eroticised leadership cult, was combined with a strong aver-sion to the modern world. This mentality was also permeated by a passionate nationalism which explains why wave upon wave of the Youth Movement's members were able to die singing as they threw themselves into the machine-gun fire at Langemarck. Their anti-modern romanticism and idealism which rejected the world as it was, alongside a collective enthusiasm for pseudo-reformist aims among those about to step into responsible positions in society, undoubtedly increased the Movement's susceptibility to a type of politics which was to radicalise the revolt against urban, industrial civilisation ten years after the war. It simulated 'movement' and the notion of a new departure; but by that time the 'blue flower' of German romantic yearning bloomed alongside the muddy roads of Soviet Russia.

The universities   Around 13,000 students attended Germany's universities in 1871. There were 320 students for every million inhabitants in a population of 41 million. Within the next thirty years their number had risen to 34,000, i.e. for every million out of a population of 56 million the figure had doubled to 640. In 1930 it was 2,100, and in 1960, 4,600. This development sparked off a lively debate after 1870 on the emergence of a new 'academic proletariat'. Of those 34,000 students, 10 per cent studied theology (compared with a mere 2.5 per cent in 1960). The study of Catholic theology represented an avenue for upward social mobility, since only 4 per cent of the fathers of these students had themselves been to university. In all other faculties, however, the students came overwhelmingly from the university-educated middle class and civil service families. Around 1900, for example, 27 per cent of all Prussian students had fathers who were university graduates. Over one-third came from civil service and teaching backgrounds. In Württemberg and Bavaria, Saxony and Baden, the statistics differed only slightly. In short: compared with their proportion of the total population, the privileged social classes were still strikingly over-represented among Germany's university students.

Even the occasional statistical anomaly of one or two sons of workers successfully completing their university education should not be taken as evidence of the relative openness of the higher educational system. It must be added, in all fairness, that access to the system in other Western countries was also very limited. The social field of recruitment for the university teachers was no less restricted. Between 1860 and 1890, for example, 65 per cent of all qualified university teachers came from the families of civil servants or professors.[31]

A general feature of the German universities at this time was pressure towards political conformity, and there was little change in this respect after 1871. In the powerful arts faculties the idealist conception of the state helped reinforce a tradition of historical writing which, if not devoted to perpetuating the legend of Greater Prussia's emergence, concentrated exclusively on political history with the aim of justifying existing conditions. In the faculties of economics, where a strong worship of the state and faith in its reformist policies was a pronounced characteristic of the 'academic socialists', a technically excellent training in obedience was imparted to the future civil servant. The comparatively mild criticism of the economic system by pupils and colleagues of Schmoller — for three decades the leading figure of this school of thought — was decisively countered by von Bosse, the Prussian Minister of Culture, Education and Church Affairs. He officially recommended that 'in lectures, the entrepreneur's point of view . . . should be given more prominence than hitherto, bearing in mind that one should not kill the goose that lays the golden eggs'.[32] After 1900 the basic reservations of middle-class elements willing to see reforms carried out had in any case weakened. The law faculties represented an 'armoury of political rule' and 'in a sense possessed a feudal character'.[33] They had always produced a narrow, stubborn mentality, displaying a strong traditionalism and continuing to uphold the legal positivism of the Laband school. In general, no critical arguments were to be expected from the medical faculties either; and, as far as trainees for the Lutheran ministry were concerned, it was to be another hundred years before they encountered a new 'critical theology'.

None of this should detract from a recognition of the high standards of scholarship and research at the German universities, which were copied the world over. (During the period of the German Empire's existence, twelve new universities were founded) In social and political terms, however, the universities remained bulwarks of the *status quo*. The committed liberal scholar in the mould of Mommsen and Virchow increasingly disappeared after the 1880s. A political and social conservatism, even if it had a National Liberal flavour, came to prevail. Ministerial and internal legal control over examinations and university affairs ensured a high degree of homogeneity. Brilliant outsiders like the Social Democrats, Robert Michels and Leo Arons, were effectively kept at arm's length. In the community of university teachers one moved within a small circle and felt 'at home among one's own kind'.

Student fraternities and the reserve officer system Another feature of the universities was linked to their informal task of 'feudalising' the bourgeoisie. The institutions which carried out this form of political socialisation were the student corporations, especially the duelling fraternities, whose role as social clubs and promoters of beer consumption can be ignored here. Their social and political function was, however, to impress a neo-aristocratic code of honour and general conduct upon the sons of the bourgeoisie, inculcating them with norms and values intended to bind the potential representatives of future middle-class politics to the pre-industrial aristocratic ruling groups. Their potential nuisance value was to be defused by instilling a new shared mentality. As it transpired, the fraternities enabled their members to adapt very successfully to a quite different way of life. In the duelling hall, an arena for masculine rites and tests of courage which had outlived their time, the students collected ornamental scars, often aggravated by the application of herbs, in highly stylised mock duels which clearly drew upon feudal thinking. Such mutilations were soon to be outlawed by enlightened British officials in Black Africa as relics of the 'bad old days'; but in the German Empire they visibly identified the bearer as a member of the academic élite.

In addition, the fraternities channelled their members into highly desirable positions via an influential 'old boy' network. The Federation of Kösener Corps Delegates (*Kösener Senioren-Convents-Verband*), which dated from 1848, eventually represented 118 so-called *Corps* fraternities, comprising 1,500 full-time and 4,000 part-time members along with 25,000 'old boys'. It functioned as the best-known dispenser of patronage in the competition for positions. Some ministries hardly ever filled responsible posts without first noting the personal recommendations of KSCV members. This typically German 'fraternity nepotism', ensured that a career in the administration and the judiciary was open only to the 'reliable' civil servant who had acquired his 'worldly wisdom' in practice duelling and by giving 'satisfaction' in duels fought in deadly earnest.[34] One can easily imagine the numerous advantages which the fraternity student gained from his many 'connections'. His scars could be used as a visiting-card to ensure an entry to 'society' wherever he went. Although there were often bitter disputes between the predominantly aristocratic *Corps* and the more middle-class *Burschenschaften*,[35] the same prejudices were rampant among both. They all had to avoid Jewish women, and an easily excitable nationalism permeated both. They all affected mannerisms of superiority and, despite all differences, the various fraternities, including the duelling *Burschenschaften*, came to renounce middle-class liberal politics.

Another institution worked similarly to ensure that the bourgeoisie would not again develop into a political threat. This was the reserve officer system, in which regular officers decided on who was co-opted from the middle class on the basis of 'acceptability'. Originally conceived as a sign of middle-class equality, this institution's change of function before 1871 into the proving ground of the newly consolidated military state, led to its adopting a socialisation function similar to the student corporations or the junior administrator's training period as an *Assessor*. Before a member of the middle class was accepted as a reserve in the officer corps, his candidature was subjected to a thorough examination. His professional and marital status was placed under a microscope or, perhaps more appropriately in this case, a monocle. A Jewish wife, for example, disqualified him outright. Only after such scrutiny was he classified as a 'reliable comrade-in-arms'. For anyone so chosen, the decision meant that he was expected to conform willingly to the norms and life-style of the professional soldier. In return, he enjoyed the prestige attached to the 'highest estate' in the nation, as his visiting-card would testify for all to see. For Germany's rulers this reserve officer system was a highly ingenious arrangement. Following the fears raised by the Constitutional Conflict, the new system was able to ensure the assimilation of ambitious middle-class elements for a long time to come. To be an academic with a doctorate, a member of a student *Corps* and a reserve officer meant — witness Heinrich Mann's representative figure, Diederich Hessling — that one had reached the very pinnacle of bourgeois achievement and happiness. The traditional élites had no real reason to fear that their pyramid of power would be undermined by a new generation of recruits to the conservative and liberal parties which had already been moulded in this manner.

3.6 *The regulation of conflict*

Should any violation of existing norms occur, the judiciary apparatus was at the state's disposal for the authoritarian resolution of conflict. At the same time, the state could also rely on the internalised reaction of a subservient mentality in the population which helped to defuse tensions, albeit one-sidedly, in disputes. Whenever this mechanism could no longer be relied upon, the state saw itself forced into making carefully calculated compensatory concessions in order to hold on to or regain the loyalty of the masses.

Class justice There is no need to elaborate here how the bureaucracy in a 'state based on the rule of law' was able to strengthen its influence during the fight against absolutism in the eighteenth and early nineteenth centuries. But the time-honoured legend that the German Empire guaranteed the *de facto* equality of all its citizens before the law has been expressly challenged by Richard Schmidt, a well-known lawyer in our own day. He concluded that the German

Empire's 'reputation as a state based on the rule of law is quite unjustified'.[36] Naturally, one would not wish to deny that the law provided for a high degree of security in the large German cities at this time, at least compared with American cities. People were certainly able to live in them without constant fear. It is also difficult not to be impressed by the strict legality with which the Prussian Higher Administrative Court, adhering to the letter of the constitution, placed limits on the authorities' chicanery at the time of the 'nationalities' struggle. But this is not to overlook the disregard, both subtle and on a massive scale, of statutory guarantees of equality. This runs through the history of domestic conflict in the German Empire like a clear thread. Countless court cases were decided in a way that can only be described as 'class justice'. The country's administration of justice was so 'influenced by the partisan interests and ideologies of the ruling class . . . that, despite the formal application of the law, the oppressed classes were adversely affected by the manipulation of justice'.[37] The prejudging of cases on grounds of social bias can in fact be traced through all trials involving industrial workers, farm labourers and, above all, Social Democrats. It could be seen in its crassest form as early as 1872 in the Leipzig 'high treason trial'. It was all-pervasive at the time of the anti-Socialist laws, and could still be clearly seen after 1890. One need only compare the excessive sentences meted out after the big industrial disputes of the Wilhelmine period, such as the 1912 miners' strike, with the courts' reaction to the military's duelling and other such transgressions, to realise that under this allegedly impartial system of justice some citizens were more equal than others. Massive bribery and corruption of the kind that existed under the old Prussian bureaucracy was unknown in the imperial legal administration; but the more insidious corruption of 'class justice' was not removed until 1918.

That this class justice could function undisturbed, was due in large measure to the conditioning which the judiciary had been put through in the course of its training. In the wake of Bismarck's campaign against liberal civil servants a new policy was adopted, particularly after the ultra-conservative purge of the 1878 Puttkamer 'reforms'. The desired effect was quickly achieved. The key positions in the courts and the legal administration were placed in 'safe' hands (III.1.4). And if one looks at the age structure and staffing of the judges' panels it turns out that quite a few lawyers of the post-Puttkamer mould were still promoting their ideas of a monarchical 'state above the law' during the Weimar Republic. Puttkamer's 'young men', it should be remembered, had in some cases just turned sixty years of age in 1918. The new generation of administrators coming up behind them, who had never known anything but the Puttkamer system, were considerably younger still. With this legal apparatus still intact, who could seriously have expected Friedrich Ebert, the Republic's Social Democratic President, to obtain justice from judges who showed great leniency towards right-wing execution squads?

The subservient mentality of the subject   A subservient mentality which passively accepted the actions and encroachments of the state and called for a timid reaction of silence when faced with the petty harassments of daily life formed a kind of psychic pendant to the authoritarian political system. It advised one to doff one's hat and make way for the lieutenant in the street and to see the greatness of the state reflected even in the humblest village policeman. In short, the maxim was to conform rather than protest. This primarily East Elbian mentality, which often aroused contempt in the more liberal Rhineland and the south-west, was the product of centuries-old political and religious traditions. Max Weber once said that to behead a prince in Germany might produce a liberating effect on the future course of history, because the nimbus of a great father-figure would no longer radiate the power as it had done previously. In this respect, Germany, he felt, was still 'the land without a revolution'. In other countries 'the emergence and continued existence of that internalised devotion to authority, which struck foreign observers as undignified, was either obstructed or had been broken. In Germany, however, it remained as the legacy of an uninhibited patrimonial princely rule which proved difficult to eradicate. 'From a political standpoint the German was and still is', so Weber concluded, 'the quintessential subject (*Untertan*) in the true sense of the word, which is why Lutheranism was the appropriate style of religion for him'. In 1919 Albert Einstein spoke contemptuously of this mentality when he said that 'no revolution could do anything to counter this inbred servility'.[38] Rationalist theology and political liberalism, Diesterweg's pedagogical theories and Mommsen's seminars, it is true, all sought to fashion the free and independent man. Social Democracy and the trade unions, too, were emancipatory movements which set themselves the infinitely laborious task of enlightenment. But after the fatal reassertion of the forces of conservatism after 1878, 'the whole of domestic politics' had 'the unmistakable features of Frederick the Great's system about it', as Otto Hintze acutely observed.[39]

As a result, the whole leaden burden of tradition weighed even more heavily — *le mort saisit le vif*. It was difficult to make any headway against a state which in no way shirked the use of repressive measures, while at the same time deliberately rewarding subjects with honours and titles. This approach did not fail to have an effect — perhaps an unavoidable one — even on the state's bitterest opponents. Critics in the Second International were largely justified in reproaching Germany's Social Democrats for having 'Prussified' their internal organisation, and observers recognised Prussian characteristics in those Poles who worked in the *Zabór Pruski*. There can be no doubt that the old Prussia long and tenaciously outlived its historical time in terms of its influence. To deny this is to ignore one of the dilemmas of German politics in the nineteenth and twentieth centuries.

The ideal of a conflict-free society   In the interaction between authority and subservience we can also discover the roots of an idea which one might term the Utopia of a society free of conflict. It sees the government and the bureaucracy as impartial guardians of the common good, as 'purely objective' courts of appeal. They act so to speak as technocratic experts, under whom all groups live in co-operative harmony. Antagonisms and class tensions have no place in this idyll. They are either negated or perceived as the product of malicious attempts to disturb society from the outside. These disturbers of the peace, who hold pride of place in every conservative conspiracy theory, must be resisted, driven out or, if necessary, eradicated. The powerful appeal of such a model is obviously based on a live historical tradition of intervention by the state in social development, and some of its fascination can still be seen in the willing acceptance of 'grand coalitions' and designs for a more regimented society in our own times.

A direct consequence of the denial that conflict is structural and unavoidable is an anti-parliamentary tendency. Parliament, as a forum for the settling of differences, assumes that conflicts of interest exist between different groups in society. If this is denied, parliament is reduced to the level of a mere 'talk-shop'. The citizen who considers conflicts of interest an aberration, instead of institutionalising and transforming them into everyday rituals following prescribed lines of debate, will be inclined not only to attack the notion of class struggle but will look to the realisation of a society 'free of conflict'. Eventually he will hail the great 'Pacifier' who promises to put an end to the factiousness of party squabbles once and for all. There are a number of historical prerequisites for this syndrome which played such a large part in radicalising the middle classes. After the 1870s the organised Left was presented as that disturber of the peace, out to disrupt the harmonious life of the community. The more the struggle against the aristocracy and the feudal state above withered away after the set-backs of 1848, 1862 and 1871, the more single-mindedly did all the aggressions and sullen hatreds direct themselves against the threat from below. These feelings finally found their release after 1933. The yearning for harmony among the middle class cannot, however, be properly understood solely by reference to the situation after the period 1918–29. The historical dimension also has to be taken into account.

3.7 *Compensatory payments to secure loyalty*

Despite all efforts to keep the structural antagonisms in German society under control, it soon became clear that the deliberate use of socialisation processes, class justice and internalised submissiveness was not enough to achieve this. After 1873, moreover, uneven economic growth led to 'the social question being subjected to the heat of the hot-house', as Rodbertus put it.[40] The radical discrediting of the free market economy during the depression up to 1879 led to an abrupt decline of confidence in the market's self-regulating mechanisms. The belief that, given enough time, the free play of social forces would inevitably result in the common good was also undermined. Instead, developments since the onset of Germany's industrial revolution had demonstrated that the gap was growing wider between owners of the means of production and those who sold their labour. This applied to virtually all aspects of life, and not just materially in terms of income. At the end of the 1870s the ruling élites became aware of the social and political dangers that would arise, were the system left to its own devices in accordance with good liberal practice. Conservatives, like the publicist Hermann Wagener or the ministry official Theodor Lohmann, therefore drew up a far-sighted government reform programme at an early stage. It is no coincidence either that representatives of the 1878–79 protectionist *Sammlung* policy — men like Kardorff, Stumm, Hohenlohe-Langenburg and Frankenberg — demanded immediate action in the field of social policy. Even Miquel, acting from the same motives, explained that what was needed was tireless energy 'to keep the lid on revolutionary outbreaks, and to create social well-being by encouraging property owners and readily fulfilling the just demands of the working classes, thereby diverting chaos into reform'.[41]

Social insurance in place of social reform   Prior to this, Bismarck had quite unreservedly argued the case for a measure of state welfare in the tradition of old-style government policies of the past. But he had run into the opposition of the liberal bureaucracy on this issue. As the crisis worsened he resorted to the typically Bonapartist method for stabilising the system. He adopted a social policy based on financial solutions. This constituted the domestic side of a policy whose foreign policy dimension was economic and colonial expansion. From the very outset his social policy was not conceived as a social reform intended to provide workers with a measure of protection or to make the industrial world of work more humane. And he most certainly did not have a restructuring of the social order in mind. Right up to 1890 it was well known that the Imperial Chancellor completely refused to extend the arrangements for factory inspection (only introduced in 1871), or abolish Sunday working, reduce the working day, restrict the use of female and child labour, or introduce minimum wages. The free hand which owners of capital enjoyed in their firms was not in the slightest affected by the share of social contributions eventually imposed on them. Instead, Bismarck, in common with countless entrepreneurs, held the view that industry should not be seriously handicapped if it were to maintain its competitiveness in international markets. Not only was his social policy, as it affected companies, put on ice. The 'furtherance of the entrepreneurs' immediate interests' was, in Schmoller's view, 'the very essence of social policy' for Bismarck.[42] The insurance legislation of the 1880s was quite openly conceived from the start as a 'necessary corollary' to the repressive anti-Socialist laws, to quote Vice-Chancellor Stolberg in 1878. In the words of Benedetto Croce, Bismarck wanted to satisfy 'physical needs' in order to 'tranquillise minds and break their will'.[43] The Chancellor made no secret of the fact that his social policy was borrowed from the armoury of Bonapartism. He had 'lived long enough in France', he told the *Reichstag*, 'to know that the devotion of most Frenchmen to their government . . . was basically connected with the fact that most of them received pensions from the state'.[44] If Napoleon III had hoped to tie the workers to his regime by means of state-run insurance schemes, medical insurance, pension-dividend receipts for small-time savers, subsidies for cooperatives, and so on, the Chancellor understood 'such intentions . . . perfectly'; just as, on the other hand, he unreservedly shared the French Emperor's distaste for workers' protection and their right of free association. Bismarck thus

introduced his 'taming' policy with the declared intention of com-
pelling the workers to give up their emancipatory struggle by
applying the 'prophylactic device' of the anti-Socialist laws. At the
same time he hoped to win their compliance with the state socialism
of national insurance measures. Material concessions also seemed
called for because protective tariffs brought about a considerable
increase in the basic cost of living. Not least, the growth of the Free
Trade Unions could be halted in its tracks by this means. The
political goal was to secure a working class whose loyalty to the state
would be ensured by virtue of their receipt of pensions — just like
the tied labourers in the Prussia of old. With typically astonishing
frankness, Bismarck confessed quite candidly that he 'wanted to
create in the great mass of have-nots the conservative frame of mind
which comes from the feeling of enjoying full pension rights'. 'The
citizen who has a pension for his old age is much more content and
easier to deal with than one who has no prospect of any. Look at the
difference between a private servant and a messenger in the Chancellery', he explained to a journalist in his own version of base and
superstructure. 'The latter will put up with far more . . . than the
former, because he has a pension to look forward to.' A revolution
which would be thus pre-empted would 'incur quite different costs'
compared with a policy which gives the 'industrial worker a substitute for land or property in the shape of a pension book'.[45]

This combination of carrot and stick nevertheless obstructed the
intended effect of social policy. The workers, fighting for political
and social equality, would not melt away quietly in the face of
repressive measures, emergency laws and the refusal to improve
safety regulations in the factories. If one considers the growth of the
SPD, the part played by social policy in the crisis over Bismarck's
dismissal, and his admission in 1890 that his failure was due to his
inability to instil an 'acceptance of the state' in the workers, then
Rodbertus's prognosis of 1871 that 'Bismarck's fame could meet its
Waterloo . . . over the social question' appears partly borne out.[46] It
was not just the Chancellor's remarkable lack of political wisdom in
combining repression and pensions which ensured that the appeal of
his social policy remained weak. It was also partly a result of the
miserably low payments made under the scheme which reached only
a very limited number of people. Over and above this, the health
insurance law of 1883 declared a majority of those in work (but by
no means all) liable to pay contributions. Yet a full two-thirds of the
total amount paid in came from those who were compulsorily
insured! In 1885 there were 4.7 million insured persons, or 10 per

cent of the population, each of whom was allotted 11 marks per annum for medical care. From the disabled and old-age pension scheme, introduced in 1889, about 598,000 pensions (including those paid to dependents), averaging 155 marks per annum, were paid out in the period up to 1900. It is simply not possible, therefore, to speak of the sick, injured and retired workers as leading an existence free of anxieties in Imperial Germany. 'You can hardly blame' the Social Democrats, the liberal Conservative Hans Delbrück conceded, 'if they scoff at this legislation' which 'has insured some — mark you, only *some* of the workers', while 'public opinion in its eternal Philistine wisdom' is saying 'too many laws are being passed nowadays and we could do with a rest'.[47]

German social policy only gradually lost something of the stigma of its Bonapartist origin. Slowly was there an accumulation of conrete achievements. In 1913 the average annual insurance benefit amounted to at least 165 marks. Legal safeguards were also slowly extended. In 1891 Sunday working was abolished and a guaranteed minimum wage introduced. This was followed by protection for child labour in 1903–05 and insurance for all salaried employees in 1911. Accident insurance was extended in 1900, followed by sickness benefits in 1913. After 1899, invalid pensions, whose amount had depended previously on the financial strength of each company, were paid out in accordance with uniform rates for the whole German Empire. In 1901 compulsory industrial tribunals were introduced, and at the same time public funds, albeit in modest amounts, were allocated to workers' housing. In 1901 the sum spent was 2 million marks. The 1908 amendment to the industrial code of practice extended the area covered by work-safety regulations. Together with the far more significant increase in real wages, the spread of revisionism appeared to confirm, within limits, the success of Bismarck's original calculation. However, the following points should be kept in mind:

(1) Social policy, as far as the political leadership was concerned, remained first and foremost a strategy for the avoidance of conflict. More technical assistance from the bureaucracy was occasionally granted from above, but at no time was there any thought of carrying out social reforms as a way of achieving greater equality. The agricultural labourers always remained the Cinderellas of social policy. As late as 1908 the Imperial Law on Associations reaffirmed that it was illegal for them to strike (and almost amounted to a ban on their right of free association). Any reduction of working hours or

improved safety regulations were combined with much resented
penalty clauses. In 1891, for example, unions were forbidden to
exert pressure on members, although workers' solidarity had always
held out the only prospect of success for the underdog in industrial
disputes.

(2) Wilhelm II appeared at the start of his reign to be willing to
contemplate reform. If he failed in this, it was not on account of the
'ingratitude' of the Social Democrats, as was argued at the time.
From the time of Bismarck's dismissal to the openly reactionary
course pursued after 1893–94, he developed no initiatives what-
soever in social policy. He contented himself instead with playing to
the gallery in close cooperation with heavy industry. After this
transparent confidence trickery failed to produce results, his 'struggle
against subversion' revealed what he was really after. The improved
bureaucratic efficiency which lay behind social and political measures
remained the work of a few active parliamentarians and senior civil
servants like Posadowsky. Yet even they sympathised more with
Bismarck's original intentions than with any notion of civic equality.
Their policies towards the master artisans and salaried employees
reveal quite clearly the principle of *divide et impera*. For tactical
reasons, preferential treatment was given to the potentially loyal
middle-class vote at the expense of a general improvement in the
living conditions of all employees.

Yet even this cautious social policy of the Wilhelmine period was
widely regarded by the ruling classes in 1913 as being too sympath-
etic to the workers! In January 1914 Bethmann Hollweg's deputy,
the acting Secretary of State at the Ministry of the Interior, Clemens
von Delbrück, swung completely over to the employers' side with his
declared intention of putting a 'freeze' on social policy.[48]

(3) Finally, it would be quite wrong to see in Imperial Germany's
social policy after 1900 any essentially increased readiness by the
state to make concessions. What men like Posadowsky were planning, Lohmann had already contemplated some twenty years previously. If, in fact, a series of tangible improvements did accumulate,
this was primarily a product of organised labour's unremitting
struggle. In spite of obstacles placed in the way of strikes, the use of
class justice, laws against free association and *Sammlung* policies, the
workers' movement worked untiringly and step by step until it
wrung concessions. It was not, as is sometimes still maintained, that
the state or the bureaucracy as such granted the minimum con-

cessions necessary from humanitarian motives. Nor did they display political insight from a position above the factions locked in conflicts of interest. On the contrary, they were forced again and again into making partial concessions only because of the pressures exerted by combinations of social forces and by the *Reichstag*. As in previous decades, fear of the 'red menace' played its part here. This was the reason why compensatory payments had to be made in ever larger 'doses'; not because the civil servants involved had studied under Schmoller, or because the idea of a 'social monarchy' performing a neutral role was generally in vogue. The concept, so important for the future, of the state as being responsible for social policy (and not just private insurance or company-run welfare schemes), remained encumbered in Imperial Germany by the authoritarian and paternalistic posture adopted towards the workers. In the long run it was only the modern style of state intervention which could bring about increased social equality of opportunity through a redistribution of the national income. Although admirably equipped for its task institutionally, German social policy was, however, long prevented from achieving its proper effect because social and political equality were completely denied.

Prestige policies as a form of compensation The overriding concern of social policy was to provide material assistance and guarantee the stability of the system. These principles were intended to generate a collective mentality of loyalty to the state. But the power élites of Imperial Germany knew fully well that, over and above this, compensatory 'payments' of a psychic nature were also called for. The rapid social changes caused by advanced industrialisation, widespread feelings of status insecurity, anxieties regarding declining or wavering status and fluctuations in the economy which called the *status quo* into question — all this created a profound insecurity, amounting in some cases to loss of orientation over long periods. This was especially true of the petty bourgeoisie and middle classes who had always upheld the ideals of stability, security and law and order. Herein lay the roots of that susceptibility to policies pursued for prestige purposes among those strata which did not actually share the ruling élite's code of honour. Of course, the latter itself placed a premium on status and the acquisition of prestige. The workers, on the other hand, being excluded from the 'imperial nation', subscribed to a quite different set of values for almost a generation. It is always necessary, therefore, to proceed from the fact that each social group possessed its own specific motives and driving forces. It is misleading to reduce everything to the common denominator of an allegedly universal, irascible nationalism. This conception obscures as much as it illuminates. It blurs the distinctive experiences, traditions and combinations of interests which determined behaviour and are thus crucial. To stress the point once more, it matters a great deal whether one looks at industrial workers, shopkeepers or district officials.

As far as the use of prestige as a device of political rule is concerned, the actual target group of this policy (i.e. all who numbered themselves among the middle class) was not only receptive on social and economic grounds, but also strongly predisposed psychologically for ideological reasons. The earlier liberal notion, formulated in opposition to a society based on estates, that the economically advancing bourgeoisie was identifiable with 'the nation' as such, became a commonly accepted view. It saw the middle class as the representative of the modern nation, its norms and values. Because of this identification of the middle class with the nation as a whole, foreign successes were perceived by the bourgeoisie as a boost to its own self-esteem. Conversely, any reverses were experienced as a direct attack on itself. The deliberate pursuit of a policy for the sake of greater prestige could, therefore, be used to compensate for social and economic grievances, within certain limits at least and for a certain length of time. Because of the ideological nexus, it could also bring advantages in winning support for government policies. More will be said later about this kind of prestige policy along with naval policy, imperialism and foreign policy. Here it has to be clearly stated that the ruling élites' need to pursue a policy for prestige purposes was closely bound up with the social changes taking place and the prevailing ideology of social stratification. To see the problem by reference to biological metaphors in terms of a young nation flexing its muscles or feeling the need to make its mark, is to miss the point. Forming part of the programme of compensatory measures, social policy at home and its complement of prestige policies abroad locked together like gear-wheels to keep Germany's class society on the rails.

4. Tax and Fiscal Policy

L'état c'est l'état — which, loosely translated, means that the state's fiscal arrangements hold the key to an understanding of its true social constitution. This is how the Austrian economist, Rudolf

Goldscheid, summed up the fundamental significance of national budgets, which he called 'the skeleton of the state, stripped of all deceptive ideologies'. 'Without being able to fall back on public finances' the ruling classes in the modern state would never be in a position to maintain their 'economic, social and political power'. The state became an instrument in their hands 'through the financial arrangements they imposed on it'.[1] No one would deny the central importance of national budgets, at least from the time when the modern 'tax state' (J. Schumpeter) began its rise alongside the absolutist territorial state. But there are two sides to this problem. There can be no doubt that interest groups imposed their will through the financial organisation of the state and its tax structures. However, Goldscheid was thinking too exclusively in terms of the effects of the capitalist pursuit of profit when he produced his analysis. In Western and Central Europe the apparatus of political rule was not simply a docile coordinating agent. It was a factor in its own right, which was closely linked in Germany to the interests of the powerful pre-industrial agrarian élites. It was therefore able to operate against the specific interests of capitalists. Under the primacy of upholding the system, the state could in time become the switch-point for a certain amount of national income redistribution. Indeed, the first hesitant beginnings of the institutional framework required for this task can be traced back to the Bismarck period. Bearing in mind that the German Empire's power structure combined the influences of traditional and modern forces, one must beware of assuming an outright domination of capitalist interests in the field of public finance. Here we encounter once more a mixture of influences from these divergent elements.

4.1   *The financing of the ruling system*

In the first two decades of the nineteenth century it became obvious that the state's permanent need for revenue could be met only through a system of regular taxation. The financial economy of the German states became a tax economy. A system of capital gains taxes developed in South Germany, while north of the river Main it took the form of personal and income taxes. The Prussian tax reform of 1820 upheld the traditional distinction between town and country and introduced a direct personal tax on six-sevenths of the rural population and the small towns by means of class taxes. The idea behind this was that annual tax quotas could be discharged on the basis of personal tax liability in place of the old system of corporate contributions. The 'obvious shortcoming' of this system was that it 'burdened the lower classes with a heavy direct tax, while placing a completely inadequate tax burden on the well-to-do'.[2] Up to 1861 the feudal estates enjoyed complete exemption from taxation. The 1851 reform of personal taxes, which came as a result of the 1848 Revolution, made some progress in taxing the rich. However, the new system continued to favour large private fortunes; a fact which may well have stimulated the accumulation of potential investment capital during this phase of Germany's industrial revolution. It was not until 1873 that taxes devised on the basis of class were replaced by a graduated income tax which ignored the town-and-country distinction and took in incomes of more than 900 marks (though only after 1883!). The 'tax burden on the less well-off . . . continued to be oppressive, however, and the lack of a common standard of assessment meant that its financial and social effects were doubly felt'. Only recently it has been shown what staggering differences there were, for example, in the assessment of large-scale agrarian incomes (including liability for land and property taxes). These assessments were determined, and in some cases concealed, by East Elbia's district officials who had close social ties with the local land-owners. There is no better evidence than this to support the contention that the neutrality of the Prussian civil servant was a myth.

After 1873 the economic depression made it difficult to improve the tax system. Above all, it was the Imperial Chancellor who, as a powerful advocate of indirect taxes inimical to the consumer, fiercely and successfully resisted direct taxes. A progressive income tax, in particular, was pure anathema to him and the ruling élites. 'A rational limitation of the principle of progressive taxation is not possible', he argued with some perceptiveness. 'Once this has been legally acknowledged, it will develop further in the direction of socialism's ideals.'[3] As a result of his opposition, tax reform came to a standstill in the largest state in the German Empire between 1873 and the early 1890s. In 1893 the Prussian Finance Minister, Johannes von Miquel, introduced a general income tax which imposed rates varying from 0.6 per cent to at most 4 per cent on citizens voluntarily declaring more than the minimum taxable income of 900 marks. In a period of advanced industrialisation, accompanied by generous state hand-outs to agriculture, this was anything but painful for those affected. And whether one should continue to talk nowadays of Miquel's 'reforms' on the strength of the standardisation they achieved is open to question. The capital gains taxes were passed back for use by the local governments. This was an unprecedented boon for the agrarians, and they knew full well in their rural communities why they allowed the new laws to go through. The reason was that the 1893 law on communal taxes effectively restored 'the feudal estates' exemption from taxation' abolished thirty years previously. This not only signified a reversal of the progress made towards a more 'democratic system of tax burdens'. The 'uniform application of taxes' across the board actually meant an enormous lightening of the tax burden for the large-scale agrarians. In short, it is certainly not enough to glance at the high-sounding reformist phraseology in the preamble to this law and accept it at face value when interpreting its text. Nor will it do to speak of a 'tremendous achievement' on account of its undeniable effect in rationalising the tax system.[4] The vested interests which stood behind this law and the concrete aims they had in mind must also be examined. Here we immediately encounter the massive preferential treatment given in material terms to the two main pillars of support behind Miquel's *Sammlung* policy: large-scale agriculture and industry. This is no surprise. Yet historians have shown much credulity, not to say partiality, in overlooking the crux of these 'reforms'. They have often presented the publicly proclaimed intentions of the legislators as the reality of the tax system in Imperial Germany. It is certainly true, and entirely in keeping with its true intentions, that Miquel's income tax did help to create the institutional preconditions for a welfare state and a tax system which could redistribute the national income. But this occurred quite contrary to the intentions of the decision-makers and entirely in the direction that Bismarck feared. In fact, Miquel's laws remained in force until 1918 and to some extent operate to this day to the benefit of land-owners in the Federal Republic.

The government revenues of the various German states were made up from taxes and the selling of government bonds. Finances were regulated by Article 70 of the Imperial Constitution and supplemented by the lex Stengel of 1904. They relied upon internal revenue drawn from three sources: (1) excise duties, (2) taxes on consumer articles and commodities (e.g. stamp duties on salt, tobacco, brandy, sugar, beer and legal documents), and (3) postal charges. Additional revenue came from (4), the membership contributions of the individual states, that is, money payments calculated according to population size, (5) imperial assets provided by the French reparations payments of 1871, and (6) borrowing via government bonds. After 1879 there was a dramatic increase in the revenue from excise duties. This came mainly from agricultural produce, as evidenced by its percentage contribution to the German Empire's total revenue. It was this latter trend which one of Germany's leading financial experts thought 'disheartening for social policy, not to say frightening'; for these duties represented an enormous burden for the average consumer.[5] The percentages of revenue from duties on agricultural produce increased as follows:

1879	13.2	million marks	=	11.8%
1881	17.1	million marks	=	9.2%
1891	176.3	million marks	=	44.7%
1901	255.3	million marks	=	46.0%
1913	413.7	million marks	=	47.0%

This system was undoubtedly unjust in social terms, and yet it functioned tolerably well until the costs of armaments began to soar after 1898–1900, thus upsetting the balance between income and expenditure in the national budget. Since direct taxes threatened the privileges of the propertied classes, rising military expenditure called for increases in indirect taxation. The problem was not dealt with, however, until 1906 when a minor reform, which strictly avoided direct taxes, put finances into the black. After 1908 this small surplus was again swallowed up, mainly by the dreadnought construction programme, with the result that it became necessary to tackle the problem once more.

The 1909 imperial finance reform raised taxes again by means of indirect taxation from an annual rate of 138 million marks in 1909 to 291 million in 1913. In place of the originally proposed estate and death duties, taxes on financial transactions and consumer articles were introduced. These not only failed to produce the hoped-for annual surplus of 500 million marks but perpetuated the unfair tax system. The real beneficiaries were the land-owners, who had pulled out all the stops in rousing popular support for their measures. Ultimately their demagogical agitation became so vociferous that even Chancellor von Bülow described them as 'unbridled egoists'.[6] Since taxation always implies the sanctioning of specific distribution mechanisms, this imperial finance reform revealed itself as blatantly inimical to the interests of the consumer and industry alike. It favoured instead the major agrarian interests of the 'land-owning caste' which had been placed on a pedestal since Bismarck's time as a 'social element upon which the structure of the state relied more than on any other'.[7]

The major portion of Germany's finances was swallowed up by armaments. While the strength of the peacetime army rose by 87 per cent between 1880 and 1913, military expenditure increased by as much as 360 per cent. Despite the sharp increase in the empire's budget, it still accounted for 75 per cent of the total revenue in 1913, as it had done ever since 1875. For every member of the population 9.86 marks were spent on armaments in 1875, rising to 11.06 in 1890, 14.96 in 1900 and 32.97 in 1913. The overwhelming priority given to armament interests can be seen even more clearly if one examines the appropriations in the imperial budget and compares them with the actual expenditure on armaments, expressed as a percentage of the former. The following picture emerges, based on pre-1914 figures supplied by Gerloff:

	Appropriations*	Expenditure*	% of appropriations
1876–80	481	485	100.8
1880–85	478	463	96.8
1886–90	700	656	93.8
1891–95	832	737	88.5
1896–1900	974	837	85.9
1901–05	1,200	1,100	84.1
1906–10	1,800	1,300	73.7
1911–13	2,200	1,600	74.7

*In million marks

To this should be added the numerous loans. The exact amounts involved are difficult to ascertain, but they can be roughly calculated from the interest payments. For army loans alone these work out at 47 million marks for the period 1891–95 and 68 million marks for 1906–10. Three-quarters of the imperial budget for 1913 went on armaments, leaving only 25 per cent for all other areas such as the administration, social insurance, education and so on. It cannot be denied, therefore, that 'over and above the sums allocated to armaments in its member states' budgets (whether made public or not), the Empire's need for revenue before the war was overwhelmingly determined by the demands of armaments'. Here we can clearly see the priorities of the Greater Prussian military state emerging from its budgetary allocations. And in these priorities are to be found the deeper causes of Adolph Wagner's well-known and dreaded 'law of expanding state expenditures'.[8]

The figures below provide a clear illustration of the general trend. Expenditure increased as follows:

	Billion marks	*% of GNP*	*Marks per capita*
1872 =	0.4	—	—
1880 =	0.5	2.6	12
1890 =	1.0	3.3	21
1900 =	1.5	4.4	29
1907 =	2.5	5.4	40
1913 =	3.4	5.8	51

In the field of government borrowing the government showed itself to be dependent on the changing direction of economic trends. Between 1859 and 1873 and, more so, between 1896 and 1913, it rarely succeeded in freeing itself from the terms imposed on it by the 'Prussian Consortium' or the other intermediate, major banking syndicates which made the loans. Interest rates were high. Between 1873 and 1896 a surplus of capital resulted in a highly liquid money market and all-time low interest rates which made loans easily and cheaply obtainable. This situation 'made authoritarian rule easier and weakened parliament's influence' over the budget. It was no wonder then that Prussia's national debt rose by 3.9 billion marks between 1880 and 1890 alone![9] This development should be borne in mind when judging the Imperial Chancellor's complaints about financial straits and tight-fisted parliaments.

4.2 The distribution of national income

Although exact and detailed statistics are not available, it is possible to discern the general trend in the way that national income was distributed. The 'disparity in the development of income distribution' resulted from an increasing inequality 'in favour of those on higher and top incomes', which became 'especially obvious during periods of economic prosperity'.[10] The overall figures for Germany's remarkable growth in national income are in themselves very revealing. It increased fourfold in the time between the late phase of Germany's industrial revolution and the outbreak of the First World War.

	Billion marks			*GNP in billion marks*	
1. 1860–69	=	10.67	1. 1872	=	16.0
2. 1870–79	=	13.59	2. 1880	=	17.9
3. 1880–89	=	18.95	3. 1890	=	23.1
4. 1890–99	=	26.20	4. 1900	=	32.9
5. 1900–09	=	35.41	5. 1910	=	48.0
6. 1905–14	=	43.11	6. 1913	=	54.7

Here we can clearly follow the effects of fluctuations in the economy. Thus industry's share in the period 1865–74 amounted to 31.1 per cent of the total GNP. Between 1875 and 1884 it fell to 26.7 per cent, and dropped further still between 1885 and 1894 to only 25 per cent! The statistical device of expressing income as a per capita average, although naturally levelling out any enormous variations, reveals the increase quite clearly:

		GNP per capita			
1. 1860–69	=	272 marks	1. 1872	=	388.7 marks
2. 1870–79	=	320	2. 1880	=	397.5
3. 1880–89	=	406	3. 1890	=	469.7
4. 1890–99	=	505	4. 1900	=	587.7
5. 1900–09	=	592	5. 1910	=	743.3
6. 1905–14	=	662	6. 1913	=	845.1

If one breaks down these figures by social class, it becomes clear that the industrial workers' share of the national income shrank by 55 per cent between 1870 and 1900, even though a third of the population was employed in industry up to the turn of the century.[11] The proportion of the total figure taken up by wages cannot be determined with any exactitude over such a long time-span; but we can conclude that it shrank more or less continuously between 1873 and

1913 (by one index point every four years), at the same time that fixed capital was increasing.

If we study the distribution of earned income, we find that here, too, Germany had become an industrial nation. Between 1879 and 1913 the percentage growth rates were 2.5% for agriculture, compared with 5.8% for mining, 4.3% for industry and commerce, 5.1% for transport and 4.9% for trade. Expressed in millions of marks, agriculture's earned income fell from 37.2 in the period 1875–79 to 25.5 in 1895–99 and 21.6 in 1910–13. But it rose in the four other sectors from 41.2 (i.e. by 2; 29.4; 2.8 and 7 respectively) in 1875–79 to 53.6 (i.e. 2.8; 37.4; 4 and 9.4 respectively) in 1895–99, and 59 (i.e. 3.9; 38.6; 5 and 11.4) in 1910–13. One can also clearly discern a structural shift in the balance of income on capital. For agriculture it constituted 29.3 per cent (of 2.8 billion marks) in 1875–79. Between 1860 and 1864 it had been as much as 48 per cent! From 1895 to 1899 it was 23.5 per cent (of 13.1 billion marks), i.e. it stagnated or declined slightly, while in trade (taking in the railways and the postal services) it increased from 46.1 per cent in 1875–79 to 48.1 per cent in 1895–99 and 51 per cent in 1910–13. These figures can be compared with those for the Federal Republic where the relationship in 1960 was 11.2 to 83.2 in favour of industry![12]

4.3 *The consolidation of inequality*

These global figures, however, give only a general impression of the overall trend. Within the major categories of 'agriculture', 'industry', and so on, it would take a detailed analysis to reveal the ever-widening gap which existed between higher and top incomes on the one hand, and middle and lower incomes on the other. We can see here at a different level how a process of concentration was taking place which Marx had predicted earlier in respect of capital. In the absence of any state intervention (e.g. in the areas of taxation, earnings and social policy), the capitalist economy, based on private industry and left to its own market and distribution mechanisms, was creating ever-greater disparities in income distribution. If we take the figures already cited and recall that the real wages of workers and lower-paid white-collar employees — virtually their only source of income — grew on average by no more than 1 per cent per annum between the late 1880s and 1914, whereas national income grew from around 18 to 50 billion marks, we gain some impression of how the 'laws of the market' powerfully attracted all the elements within the magnetic field of income distribution and capital formation towards the one pole and drew them tightly together. Inequality among the German Empire's citizens, who were already sharply divided by the traditions of a society based on estates and the new barriers of social class, was constantly reinforced in material terms by the fact that the mechanisms for distribution were determined by natural, unrestricted economic growth, the interests of the ruling élites, and the almost complete absence of any influences later associated with the welfare state.

5. Armaments policy

The 'Greater Prussian Annexation Conglomerate' of 1866 to 1871 emerged as the result of three victorious wars which enormously strengthened the prestige of the military. These wars also opened up the way for the logical extension of the military politics of absolutism, which were given full expression in the Empire's 'statute of organisation' (Ridder). A crucial role in this process was performed by configurations of forces which acted quite independently of the Imperial Constitution's written text. Up to 1918 the problem of how power should be distributed internally was resolved in favour of the army under the monarch's command and kept free of any control by representative organs.

5.1 *The army*

After Prussia's success in the 'iron game of dice' — which was how Bismarck described his policy of calculated risk[1] — the way was prepared in 1866 for the 'iron' army law of the following year. It stipulated that the strength of the standing army (initially up to 1871) should be equal to 1 per cent of the population. The annual allocation of 225 thalers per man plus other military expenditure absorbed 95 per cent of the North German Confederation's entire revenue. It has already been pointed out that the parliamentary debate on the military proposals, anticipated for the autumn of 1871, was postponed because of the convenient timing of Bismarck's third war. The result was that the 'iron' law was extended without much fuss by three years up to 1874. The Imperial Constitution (Articles 60–62) clearly set out the established strength of the peacetime army and its financial allocation, though it was also implied that the figures were to be 'authorised at a later date through the proper channels of the Empire's legislative procedures'. But Article

63, para. 4 of the Constitution flagrantly contradicted this statement. Since 1867 the Emperor, as King of Prussia, had performed a
dual role as 'commander-in-chief of the Confederation's army and
its presidential head', with the latter's decisions requiring a ministerial counter-signature. Subsequently the King was also made
Supreme Commander of 'all the Empire's land forces in peace and
war' (by Article 63, para. 1), with Bavaria and Württemberg
retaining special privileges. Article 63, para. 4 now granted him the
sole right to determine the 'effective strength of the imperial army'.
This provision shows what the true motives of the victors in the
Constitutional Conflict had been. 'The original intention of the
Imperial Constitution', Bismarck openly admitted, 'had been to
make the Emperor free and independent of the *Reichstag*'s resolu-
tions.' These would be 'a limitation on the Emperor's sovereign
powers' if after 1874, as a result of new concessions to the legislature,
there were to be any new periodic trials of strength which questioned
the army's absolutist isolation as 'a state in its own right' (Lucius).[2]
In 1874 the imperial government went all out to settle the issue. It
demanded a 'perpetual budget' to give the Emperor the sole right to
determine the strength of the army. This would have made parliamentary approval automatic and, in view of the size of the
military budget, would have effectively abolished the *Reichstag*'s
right to scrutinise the budget. This led to the clash which both sides
had anticipated. The outcome failed to satisfy the *camarilla* of officers
around Roon. But, since the so-called 'septennial bill' granted the
government its desired army strength for the next seven years, it
meant that the *Reichstag* had climbed down over a fundamental issue
and, in doing so, had tied the hands of its successors. Not surprisingly, the old lines of the Constitutional Conflict had been drawn up
once again. Eugen Richter, speaking for the left-wing Liberals,
accused the septennial law 'of preserving absolutism against the
parliamentary system in military affairs'. He prophesied that 'this
piece of absolutism will inevitably grow like a cancer'. That 'militarism is more and more taking on a shape in flesh and blood' was
the criticism voiced by the Centre Party deputy Mallinckrodt in
attacking the bill. And the leader of the National Liberals, von
Bennigsen, made a shrewd protest on the principle involved. After
the attempt to increase the legislature's influence had failed, he
summed up by saying that 'the military arrangements and institution of the army represent . . . to a considerable degree the skeletal
structure of any state's constitution . . . so that if one fails . . . to
accommodate the army and defence arrangements into the political

constitutional framework, constitutional conditions in a country can never become a reality'.[3] In this sense, the German Empire still did not possess a proper constitutional framework forty years later.

Following the conservative swing of the previous year, the second septennial bill of 1880 was quickly approved. The third septennial was also hurried through in 1887 against the background of another war scare conjured up by Bismarck. Since, after 1893, the *Reichstag* was re-elected every five years, the demand for a quinquennial bill was soon raised, along with a proposal for a two instead of three year period of military service. Even though the government eventually did give in on both these issues, its concessions should not be interpreted as a sign of weakness. On the contrary, its conciliatory attitude reflected a self-confidence which showed that the placing of the army under the monarch's exclusive control was regarded as assured.

The strength of the peacetime army grew steadily with each new military law that was passed. Its authorised strength in officers and men in relation to the total population was:

1870	40.9 million	approx.	400,000 men
1880	45.1		434,000
1890	49.2		509,000
1900	56.1		629,000
1913	67.0		864,000

This means it increased by almost 100 per cent between 1880 and 1913, although its actual strength usually lagged somewhat behind the authorised figures. As already noted, military expenditure increased by 360 per cent during the same period, and accounted for 75 per cent of the imperial budget before the war.

The German Empire retained the old Prussian distinction between the monarch's right of command and the authority of the military administration, by way of which the Prussian Minister of War passed on information to the *Reichstag*. From the time of the Constitutional Conflict onwards the issue at stake was whether the monarch's right of command, kept free of any representative control, could be maintained, or even extended, in the face of parliamentary demands for a say in this sphere. In fact, it was decided that 'on the question of the right of command, the Emperor's orders' were 'exempt from ministerial endorsement', although both the Imperial

Constitution and the Prussian Constitution made the validity of royal decrees formally dependent on this. The sovereign's right of command survived as an essential element of late absolutist rule and, consequently, could scarcely be given a defined place in liberal constitutional law. It represented a stubbornly preserved relic of the old feudal order, with the King as the charismatic leader of a warrior host by virtue of his royal blood, to whom the latter was bound by a bond of personal loyalty. Throughout the nineteenth and twentieth centuries this notion persisted in the ideal of the Prussian ruler as a 'Supreme War-lord', a title which Richter aptly described as a 'constitutional-cum-mystical concept'.[4] This warrior chieftain figure-head stood above a network of institutions, of which three were particularly important: the Military Cabinet, the General Staff and the Ministry of War. The Military Cabinet inserted itself, quietly but effectively, as an instrument of royal control into the gap not covered by the constitution, i.e. the sovereign's right of command free from parliamentary control. Originating as a department assisting the monarch in an administrative role, it was given separate status from the Ministry of War in 1824, and worked alongside it as a permanent rival after 1850. In 1883 the Chief of the Military Cabinet managed to have the personnel division of the Ministry wound up, and the Cabinet took charge of personnel matters itself. As a result of this move, the Chief of the Military Cabinet, who was directly under the King's authority, gained a crucial say in matters relating to the royal command. This enabled him to exercise a far-reaching influence in various departments, either directly or as an *éminence grise*. The Cabinet remained true to the motto of its long-standing Chief, Wilhelm von Hahnke (1888–1901), that the army 'should remain a separate body, into which no critical eyes should be permitted to gaze'.[5] Following the departure of the elder Moltke the Military Cabinet usually got its way, even at the expense of the General Staff.

The latter had been formed in Prussia in 1816 after the Napoleonic Wars, but was completely insignificant until Helmuth von Moltke took charge in 1858. Up until 1859 the Chief of the General Staff was not even allowed to report directly to the Minister of War. In June 1866 a royal order decreed that the General Staff should not be allowed to give direct orders to the troops without first going through the Ministry of War. However, Moltke's personal success in the German 'civil war' of 1866 gave his department an enormous boost. During his well-known quarrel with Bismarck at the time of the French campaign, he said in January 1871 that he had believed that he and the Chancellor stood on an 'equal footing' in their dealings with the King; but in the end the latter threw his weight behind Bismarck. The first victories on the battlefield made a much greater impression than the long-drawn-out guerilla warfare that followed. Moltke's hate-filled remarks about 'a war of extermination' against France did not reach the ears of the public,[6] and from the time of the Berlin victory parade on, the Moltke myth, carefully cultivated by 'the great taciturn figure' himself, began to gain complete acceptance. Certainly, the areas of responsibility between the General Staff, the Military Cabinet and the Ministry of War continued to be disputed. But after a dozen years of almost classical 'Empire-building' by these departments, the issue was finally decided. When a carefully contrived quarrel between von Albedyll at the Military Cabinet and von Kameke at the Ministry of War led to the latter's dismissal, the former imposed two conditions on Kameke's successor, Paul Bronsart von Schellendorf. Firstly, the Military Cabinet was to be strengthened at the expense of the Ministry, and secondly, in return for the support and helpful intrigues of the General Staff, he demanded that the Chief of the General Staff have the right to report personally to the Emperor without the Minister of War being present. Bronsart agreed to these conditions. Henceforth, the Ministry of War became a relatively insignificant power factor. The General Staff, on the other hand, suddenly became a factor in its own right. The important consequences of this inter-departmental power struggle will be discussed shortly in connection with the Schlieffen Plan.

But first, it is worth noting that the new arrangement in 1883 fitted in well with Bismarck's designs. He had readily made use of the army as an instrument of his policies, e.g. before the earthworks at Düppel, during the 1866 Prussian War of Secession and against Napoleon III. But he had done so always in the interests of Greater Prussia's expansionist programme. In return, he constantly defended the military's privileged status, and it was partly in order to defend their interests that he assumed office in 1862. Thereafter the Chancellor continued to support the military. But, whenever possible and wherever necessary, he flatly refused to allow them to interfere in politics. This is why the Constitution, which reveals his touch at every turn, made no provision for an *Imperial* Minister of War. He had every reason to fear the competition which would come from a potential political rival who could use the traditions of the military state for his own ends. He put it in a nutshell when he remarked that an acting imperial minister 'would continually be at loggerheads with the Chancellor'.[7] By contrast, the Governor of Alsace-Lorraine could be granted full equality on paper with the Chancellor *vis-à-vis* the Emperor, without this causing the least offence. But despite Bismarck's vigilant distrust, the military did exert political influence, and this undeniably increased after 1890. Thanks to the office of military attaché (i.e. the traditional Prussian *aide-de-camp*) in St Petersburg and elsewhere, the official channels of the Foreign Office could be easily bypassed and the Emperor kept directly informed of developments.

Of much greater importance were the proposals to launch a preventive war which were frequently put forward by high-ranking officers. At an early juncture, Moltke envisaged a war on two fronts and, like von Waldersee, often promoted the idea of exploiting the advantages of attack. Plans of this kind culminated in the preparations of 1887. Since Russia's internal weakness meant that 'the timing of an attack was more favourable for us', and since chauvinist agitation in France bode ill, Moltke advised launching a winter campaign against Russia. However, he failed to get his way once again because of Bismarck's determined opposition.[8] This opposition was not the product of any moral or ethical considerations which led the Chancellor to rule out a pre-emptive strike on principle (as the orthodox view of Bismarck would have us believe). It was based on a cool calculation of interest which owed nothing to Christian principles. From 1875 onwards the potentially adverse effects that going to war would entail were regarded as too dangerous because they had become incalculable. It was this kind of restraint, based on considered judgements and taking account of all the political factors, that was abandoned after Bismarck's dismissal in 1890. Up to that point his views had prevailed because of his special position of long-standing. When political restraints weakened, however, there was an increased tendency among the General Staff under Moltke to think purely in terms of military efficiency and expediency.

In an age of rapid developments in weaponry, the efforts of the Prusso-German military to prepare for a future war by meticulous planning were typified by the Chief of the General Staff, Alfred von Schlieffen (1891–1905). The operations plans named after him were the product of a striving for purely technical perfection, which tacitly ignored the priority Clausewitz had given to political considerations. The Schlieffen Plan, which was worked out in several different versions between 1895 and 1906, was supposed to offer a miracle solution to the problem of a war on two fronts. Its first main objective was the defeat of France. To achieve this aim, the right wing of the German armies was to push through Belgium, Luxembourg and Northern France in a great sweeping movement within approximately six weeks and in such massive strength that the French armies would be encircled. Consequently, this wing was eventually equipped with a strength seven times greater than that on the left. To use Schlieffen's favourite analogy, the aim was to inflict a 'modern Cannae' (a total anihilation of the enemy), in the west, before turning to the push in the east. The final version of this blueprint for victory, regarded as utterly infallible, was drawn up between December 1905 and January 1906, at a time when the Tsarist Empire was weakened by the effects of revolution. The Plan finally provided, therefore, for the German armies' ratio of strength to be 8 to 1 in the west compared to the east.

Long before it dawned on Moltke that the Battle of the Marne signalled the failure of the Schlieffen Plan, three serious problem areas could be discerned which made this blueprint for success somewhat dubious from the outset.

(1) The German army was never strong enough to carry out successfully an operation of this kind on such an enormous scale. Schlieffen himself never pressed insistently enough for the requisite increase in the army's manpower, although the General Staff could hardly have forgotten how the elder Moltke's victories had always depended on numerical superiority for their success. Planning, therefore, was based on a Utopian and militarily irresponsible belief in miracles which is not easy to reconcile with the much-vaunted realism of the General Staff. Without an overwhelming superiority in troop strength the right wing was simply never adequately prepared for its crucial role. Thus, the 'great Schlieffen Plan . . . far from being "a safe recipe for victory" enjoying "a surfeit of chances for success", was instead a "reckless gamble" '.[9]

(2) From the very beginning it was a mistaken belief that the problem of a war on two fronts could be decided for good by a Cannae in the west. To begin with, there was still the vast Russian Empire, which, especially after its alliance with France, was an enemy still to be reckoned with. It was hardly likely to throw in the towel the moment its French ally was defeated. Moreover, no provision was made for the guerrilla warfare one could expect to occur in a defeated France, with all its unpredictable consequences, even though most of the planners had seen this happen before when

they were young officers in 1870–71. Finally, all the historical experience pointed to the inevitable entry of Great Britain into the war, if Belgium were invaded.

(3) From 1897 on the disregard for Belgian neutrality was included in the Plan and remained a permanent feature right up to its actual violation in 1914. In 1905 Schlieffen himself touched on the enormous problem posed by the possibility that Great Britain would immediately come to the assistance of France, though only in a footnote. Yet after his dismissal he recommended the deliberate use of terror if Belgium were to offer resistance — for example, by bombarding its fortress towns. He was firmly convinced that it would not be necessary to deploy German troops against Russia, since it would be deterred from any action by Germany's victories in the west. Both these ideas betray an almost ridiculous lack of sound judgement in appraising the situation by a man who exercised the highest authority in German military planning. His successor, the younger Moltke, saw quite clearly from Schlieffen's desk in 1913 that the attack on Belgium would turn Great Britain against Germany. He wanted, therefore, at least to guarantee Belgium its economic assets and forgo any annexations by Germany. But he, too, clung to Schlieffen's decision. He was thus not only unbelievably naïve politically but showed a blindness towards the military implications. The Schlieffen Plan with its 'enormous inflation of a purely strategic principle' ignored the question of what political, and consequently also what 'military ramifications the invasion of Belgium' was bound to have and how these 'would alter the whole situation'.[10]

That such a one-sided emphasis on technical military thinking could come to prevail in the Greater Prussian Empire was mainly a result of two developments:

(1) The militarisation of Prussian society since the eighteenth century had placed the army at the top of the pyramid of prestige and had also led to military norms, patterns of behaviour and ways of thinking taking an increasing hold over bourgeois society. This, along with an excessive respect for the army, smoothed the way for the triumph of a narrow military departmental and specialist way of thinking. The successful wars of the 1860s and Germany's position of hegemony in Central Europe led to a further increase in the 1870s in the esteem enjoyed by the military. After 1894, moreover, the chances for the German Empire's survival in a future war on two

fronts seemed to depend more than ever on its military strength and effective military planning. All these factors were fully exploited by the army, surrounded as it was by an aura of mystery because of its expert knowledge. But these factors were effective even without the military's active encouragement, and it did not encounter any stiff political opposition.

(2) The reason for this was that, parallel to this development and since Bismarck's dismissal, the politicians had come to capitulate in the face of military arguments which were dressed up as the only logical option. Schlieffen and the younger Moltke were able to point out convincingly that neither Chancellor Hohenlohe nor his successor Bülow had insisted on the primacy of civilian decision-making. And Bethmann, the bureaucrat in the Chancellor's office, continued to tell his critics after the First World War that as a 'layman in military matters' he simply could 'not presume to pass judgement on military options, let alone military necessities'.[11] This meant he had abdicated responsibility in favour of the military, had betrayed his task of political coordination and had failed to ensure that political considerations were given priority. To Bismarck, as to Clausewitz, who had devoted himself to this problem, this priority had always been an inalienable right of the political leadership.

No wonder then that the political options were further narrowed down in 1913 when work on planning the proposed eastern campaign was discontinued. This decision implied that any German success in a future war depended quite fundamentally on a quick pre-emptive strike being carried out against France. Given the main thrust of the Schlieffen Plan, it also meant an attack on Belgium which would in turn force Great Britain into entering the war. This was to set in motion an almost automatic chain of events which narrowed down the options still further in the summer of 1914. However, this chosen course cannot be properly explained without reference to the internal distribution of power between the civilian politicians and the military. Great decisions of strategy have always been inextricably bound up with the elaboration of political aims which, while not requiring a knowledge of military affairs is obliged to incorporate the military's counsels. Long before the July crisis of 1914 Berlin had committed itself to a basically unsound war strategy which in political terms represented 'the worst of all the available options',[12] in that it forced Great Britain's entry on the side of the Franco-Russian alliance. The argument that the threat of a French invasion of Belgium forced Germany to take counter-measures, or even justified its actions, is completely unfounded. Belgium was firmly resolved to defend its neutrality from 1906 onwards, and Britain, for political reasons, refused to agree to French proposals to invade right up to 1914. The constellation of social forces in Germany, the actual constitutional framework of the country, and the whole weight of historical tradition, all ruled out a politically more sensible preparation for the event of war. The fact that it was not the alignment of forces outside its borders which imposed a certain course of action on Germany, but that this was primarily a product of decisions arising from its internal political situation, will be shown later, though without moralising about guilt or seeking to lay the blame on individuals (III.7).

One military development outside Germany should, however, be mentioned at this point. In the first war it ever conducted, Wilhelmine Germany practised an early form of 'total war', i.e. in the crushing of the Herero rising of 1904–07 in its colony of German South-West Africa. The military administration, which took over control from the civilian governor, brutally put down the rising, using all the means at its disposal. The objective here was no longer merely victory, but 'annihilation' (*Vernichtung*), as it was referred to in revealing language. The military waged a 'campaign which left no possibility for peace'.[13] Almost half the natives were wiped out. Many were killed by being deliberately driven into the waterless Omaheke Desert. A quarter of their number were deported and abandoned to a deliberate policy of extermination in the prison camps. Once the direct costs of the operation had risen to almost 590 million gold marks, the troops set about creating 'peace and order'. But over wide areas it was the peace of the graveyard. Hatred and fear reigned between blacks and whites. Only in the latter part of the American Civil War had a Western nation in the nineteenth century previously conducted a campaign of such radical ferocity. This German colonial war confirmed the worst fears, felt first by liberal and then by socialist critics, about the consequences of colonial rule. The form that warfare would assume in the not too distant future was already plain to see.

5.2 *Militarism*

Gerhard Ritter, for twenty years the doyen of West German historians, took the view that militarism, in its true sense, prevails 'when the primacy of the political leadership over the military, i.e. of its thinking over the army's, is endangered'.[14] This has long been criticised as far too narrow a definition, and, especially where Prusso-German history is concerned, one is bound to agree. The overriding problem is not simply one of political decision-making being temporarily eclipsed by military considerations. Rather, it is the spread of military thinking in social groups exercising an important influence on society as a whole. The exceptional role of the soldier in modern German history before 1945 can be understood only by reference to the spread of military values throughout German society. This 'social militarism' not only placed the military highest on the scale of social prestige but permeated the whole of society with its ways of thinking, patterns of behaviour, and its values and notions of honour. Developments in eighteenth-century Prussia had a crucial influence on the character of its society and its constitution. The feudal land-owner also appeared in the role of military commander. Together with his role as judge, and frequently also rural employer, he embodied an authority encountered in all aspects of social life. The structure of the army was inextricably bound up with the land-owner's authority. Whether as a tied labourer or army recruit, the citizen of the state found himself continually confronted with the same authority. Even the Prussian reforms and universal military service did nothing to break down this fundamental relationship in German rural life. The land-owning aristocracy, accustomed to exercising power, continued to provide the military élite of the state, under whom the citizens of the towns were also obliged to 'serve'. After its position had been challenged in 1848 and 1862, the land-owning aristocracy's successes in the years leading up to 1871 preserved the hierarchy of privilege, with the military exercising power at the top. If even an historian like Ritter recognises that one consequence of events in the period 1866–71 was a process of militarisation of a kind common throughout Europe,[15] it may be assumed that, quite apart from the problem of stepped-up armaments, there were even more important changes that resulted from Prussia's historical traditions. And indeed there were. They can be observed in the many highly revealing outward signs of militarism. For example, every imperial chancellor in Germany wore a uniform when appearing in the *Reichstag*. At royal banquets Chancellor Bethmann Hollweg, as a mere major, was seated at the lower end of the table beyond the colonels and generals present. The hard-working Minister of Finance, Scholz, thought it the happiest moment of his life when, by royal favour, he was allowed to exchange the uniform of a sergeant — the highest rank he could attain as a member of the middle class — for that of a lieutenant. But one of the most important effects of this social militarism is revealed by the institution of the reserve officer. Placed under constant threat by socio-economic developments, the officer corps became gradually more and more segregated in its role as 'the estate which upheld the nation'. Indeed, it became an almost separate, self-perpetuating caste.

Germany witnessed the general phenomenon of a spread of military values and codes of conduct throughout society. This engendered a sense of inferiority in civilians, of which Bethmann Hollweg was a typical example. Social militarism could be seen at every turn; in the precedence at Court of the most junior of nobles in lieutenant's uniform, in the way one stepped aside to let an officer pass in the street, in the employment of ex-NCO's as postal officials, in the drills which formed part of physical education in the grammar-schools. All this performed a highly desirable disciplining function which benefited the ruling classes. However, there were several other aspects of this militarisation of society which deserve to be highlighted.

The army as an instrument for use in the struggles of internal politics   It goes without saying that the army was regarded first and foremost as an instrument for attack and defence in the event of war. But alongside this role it should also be realised that it was expected to be 'the armed supporter and main pillar of quasi-absolutist government'. 'To this end, military training had to be turned into a school' to inculcate 'blind obedience to superiors and an attitude of loyalty to the Crown'. Thus, from the time of the Constitutional Conflict onwards, the lengthy period of military service was meant to guarantee the government 'a reliable army at its disposal in the event of internal revolution'.[16] On this question the high-ranking military made no attempt to camouflage the army's role in preventing internal disturbances. 'An efficient army', von Roon said during the debate on the perpetuity bill, 'is our only conceivable protection against the red and black [i.e. Socialist and clerical] threats. If they [the politicians] ruin the army, it means the end for us.'[17] This view took a firm hold from then on. As the Social Democrats grew in strength, so the concept of the army as a kind of Praetorian Guard became more attractive. This meant that many regular officers saw universal military service as a dangerous institution which conscripted more and more Social Democrats into the army. In 1892, in a secret memorandum to the Minister of War, von Gossler, the recently appointed Chief of the General Staff, von Waldersee, argued for 'small professional armies' which, 'given good pay, could be deployed primarily against internal enemies'. What was meant by this, he went on to explain in greater detail to the Emperor. He envisaged a pre-emptive strike against the SPD. One could not 'leave it to its leaders to choose the timing for the great settling of accounts'. Instead, one had 'to force the issue quickly, if at all possible'. Waldersee put forward proposals to deport prominent socialists, limit the rights of free association and assembly, suppress 'undesirable' newspapers and periodicals, and change the law on suffrage for the *Reichstag* elections. All of these were measures which could be carried out only with the help of the army.[18] In 1907 the General Staff's Second Section for Military Studies produced a study concerning its strategy for 'fighting in insurgent towns'. It unequivocally posited the SPD as the enemy in any future civil war situation.[19] As far as the officer corps was concerned, the political Left was still 'the Fatherland's enemy within', and army fears of the threat it posed received a fresh stimulus after its victory in the elections of 1912. These fears influenced armaments planning and the debates on armaments levels in the years 1912 and 1913. They persisted throughout the years leading up to 1914, regardless of the fact that Noske's line had long asserted itself in the SPD over the radical anti-militarist stance represented by Karl Liebknecht.

Social composition and behaviour controls   After 1848 the feeling of being threatened, first by the liberal bourgeoisie and later by the socialist proletariat, became firmly established among regular army officers. Roon's slogan took hold: 'The army is now our fatherland, for it is the only place which has not yet been infiltrated by impure and restless elements.'[20] Personnel policy was conducted accordingly. During the Constitutional Conflict Moltke constantly insisted that middle-class aspirants to the officer corps should be rejected, 'because they do not bring with them the outlook the army has to preserve. And it must stay that way'.[21] Recruits of aristocratic origin were regarded as reliable; especially those who had attended the cadet schools. The army's policy was to give them preference and protect them from 'harmful' influences. Speaking in 1870, General von Schweinitz remarked that 'our power comes to an end when we run out of *Junker* material to fill our officer posts'. To this Bismarck replied: 'Although I'm not allowed to say as much, I have always acted accordingly in my dealings.'[22]

Taking the same line, Waldersee demanded in 1877 that 'the caste-ethos be further developed among us, and we, the officer class, should cut ourselves off more from the other classes as a self-sufficient estate'. For only by 'keeping our distance from other social groups and creating a firm sense of community among officers' could the goal of keeping the army equipped to strike effectively in the struggle between 'the haves and the have-nots' be achieved. Even at this early juncture von Waldersee demanded an end to 'the system of universal military service' on the grounds that 'only a professional army' could 'prevent the total collapse of the existing social order', or 'in short, . . . could shoot down the rabble without hesitation when ordered to fire. This would be the evidence that we had our warrior caste'.[23] In 1900 Schlieffen also expressed agreement with the basic principle of social exclusivity, and in 1903 the Minister of War, von Einem, concurred when he said that 'the shortage' of officers could be alleviated only by 'lowering the standards regarding social origins; but this is not advisable because we could not prevent taking in greater numbers of democratic and other elements which would not be suitable in our ranks'.[24]

The results of this personnel policy, which was guided by socially defensive considerations, confirm the intensity with which the various branches of the army officer corps sought to ensure a preponderance of reliable *Junker*. In 1865 the nobility accounted for 65 per cent of all Prussian army officers. In 1913 it was still 30 per cent. This group occupied virtually all the army's senior positions. In the same year 80 per cent of all cavalry officers were nobles, as were 48 per cent of all infantry officers and 41 per cent of field artillery officers. Only in the case of the pioneers, who, because of their emphasis on technical skills, were traditionally middle class in origin, was the figure a mere 6 per cent. In 62 per cent of the Prussian regiments more than 58 per cent of the officers were from the nobility. Sixteen regiments had an exclusively aristocratic officer corps. In 1913 only 59 officers in the Guards units were of middle-class origin. In 1908 it had been as few as four. In 1900, 60 per cent of all ranks above colonel were occupied by nobles. In 1913 the figure was still 53 per cent. Of 190 infantry commanders in 1909 only 39 were middle class and half of all the majors were nobles. Prussian officers, mostly of noble origin, enjoyed the lion's share of General Staff posts, numbering 239 officers in 1888 and rising to 625 in 1914.[25] Thus, up to 1913 the upper echelons of the Prussian army, and hence the core of the imperial army, were completely dominated by the nobility. Nevertheless its share of posts was unmistakably declining as the overall strength of the army increased.

This explains why the debate over the major new army bill in

1913 immediately developed into an issue concerning the social composition of the officer corps. The Minister of War, von Heeringen, defended the army as a traditional bastion of the nobility against the requests of the General Staff, represented in particular by the middle-class planner Erich Ludendorff, for an increase of three army corps to meet the requirements of the Schlieffen Plan. Heeringen maintained that 'if an expansion of the Prussian army by almost a sixth of its strength' was being asked for, 'such a drastic measure' would require 'careful and detailed consideration'. 'This exceptionally large increase could come about only by drawing upon social groups' which were 'not really suitable for supplementing the officer corps, which would be exposed to democratic influences'.[26] Supported by the aristocratic Military Cabinet, the Minister was able to reject the proposal. As in the case of the military's policy towards Russia (III.7.2), armaments policy was not determined by military requirements, but by the power struggle in domestic politics. It was later said that the absence of the three army corps in question had a crucial effect on the outcome of the First Battle of the Marne. The reason they were not there was not because their creation had been opposed by the *Reichstag*. It had, in fact, been willing to approve them. The explanation is rather to be found in the distribution of power in Prusso-Germany and the fears and inactivity it engendered. Members of the middle class were regarded with the greatest suspicion as crypto-democrats. Jewish citizens were kept totally at arm's length. Between 1878 and 1910 there was not a single Jewish regular officer in the entire Prussian army. In 1911 there were in all only 21 Jews in the officer reserve. Here was the proof of Rathenau's remark that the Jews were treated as 'second-class citizens'. Whether held overtly or covertly, antisemitism was certainly practised effectively. It was a dominant feature of the imperial officer corps, and in this area National Socialism had no need to introduce into the army of its own day what was already a well-established practice.

It was not only officer candidates who were subject to a policy based on clear selection criteria. The army tried to operate along similar lines when it came to recruiting NCO's and the ordinary ranks. In 1911, for example, 42 per cent of the Germany population lived in the countryside. Yet, in spite of 'universal' military service, 64.1 per cent of that year's recruits were drawn from rural districts along with a further 22.3 per cent from small towns which were unmistakably rural in character. Only 6 per cent came from the big cities and a further 7 per cent from Germany's middle-sized towns.[27]

Here, too, the army relied on that internalised subservient mentality which was the product of centuries of feudalism, and attempted to keep the proportion of city-dwellers 'tainted' by socialist ideas to a minimum. The traditional method of meting out cruel treatment to the common soldier could not be used without the risk of a Social Democratic deputy bringing such cases to the attention of the public. The Prussian tied farm labourer, who was long accustomed to obeying his superiors, was much more easily 'broken in' as a recruit. He was also much more receptive to the talk of military chaplains with their 'theology of war' and royalist sermons which justified the structure of authority in a military world order descending from the King and Emperor as *Summus Episcopus* and 'Supreme War-lord'.

Over and above this personnel policy, which operated at all levels, there were other institutions which sought to control behaviour in the interests of a neo-feudal code of honour and social exclusivity. Up until 1918 duelling was still an informally prescribed method for regulating conflicts between army officers. Any refusal to perform this archaic ritual resulted in dismissal from the army. Courts of Honour were set up to deal with internal quarrels and to issue challenges to single combat. As late as 1913 the Prussian Ministry of War decided that these Courts of Honour were subject only to royal authority. Every attempt by the *Reichstag* to exercise jurisdiction on the matter was strongly resisted. The actual workings of military justice remained secret. Its procedures excluded the civilian courts and gave more prominence to displays of *esprit de corps* and feelings of solidarity than to the actual offences committed. If a soldier of ordinary rank offended against army regulations, he faced a period of harsh imprisonment. In several controversial cases even reservists were given prison sentences. Officers, on the other hand, were legally exempt from imprisonment, providing yet another example of how the principle of equality before the law was violated. When criticisms voiced by Social Democrats, especially Karl Liebknecht, brought numerous abuses to light, they were seen as 'attacks on the King's uniform' and resentfully rebuffed. The substance of these criticisms was denied — even when known to be true. And so the impenetrable barrier preserving the military *imperium in imperio* was reinforced, sealing them off still further from the rest of society.

The military's privileged position was suddenly highlighted shortly before the war by the Zabern affair of 1913. A twenty-year-old Prussian lieutenant in the Alsatian garrison town of Zabern (Saverne) swore at some civilians and incited recruits to acts of violence against them. The incident became a public issue, caused a stir throughout the German Empire and, following mounting excitement, resulted in the deployment of armed military patrols which arbitrarily arrested some of the townspeople. Press criticism of the government's handling of the affair reached a peak of frenzy, as had happened only once before at the time of the *Daily Telegraph* affair. Sharp exchanges in the *Reichstag*, which passed a vote of no confidence in Chancellor Bethmann Hollweg, demonstrated just as clearly as did many newspapers the disillusionment felt at the complete impotence of the civilian authorities, and, in a wider sense, of civilians in general *vis-à-vis* the military. This disillusionment was further underlined when, following a farcical military trial, the officers responsible were acquitted. The 'portent of Zabern' laid bare a structural crisis in the constitution of the German Empire. It showed that, whenever it came to a borderline case, the army could arrogantly defend its special position regardless of the private citizen's constitutional rights, to say nothing of its lack of basic political reasonableness. Neither the Imperial Justice Department nor the Ministry of War had any doubts that the actions of the military authorities had no legal basis. Nevertheless, the Minister of War, von Falkenhayn, was able to persuade the Imperial Chancellor of the need to defend the military. The powerlessness of the *Reichstag* to do anything, the military's open display of arrogance, the rapid collapse of the parliamentary opposition, and the defence of the army's traditional role in the state, all threw into sharp relief Germany's constitutional reality before 1914. They also highlighted the consequences of a social militarism which had seriously weakened any middle-class protest.[28] Only a few years before the German Empire's collapse, the true face of the military state's semi-absolutism revealed itself on the soil of the 'imperial province' of Alsace Lorraine. The Zabern affair laid bare its true character.

'The mobilisation of petty-bourgeois militarist sentiment'[29]   The army was regarded as the 'school of the nation' in arms. It worked constantly to train and indoctrinate each annual intake of recruits, thereby wielding an influence which reached far beyond the confines of the barracks. It participated fully in the political socialisation of citizens in a variety of different ways. Compulsory military service and social militarism should, therefore, be dealt with in the context of institutions of socialisation as an additional means of ensuring discipline and shoring up the *status quo*. It is not so much a question of investigating, for example, the content of school instruction with its

glorification of anything military, but the institutions themselves. On a local level, for instance, the ex-servicemen's associations attempted to organise all 'veterans' after their return to civilian life, and were an appreciable factor in the formation of public opinion. In 1910 there were 1.5 million members in 16,500 Prussian veterans' associations alone. The membership of the German Federation of Ex-Servicemen's Associations (*Deutscher Kriegerbund*), which began in 1873 with 214 associations and 27,500 members, passed the million mark around 1900 and numbered 1.7 million in 1910. A further 2.5 million men were organised in the so-called *Kyffhäuserbund*. Beyond these there were countless other organisations which were not actually organised into nation-wide federations. What they all had in common was a carefully nurtured militant attitude that was basically anti-Social Democratic and often also anti-Semitic. Bismarck had recognised at an early stage the possibility of moulding these associations into instruments for his campaigns in domestic politics. He made use of the 'strong defence' they offered 'against tendencies endangering the state'. The specific nature of these organisations meant that the government always had a pillar of support loyal to the German Empire. In addition, there were also the paramilitary youth organisations like Young Germany (*Jungdeutschland*) and the Young Defenders (*Jugendwehr*). If one includes the supporters of the Navy League and the Army League — also mobilised at election time as groups 'loyal to the Empire' — then, alongside its own troops, the army was able to keep a grip on at least 5 million Germans before 1914, i.e. a sixth of all adult males and youths.[30] One has to be aware of these figures and realise what they mean in terms of the influence and collective mentality that lay behind them, to appreciate the significance of the military and all its ramifications in Imperial Germany.

5.3 *The navy*

During the latter half of the German Empire's existence the navy assumed an importance which few could have predicted. During this period armaments policy and military policy cannot be viewed in isolation from naval policy. Ever since the 1870s German ships had operated in East Asian waters, the Pacific and around the coast of Africa in order to provide protection for imperialist expansion; but these had been only light cruisers and gunboats. In 1889 an Imperial Navy Office was set up along the lines of existing government departments. However, it carried no weight in the decision-making machinery of central government in Berlin. The expansion of the German battle-fleet after 1898 was, therefore, a major turning-point. It was the result of several different factors, all contributing to a highly important development that was to play a fundamental part in shaping German domestic and foreign policy in the years before 1914. At this point the name of Alfred von Tirpitz immediately comes to mind as one of the Wilhelmine period's key figures. Originally responsible for developing the navy's torpedo-boat flotillas, he held the post of Chief of Staff of the Supreme Naval Command between 1892 and 1895. He showed a lively and active interest in imperialist expansion, especially in East Asia, and in 1897 was appointed the new Secretary of State at the Imperial Navy Office. It would be wrong to assume that he promoted the cause of fleet construction out of an exaggerated desire to see his department grow and eventually close the gap between the navy and the army with its long-established traditions. His thoughts revolved around other aims, and the course of naval policy in practice immediately revealed the two main functions it served.

(1) The first was the navy's combat role, directed against rival states, especially Great Britain as the dominant naval power in the world at the time. This role became less prominent later on, following the development of a calculated risk policy which was primarily defensive in intention. Tirpitz's deterrent strategy envisaged that the German fleet should be sufficiently powerful to avoid defeat in a straight fight against its nearest rival in terms of fleet strength. In keeping with its offensive role, the fleet was intended to provide a deterrent by virtue of its existence; but, if war could not be avoided, was expected to overcome any opposition, help in the opening up of overseas markets, provide safe access to them, and so contribute to securing the economic gains of colonialism.

(2) From the very outset this offensive role was closely connected with the navy's function as an instrument for use in the conflicts of domestic politics where it served the interests of social imperialism (III.6). Its main advocates, including Tirpitz and the Emperor, intended the navy to satisfy material interests, in particular those of heavy industry and shipbuilding, as well as their workers. Beyond this, however, and partly as a result of it, the navy was to help undermine the political ambitions of the bourgeoisie and the proletariat, thus stabilising the existing power structure. Its social basis was, in fact, a fusion mainly of concrete industrial interests and

bourgeois enthusiasm for the fleet which was much more broadly based than Bismarck's imperialism of the 1880s had been. Where the economy was concerned, naval contracts had a long-term stabilising effect, at least on a psychic level. The fleet symbolised Germany's ambitions to become a world power. It attracted nationalist energies and enabled certain groups to identify with a 'national' mission. It also acted as a compensatory diversion from the German Empire's internal problems. No wonder then that the Caesarist tendencies of the Wilhelmine political system were closely tied in with the navy. Behind the facade presented by the most advanced weapons technology of the time 'an Emperorship shored up by plebsicitary approval of the fleet' served 'as a counterweight to the dreaded growth of parliamentary influence',[31] and obstructed Germany's social and political modernisation. Naval policy was, therefore, also designed to affect society as a whole.

After the prestige gained from the events of 1870–71 had faded away, Tirpitz argued in 1895 that the nation was yearning 'for a goal — for a patriotic rallying slogan'. Bismarck's imperialism of the 1880s had tried to provide one, but now the pronounced social effects of industrialisation and the rise of the SPD since 1890 made the need to supply slogans all the more urgent. Political lobbying on behalf of the fleet would put 'life' back into 'the debate in national policies'. It would create 'a healthy counterweight to unfruitful and Utopian social policies'. Tirpitz had in mind an internal political crisis strategy in which the battle-fleet played the main part. It would enable the German Empire to pursue its political ambitions to become a world power (*Weltpolitik*). At the same time, this 'new and great national cause and the economic benefits' it entailed, would, he hoped, provide 'a strong palliative against educated and uneducated Social Democrats'.[32] Here the effect of ideological integration which this policy was to have on the nation — indeed the campaigning for the navy in itself — was every bit as important as the tangible benefits of overseas expansion. It would provide a diversion from the power struggles of domestic politics and the pressing problems of Imperial Germany's class society. The advocates of naval policy, therefore, saw its main objective, in a narrow sense, as the preservation of the country's class structure. Its all-important reference group was the propertied and educated bourgeoisie, whose position was to be defended socially and politically against the danger 'from below'. At the same time, the pre-industrial élites, especially the East Elbian landed aristocracy, also benefited from 'the ghastly navy', not directly, but indirectly through the compensations to be gained from a reactionary policy of *Sammlung*. Naval policy found that its greatest appeal lay with the bourgeoisie, which was helped by the Imperial Navy Office to discover its 'very own' branch of the armed services, thus providing the middle class with compensation for its frustrated desire for parity of esteem in the army.

The groundwork for the navy's defensive function in both the external and internal spheres was laid by the conversion from a cruiser fleet to a battleship fleet. This was part of a general phenomenon at the time which could also be observed in other countries like Japan, Britain, France and the USA. The historical and ideological justification for this development was provided by the arguments of Alfred T. Mahan, who was the most influential prophet of the new 'navalism' in the Anglo-Saxon countries. At the express wish of Wilhelm II, Mahan's books were made required reading for German naval officers. His *Influence of Sea Power upon History* was Tirpitz's 'naval bible'.[33] Behind the demands for such conversion programmes lay the assumption, which gained strength after the Sino-Japanese War of 1894–95, that the future belonged to heavily armour-plated battleships, fitted with guns of an unprecedentedly large calibre for engagements on the high seas and the bombardment of coastal towns. At about the same time (within a dozen years in fact), all the great sea powers, including the USA, Germany and Japan, began constructing heavily armoured cruisers. When Tirpitz followed this powerful trend with his own programme he was able to argue with complete justification that it would place the German Empire in the forefront of modern naval development. But since the extremely costly building of a new fleet would have to compete for funds with the army's financial requirements, when the navy was unsupported by a past tradition of success, the Imperial Navy Office began to develop a new, modern style of influencing parliamentary opinion. It used mass-propaganda techniques and launched a carefully planned public relations campaign, all in order to mobilise public opinion and, with its help, win the *Reichstag*'s approval for increased naval expenditure. A new type of cooperation between the Imperial Navy Office's public relations department and the Navy League, with its 'navy academics' willing to propagate its message, newspapers, periodicals, individual politicians and parties, certainly proved technically successful. However, the enormous political costs soon became apparent.

First of all, a new six-year construction programme was approved in the first Navy Law of 1898. It provided for two squadrons of eight battleships each. In practice it meant a tacit acceptance of the idea of 'perpetuity' for which Tirpitz deliberately aimed, because from now on the navy's strength, measured in its number of ships, was to be maintained to modern technical standards. This would be achieved by placing statutory limits on their period of commission, thus providing deadlines for their eventual replacement, the timing of which would be a matter for the navy to decide. This showed the political and psychological skill of Tirpitz and his colleagues in pursuing aims which to all outward appearances gave the impression of being limited. Only two years later, however, the Supplementary Naval Estimates Law of 1900 openly called for the attainment of world power status for the navy. The Imperial Navy Office insisted on four squadrons of eight battleships each, two flagships, eight battle-cruisers and twenty-four cruisers, as well as a fleet for deployment outside home waters consisting of three battle-cruisers and ten cruisers. In terms of quantity and expenditure this represented an enormous burden on finances, especially as the *Reichstag* had already agreed to a construction programme stretching over seventeen years and involving huge costs. But this proposal around the turn of the century for an expansion of the fleet also represented a new departure in qualitative terms. A new 'risk theory' was developed in connection with the concentrated naval programme, the barely concealed aggressive intentions behind the building of battleships emerged at the same time that the social imperialist aspect was becoming increasingly evident in the long-term 'Tirpitz-Plan' and the campaigning for a bigger fleet. The middle-class liberal parties gave it their massive support. With the backing of even the left-wing Liberals and the Centre, the battleship-building programme was carried along on a great tide of approval. Friedrich Naumann, the fading figure-head of German liberalism, who was still influenced by his ideas as a Protestant pastor, provided a particularly quaint justification: 'It's as if I can hear Jesus speaking', he wrote in the 1890s when defending his 'joyful faith in Tirpitz' (Theodor Heuss). 'Go forth, build the ships, and pray to God that you won't need them.'[34] This religious faith in armaments was not, however, what decided whether or not the first Supplementary Naval Estimates Bill was approved. True, the propaganda campaign for the navy went all out for results. Fifteen years later, Bethmann Hollweg recalled that 'the policy of encouraging chauvinist tendencies' had been necessary in order to 'win over' the nation to 'the building of the fleet'.[35] But the campaigning by itself was not enough. In March 1900, the American naval attaché in Berlin, who was familiar with the hard political bargains struck at home, knew what constellation of forces was necessary to get 'the bill for increased naval estimates through. The agrarians use their support for the bill to wring concessions to protect their own interests and, where possible, to get a tariff on agricultural imports which will be framed in future trade agreements'.[36] For some years previously, government ministries had already been preparing for a new increase in protectionism. This came into effect with the Bülow tariff of 1902. In fact, the Supplementary Navy Bill and the customs tariff formed a package put together by the majority of deputies in the *Reichstag*. The middle classes and heavy industry were given a naval construction programme, the large-scale agrarian producers a more favourable tariff system. Together they placed the seal of success on Miquel's *Sammlung*, which was carried along by the navy. In their combined effect, however, they set the course taken by foreign trade policy and armaments policy throughout the years before 1914. Both were in keeping with the overriding priority of stabilising the system from within for the benefit of specific interests. Following in the tradition of Bismarck's 'cartel of the productive estates', this arrangement meant that decisions which had important implications for foreign policy had become instruments for use in combating internal political problems through the demagogic exploitation of popular nationalism.[37]

The second Supplementary Naval Estimates Bill of 1906 marked another important turning-point. The German Empire now changed over to the building of dreadnoughts. This powerful new class of capital ship (of approximately 25,000 BRT, equipped with 30–38 cm guns and capable of increased speeds up to 21–28 knots) was developed in the British naval dockyards in response to Germany's fleet-building programme in the years before 1906. It rendered all existing battleships obsolete, and produced an escalation in the Anglo-German naval arms race. Britain could hold on to her lead only on the strength of her superior number of dreadnoughts, while Germany could close the gap between the two navies only by building its own ships of the same class. But several of Tirpitz's original assumptions had already proved erroneous. Britain was fully capable of outstripping Germany's pace of construction with even more modern ships. It was also able to overcome its political isolation. In contrast, Germany's financial position worsened just at the point when the dreadnoughts were beginning to make new demands on its economy. Its room for manoeuvre in foreign affairs was also becoming more restricted. Nevertheless, a *Reichstag* majority was formed, including even the left-wing Liberals, which not only approved the dreadnoughts as replacements for obsolescent ships but gave the go-ahead for the building of three new battleships and six battle-cruisers.

The third Supplementary Naval Estimates Bill of 1908 reduced the lifetime of all the navy's commissioned ships to twenty years, allowing the new classes of ships to be brought into service sooner. At the same time, it introduced the building tempo of four dreadnoughts per annum up to 1912. In fact, it proved difficult to keep up this pace of construction. Nevertheless, between 1908 and 1913 fourteen battleships and six battle-cruisers rolled down the slipway. Because of this relative success by the naval planners, negotiations with Britain on comparative naval strengths broke down in 1912. By exploiting the momentum of the building programme and the alleged requirements of naval armaments, Tirpitz was able to make his views prevail over those of Bethmann Hollweg at the crucial moment. Concessions by Britain were turned down as inadequate. The Chancellor had been working hard for conciliation with London on the basis of mutual armaments limitations, and even threatened to resign if the talks failed, but to no avail. Tirpitz got his way.

The political leadership responded to the outcome of these negotiations by introducing a new, fourth Supplementary Naval Estimates Bill. The *Reichstag* approved three new dreadnoughts and two cruisers, as well as a reorganisation of the fleet which enabled a fifth squadron to be put into service. As with the army's proposed estimates, a large majority of deputies were prepared to go along with the government. In the last years before the war 60 per cent of the German Empire's armaments budget flowed into the fleet-building programme. By 1914 the ratio of ships between the German and British battle-fleets was 10:16 — that is, the target of a 2:3 ratio of strength, as desired by Berlin, had been more or less reached. As for domestic politics, the fleet did not actually fulfil the euphoric hopes placed in it at the turn of the century. It did, however, shore up the policy of *Sammlung*, though it proved incapable of significantly reducing Germany's class antagonisms. Its failure to do so signified 'the bankruptcy of Wilhelmine social imperialism by peaceful means'.[38] In foreign policy its effects can only be described as catastrophic. Relations with Great Britain, the only European power with which it could reach an understanding, no longer possible with France or Russia (see III.7.2 below), were strained beyond repair. Leaving the Schlieffen Plan aside, the aggressive policy of battleship construction, with its obvious anti-British intentions, was bound to arouse deep suspicion in London and the feeling that Britain's vital interests were being threatened. In military terms, the battle-fleet proved a complete failure. It was unable to affect significantly the course of the war at any point, and certainly did not succeed in turning events in favour of the Central Powers. As a revolutionary groundswell spread throughout the navy after the undecided Battle of Jutland in 1916, later to find its release in 1918, Grand Admiral von Tirpitz, professionally a failure, who had resigned as early as March 1916, took a step which was entirely consistent with his social and political outlook when, in 1917, he founded the proto-fascist German Fatherland Party.

6. Imperialism

Western imperialism, viewed here as both the direct and indirect, formal and informal rule exercised by industrial countries over undeveloped regions by virtue of their socio-economic, technological and military superiority, is a complex phenomenon. Its prerequisite is the process of industrialisation, which forms a watershed in world history and which, despite all the undeniable elements of continuity, distinguishes imperialism from earlier forms of European colonialism. It can best be discussed within a theoretical framework which — as outlined in the introduction in general terms — enables us to analyse the central and interrelated problems raised by it.

(1) Nowadays it must obviously seem inadequate to discuss imperialism purely in terms of 'the economy' or 'industrialisation'. This is far too general an approach, leading to findings that are vague and usually inconclusive. Instead, we should try to comprehend, in terms that are as exact as possible, the significance of industrial and agricultural growth in those states which become involved in expansionist drives. It is in the historical nature of such growth that it follows an uneven pattern. The long-term secular trend of a continuously prospering economy shows only one side of the picture. Periodic interruptions to growth (e.g. recessions, depressions, seasonal fluctuations), variations in the business cycle ('Kitchins' over forty months, 'Juglars' over ten to eleven years, Kuznet's twenty-year cycles, or even the long waves of 'Kondratieffs') — in short, the irregular rhythm of boom, crisis, downturn, depression, upturn is on the whole more important for contempor-

aries and historians than the mathematical and statistical overall trend which obscures the violent oscillations.[1]

(2) Social change is one of the preconditions of the economic processes involved; but it also accompanies them and is affected by them. It should, therefore, be examined as a specific social structure in its own right. Changes in the constellations of social forces and the problems of a nation's class structure become, therefore, the focus of analysis.

(3) This, in turn, raises the question of the political contest for the acquisition, maintenance and extension of opportunities to wield power. In other words, we must also analyse the inner dynamics of the ruling political system. At this point imperialism emerges as a strategy and means for defending and stabilising political domination, and must be seen against a background of conflict generated by attempts of either upholding or changing the system. In this respect, domestic and foreign policy become two facets of one and the same national policy. In this context the effect of ideologies such as Social Darwinism can be determined. Their impact cannot be adequately accounted for if they are seen only as quasi-autonomous factors or dealt with purely in terms of the history of ideas. The approach adopted here enables us to account for the astonishing simultaneity and similarity of the West's imperial expansion. If, on the other hand, one reduces the decisive driving forces behind imperialism to specific national 'urges', the historian's concern with the particular is turned into a dogma. It leads inevitably to a distorted picture, since it makes a comparative analysis which can elucidate problems by stressing common structural elements difficult, if not impossible.

6.1 *Uneven growth and the legitimising of political domination: social imperialism*

If we adopt the above approach to imperialism, particular attention should be paid to two things when dealing with problems of economic growth. To begin with, the historically unprecedented dynamism of the industrial economies released forces which were widely perceived as compulsive drives emanating from the system itself. A pragmatic expansionism responded to these forces and led to the acquisition of new markets. These were secured either by informal means or by direct colonial rule over territorial possessions. There is no need to make a distinction here between the imperialism born of economic depression (up to about 1895) and that born of the trend-period of economic prosperity which followed. Nor is there any point in denying the connection between imperialism and economic development. Empirically, the genesis of modern imperialism is inseparably linked — subjectively in the consciousness of contemporaries, but also objectively for subsequent research — with the variations in the economic cycle. This is true not only of Germany's imperialist expansion but equally valid for the American, French and Belgian cases, and — allowing for its divergent historical time scale — the British example as well. But even in the period of world-wide economic boom between 1896 and 1913, the most important element common to both phases of expansion was the experience of irregular growth, i.e. the constant difficulties of arriving at a rational advance calculation of opportunities for profit. This helps explain the high expectations placed in foreign trade, which virtually became an ideology in themselves. A trend-period of prolonged prosperity never implies a continuous development free from interruptions. After 1896 the upswing was interrrupted by crises and, to some extent, depressions: in 1900–01, 1907–08 and 1913. These provided painful reminders that there was no such thing as a continuous and even rise in economic development. What is historically illuminating, indeed critical, is not only the losses involved in colonial trading (felt at the time, though calculable only nowadays), but the sometimes slight, sometimes exorbitantly high profit margins of parasitical groups representing vested interests. Equally important is the fact that for those involved in the decision-making processes the undeveloped regions of the globe appeared to offer new markets and investment opportunities, as well as the possibility of stabilising the domestic economy. The pragmatic expansion referred to was, therefore, part of those actions by which an emergent state interventionism, aimed at sustaining and controlling economic prosperity, sought to contain the effects of uneven economic growth. State-sponsored export drives and the acquisition of new markets, leading to an 'informal empire' or direct colonial rule, aimed at restoring and sustaining economic prosperity in a gradually expanding domestic market whose absorptive capacity was long underestimated. The material well-being of the nation came to depend on various forms of successful expansion, including, of course, trade with countries at a similar stage of development. It was also served by a preventive imperialism which tried to secure long-term opportunities by, for example, precautionary annexations of the kind envisaged by Lord Rosebery when he spoke of 'staking out claims for the future'.

But the various economic motives behind this expansionism, however prominently they may figure in economic theories, represented only one element behind imperialism. The desire, indeed the decided aim, of legitimising the *status quo* and the political power structure by a successful imperialism was intimately bound up with an expansionist programme. The intentions behind Germany's overseas expansion, and the function it performed, served the interests of a 'social imperialism'. This amounted to a conservative 'taming' policy which sought to divert abroad reform attempts which found their expression in the emancipatory forces of liberalism and the socialist workers' movement, and endangered the system. It was a defensive strategy which aimed at the social goal of a conservative Utopia and attempted rigidly to defend traditional structures against continual change. It made use of modern propaganda techniques, but aimed at preserving the inherited pre-industrial social and political structures of the Greater Prussian Empire, while defending the industrial and educated middle classes against the rising proletariat. Social imperialism could be applied on several fronts. It promised either real gains from overseas which could be exploited for the purposes of domestic politics, or it held out the rewards of activity — often no more than the illusory successes of activity for its own sake — which could effectively provide ideological satisfaction in terms of national prestige. It was precisely this calculation which made social imperialism an ideology of integration which could be deliberately applied from above to combat the antagonisms of German class society. It diverted the political activities of the bourgeoisie into a 'substitute sphere' and practically became 'the areas in which its accommodation . . . to the existing national state, its structures and needs' took place.[2] At the same time, the more far-sighted large-scale agrarian producers found that social imperialism offered them a new guarantee for the maintenance of their position of social and political domination in the shape of a socially reactionary *Sammlung* policy with its programme of overseas expansion.

Economic and social imperialism, as an instrument for stabilising and legitimising political domination, is associated with the birth of modern state interventionism, as outlined above (II.2) In a system of state-regulated capitalism political authority is increasingly legitimised by the political leadership's efforts to ensure constant economic growth, and, in so doing, to maintain the essential conditions for social and political stability. This, together with the manipulatory technique of social imperialism, consistently formed the basis of Germany's overseas expansionist policy. At a time when the traditional or charismatic authority of the government was being challenged, Bismarck's early economic and social imperialism was designed to improve the conditions for stability on behalf of the economic interest groups and social allies of the neo-conservative 'joint-protectionist' front of 1879 (Hans Rosenberg). It hoped to defuse the conflicts which had grown since 1873 over national income distribution and redirect political and psychic energies towards new and distant goals which would provide rallying-points. It would also revitalise ideas of a 'national' mission and the 'national' interest. The overall effect would be to consolidate the position of the authoritarian head of state, and with it that of the privileged social groups upholding his rule.

The problems caused by uneven economic growth and the need to legitimise Bismarck's Bonapartist rule coincided, and, as events were to show, made an imperialist policy appear inevitable. After the six-year-long depression up to 1879 had made way for a short-lived recovery, a further depression between 1882 and 1886 proved to be a traumatic experience in this respect (as was also the case in the USA and France). A broad ideological consensus, which had been emerging since the late 1870s, cut across pressure groups, the press, the *Reichstag* and the civil service. It was most prevalent in the 'strategic clique' (Ludz) of politicians supporting the 1879 *Sammlung*. This consensus united the growing demand for a stepping-up of foreign trade with that for fresh colonial acquisitions. Both were intended to help Germany out of the economic crisis and reduce social conflict at home. 'If regular, broad outlets are not created' to cope with 'the overproduction of German labour', ran one typical forecast, 'we shall move with giant strides towards a socialist revolution'.[3] Some liked to use the analogy of 'safety-valves', comparing Germany's internal development to an 'overheated boiler'. The President of the German Colonial Association (*Deutscher Kolonialverein*) of 1882, Prince Hermann zu Hohenlohe-Langenburg, was convinced 'that we in Germany cannot combat the danger of social democracy any more effectively' than by the acquisition of colonies. Apart from the direct economic advantages to be gained, the intensive agitation for colonies also promised 'greater security against communism' as a consequence of overseas expansion. The connection between economic prosperity and a situation of internal social stability was always present in the minds of the exponents of this ideological consensus.

It was also in Bismarck's mind when, encouraged by the favourable international situation and confident of success in view of the state of the economy, the existing ideological climate and the *Reichstag* election results of 1884, he combined his foreign trade policy, which had been building up over the years, with his methods for stabilising the domestic situation, and augmented them with a colonial policy. In a short space of time between 1884 and 1886 Germany acquired its 'protectorates' in South-West Africa, Togoland, the Cameroons, East Africa and the Pacific. Originally intended to be run by private syndicates enjoying the state's protection, they had almost all become Crown colonies by 1889. This was because the interested parties had balked at the initial costs involved and had expected the state to take over the expense of improving the infrastructure as well as provide protection against foreign competition. In any case, rebellions inevitably led to military interventions which involved the state. Apart from Samoa in the Pacific and Kiao-chow, with its 'protected zone', in China, little was added to the German Empire's first colonial acquisitions. Small parts of its African territories were gained later by way of concessionary agreements. Even in the 1880s the setting up of formal colonial rule would probably not have come about, had it not been for the intense competition from Germany's rivals who were advancing into the world's markets because of similar pressures. The advantages of an 'informal empire' were ever-present in Bismarck's thinking throughout his political life. In this respect, the 'Congo free-trade zone' and China's 'open door' corresponded most with his own ideas. But, caught between the pincers of international pressures and international competition, he decided to follow a policy of establishing protectorates which soon ended up becoming colonies of the German Empire. However, by virtue of his exceptional authority, he was still in a position to stem any dangerous overflow of the drive for colonial expansion which might provoke direct conflict with Britain or France. This was shown quite clearly, for example, in his refusal to establish protectorates over certain areas and in his opposition to the idea of a Central African Empire (*Mittelafrika*), as proposed by Carl Peters and his Society for German Colonisation (*Gesellschaft für deutsche Kolonisation*) of 1882. This attitude, however, made him powerful political enemies at home who appreciably strengthened the coalition of forces which prepared the ground for his dismissal. His successors proved incapable of continuing to play the role of lion-tamer as effectively as he had done, especially when the antagonisms within Germany's class society increased and confronted them with problems for which the growth of the SPD was only the visible sign.

6.2 *Wilhelmine 'world policy' as domestic policy*

As events soon revealed, not only had the economic imperialism of the 1880s pointed the way for future developments to take, but the social imperialist technique of government began to determine the shape of things to come. Henceforth, imperial policy continually and deliberately fell back on the latter, once Caprivi's uphill struggle of partially adjusting economic conditions to the realities of Germany's industrial development had been thwarted by the agrarians. Miquel's *Sammlung* rested, as he himself said in 1897, on diverting 'revolutionary elements' towards imperialism, in order to turn the nation's gaze 'abroad' and bring 'its sentiments . . . on to common ground'. This functional advantage of social imperialism was also part of Holstein's thinking (from the 1880s) when he argued that 'the government of Kaiser Wilhelm II needs a tangible success abroad which will have an effect at home. This success can come about only as the result of a European war, a world historical (*weltgeschichtlich*) gamble, or else some acquisition outside Europe'.[4] Between 1897 and 1900, by acquiring Kiao-chow in the Shantung Treaty, German policy in China took account of these strategic considerations, as did the emerging naval construction programme. This sort of thinking was also clearly in evidence among the so-called 'liberal imperialists' like Friedrich Naumann, Max Weber, Ernst von Halle (Tirpitz's chief propagandist) and the political scientist, Ernst Francke, to name but a few. A successful social policy alongside an increase in parliamentary influence would make it possible to conduct a powerful *Weltpolitik* by first satisfying the workers. In this case internal reform would underpin imperialism as the main priority, for the integration of the social classes was seen as the prerequisite of strength abroad. *Weltpolitik* would, moreover, facilitate an effective social policy through tangible material concessions. Successes abroad were expected to lead to a kind of truce on the home fronts. Admittedly, these Liberals did not participate in the decision-making processes of the German monarchy; but they did lend their support to the expansionist programme to which Berlin was committed.

The true significance of Wilhelmine 'world policy' can, it seems, be appreciated only if viewed from the perspective of social imperialism. Its precipitate character should not obscure the fact that it was based on the deliberate and calculated use of foreign policy as an instrument for achieving domestic political ends. Whenever concrete economic interests were not involved, the prestige element figured even more prominently than ever. As the professor of law at Freiburg University, Hermann Rehm, said with considerable foresight in 1900, 'only the idea of Germany as a world power is capable of dispelling the conflicts between rival economic interests in internal affairs'.[5] The problem was not just one of overcoming conflicts by means of *Sammlung* policy, but as much a matter concerning rights of political participation and social equality for the workers, against whose political representatives it was easy to mobilise a 'pro-Empire' imperialism after 1884. In view of the nation's internal fragmentation into a class society and the strong tensions between, on the one hand, the authoritarian state, the ruling élite of landowners and the feudalised bourgeoisie, and, on the other, the advancing forces of parliamentarisation and democratisation, it seemed to the Berlin politicians, operating within their own horizon of experience, that there was no alternative to the 'taming' policy of social imperialism in terms of the success it promised. From their defensive positions they no longer wanted to — nor could they — modernise Germany's social and political constitution to the extent required. It was this seeming lack of any alternative which proved to be the decisive factor, and a most unfortunate one at that; for it was not left to their free decision, as many have argued since, to exercise moderate restraints by scaling down Germany's overseas involvement. As a result of Germany's social and political tensions, there was a constant pressure from within the system to fall back repeatedly on the proven technique of social imperialism. To this extent, von Waldersee hit the nail on the head when he set his hopes on 'a foreign policy' which would have 'a positive effect on internal conditions', and thought it 'a sign of malaise that we cannot help ourselves out of the situation through our domestic policy'. Surveying the situation from his position at the centre of decision-making machinery Bülow also insisted that 'only a successful foreign policy' could 'help, reconcile, calm, rally and unite'.[6]

All this serves to emphasise the objective function of Wilhelmine world policy's frantic and hazardous desire to be 'part of the action'. It also throws light on the avowed purpose of Germany's decision-makers and, thus, their conscious intentions. Shortly before the outbreak of war in 1914, Bülow, for example, showed unsurpassed candour in setting out the detailed arguments for this 'vigorous national policy' in his widely-read book, *German Policy. Weltpolitik* was presented as the 'true antidote against social democracy'. This amounted to an admission that the way of domestic reform was bankrupt. At the very least, it implied the abandonment of attempts to establish a modern society of freely participating citizens.[7] From the 1880s onwards, social imperialism remained embedded in German politics as a pattern of political behaviour. With the abrupt transition from Bismarck's Bonapartist rule to the polycracy of the Wilhelmine era, 'the tendency grew to neutralise' the inherited 'deep discrepancy between the social structure and a political order which had hardly taken account of the changed social situation since the industrial revolution'. This was done by 'diverting internal pressures outwards in a social imperialist fashion' which concealed 'the long overdue reform of Germany's internal structure'.[8] Can one find a more convincing interpretation than this of German 'world policy' as domestic policy? Or, to put it differently, of 'world policy' as a continuation of the defence of the domestic *status quo* in the world arena?

One thing should, nevertheless, be noted: however clearly this social imperialism represented in functional terms a conservative response to the challenge of the problems posed by a class society and its anachronistic distribution of power, it should not be reduced solely to its manipulatory element. Economic interests in a narrow sense almost always played their part and helped justify overseas expansion. While Germany's China policy after 1897 certainly provided an opportunity for brilliant moves on the chessboard of domestic politics, the Shanting Treaty, which arranged the 'lease' of Kiao-chow, also secured one of China's richest provinces for German economic penetration. It gave heavy industry and an ailing railway construction industry at home the prospect of a share in the opening-up of the massive Asian market. We cannot ignore the political aspects of the Berlin–Baghdad Railway scheme either; but it also provided tempting opportunities for specific economic interests which were always served by this kind of expansion. If the political leadership often pushed economic interests to the fore, exaggerated their importance and formally egged on businessmen into entering agreements, the state soon followed in their footsteps once they had acquired importance and influence abroad. If one narrows down the question to determining the relative importance of the different factors which motivated imperialist expansion, and attempts the same regarding the decisions that were made, the conclusion will be that the element of social imperialism was either dominant or at least of equal importance alongside economic factors prior to 1914. In the final phase of Imperial Germany's expansionist policy, namely the formulation of its war aims in the First World War, social imperialism again assumed prime importance.

6.3 *Social Darwinism and pan-Germanism as imperialist ideologies*

In his *Principles of Realpolitik*, published in 1853, Ludwig August von Rochau recommended contemporaries to adjust to the existing realities of the new configuration of interests in the post-revolutionary era. Nevertheless, he admitted that 'ideas . . . have always had as much power as their holders care to vest in them. Therefore, the idea that . . . inspires an entire people or epoch is the most substantial of all political forces'.[9] One such idea, often said to have possessed this power during the age of Western imperialism, was Social Darwinism: the transfer to the social and political sphere of Darwin's biological theories of 'natural selection' and 'the survival of the fittest' in 'the struggle for existence'. After the 1870s and 1880s this Social Darwinism spread throughout the Western industrialised nations where it exerted a considerable influence before reaching its apogee in the radical racialist theories of National Socialism. It provides the historian with an excellent example of the indissoluble interconnection of influential ideas with social development, and an ideological critique is particularly suitable for placing Social Darwinism into this context.

Marx and Engels grasped the connection early on. In 1862 Marx commented: 'It is noticeable that Darwin recognises among plants and animals his own English society, with its division of labour, competition, opening-up of new markets, "inventions" and the Malthusian "struggle for existence". It is Hobbes's *bellum omnium contra omnes*, and it reminds one of Hegel's *Phenomenology*, where bourgeois society figures as "spiritual animal kingdom", while with Darwin the animal kingdom figures as bourgeois society.' 'The whole Darwinian theory of the struggle for existence', Engels wrote in the mid-1870s, 'is simply the transference from society to animate nature of Hobbes's theory of *bellum omnium contra omnes* and the bourgeois economic theory of competition, as well as the Malthusian theory of population. Once this feat has been accomplished . . . it is very easy to transfer these theories back again from natural history to the history of society, and altogether too naïve to maintain that thereby these assertions have been proved as eternal natural laws of society.' Like Nietzsche and Spengler after them, both men recognised in Social Darwinism an eminently suitable 'system for justifying bourgeois capitalism' (H. Plessner).[10] In addition, they set out a framework for its analysis which can scarcely be improved upon even today.

By reading Malthus, who as an amateur natural historian believed he had deduced his ideas from nature, both Darwin and the biologist, A.R. Wallace (whose researches led Darwin to publish his *Origin of Species*), were inspired at a psychologically critical stage in their work into developing their own theories of evolution. It cannot be said that these evolved purely from their own findings. Darwin, who stood Malthus on his head, himself became the first Social Darwinist when he advanced the rise of the so-called 'Aryan race' in Europe and particularly the United States, as conclusive proof of the validity of his theories as applied to human society. It could even be said that he openly prepared the way for a racialist interpretation of Social Darwinism.[11] No doubt this world-view (*Weltanschauung*) based on the circular conclusions of Malthus and Darwin through to a vulgarised version of Social Darwinism, which presented itself as a summit of scientific reasoning, struck a responsive chord in providing a justification for bourgeois economic activity and the competitive capitalist system, the absolutism of the entrepreneur and national self-assertiveness. As a manifestation of the decline of positivism, it banished hopes for a more open society and put the fixed laws of an anti-egalitàrian system of a social aristocracy in its place. Its functional significance lay in the fact that it enabled the ruling élites to appear compatible with progress, while providing a justification for the immutability of the *status quo*. At the same time, it allowed the emancipatory aspirations of the workers or colonial peoples to be dismissed as the futile protestations of inferior subjects in the struggle for existence. Vested with an aura of 'irrefutable' scientific knowledge, it was this versatility of application that gave Social Darwinism its power in its very real connection with the ruling interests. As an ideology which proved virtually ideal for justifying imperialism, it was kept alive by a host of popularisers in the industrialised nations. If one were to remove it from its specific social context, it could be evaluated as an independent factor. But this would lead only to its being seen as a mere distortion of pure science and would fail to account for its social impact.

Similarly, pan-Germanism can be seen as a variation of attempts to justify imperialist expansion, and one that drew increasingly on racialist theories for this purpose. A weed like this could only flourish in such lurid colours in a specific social environment. The processes of economic concentration and social polarisation were to some extent reflected in the 'preferential position befitting one's own nation'. Economic progress and the subjugation of overseas territories seemed attributable to the 'special natural qualities' of the nation, 'that is, its racial characteristics'. At any rate, enormous claims were made on the basis of this belief. Racist pan-Germanism, which would 'cure' the world (Paul Rohrbach), gave rise to a pseudo-scientific 'concealed justification' for ongoing expansion. It demanded sacrifice for the sake of a 'higher common interest' — that of a Teutonic world mission. The originally circumscribed idea of the 'nation' was placed 'in the service' of these new goals as 'a propelling force', within the blurred parameters of which everyone from a banker like von der Heydt to a rabid nationalist schoolteacher, from a swaggering soldier to a middle-class enthusiast of colonialism, could project his own aspirations.[12] Although it has not yet proved possible to demonstrate conclusively that pan-Germanism had a direct influence on Berlin's political decision-making machinery, it was an important factor in the public opinion of groups loyal to the Empire. For political reasons it was very rarely criticised by the government. It flourished mainly in the upper and middle classes who had a strong influence on public opinion and received its main backing from their militant organisations like the Pan–German League, the Navy League and the Army League. Without doubt it was one of the poisonous ingredients in that ideological mishmash which later propelled the *völkisch* nationalists and whose extremism was supposed to make good its obvious intellectual inferiority.

7. Foreign Policy

7.1 *Foreign policy in the system of states*

Germany's emergence as a Great Power in Central Europe between 1866 and 1871 encountered no serious objections from either Russia or Great Britain. It might almost be said that they 'allowed' it to come into being. The new German Empire took up its position in the existing international system, whereupon the other states responded by adjusting themselves to the new arrangement with moves and counter-moves in keeping with the system's traditionally competitive structure. The position approaching hegemony which Imperial Germany attained in terms of political and economic strength was played down by Bismarck in his claim that Germany had reached 'saturation' point. However, the fact that within the space of a few years Berlin had become the venue for the most important international conferences of the time clearly showed how the centre of gravity had shifted. As in a system of interconnecting pipes, the equivalent in the external sphere of Bismarck's socially conservative 'taming' policy at home was, after 1871, a policy of inertia on the European stage aimed at consolidating what had been gained. If the continued existence of the Bismarckian Empire was not to be jeopardised again by a militant foreign policy of calculated risk like that of 1864 to 1871 — and this was completely ruled out by the conservative priority of preserving the system — three possible strategies were left for Berlin to follow. The aim was still one of diverting 'the ominous consequences' of the German Empire's creation 'into the international sphere' while bringing about an equilibrium in the initially 'unsettled situation among the concert of powers' at the same time as preserving the 'outmoded social order'.[1]

Firstly, it would be possible to follow the traditional principle of reaching agreement on defining spheres of influence in order to avoid or reduce friction with rival powers. Secondly, the precarious possibility existed of playing off the interests of one Great Power against the other and of diverting these rivalries to the geographical periphery of Germany's sphere of influence or into imperialist expansion. Thirdly, potential enemies could be countered with quick pre-emptive strikes, thus nipping prospective alliances in the bud. This could well conjure up the danger of these very alliances being formed from a fear of being threatened by Germany at some point in the future. For this reason, the third possibility was never considered by Germany's leaders for over forty years because of the unforeseeable risks involved, though after Moltke's time this option was often advocated by the military. The two other strategies did play their part. As is well known, Bismarck tried for years to put into practice his idea of diverting competing interests to the periphery. This thinking runs like a thread through his endorsement of French colonial policy in North Africa and Indo-China to his position on the problem of Egypt and the conflict of interest between Russia and Britain in Central Asia. His favoured tactic became risky, however, when Germany's interest in a programme of overseas expansion increased, i.e. when the social imperialist character of Wilhelmine 'world policy' virtually dictated the necessity of constant foreign involvement. Since German foreign policy soon lost its static character imposed by the notion of 'saturation', this tactic could be in the nature of only a temporary expedient. The carving out of permanent geographical spheres of interest was essentially frustrated by forces at work within Germany itself. Scarcely had half a dozen years passed since 1871 before it became clear that an expanding industrial capitalism was giving the lie from within to all the claims that Germany had reached a state of 'saturation'. While it is true that no new territorial claims in Europe were officially envisaged, the dynamism of industrial development took no account of national frontiers. The qualitative change in Germany's foreign trade interests which had come about during the period of advanced industrialisation introduced a disturbing factor into foreign policy which the traditionalists in the *Wilhelmstrasse*, accustomed to thinking in national terms, probably underestimated. The Austro-German negotiations of 1878 and 1879, which finally produced the Dual Alliance in October 1879, revolved at first around the larger issue of a projected customs union which would have created a massive Central European bloc as a domestic market for German industry. Until the caesura of 1887, Russo-German relations reflected these economic problems, as did Germany's growing involvement in the Balkans. Early German imperialism, protective tariffs, Caprivi's trade agreements, and so on, all demonstrated each in their own way the continuing and apparently unstoppable involvement of Germany in the world economy and its markets. Compared with this reality, the relatively static concept of Germany as a 'satiated' state soon showed itself to be wholly inappropriate.

The overall defensive strategy which combined social conservatism at home with a foreign policy of avoiding conflict abroad was exposed to constant erosion from the end of the 1870s onwards. This cannot be put down primarily to the other participants in the international system or to mistakes and miscalculations by their leaders. The erosion was, as the last six years of the Bismarck period already seemed to demonstrate, a logical outcome of Germany's internal social and economic problems together with the need to redefine its main areas of interest. As outlined above, German imperialism can be seen on the one hand as a defensive strategy in domestic politics. On the other hand, it introduced an aggressive component into Germany's foreign relations. This ambivalence can be observed on more than one occasion. Indeed, the Janus-faced character of such intentions and actions are virtually the hall-mark of the period after 1879. They can be adequately explained only by an analysis of what Kehr called 'the home front' of foreign policy. To use makeshift phrases like 'basic power politics' comes nowhere near to explaining the real problem. What additional light does this

approach throw on the subject? Does it imply the existence of a
dubious 'ideal type' of political behaviour or a similarly dubious
socio-psychic constant which defines the enjoyment and exercise of
power — as in Hobbes's 'restless desire for power after power' — as
a primordial instinct, in short an anthropological factor? Should we
not rather investigate class-based systems of social values and
norms, processes of political socialisation and uses of stereotyped
language, in whose ciphers are contained beliefs and unconscious
assumptions, with a view to laying bare the different conceptions of
power held by the various social groups? Should the concept of
'power' not be set as precisely as possible in its social context, i.e. in
the web of interests surrounding it? Should we not try to discover the
functional nexus of structures embodying political domination, so
that this ahistorical notion of 'basic power politics', which is allegedly not subject to change, may be replaced as soon as possible by
an analysis of how it manifests itself in concrete situations, thus
rendering the term superfluous? The concern for 'the eternal recurrence of the identical' (Nietzsche) in history, implicit in the idea of a
'basic' power instinct, may fascinate the behavioural scientist. If,
however, the historian contents himself with this kind of termino-
logical shorthand, he fails to undertake an investigation into its
concrete manifestations and produce a systematic explanation of it
in a framework of historical theory. It is worthwhile, therefore,
taking serious note of the judgement of a man who can hardly be
accused of prejudice when approaching this subject: 'One will not
become acquainted with the world', said Leopold von Ranke, 'if one
cares to take only internal relationships into account. We note the
external ones as well, but then only as secondary. They are tran-
sient, the former are enduring'.[2]

7.2   *Foreign policy under the 'primacy of domestic politics'*

The unstable mechanics of foreign policy, its anaemic kinetics of
action and reaction and diplomatic procedures for the avoidance of
conflict or its escalation, are deliberately not pursued in this enquiry. A wealth of literature awaits anyone who, for example, wishes
to learn more about the Bismarckian system of alliances or Wilhelmine diplomacy. The configurations of forces behind these alliances
at any particular time lead us directly back to the primary 'enduring' conditions — that is, back to 'the primacy of domestic politics'.
This can be shown by a cursory look at the problems which influenced Germany's relations with the three Great Powers: France,

Great Britain and Russia.

France The decision to annex Alsace-Lorraine in 1870 rested on a variety of motives. Domestic political considerations, in the broadest sense, together with military demands were far more important than the general notion of improving Germany's strategic position and external security *vis-à-vis* a traditionally more powerful France. The separation of these regions from France was carried out against the will of the vast majority of their inhabitants and permanently damaged Franco-German relations. To some extent the return of the 'imperial province' to France was still an aim behind the fighting in the First World War forty-five years later. In view of its fateful consequences for foreign policy, it would have been sensible to have revised the decision of 1870–71. However, this would have been suicidal in its effect on Germany's domestic politics. These consequences were immediately recognised. The argument that the annexation had been necessary in order to provide a 'material guarantee' against future French aggression was dismissed by Marx in the autumn of 1870 as a pretext for 'the feeble-minded'. He saw that in military terms the campaign of 1870 had shown the ease with which France could be attacked from German territory. German history itself, from the time after the Treaty of Tilsit, testified to how a defeated nation would react to dismemberment of its territory. Was it not an utter 'anachronism', he asked, 'to make military considerations the principle by which the boundaries of nations are to be determined?' Austria would then have been justified in claiming the line of the Mincio, and France the left bank of the Rhine. 'If boundaries are to be determined by military interests, there will be no end to claims raised, because every line drawn by the military is necessarily faulty and can be improved by annexing some more outlying territory; and, moreover, they can never be fixed finally and fairly, because they are always forcibly imposed on the vanquished by the victor, and so already carry within them the seeds of a new war.' The taking of Alsace-Lorraine, Marx concluded, would virtually turn war into a 'European institution', since France, even after a sham peace which could at best be only a truce, would demand the return of its lost eastern provinces. That meant perpetuating war between two of the great European nations and their ruin as a result of 'reciprocal self-mutilation'. Until then, he feared, Prusso-Germany's 'military despotism' would stiffen in order to maintain its hold on Western Poland. What was decisive in Marx's view was the spread of conflict to the east. He saw this prospect as 'unavoidable', since 'the war of 1870 carried a war between Germany and Russia in its womb just as surely as the war of 1866 had carried that of 1870'. There was no doubt that Germany would have to defend its conquests, either as 'the obvious lackey of Russian aggrandisement', or else by arming itself 'not for one of those half-baked "localised" wars, but for a racial war against the allied races of the Slavs and Latins'. And in such a war on two fronts against a Franco-Russian alliance the German Empire would go under.[3]

Few predictions of this clear-sighted critic living in his London exile were to be realised as fully as this one. Apart from Marx, only the Baltic German writer, Julius von Eckhardt, recognised in a similarly sceptical vein and at an early juncture, the problems of assimilation posed by the 'imperial province', the permanent hostility of neighbouring states armed to the teeth and the danger signs of a Franco-Russian alliance. Bismarck might for a time rely on the slogan, as brutal as it was foolish, of 'let them hate me as long as they fear me'; or issue the directive: 'In everything that does *not* concern Alsace, I should like a conciliatory approach towards France.'[4] But his was not the way to heal the breach, and already during the 1880s even the high-ranking German military shared the criticisms that were levelled against the annexation of 1870. They deplored the 'European quandary' they had got themselves into as a result of conquering Alsace-Lorraine, since it had established 'a permanent state of war between France and Germany'. As early as 1892, Moltke feared a war on two fronts, and five years before the conclusion of the Franco-Russian military agreement of 1872 Bismarck admitted to the Prussian Minister of War 'that in the not too distant future we shall have to face a war against both France and Russia simultaneously'. It was going to be 'a war of survival'.[5] This was how, seventeen years after the annexation, and twenty-seven years before the outbreak of the First World War, Bismarck described the dangerous long-term effects of the decision of 1870.

The suggestion was often made from a variety of different quarters that the problem of Alsace-Lorraine, which prevented an improvement in Franco-German relations — thus jeopardising the peace of Europe — should at least be neutralised. There was talk of this in the press, in the *Reichstag*, where Wilhelm Liebknecht took up the subject, and even in a diplomatic démarche from Vienna in 1897. But just as French nationalism rejected any compromise after the turn of the century, insisting on the return of the provinces, so in Germany any questioning of the *status quo* on this matter was taboo. In 1905, after the first Moroccan crisis had passed, the Chief of the

General Staff, von Schlieffen, soberly worked out the alternatives. Germany had either to fight a preventive war against France or finally come up with a new settlement for Alsace-Lorraine. No other options were open to imperial policy.[6] Since Berlin never seriously considered finding a new *modus vivendi* with France, the alternatives were narrowed down even further at a critical point in time. There was now only one possible option.

Great Britain The persistent legend of the British Empire as 'perfidious Albion', following Germany's development after 1871 with suspicion and intrigue until it achieved the latter's 'encirclement', has long obscured the fact that it was Berlin that first rejected serious cooperation and then made it simply impossible. Certainly, the deep-seated antagonisms that existed during the nineteenth century between the British and Russian world empires, between the whale and the bear, were a constant factor which always had to be taken account of in the design of German foreign policy. Nevertheless, Germany's freedom of action in the late nineteenth century became considerably broader in scope, as the period 1884 to 1889 testifies. More important, however, than these antagonisms or any geopolitical considerations was the fear felt before 1890 by Bismarck and the 'strategic clique' around him of the liberalising repercussions that might result from any Anglo-German cooperation. It was not trade rivalry, which became apparent only gradually, that proved to be the most important factor here. It was the contrasting political values of the two countries — that is, their quite different historical traditions, political cultures and their underlying social configurations. The historical alternative to Germany's Bonapartist semi-dictatorship and rule by pre-industrial oligarchies was, in the first instance, a parliamentary monarchy, regardless of whether its character was determined by 'National' and/or 'Progressive' Liberals. The Constitutional Conflict and the strength of the National Liberals in the early 1870s meant that, unpredictable obstacles aside, a transition to a parliamentary monarchy could become a reality. Neither Bismarck nor the Liberals could rule out the possibility. The latter could still count on widespread support in the towns of South Germany and west of the Elbe, as the election results of 1881 and 1884 testified. We need only speculate on a few of the possible consequences which might have resulted from Crown Prince Friedrich taking over the government after the two assassination attempts on his father, Wilhelm I, to realise how unstable the balance of power was in Berlin. Whatever one makes of hypothetical

questions of this kind, Bismarck took political liberalism seriously as
an opposition force, along with the imponderables that could work
in its favour, for example, the Anglophile sympathies of the Crown
Prince and his English wife, the continuous object lesson provided
by English parliamentary life, and the symbiosis of the English
landed aristocracy and the commercial and industrial middle classes,
so different from Germany. These were the straightforward factors
which, if there were a closer association between the two countries,
would be predictable but extremely difficult to control. At the
beginning of the 1880s 'the Crown Prince hadn't become ill yet',
Herbert von Bismarck is reputed to have said. 'We had to be
prepared for a long reign, during which English influences would
dominate'; by which he meant the so-called 'English intimacy'
resulting from Crown Princess Victoria's presence in Berlin and the
threat of a liberal prime minister in the style of Gladstone emerging
in Germany. In view of 'our internal situation', Bismarck thought
this worrying.[7] The Chancellor himself is reported to have had a
conversation with Ambassador von Schweinitz in which, like his
son, he considered occasional political friction with Britain necessary 'to keep alive German annoyance with England'. This would
inhibit 'the influence of British ideas of constitutionalism and liberalism in Germany'.[8] What Bismarck hated about Gladstone was not
just that he stuck to his principles and believed that politics served
moral ends. He also saw in him, quite rightly, a great rival counterpart representing a bourgeois liberalism that was much closer to the
people and more in keeping with the powerful currents of the age.
Bismarck would not, therefore, allow Anglo-German relations to
develop beyond a certain point, namely that of a restrained coëxist-
ence which appeared compatible with conflict of a limited nature.
And if the sheer presence of the vast Russian Empire on Germany's
eastern border appeared to justify his adopting this stance, it was
more the result of the shared conservatism of the eastern monarchies
and the Tsarist autocracy than any consideration of it as a potential
power factor. As for the legitimising effects of political traditions, the
keeping of a conscious distance from London was part and parcel of
Bismarck's strategy during his period of office, as was the Anglopho-
bia that resulted from conflicting colonial interests between 1884
and 1889.

In the 1890s, commercial rivalry in the world's markets increased
dramatically. Above all, German policy embarked on a collision
course with Britain's vital interests when the decision was taken to
expand the battle-fleet. From the time of the first Supplementary

Navy Bill of 1900, there was no doubt as to Germany's aims, with their sometimes openly declared, sometimes carefully concealed, aggressive intent. Nor was there any inclination in London to meet this new danger with a trusting naïveté. Germany's naval policy was too unmistakably bound up with the image of 'the enemy across the Channel' for the British to sit back and wait for things to happen. Bearing in mind the domestic political dimensions of the 'Tirpitz-Plan', as well as the German decision not merely to yield to the international trend of battleship-building but, without cause from London, to arm against Britain on such a massive, concentrated scale, we can see how Germany's moves on the chess-board determined the rules of the game up to 1914.

Russia   As for Russia, there were of course the social and ideological factors of the 'monarchical principle' common to both countries, as well as the bond uniting the accomplices in the Polish partitions. Together these created certain affinities. But political, military and economic interests advised caution on the part of German policy with regard to its massive neighbour in the east. The expansion of Greater Prussia between 1864 and 1871 had been allowed to proceed, partly owing to Russia's acquiescence. 'That the Russians let us take Alsace-Lorraine', Bismarck admitted, 'was directly due to Alexander II's personal policy.'[9] Export considerations and the General Staff's planning also induced a policy of cooperation with the least possible friction. But friction was never far from the surface. The disappointment which the outcome of the Congress of Berlin meant for St Petersburg's policy was blamed, perhaps too one-sidedly, on the 'honest broker' of the *Wilhelmstrasse*. The German tariffs on agricultural produce, in force after January 1880, directly affected Russian grain exports which had already been forced to fight hard for the lion's share of the German market following the arrival in Europe of American wheat. In 1885 Germany's tariffs were trebled. In March 1887 they were almost doubled again. German agricultural protectionism with its inevitable, indeed conscious, anti-Russian intentions, reflected the social configuration of forces in Germany since the end of the 1870s and was seen as an unavoidable necessity by the leadership. Its impact on Russia was painful for the following reason: the first steps towards modernising the Tsarist Empire after the débâcle of the Crimean War were increasingly dependent upon the country's successful industrialisation. The financing of this came largely from the proceeds of Russia's agricultural exports. To the extent, however, that high tariff walls made access to the neighbouring, receptive German market extremly difficult within the space of a few years, one of the main props of Russia's intended modernisation — and with it all the hopes of the Tsarist oligarchy in its internal and external affairs — began to totter. A growing Germanophobia, which German diplomats could not avoid noticing, was accurately put down to 'the question of grain tariffs'. Yet Germany's internal power relationships ruled out the possibility of any reversal of Bismarck's policy, despite the explosive effect it was having abroad.

Worse still, six months after the third tariff increase, Bismarck's government delivered a serious blow to the second prop of Russia's early industrial modernisation programme. Lacking liquid capital of its own, Russia depended essentially on capital from foreign sources. By 1887 the German money market had come to occupy a key position. At a time when savings bank deposits in Prussia amounted to no more than 2.2 billion marks, between 2 and 2.5 billion marks' worth of Russian securities were in German hands. In November 1887, however, a virtual ban was placed on trading in Russian securities on the Berlin stock exchange. Bills of exchange were no longer honoured and Russian stocks were no longer recognised as guaranteed, safe investments. This led to a panic on the Berlin stock exchange, resulting in a massive drain of funds to Paris where some of the French banks took on most of the Russian government securities. This meant that Berlin itself partly laid the economic foundations of the Franco-Russian alliance. Thus, a financial war broke out on top of the tensions over agricultural tariffs at a time when Russia, after 1890, was on the brink of its own industrial revolution. This meant that, in a phase when its need for capital was almost without limit, only the way to Paris remained open. The City of London was closed to Russian loans and an abandonment of the Tsar's modernisation programme was no longer politically possible.

Several of the factors behind this ruthless German policy concerning the movement of capital can be identified as belonging to conventional, foreign policy practice. Bismarck's drastic medicine was supposed to dampen down a pan-Slavism which appeared belligerent, but was doubtless exaggerated. It was also intended to undermine the Francophiles in St Petersburg, thus strengthening the Germanophiles, by a drastic demonstration of the importance of Germany's friendship. Finally, there was the idea of discouraging Russia's expansionist policy in the Balkans which conflicted with Austrian interests. It was a case of 'consistently' holding down 'Russia's credit' in order 'to calm down its belligerence, and, if possible, counteract its effects'. At least this was how the harsh measures were defended by the Russophobe Secretary of State at the Berlin Foreign Office.[10]

However, this readiness to take on the undeniable and unpredictable risks of 'brinkmanship' in foreign trade relations was more the result of factors stemming from the domestic political situation. The massive economic interests of the East Elbian grain producers and the accompanying social and political concerns of the land-owning stratum demanded agricultural protection. But they also deemed it necessary to exclude their Russian competitors from the German money market which was helping to finance railway construction in Western Russia. This was a development which also aroused the fears of the military. For its part, export-orientated industry had long since declared that retaliatory measures against Russian import duties were long overdue, since these had been rapidly increasing ever since 1877. German exports to Russia fell by half between 1880 and 1887, from a 24 per cent share of Germany's total foreign trade in 1875 to only 5 per cent in 1885. The two crucially important interest groups within the conservative *Sammlung* policy could be tied even more closely to Bismarck's government as a result of increased tariffs. At the same time, the crisis in Russo-German relations, together with the fabricated danger of a war with France, worked politically to ensure the safe passage through parliament of the proposed increase in army strength, approved in November 1887 by the so-called 'cartel *Reichstag*'. Bismarck, to be sure, opposed those who advocated a 'preventive' winter campaign by Germany in the east with his categorical refusal to contemplate any attack of this kind, arguing that 'we can . . . only lose and shall gain nothing'. But the economic cold war also had the effect of weakening these demands, by showing Bismarck's readiness for concessions to the hard-liners.[11] Thus we can discern the overall strategy which united both domestic and foreign policy. And we can also see the aggressive consequences of measures taken for the defence of the *status quo*; for in these was expressed the dialectic of the conservative Utopia. Anachronistic power relationships were so unconditionally preserved that 'the very means which Bismarck employed to preserve the peace . . . ' became a factor which 'contributed to threatening the peace'.[12] Regardless of whether the Chancellor might have originally trusted himself to correct a manoeuvre leading once more to a collision with Russia, or whether he believed it possible to separate foreign policy from foreign trade relations, the effects were to prove extremely unfortunate after 1887. Instead of providing the stopgap moratorium of the Reinsurance Treaty with the only possible firm economic base the intransigence of the agrarians would permit, namely Russia's reliance on the German capital market, Berlin itself placed the seal of success on the negotiations for the Franco-Russian alliance. German policy not only increased the danger of a war on two fronts; it practically guaranteed it. In 1887 the points were set for 1894 and 1914. It seemed that the chief priority of maintaining the social and political system, as defined by Berlin, permitted no other possible alternative. Over and above this, the decisions of 1887 and their consequences prevented any possibility of the Russian market's becoming the great continental alternative to overseas imperialism for the export of manufactured goods and capital. From now on this route was barred.

8. The First World War: escape forwards

During the Weimar years after the First World War, a passionate debate took place in Germany, in which almost every German historian of note attempted to refute the moral and legal accusations of war guilt contained in Article 231 of the Treaty of Versailles. In the 'July crisis' of 1914, so the argument ran, the German Empire had acted in self-defence, especially in the face of the advancing Russian 'steam-roller'. Later, through no fault of its own policies during the war, it finally succumbed to the superior might of its enemies. The view which gained most acceptance in the 1930s, particularly in English and American research, was that all the European capitals, Berlin among them, shared equal responsibility for the breakdown in diplomacy in 1914. This comforting opinion, which removed the burden of sole responsibility, was put forward with some effect in the voluminous narratives of von Wegerer, Fay, Renouvin and others. No critical research on the subject was possible under National Socialism, and the excesses of the Nazi dictatorship raised more urgent problems for historical research in the immediate period after 1945. It was not until 1961 that the work of the Hamburg historian, Fritz Fischer, appeared, entitled *Germany's Bid for World Power* (*Griff nach der Weltmacht*, now translated as *Germany's Aims in the First World War*). As a massive critique of the conduct of Germany's leaders in the summer of 1914 and their uncompromising war aims policy up to 1918, it provoked an acrimonious discussion. Although Fischer's thesis that, as in 1939, Germany bore the main share of guilt in 1914 was open to various criticisms on both theoretical and empirical grounds, the strident, venomous, nationalistic tone adopted by most of his critics showed it was high time that the taboos on this subject from the inter-war period were finally dispelled. Once the initial excitement had died down, two opposing schools of thought confronted each other. The first insisted not only on the accuracy of Fischer's overall criticisms, but accepted that Germany had deliberately prepared, and indeed planned for war in the years before 1914. Its protagonists argued that a continuity of aggression had existed thoughout the entire period of the German Empire's existence. The other side, while gradually conceding a great deal, insisted on drawing a distinction between vague expressions of opinion, not necessarily involving any form of commitment, and consciously taken political decisions; between calculations made in peacetime and the actual implementation of plans in wartime; between expansive imperialist aims and a fictitious monolithic unanimity. In the final analysis they stressed the defensive character of the political decisions made in Germany at the time.[1]

8.1 *Aggressive policies of defence*

Neither of these two schools, whose positions are simplified here to highlight their differences, can provide a definitive explanatory model which adequately accounts for the peculiar blend of aggressive and defensive elements in the making of German policy. There can be no serious doubt about the 'will to become a world power' which was shared by the bourgeoisie and influential sections of the old ruling élites and which became increasingly evident after the 1880s. But showing a determination to belong to the small circle of Great Powers in the international political system, is a long step away from planning to unleash a war long in advance. It is also too hasty a conclusion and one which empirical studies have not yet verified. As for Germany's expansionist aims in 1914, it is necessary to distinguish clearly between formal and informal influences. For example, the active involvement of German firms and German banks in French industry gave rise to a specific web of interests; but this had no direct relevance for plans involving annexation. True, there was excited talk here and there about acquiring France's ore deposits in the Longwy-Briey basin, or of the need to take over Antwerp's port installations. Pan-German spokesmen demanded the annexation of the Flemish part of Belgium. But it is a myth that, as a result, war was deliberately planned and engineered by the

German decision-makers on the strength of such demands. True, much was writen before 1914 about carving up the Ottoman Empire — a *cause célèbre* going as far back as the Crimean War. But, like other governments, Berlin did not want to be the first to burn its fingers on this particular iron. True, there were vague, and sometimes not so vague, ideas for a Central European customs union (*Mitteleuropa*) from the end of the 1870s onwards; but hopes for a competitive and wider European market dominated by Germany were outweighed by fears. It was these fears which led the German Empire to try to overcome the industrial and agricultural competition of giants like the USA, the British Empire and Russia through a policy of national isolation. True, the fanatics of the Union of the Eastern Marches speculated about a programme of imperialist expansion and Germanisation in the east; but Wilhelmine Germany was not the only country to possess this sort of lunatic fringe. In short, wherever we look for a continuity of aims we have to remember that there was without doubt a profusion of sometimes concrete, sometimes bizarre, calculations before 1914: but a straight line cannot be drawn between these and the political decisions taken in the summer of 1914. The undeniable existence of deliberate intentions to expand Germany's economic influence cannot be equated with concrete plans for territorial annexations. The very general and, at the same time, amateurish deliberations of several Berlin ministries, whose task was to prepare for the event of war, and the few moves which actually followed, could also be observed in other countries. At no point did they have anything to do with the outright economic and financial preparation of war, to be unleashed by a certain date. The notion of a dead-straight, one-way street, down which imperial policy consciously proceeded for years in advance towards the Great War, is unconvincing. It crumbles when confronted with the reality of the pre-war years. What is more, the advocates of this argument fail to recognise that war on such a grand scale opens up the possibility of new goals. They may believe that schemes and blueprints provide an evolutionary link between the period prior to 1914 and the war itself. But the specifically extreme form of, for example, the megalomaniac 'September Programme', which summarised Germany's war aims in 1914, becomes intelligible only if one appreciates the discontinuity which the war itself produced. On the other hand, we can readily assume today that German policy accepted the risk of a continental European war which could no longer be localised, when it quite deliberately escalated the 'July crisis' and drove Vienna on into its fateful confrontation with Serbia. If, however, the thesis of direct continuity proves untenable on theoretical grounds, because the deliberate pursuit of aims it assumes takes no account of the human and institutional constraints on the actions of the decision-makers; and also on empirical grounds, because the rhetoric of peacetime war aims fails to explain adequately the relative importance of influences which produced the decisions taken in the summer of 1914, we must look elsewhere for the determining factors which induced the decision-makers to risk war.

At this point we can relegate the traditional cliché of the paramount importance of foreign policy, and in particular the mechanics of treaty obligations, to a subordinate role. Everyone at the time was aware that Europe was divided into two armed camps. They all knew full well that once a certain point had been reached any escalation of conflict would transform the cold war into a 'hot' one. Berlin was no exception. Consequently, there must have been motives bringing themselves to bear here, which seemed to make an escalation necessary in spite of the foreseeable responses this would produce. A colonial conflict of the kind that would embroil the world — for years a fear of the European Left — was not one of the causes of war. In Latin America the competitive economic struggle continued in the shadow of the Monroe Doctrine. Political calm reigned in the Pacific. In East Asia the Manchu dynasty made way for the Chinese Republic in 1911–12 without its disintegration resulting in any intensification of imperialist rivalries among the Great Powers. As for African colonies, agreements had recently been arrived at, also between Berlin and London, which meant there was no increase of friction in that sphere. Instead, it was the provisional nature of the consensus on carving up the globe which effectively charged up the traditional areas of conflict between the European powers and their client states with renewed tension. After the Bosnian Crisis of 1908, or at the very latest after the Second Balkan War, any perceptive observer could see that this trouble-spot was a minefield which had to be made safe. The assassination of the Archduke Franz Ferdinand at Sarajevo and the subsequent breakdown of Austro–Serbian relations provided Berlin, only indirectly affected, with a pretext to pursue its precarious crisis strategy. How this dangerous brinkmanship, which placed so much at stake, could come about can best be explained by looking at the complex web of sensitive factors in domestic politics.

For decades German policy had relied essentially on the beneficial spin-off effects of a successful foreign policy on internal politics and on the social imperialist policy of deflecting domestic antagonisms abroad. As the résumé of Fischer's argument puts it, 'an energetic foreign policy was meant to help strengthen the endangered *status quo*'. 'Large-scale industry and the *Junker*, the army, dominated by a conservative ethos, and the civil service, ideologically and socially all interwoven in terms of their members' social background, became the specific and reliable supporters of an "idea of the state" which viewed world policy and national power politics essentially as a means of dissipating social tensions at home by campaigns abroad.'[2] The German Conservatives and the Free Conservatives, like the Centre, learnt to champion imperialism as a means of furthering their own interests once they realised the use to which Bismarck's colonial policy, Wilhelmine world policy and Tirpitz's battleship-building programme could be put in the field of domestic politics. After 1884 it became an important plank in the National Liberals' party programme, and after 1907 virtually a 'kind of electoral sheet-anchor'. As one of their number, Friedrich Meinecke, wrote in 1912, it was 'after all . . . precisely the idea of imperialism which today holds our party together from within, and which is bound to bring together not only our right and left wings, but all our compatriots in times of dire need'.[3] To be sure, there was soon to be no lack of this 'need'. Even among the so-called Left-Liberals, notions of a 'liberal imperialism' derived from Naumann and Weber were widespread, and Germany's expansionist policies often occupied a central place in the programmes of large pressure groups representing vested interests and the organisations devoted to political lobbying. Only the SPD retained its capacity to take a critical view on matters of principle; though it is true to say that this sometimes took second place to its purely pragmatic objections to German colonial policy. The high degree to which German imperialism was a product of internal socio-economic and political factors has already been stressed several times over. On the whole, it created, particularly among the power élites, an overt or latent predisposition to rely on foreign policy successes as the best means, in the absence of reformist alternatives, of combating Germany's domestic problems. With complete frankness, Bülow described this tendency as the basic orientation of imperial policy in his book, *German Policy*, published in 1913. After the fleet-building strategy failed to produce its desired effect in domestic politics, the massive election victory of the Social Democrats in 1912, who along with the Progressive People's Party (*Fortschrittliche Volkspartei*) now formed the largest bloc in the *Reichstag* (with 152 out of 397 deputies), constituted, as did the great strikes of the same year, an unmistakable danger signal. As a result, the major industrial and agrarian interests closed ranks. An attempt was made to create a coalition of the Right based on patriotic policies, and social policy was 'frozen'. The rival political camps in the *Reichstag* continued to obstruct each other, leaving little prospect for the parties of the Right and their closely allied pressure groups to push through their policies. Henry Axel Bueck, for many years the General Secretary of the Central Association of German Manufacturers (CdI), declared at the end of 1910 that German industry's main task was 'the defeat and destruction' of Social Democracy. Matthias Erzberger, the leader of the Centre's left wing echoed him early in 1914 in describing 'the destruction of the enormous power of Social Democracy' as the 'central issue in domestic politics'. From 1912 onwards, the SPD relied more than ever on old 'Comrade Trend' to provide them with an even greater increase in seats at the next *Reichstag* elections. But nowhere was there any personality in evidence who could have galvanised the Left into action and helped them show more enterprise in their dealings. Nor was there anyone who could have forcefully shown their opponents a way out of their predicament. Bethmann Hollweg's 'policy of the diagonal' could cope with the German Empire's problems, but rarely did it find a solution to them. It certainly could not provide one within a system that was fast becoming ungovernable. The recession which began in 1913 and continued throughout 1914 strengthened the impression — less because of objective difficulties than the psychic insecurity induced by the crisis — that the way ahead was extremely uncertain. Also, the noticeable shortage of capital which was only now beginning to cause problems for German finance capitalism, especially in the Balkans and in the Turkish trade, which was a major long-term concern, further contributed to this mood. Viewed as a group, the German bankers representing high finance, were, with a few significant exceptions, inclined to adopt a policy of caution, preferring to operate in areas of informal influence and rule. At the critical moment they remained outside the *arcana imperii* of Germany's ruling élites. The shortage of capital did not, therefore, constitute a genuine reason for going to war, though it did add to the sense of crisis. After 1912 major and dangerous developments seemed to multiply, giving rise among the ruling élites to a sense of being forced into a corner. The result was that they were increasingly prepared to fight tooth and nail in defence of their position. They became more and more determined not to give up their anachronistic privileges willingly.

The British élites, in contrast, demonstrated their ability to learn from experience by showing their readiness to make concessions, before they too adopted an inflexible and irresponsible attitude to the problem of Irish Home Rule. Ruling élites who find themselves in a defensive position with their backs to the wall become greatly predisposed to taking considerable risks in order to hold on to their position of dominance. Here, it seems, we have a general model of political behaviour in front of us whose validity extends to our own age. Subjectively, it takes the form of a defensive mentality which finds its expression in letters, diaries and other documents. Objectively, the point to be recognised it that a position can be defended by aggressive means, and this can even mean open conflict. This behaviour has nothing to do with deliberately planning for war. But a defensive struggle of this kind, as ruthless as it is desperate, does not shrink from the extreme risk of war just because the possible consequences cannot be calculated in advance. The key to the policy pursued by Germany's statesmen in the summer of 1914 lies in the predisposition of its ruling élites to continue their defensive struggle by aggressive means.

This predisposition, which had been growing increasingly since the second Moroccan crisis and could look back to the apparently successful policy of risk pursued during the period 1864–70, was given the support of the influential high-ranking military at the decisive moment in time. Their arguments, along with the 'unspoken assumptions' of the power-élites, were the weight that tipped the balance in their decision to use the fresh Balkan crisis of 1914 as the lever for a spectacular foreign policy success which was intended to have a positive effect on Germany's internal situation. They therefore embarked upon a policy of 'escaping forwards' from the country's internal problems; they refused to place their trust in the gradually emerging, albeit long-drawn-out, procedures by which the Great Powers attempted to 'manage' such crises. To the high-ranking military it seemed as if their freedom of action to arrive at any alternative decision was extremely limited. They had put a ceiling on the army's military preparations because of their socio-political preoccupation with the need to find the right type of 'reliable' officer recruit. By placing their trust in the success of the Schlieffen Plan in the west, and on account of the still inadequate increase in army strength, they postponed the proposed deployment of troops in the east. The desired effect of a 'Cannae' by the right wing depended on mobilisation proceeding according to plan and on a successful, quick pre-emptive strike. Their most recent intelligence appeared to confirm that Russia's military preparations would give the Tsarist Empire an outright superiority by 1916 or 1917, which would tie down a large part of Germany's forces on its eastern border. At the same time, Germany could maintain its lead over France only up to 1915. With time working against them, therefore, the German military, trapped by their own timetable of planning and deployment, had no wish to see the opportunity pass and to issue the threat of a trial of strength. This was especially the case when a renewed increase in the rate of Germany's armaments build-up now appeared out of the question for political and socio-economic reasons. If the bluff succeeded, the German Empire would gain a longer breathing-space. If, however, the fuse burnt down as far as the powder-keg, an early deadline — the earlier the better — seemed at any rate preferable to postponing the conflict to a later and almost certainly less favourable point in time. In the judgement of 'the military', as they informed the Chancellor, defeat would 'no longer' be avoidable 'in two years' time'. At this juncture their calculations and fears joined forces with the growing readiness of the traditional power-élites to pursue a policy of risk. This readiness was one of those mainly unspoken assumptions which decision-makers fall back on in times of crisis once rational considerations can no longer provide a sound basis for decision-taking.

This study has attempted repeatedly to describe the complex syndrome of fears which prevailed among the ruling élites of the time. In the spring of 1914 the Duke of Ratibor disclosed to the French ambassador, Cambon, that 'the commercial and bourgeois classes' were 'about to gain the upper hand at the expense of the military and land-owning classes. In view of this, a war was called for to restore order to existing relationships'. Since, moreover, 'the wars of '64, '66, and '70 . . . had strengthened the position of the military and the agrarians' political parties', a war would now be 'necessary to put things back on the right track'. As the Bavarian diplomat, Count von Lerchenfeld, noted after a conversation with Bethmann Hollweg, there were certain 'circles in the Empire' who, with more of an eye on the 'red menace', expected a war to lead to 'a restoration of internal conditions . . . along conservative lines'. Similarly, the Prussian 'Old Conservative', von Heydebrand, connected a war with 'a strengthening of the patriarchal order and mentality'.[4] Such ideas had been a feature of conservative thinking ever since Bismarck set out to solve the Constitutional Conflict through the use of war. Now that the situation of crisis in 1914 was seen as comparable to this in terms of the threat it represented to the interests of the ruling élites, their tendency to indulge in a desperate gamble once more gained ground. Against this background, Bethmann Hollweg's remark is easy to understand when, looking back in 1918, he said that the war had 'in a certain sense' been a 'preventive war'.[5]

Yet it should not be overlooked that in the summer of 1914 the Imperial Chancellor personally feared that war on a major scale would have a quite different effect on internal politics. At the beginning of July he commented sceptically that a 'world war with its utterly incalculable consequences could enormously strengthen the power of the Social Democrats, because they preach peace, and could topple many a throne'. He dismissed Heydebrand's expectations of a stabilisation quite bluntly as 'nonsense' and expected 'a war, whatever its outcome, to result in an upheaval of all existing arrangements'.[6] But this realistic prognosis had no real influence on his actions, nor could it have. Put another way, in the web of formal and informal decision-making agencies, Bethmann, the bureaucrat in charge of the imperial bureaucracy, possessed neither the weight nor the outstanding personal qualities necessary to translate his personal fears into a policy for peace which would have conserved social arrangements in line with his own views. During the July crisis it became obvious once more that this imperial chancellor could no longer conduct imperial policy in a clearly coordinated manner.

In view of the structural constraints hampering coordination, any apportioning of individual blame would fail to identify the true source of the problem, which was to be found 'in the deeper layers of social development'. As far as Germany is concerned, the First World War did not result from many years of deliberate planning, but simply from its ruling élites' incapacity to cope with growing problems in a world which was rapidly heading in the direction of democratic forms of government. On top of this, the historically conditioned tendency to react to internal difficulties with an aggressive form of defence was to prove disastrous. In the field of foreign policy, by war if necessary, this aggressive defence was meant to put an end to Germany's internal problems, or at least provide a breathing-space, so that the ruling élites could 'continue to further their own narrow interests and halt the advance of Social Democracy'.[7] Since the conflict between Austria–Hungary and Serbia, encouraged by Berlin for these reasons, caused the complex system of alliance commitments to be set in motion, the policy of 'calculated risk' failed. It revealed itself in August 1914 as an almost desperate crisis strategy which had not only toyed with the possibility of a major war but consciously risked one. It had therefore played a direct part in unleashing it. 'If the same goal' of averting a loss of political and social power 'requires another war', Burckhardt had prophesied in 1872, 'then we shall have one.' Engels had already predicted with some foresight what this would mean in the twentieth century when he wrote in 1887 that it would

> . . . no longer be possible for Prussia–Germany to have any war other than a world war, and a world war at that of a scope and violence hitherto undreamt of. Between eight and ten million soldiers will tear at each other's throats and devour the whole of Europe until they have stripped it barer than any swarm of locusts could ever do. The devastation of the Thirty Years' War compressed into three or four years and spread over the whole Continent; famine, pestilence, the general demoralisation both of armies and the mass of the people produced by acute distress; hopeless confusion of our human activities of trade, industry and credit, ending in general bankruptcy; the collapse of the old states and their traditional political wisdom to such an extent that crowns will roll by the dozen across the cobbles, and no one will be there to pick them up.

In such a catastrophe, one of Bismarck's wishes, which he is said to have uttered in 1897, seven years after his dismissal, would be fulfilled: 'He might yet live to see revenge in the destruction of the work whose foundations he himself laid.'[8]

8.2 *The financing of the war and the war economy*

There are a great many concise and detailed accounts of the military history of the First World War and the various diplomatic manoeuvres associated with its course. Rather than deal with these, however, this study focuses on some of the basic features of Germany's war-time finances and war economy. The financing of this war, which, contrary to expectations everywhere, did not turn out to be a short, sharp exchange of blows lasting only a few months, was settled after 4 August 1914 by the passage of an enabling act in the *Reichstag*. Of the estimated direct costs of the war, amounting to between 152 and 155 billion marks (i.e. between 98 and 100 million per day), about 60 per cent was covered by nine issues of long-term war-bonds with a nominal value of 99 billion marks (97 billion in real terms). The rest was made up by treasury bonds, whose balance at the end of November 1918 was 51.2 billion marks, together with tax revenue. The famous Spandau war-chest, housed in the Julius Tower in Berlin, where the remainder of the French reparations from 1871 was kept, contained only 205 million marks. This was just enough to pay for two days of the war.[9] As in the war of 1870–71, the basic principle of charging the main portion of Germany's war-debt to her defeated enemies at a future date remained unchanged. The Secretary of State, Helfferich, explained quite openly to the *Reichstag* that 'we can cling to the hope that, once peace has been concluded, we can present our enemies with the bill for this war which has been forced upon us'.[10] High taxes to pay for the war, of the kind eventually introduced in Great Britain, which would mainly have fallen upon the propertied classes, were not imposed. This made an increase in the money supply inevitable, which was brought about by thirteen separate banknote issues. The resultant excess in purchasing power was partially absorbed by the sale of war-bonds. However, since the newly created paper currency, along with deposit holdings, was not matched by a sufficient supply of consumer goods, the full effect of this policy emerged only after the collapse of Germany's war effort. It can therefore be justifiably argued that Germany's post-war inflation began in August 1914.

The war-bonds were without doubt the most important feature of Germany's financing of the war. The government was granted a legal monopoly on their issue and no other borrowers of capital were allowed to operate. 'If Germany's political leaders had got what they desired, the proportion of long-term borrowing in the total national debt would have been higher' (Lütge). Up to the fourth issue in March 1916 the sums raised were more or less sufficient to fund the German Empire's floating debt. But from the fifth issue to the ninth issue this became more and more impossible. By November 1918, an unfunded surplus debt of 51.2 billion marks had built up. In effect, this meant the conversion of the floating debt into a long-term debt; leading to 'the creation . . . of titles to assets in the hands of numerous government creditors' who were usually already among the materially better-off. The actual national debt of 156 billion marks in 1919 would, on a 5 per cent rate of interest, have imposed on the imperial budget an ongoing annual amortisation expense of 5 billion marks.

In Britain, where, after 1917, 80 per cent of all war profits made by joint-stock companies were taken in taxes, high taxes designed to pay for the war covered 30 per cent of its total costs. This system, had it been adopted in Germany, would have offered several advantages; but it could not be adopted because of its internal distribution of power. It would have immediately taken money out of circulation, thereby keeping the money supply in line with the declining production of consumer goods. Its effect would therefore have been to hold down inflationary price increases and the cost of living. Above all, war profiteers would not have been able to lend the state such massive amounts of money earned from armaments contracts in the expectation of making large return profits later on the interest. Such a partisan misuse of national wealth did not permit the adoption of a policy to serve the common good. Not only did the German power-élites manage to ensure the government's war-bonds policy continued up to 1918; they were even able to prevent any taxation of war profits being introduced before 1916. In 1917 taxes of this kind produced 4.8 billion marks of revenue. In 1918 the figure was 2.5 billion. Altogether, only 16 per cent of the costs of Germany's war effort were covered by taxes. As a result of the methods adopted to finance the war, an unprecedented crash was bound to follow once it ended. It did; and it struck severely at the economic roots of the middle classes in particular. What remains astonishing is the fact that a similar occurrence was repeated some twenty-five years later without in either case the frustrations it engendered being directed against those who were actually to blame.

The basic character of Germany's war economy remained the same throughout the four years of the conflict. It suffered from a dependence on imported raw materials and food supplies, a shortage of industrial manpower and an increasingly effective Allied blockade. In 1913 essential quantities of nitrate (for munitions), manganese and rubber were entirely imported. Ninety per cent of cotton, wool and copper was imported, as was 60 per cent of leather and 50 per cent of iron-ore. Germany had an adequate supply of coal, and right up to the end was able to make up the deficiency in iron ore by imports from Sweden. Beyond this, however, its obvious need to organise and administer the procurement of raw materials on a central basis soon made itself felt. The head of the AEG electrical engineering trust, Walther Rathenau, managed to have a special section of the War Ministry set up as early as August 1914, charged with the specific task of procuring raw materials for the war. He himself took charge of the new department until April 1915 when his place was taken by Major Koeth, a military technocrat who ran the section with considerable skill up to 1918. From this office and other agencies a limited form of planning was gradually built up; but it was one which at no time interfered with the ownership of private capital, private investment, price fixing and depreciation, despite the obvious damage private economic decisions did to the German war effort. Rathenau's plans for more extensive controls remained a blueprint that was never put into effect.

In terms of food production the German Empire achieved self-sufficiency only partially. In 1913, for example, 2 billion marks' worth of foodstuffs had to be imported. Although 90 per cent of its bread cereals were produced at home, yields steadily declined throughout the war years, until in 1917 the harvest was only half that of 1913. Since grain and potatoes were the main crops affected by this drop in yields, starvation, resulting in the first place from the blockade of Germany's ports, proved to be one of the Allies' most effective weapons. Imports from neighbouring and neutral countries reached Germany in only very limited quantities. Even so, it was relatively late in the war before the first steps were taken to establish a controlled economy in agriculture. As a result of the land-owners' resistance, controls were obstructed until 1916, and the half-hearted measures that were subsequently introduced could not prevent the terrible 'turnip winter' of 1916–17. (Germany's population was without doubt far better provided for during the Second World War, up to the end of 1944, because plans had been worked out well in advance, the *Reich*'s occupied territories more systematically plundered and stocks of provisions better organised.)

Germany's towns were discriminated against as a result of these developments. Black markets sprang up everywhere. Their exorbitant prices once more favoured the well-to-do in society. A stark contrast arose between conditions in town and country. At the same time, the antagonisms which were increasing between rich and poor sharpened the divisions within urban class society. In the spring of 1916 the first public protest meetings against food shortages were held, and in May of that year a government department was finally set up to deal with wartime food supplies. Its results were generally disappointing. Following a particularly bad harvest, it found it could not guarantee a daily bread ration of more than 170 grammes per person during the winter of 1916–17. Infant mortality rose by 50 per cent over the figure for 1913. The accepted official figure of 700,000 deaths by starvation during the war is more likely to be too low an estimate. This was the reality of the 'fighting homeland', not the idealised picture later drawn by writers of the political Right like Jünger, Beumelburg and Zöberlein.

If the wartime food shortages showed up the hollowness of the bombastic phrases, banded about *ad nauseam* by the agrarian pressure groups, concerning the efficient 'food producing estate' serving the common good, the methods used in organising industrial manpower caused problems of a quite different order. At the start of the war about 5 million men were enlisted. The figure rose gradually to 11 million, i.e. from 7.5 per cent to 16.5 per cent of the total population between 1914 and 1918. This meant that, instead of the unemployment which, it was widely feared, would result from the war, there was soon a shortage of manpower. The demands of the war economy, especially the armaments industry, not only led to an increase in the power of the employers but augmented the influence of the Free Trade Unions. Under the guidance of the military commanders, who assumed executive powers in their army corps districts from the very first day of the war, following the declaration of a state of siege, cooperation of a tentative nature took place between employers and employees. To achieve the main objectives of increasing production and avoiding strikes, the representatives of the military and the employers were forced to grant social and political concessions. These worked, on the whole, to the advantage of their adversaries and ultimately led to an informal system of wage bargaining. This internal industrial development intensified conflict within the opposing camps. In the SPD and the Free Trade Unions the gap widened between the right wing, which supported the war almost without reservation, and the left wing which, because of its growing numbers, was able to make its opposing views increasingly heard to the point where it could no longer be ignored. In the employers' camp, too, where the Central Association of German Manufacturers (CdI) and the Federation of German Industrialists (BdI) merged in 1914 to form a War Committee for German Industry, there was conflict between the uncompromising position that the entrepreneur should be 'master in his own house' and the belief in the need for limited concessions. The ideological façade of a 'civic truce' (*Burgfrieden*) concealed the problems, but only temporarily. The policies of the government proved incapable of bringing about the effect of reconciling conflicting interests, which a powerful parliament and political parties could have achieved; and the thin concoction of the so-called 'ideas of 1914' was no substitute. Consequently, the power of the pressure groups continued to increase throughout the war years. One of the ways in which this expressed itself was that state controls over the war economy remained weak. This in turn immensely benefited the propertied classes and caused the cost of living to rise much faster than real wages. The kind of precarious compromise both sides found themselves forced into as a result of the structure of power relationships and opportunities to gain influence was exemplified by the Hindenburg Programme of

1916. It represented an intensified attempt to wage total war for the first time and according to definite plans. Breaking with the kind of *ad hoc* improvisation which had prevailed up to that point, the Third Supreme Command of the Army (*3. Oberste Heeresleitung*) under Ludendorff and Hindenburg aimed at a radical stepping-up of the war effort.

(1) Armaments production was, as Ludendorff's right-hand man, Colonel Bauer, put it, to be increased 'at all costs', to be between two and three times previous levels.[11] The firm orders placed by the military satisfied almost all the wishes of heavy industry, with whose needs the Supreme Command fully coordinated its plans.

(2) Closely connected with the programme of production targets was the so-called Auxiliary Service Law which attempted to enlist every adult citizen for the war effort. Ludendorff originally called for the universal direction of labour (including women) to be introduced, along with an extension of military conscription to include all men up to the age of fifty, premilitary training for the country's youth, closure of the universities and the shutting down of all factories not involved directly in war production. These measures were tantamount to a complete militarisation of society.

As far-reaching demands they immediately provoked opposition from the politicians of the Left and Centre, but more particularly from the trade unions which demanded concessions in return for having to give up the worker's right to choose his place of employment. They insisted on the setting up of workers' committees, along with arbitration and mediation boards for every factory. During the negotiations over these proposals, the head of the Supreme Command's Railways Section, General Groener, representing the military, spoke in favour of making these concessions. He was a South German and had, in his own abstract way, a sense of justice. Helfferich, on the other hand, as Secretary of State at the Imperial Ministry of the Interior, in his transparent role as guardian of heavy industry's interests, obstinately opposed a more flexible policy. For the moment he got his way in the framing of the draft bill to be presented to the *Reichstag*. This was, however, subjected to fierce criticism by the majority of deputies, as a result of which various amendments were eventually adopted. The government's defence of the bill was of no avail. It eventually became law in December 1916 by a vote of 235 in favour to 19 against. It provided for compulsory labour service for all sixteen- to sixty-year-olds and gave powers for labour to be directed into the armaments industry. A change in one's place of work was made subject to approval by a factory arbitration committee, which also assumed responsibility for mediating in internal disputes. The government saw to it that no ceiling was put on the employers' profits, but neither were controls introduced to check rising nominal wages. While heavy industry got its way in the production programme, the Auxiliary Service Law led to an enormous gain in the position of the trade unions as a power factor of equal importance alongside the employers. The *Reichstag* not only refused to accept the proposals by withholding the plebiscitary approval desired by the Supreme Command; it created institutional procedures instead, which can be interpreted as anticipating the judicial system for the settling of industrial disputes once the war ended. For the first time a majority was formed between the SPD, Left–Liberals and the Centre to support the measure. This majority was later to adopt the 'Peace Resolution' of July 1917, thus prefiguring the 'Weimar Coalition' of parties which supported the Republic. Although this outcome was a great disappointment to the Supreme Command, the government and the employers, the party politicians and trade unionists had paid a high price for their successes, which were in any case of only a limited nature. It is, of course, possible to speak of a progressive integration of the workers and their organisations into the state; but in reality, and in the perceptions of those concerned, it meant their accommodation to a 'chaotic political system' (G. Feldman) and an acceptance on their part of the essential conditions of a capitalist economy. It was at most, therefore, a continuation of the 'negative integration' of the pre-war years. The few Social Democrats who expressed their dissent saw this much more clearly than the pragmatists of the trade-union movement who were so desperately eager to gain recognition as equal partners. In next to no time their opinion was shared by many thousands of supporters, especially those in the ranks of the Independent Socialists (USPD).

The newly created War Office under Groener practically supplanted the old Ministry of War, though it found itself continually paralysed by disputes over areas of responsibility. Furthermore, the débâcle of the crisis in raw materials, coal and transport during the winter of 1916–17 already showed that it would be impossible to fulfil the requirements of the Hindenburg Programme. And instead of helping to unite them behind the total war effort, the Auxiliary Service Law led to a worsening of relations between the employers and the trade unions. Although wages in the armaments industry rose by about 150 per cent within four years, this was a simply pitiful increase compared with the rates of profit enjoyed by the manufacturers. Right to the very end of the war, the state in its role as sole customer was willing to pay any price for their products. Resentment at this, together with the problems of food supply and the military stalemate on the Western and Eastern Fronts, led to increased instability at home.

The strikes which began to occur from 1917 onwards provide a reliable indicator of this instability. In that year the number of strikes shot up to 562, compared with only 240 in 1916. Some 1.5 million workers were involved in these strikes. The first major stoppage in April was as much sparked off initially by news of the Russian Revolution as by the cutting of bread rations. Although the strike was crushed by the military, the strength of the Independent Socialists, who now openly spoke out against the government's annexationist aims and the Prussian Three-Class voting system, suddenly became evident, especially in Leipzig. The wave of strikes continued well into the summer. They were particularly violent in Upper Silesia and Cologne, where the employers stuck to their traditional attitude of hostility towards the unions. From now on a rapid polarisation took place in politics and society. The Supreme Command, the employers and the right-wing parties loudly demanded a policy of uncompromising repression; and this was certainly put into practice often enough. On the other hand, the Left managed to make advances, especially in the Metal Workers' Union. Right-wing trade union officials found it increasingly difficult to control their members' moods and actions, as is evidenced by the various unofficial strikes which occurred. If they did not wish to sit back and watch all real influence slip from their hands, they were obliged to adjust gradually to the radicalisation taking place in their movement. The massive strikes of January 1918 formed a new climax with half a million workers in Berlin and over a million more in the rest of the country coming out in a partly spontaneous protest. Up to the revolution in November there were a further 499 strikes in 1918 alone! It was symptomatic that Groener, who came out not only in favour of mediation but of the inspection of war profits and increased taxes on them, was soon ousted from his position by the Supreme Command and heavy industry in the summer of 1917. Those who, like him, were intent on some degree of conciliation, were scarcely to be found any longer in key posts. As the German Empire entered its last year of war, social and political confrontations, intensified on the one hand by fanatical annexationist demands and the Fatherland Party, and on the other by war weariness, starvation and the Independent Socialists, became more and more insoluble.

8.3 *War aims and class society*

This fundamental conflict revealed its class character clearly as the contradictions of German society's class structure grew immeasurably worse during the course of the war. Without considering those social and structural aspects which were constitutional and political in nature, it is impossible to appreciate the central feature of Germany's war policy, namely the significance and function of its war aims. Much has been said and written on this subject over the past two decades. Here we are not concerned with whether the opposing sides in this war outbid each other in the scope of their war aims, or the extent to which they became entangled in a fateful web of demands and counter-demands; or whether any one of them has the right to reproach the others, given the lack of moral clarity which prevailed in circumstances that were exceptional. The focus of interest here is the continuity of the German Empire's social imperialism, and, indeed, its intensification. It can no longer be seriously denied that from the fantastic catalogue of German war aims contained in the so-called 'September Programme' of 1914, right through to the last offshoots of its chimerical schemes in the autumn of 1918, the German Empire's war aims were always associated quite clearly, and at times with brutal frankness, with hopes for concrete gains, whether economic or strategic in nature, or concerned with new settlement programmes and national minorities. Whether the subject of discussion was the iron-ore deposits of Longwy-Briey in Lorraine, the Belgian channel ports, the Russian granary or the Polish 'border strip' there was no attempt to conceal the fact that the advocates of formal annexations and informal domination represented very real and massive material interests. Yet it would be quite misleading to reduce Germany's war aims to these interests alone and to content oneself with a kind of fashionable economic determinism which would see the dominant motive purely in terms of the pursuit of profit by heavy industry's expansionist lobby or in the acquiring of the so-called 'strategic outlying areas'. Motives like these were certainly not just the prerogative of the many politicians who desired hegemony. Nor were they restricted to the power-seeking ideology of pan-German professors.

From the initial euphoria of 1914 to the final disillusionment of 1918, hopes were pinned on Germany's war aims as a means of once more diverting attention from the need for internal reform. Its traditional power relationships and, hence, the position of the privileged élites, were to be legitimised anew by means of successes abroad. For decades this crisis strategy had constituted a fixed pattern of thought and action in the policies pursued by Berlin. Now the war opened up new and unprecedented possibilities for its application.

These motives run like a clear thread through countless memoranda, submissions to the government, exchanges of correspondence and reports — in short, through the whole gamut of source materials which have become known as a result of the debate stimulated by Fischer's work. This is true not only of the policy of the Empire as a whole but of 'the war aims policies of its member states',[12] where fantastic schemes and grotesquely anachronistic notions lost all touch with reality and where attempts to salvage the old order and its representatives stood in the forefront of deliberations. Interminable debates as a distraction from reality, projects vested with boundless fantasies of new German vassal states along the Baltic coast, plans for partitioning Alsace-Lorraine, giving Flanders to Prussia, Lithuania to Saxony, placing a King of Württemberg on the Polish throne — nothing was too improbable for it not to be heatedly discussed for years in the cabinet councils and among the advisers of the German princes. Certainly, dynastic ambition of a literally 'late-feudal' character played its part here. Certainly, too, the need to keep a watchful eye on Prussia's growing power provided a constant stimulus. But here, too, the true rationale behind such schemes and manoeuvres was the need to stabilise a world of aristocratic and monarchical tradition which had outlived its time. Behind the profusions of a rich tapestry of bizarre juxtapositions (if one may use such 'reserved' language to describe the almost pathological frenzy with which these plans were forged) the defence of the *status quo* remained the central consideration. For this reason the debate on Germany's war aims highlights not only the extreme degree of megalomania and ambitions for world power behind the bewildering amount of unrestrained rhetoric and loss of contact with reality. It also points to the extremely limited freedom of action and the narrow range of options left to the ruling élites as a result of the profound internal changes they faced. Since they could see the fatally dangerous threat to their position growing — as Bethmann Hollweg had done in June 1914, and which Friedrich Engels had foretold in 1887[13] — they increased speed on their chosen course for fear of the open or latent pressures from the broad masses for political and social reform. They hoped to save themselves through grand expansionist successes dictated by fantasy, and so prolong their existence beyond its due time. There was, therefore, also an element of inevitability in these war aims — *rebus germanicis sic stantibus*, as it were, in view of the way that power was distributed at the time. It was not the desire to take an aggressive leap into the dark which proved to be the only decisive factor, but the feeling, ever-present since the imperialism of the 1880s, that they were obliged to defend their position by actions in the external sphere. The difference was that this time the pressure was greater than ever before.

The functional aspect of Germany's war aims can scarcely be overestimated. They were without doubt seen by the power-élites as a means of ensuring political and social unity; and to this extent, the planners' excesses provide a true reflection of the fact that society in Imperial Germany was socially and politically deeply divided. Nor should one fail to appreciate that the concrete expansionist interests and programmes after the spring of 1918 involved a qualitative leap towards new kinds of goals. It is because of these that it might be said that 'the pre-history of the Second World War' began already 'during the First World War'.[14]

Following Russia's two revolutions in 1917, the Third Supreme Command succeeded in placing the Soviet government under the yoke of the 'dictated peace' of Brest-Litovsk of 3 March 1918. Thereafter, Germany's war aims became the subject of decisions actually taken over the next few months. The Treaty of Brest-Litovsk provided the German government with the first real opportunity of putting its war aims into practice. Nothing reveals more clearly the terms which a victorious Germany would have imposed on its enemies than this truly Carthaginian peace. It provided for the territorial dismemberment of Russia by, for example, granting independence to the Ukrainian People's Republic, Finland and the Baltic states, and imposed harsh economic terms, intending to place all of Russia west of the Urals under German domination following a period of transition. A Pan-German League memorandum which in 1914 had called for Russia to be pushed back to the frontiers of Peter the Great's time, though at first banned from publication, had by now been printed and circulated in large numbers thanks to Ludendorff's intervention. Now that pamphlet's main demands had been more than satisfied. After March 1918, when the war in the west had again reached stalemate and the prospect appeared of a collapse on the Balkan front, the idea of 'taking over all of Russia and holding this giant empire in permanent dependence on Germany' began to win general acceptance 'throughout the German leadership'. This 'axiom' stood, of course, in 'complete contrast' to the exaggerated estimates of the strength of Tsarist Russia prior to 1914. The Treaty of Brest Litovsk made possible a realisation of this 'grand design' in several respects. In addition, the supplementary treaties signed between Germany and Russia on 3 August 1918 increased the former's direct influence over Russia's unoccupied areas. German troops held a front stretching from Narva through Pleskow, Orsha and Mogilev to Rostov. They controlled the Ukraine, and advance detachments occupied the Crimea and had penetrated as far as Transcaucasia. Germany's plans for a 'Greater Territory' in the east had therefore taken on a tangible form. Because it seemed that its massive war aims had been realised for all time, the collapse of Germany's war effort in the summer of 1918 came all the more as a sudden jolt and shock. The 'strategic outlying areas' in the east seemed to vanish like some apparition. When Hitler's 'ultimate objective of building a German Empire in the east on the ruins of the Soviet Union' was propagated only a few years later, it was not simply the hallucinatory vision of a dreamer. There were already sufficient 'concrete points of contact in what had been realised in 1918. The German Empire in the East' had, if only for a short time, already been 'a reality once before'.[15]

Apart from domestic political considerations and the desperate need for direct, even though barely usable, access to grain supplies and sources of raw materials, there were further motives at work which influenced the decisions taken by Germany's military and political leadership. These also justify our speaking of a qualitative change at this time.

(1) After the Allied blockade had cut Germany off from the world's markets for almost four years and severed its trade connections, and after the Entente's plans for the postwar economic division of the world became known in Berlin from the spring of 1916 onwards, ideas of achieving autarky began to generally dominate thinking. These went far beyond the original plans for a Central European customs union in the shape of *Mitteleuropa*. It now seemed essential for Germany to pursue expansionist aims in Russia, with its massive potential in foodstuffs and mineral resources. Indeed, this strategy appeared to offer virtually the only prospect of success. In particular, the exponents of German autarky were able to operate

in the vacuum caused by the collapse of Tsarism.

(2) Up to this point the view had prevailed among the German Empire's influential ruling élites that the world war should be regarded only as a prelude to 'future major wars' in which the world powers would continually redefine their spheres of influence in constant competition with one another. This Social Darwinist variant of the belief in an international system of antagonistic states called for territorial acquisitions for the purpose of strategic defence on such a gigantic scale that the whole of Russia was dealt with like the estate of a bankrupt, to be disposed of as seen fit.

(3) In the newly acquired 'eastern territory', not only the Pan-German League and the Union of the Eastern Marches but also Ludendorff envisaged both a ruthless resettlement of the Slav population and its complement of 'a reallocation of land' on an ethnic basis to the benefit of all the German settlers in Russia. Already in December 1915 Ludendorff, as the real power behind the army's Third Supreme Command, had said of Russia: 'Here we shall acquire the breeding stations for the people who will be essential for further struggles in the east. These struggles will come inevitably.'[16] His choice of words is highly revealing. In 1918 the green light was given to a racialist policy of Germanisation. Even this analysis of motives, which can easily be taken further, sufficiently shows how the important prerequisites of the programmes and practices of National Socialism arose, or were created, during this period.

Apart from Germany's war aims policy, other ideologies intended to reconcile differences at home played an important part for a time at least. The 'civic peace', proclaimed in August 1914, was meant to put an end to the conflicts of domestic politics. An entirely fictitious 'national community' (*Volksgemeinschaft*) was invoked in order to ensure the unity of the 'fighting nation'. In the commercial middle classes, where the ideal of a conflict-free society was firmly established, and even among the SPD's *vaterlandslose Gesellen*, who were seen to be absorbed into the nation on 4 August 1914, the vocabulary of the 'civic peace' gained considerable influence throughout the first year of the war. By 1916, in contrast, the tissue of grand-sounding phrases had all but disintegrated.

The academic world held on longer to the so-called 'ideas of 1914'. If they could not look back to a tradition of revolution, they wanted at least a defensive ideology against the English shopkeeper mentality, Gallic shallowness and Slavic barbarism. These 'ideas' were a continuation of all the pernicious phobias of the pre-war period, ranging from hatred of England and antisemitism to Teutonic arrogance and a romanticising Germanomania. Leading scholars vented their spleen in the language of the gutter. Once again Germany's separation from the intellectual and political culture of Western Europe appeared confirmed: the connecting threads were severed, and an arrogant self-righteousness praised the isolated German way of life, seeing it as a quality which would 'cure' the world. The war theology of the two main Churches flowed into this poisonous brew which was regurgitated in countless brochures, war speeches, letters to the front and the like. It was here that the concepts of total war were disseminated in an insufferably idealised form. Total mobilisation and the waging of war not only provided a compensation for Germany's quantitative inferiority in the face of the enemy alliance but held out pseudo-solutions for the problems of its own class society. The excessively idealised 'community of the trenches' had positive features ascribed to it which were denied to the majority by capitalism in peacetime. In an unprecedented perversion of human values the abnormal social relationships which can develop at the front, in the omnipresence of death, were presented as a model for an ideal society in which authoritarian, disciplined and anachronistic forms of community life would prevail. The ideological spokesmen of the 'nation in arms' took refuge from the modern world in a social romanticism imbued with military values and social norms. Class conflict would be eliminated by the visible command structure of a state hierarchically organised for war. The right-wing conservative advocates of the 'total state' before 1933, like Freyer, Jünger, Forsthoff and many others, were as able to refer to this concept without a sense of strain as the National Socialists themselves.[17]

In 1918 many of the propaganda hacks were overcome by sudden bewilderment at Germany's defeat. Few were sobered by the experience, as the political climate of the Weimar Republic testified. 'I have often thought', Karl Kraus said later with biting sarcasm, 'that no greater torture could have been devised for the whole pack of poets and literati of the Central Powers than to publish sentence for sentence now what they scribbled then, partly as a result of benighted stupidity, partly in the speculative hope of sparing their own lives by praising the heroic deaths of others.' Perhaps it would have a 'salutary effect', he thought, if one reminded them 'of the method by which they hounded to their destruction all those who did not have the good fortune to be able to transpose their mental confusion into literature. My proposal to round up the war writers once peace had been declared and have them flogged in front of the war invalids has not been realised. . . '.[18]

8.4 The final 'revolution from above'

The growing dichotomy in the development of German society during the war can be discerned in several areas: in the relationship of the industrial employers to their workers, in the widening social gap between the 'middle classes' and the upper class, in the narrowing gap between the former and the proletariat, in the relations between all the social classes and the state, in strikes, repressive measures, the disparities of real income, and so on. The polarisation in politics also increased after 1916. In March 1917 a minority in the parliamentary party of the Social Democrats, which had made its views increasingly heard since the first debates on war credits in August 1914, formally left the party. Their secession made public the internal split which had existed within German Social Democracy for some time. In January 1917 the so-called 'Spartakus letters' of the *Gruppe Internationale*, written mainly by Karl Liebknecht and Rosa Luxemburg, began to appear. It was from this group that the Spartakus League emerged in the same year. This compromised a tiny left-wing group, at first forming part of the Independent Social Democratic Party of Germany (*Unabhängige Sozialdemokratische Partei Deutschlands* — USPD) which was founded, again at Gotha, in April 1917. The split within the organised labour movement had become final.

On the opposite side of the political fence, the Third Supreme Command of the Army, set up in August 1916 under Ludendorff and Hindenburg, supported the trend to the right in German domestic politics. From the very beginning Ludendorff considered a 'dictatorship' of the Army Command 'a distinct possibility'. His close associate, Colonel Bauer, also spoke openly in favour of one in the autumn of 1916. In December he thought that one would arrive 'at a military dictatorship as the only way out', and that Ludendorff 'belonged at the top also, nominally'. He added that only 'an absolute military dictatorship' could be of any further help in the situation. Bethmann Hollweg's fall in July 1917 signaled the rising dictatorship of the army. Though not yet directly established before that point of time, it had begun effectively to operate in certain areas. Ludendorff was also apparently offered the imperial chancel-

lorship at this time. The Emperor — at the very latest after Bethmann's forced dismissal — was turned into a kind of 'shadow Kaiser
by his own generals'.[19] As it transpired, the Supreme Command's
dictatorship could not always get its own way in domestic politics —
witness the Hindenburg Programme! — and after the end of September 1918 it also lost its plebiscitary support. But, up until then,
so many opportunities to exercise power had been built up and
made use of that its position in the complex web of power factors,
some of which had been by now reduced to a useless role, can be
justifiably described as dictatorial. This development was not without a certain logic. Ever since the 1890s the power vacuum at the top
of the Greater Prussian Empire had not been properly filled. The
Emperor had proved incapable of filling it; the parliament and the
political parties had been kept out in the cold, and the civilian
politicians had shown themselves incapable of providing leadership.
And since it had been the military who had made the founding of the
state possible in 1870–71, tenaciously defending their own privileged
position within it ever since, and since rival power factors proved
incapable of challenging the army between 1914 and the autumn of
1918, the basic principle which had brought the German Empire
into being emerged once more at this time of external and internal
crisis: the militarism of Prussia–Germany showed its true face in
Ludendorff's 'military dictatorship'. This dictatorship inaugurated
the final phase in the history of Imperial Germany, just as Moltke's
armies had inaugurated its beginning. The wheel began to turn full
circle.

Behind the Third Supreme Command stood the German Fatherland Party (*Deutsche Vaterlandspartei*), which emerged in the summer
of 1917 and was supported by the army's leaders for the same
reasons they had backed the Prussian Diet in its defence of the
Three-Class voting system. After a majority had been found to
support the Peace Resolution of July 1917 in the *Reichstag*, the East
Prussian civil servant, Wolfgang Kapp, and Grand Admiral von
Tirpitz, now a professional failure, worked together with various
pressure groups and nationalist organisations to create the Fatherland Party as a new right-wing rallying point for a nationalistic,
imperialistic mass movement with proto-fascist features. When the
meeting to found the party was held in Königsberg on 3 September
1917, Kapp and Tirpitz were elected Chairman and Vice-Chairman
respectively. The executive committee was granted full powers and a
vigorous membership campaign was launched.

The declared aims of the Fatherland Party, which by July 1918 was said to have 1.25 million individual and corporate members in 2,536 local branches, were: a massive programme of annexations in the east and the west, which surpassed all previous war aims in scope, control of the Dutch and Belgian coasts, a Central African colonial empire (*Mittelafrika*) and expansion in Russia and Turkey 'as far as the Pacific and the gates of India'.[20] At long last a broadly based party of the Right, which had been aimed at in 1913 and which could be traced back to the *Sammlung* policies of 1879, 1887 and 1897, had become a reality. Heavy industry (represented by, for example, B. Stinnes, Kirdorf, Hugenberg, Roetger, Röchling), the electrical, chemical and machine-manufacturing industries (B.C. Duisberg, W. von Siemens and E. von Borsig), North German wholesale traders and shipyard owners, the Federation of German Industrialists (BdI), the Central Association of German Manufacturers (CdI), the Imperial German Association of the Middle Classes (*Reichsdeutscher Mittelstandsverband*), various peasants' associations, the Pan-German League and other chauvinistic organisations — all formed the broad institutional, but nevertheless morbid, basis of the Fatherland Party. There was no lack of funds, nor of propagandistic skills, which would have been worthy even of Goebbels. The party took full advantage of its members' excellent connections with the civil service and the armed forces, where the 'patriotic instruction', first introduced by Ludendorff, was now supplemented by the illegal but tacitly approved propaganda of the Fatherland Party. A massive attempt was made to dominate public opinion and mobilise those sections of the public which were susceptible to slogans about holding out to the bitter end and persevering with Germany's war aims. The hitherto reticent Meinecke wrote in September 1918 of this 'monstrosity of the misplaced egoism of self-interest and misplaced idealism, which is one of the greatest examples in the history of German party politics of duping the gullible'. He found 'in the annexationist nationalism, an excellent way of implementing uncompromisingly a rigidly authoritarian policy both at home and abroad'.[21] In a last blind fit of rage, brought on by despair behind an outward show of confidence in final victory, the forces united in the Fatherland Party attempted the impossible in the last year of the war: to preserve the authoritarian structures within the German Empire at the same time as obtaining a victorious peace externally. Brest–Litovsk was to be only the first step on the road to a German world empire.

This hubris lasted barely a year. But in terms of organisation and propaganda a clear path had been marked out for a radical German fascism to follow. To some extent, this fascism took up where the Fatherland Party had left off. Anton Drexler, both as functionary in the Fatherland Party and as the original founder of the Nazi Party, perfectly symbolises the connection. When Meinecke looked back on the catastrophe of the Second World War, it seemed clear to him that both 'the Pan-German League and the Fatherland Party had been true curtain-raisers for the rise of Hitler'.[22]

As the short-lived history of the Fatherland Party reached its unfortunate climax in the spring of 1918, the failure of the last major German offensive on the Western Front appeared imminent from the end of April on. In mid-July this offensive, code-named 'Michael' in Germany, collapsed; the Allies began their counter-attack along a broad front. On 14 August the Supreme Command at its headquarters in Spa acknowledged for the first time that, despite the German advance in the east, the situation was now becoming 'hopeless'. By 29 September demands for a cease-fire had been drawn up. It was admitted that the 'German army . . . was finished' and Germany's 'ultimate defeat simply unavoidable'. Suddenly the army leaders took note of the peace proposals of the US President, Woodrow Wilson, whose Fourteen Points were in fact not even known to them in precise detail until 5 October. The Supreme Command practically issued an ultimatum to the Imperial Chancellor, insisting that he send off their offer of a cease-fire 'without the least delay'. The Conservatives were informed of this on 30 September, followed by the leaders of the other political parties on 2 October. The overwhelming disappointment they felt at this move knocked the enthusiasm for Germany's war aims out of many of them. Stresemann, for example, suffered a nervous breakdown. 'Enslavement for a hundred years to come', wrote Bethmann's confidant, Kurt Riezler, on 1 October. 'The end of the universe for all time. The end of all hubris.'[23] This was all somewhat premature. But it did reflect the general change in mood.

After 1917 there was talk in the Supreme Command of troops at the front being 'stabbed in the back' by left-wing elements at home. By July 1918 — long before the revolution! — the 'stab-in-the-back' legend had been elaborated. On 1 October Ludendorff declared cynically that the politicians would have to 'eat the soup they've landed us in', since it was 'thanks mainly to them' that 'we have come to this'. Summing up his impressions, Groener remarked that 'the Supreme Command took the view' that it would 'refuse to accept any responsibility for the cease-fire or subsequent events'. And, as it turned out, the political leadership, obliged as it was to intervene, allowed itself to be burdened with the odium incurred as a result of this all too hasty action. At the same time as this, the President of the Pan-German League, Heinrich Class, was proposing a more pernicious way of dealing with the situation. He called for a 'ruthless campaign against Jewry, against which the all too justified wrath of our good, but misled, people must be directed'.[24]

While the military was shamelessly divesting itself of the responsibilities it had once sought, there was a sudden change in the whole political scene. The Supreme Command developed a new evasive strategy when it suddenly proposed that civilian politicians should be brought into the government executive and be made responsible to the parliament. The idea was to unload the responsibility for defeat and the problems which would follow after the end of the war onto the majority parties in the *Reichstag*. Admiral von Hintze, recently appointed Secretary of State at the Foreign Office and in very close contact with the Supreme Command, described this constitutional change as the last 'revolution from above' and the only 'means of forestalling a revolution from below'. Speaking of the role of the Supreme Command in this, he said, 'if pushed into the limelight, it ought to provide a temporary transition and make the change-over from victory to defeat bearable . . . this would be its palliative effect'. A man like Groener, who was familiar with the true position, made no bones about 'the parliamentarisation being brought about by Hintze'. The conservative bastions of the monarchy and the army were to be preserved as far as possible behind the facade of new arrangements intended to prevent the radical overthrow of the system and prove acceptable to the Allies. Once achieved, the military believed, as Ludendorff put it on 7 October, that 'we can climb back into the saddle and govern according to our old ways'.[25]

In opposition to this interpretation, recent scholarship has argued that this tactic of the Supreme Command coincided with a strong, separate initiative by the *Reichstag*. This view, it would seem, owes a great deal to the desire to trace the beginnings of Weimar's parliamentary government as far back in time as possible. In the spring of 1918 the General Assembly and Central Committee of the *Reichstag* were willing to adjourn until the autumn, while the recently chosen 'Inter-Party Committee' agreed not to meet for two months; all acted in deference to Ludendorff, and with his 'Spring offensive' on the Western Front in mind. In short, the struggle for parliamentary control was not all that impressive. By the end of September the Imperial Chancellor, von Hertling, a cardboard figure-head set in place by the Third Supreme Command, was forced to resign. He had lost the support of even the party politicians; but by this time Hintze's pressure — to use his name as a kind of shorthand — to achieve greater parliamentary control was making itself felt. Each of the possible candidates from the majority parties in parliament, considered for the post of chancellor, refused the chancellorship. Even taking into account the highly unfavourable circumstances at the time, can it really be said that this was evidence of a confident campaign to achieve parliamentary control? Prince Max von Baden, who was finally thrust into the limelight, was a little-known figure — not suprisingly, for he had, after all, disapproved of the July 1917 Peace Resolution and still would have nothing to do with it in the spring of 1918. Instead, he demanded that the military's achievements to date be exploited to the full and a parliamentary-style government resisted. Men skilled in the art of manipulation helped him into the office of imperial chancellor, a post which had never been so little coveted by anyone since 1871. He accepted, but even then only, so it was said, after 'Hindenburg and Ludendorff had "approved" his candidature'.[26] What, one might ask, would have become of the *Reichstag's* initiative if the military dictatorship, which had been crumbling since 29 September, had rejected this colourless but well-meaning candidate who, so it seemed, could not in any case have become a danger to them? This was how Prince Max von Baden was appointed Chancellor on 3 October. On the very same evening he signed the telegram to the Allies, which had been drafted by the Supreme Command. 'This was tantamount to capitulation', he said later, but the concluding sentence, which he angrily added, to the effect that for this step 'the Supreme Command would be just as responsible as for the consequences' was a piece of wishful thinking. It was highly doubtful that the *Reichstag* could by itself have initiated the successful first moves towards parliamentary control, in spite of the existence and gradual acceptance of the existing parliamentary groups, which slowly gained influence. Even Arthur Rosenberg therefore judged that 'the extension of parliamentary influence was not something wrested by the *Reichstag*, but something decreed by Ludendorff. This kind of revolution has no precedent in the whole of world history'.[27]

The October Reforms of 1918 resulted, two days after Ludendorff's dismissal, in, among other things, a law to introduce a parliamentary monarchy. However, there can be no suggestion of this having brought about any definitive change in the structure of power, let alone a firm basis for parliamentary rule. The navy leadership withdrew entirely from the government and gave orders on 29 October for the High Seas Fleet to weigh anchor. This was the final action in the chain of events leading to revolution. On the same day the Emperor fled to the army's General Headquarters, back to the very heart, as it were, of the Prussian military state. But the trial of strength between the old regime and the new political order was by no means decided yet. On the contrary, there were clear signs from the end of October onwards that a conservative counter-move in the form of a *coup d'état* was imminent. With a sense of fairness, not normally encountered in his social class, the head of the Naval Academy at Mürwik judged that it was 'not manly and . . . above all, not decent, when one has ruined things (as "we" have done) and is forced to leave the stage, to want to continually stick spokes in the wheels of others who have jumped on to keep things going at a dangerous moment in time. For we have certainly ruined things'. When it became clear, therefore, that the reforms went dangerously far and that a monarchy under parliamentary control might become a reality rather than a useful deception for Woodrow Wilson's benefit, thus ruling out a return to the *status quo ante*, it began to look increasingly less likely that the monarchy and the military would give up without a fight.[28] In the event, Germany's parliamentary monarchy lasted for just three days. The revolution pre-empted the counter-moves of the old forces. The sailors refused to be sacrificed in their thousands for the sake of a completely futile gesture by the navy to win prestige, and simply to satisfy the hara-kiri mentality of a Naval Command, prepared, in a last act of desperation, to risk the loss of all its ships rather than capitulate. Their refusal led to an open revolt between 28 October and 3 November, which immediately spilled over from Kiel to the other cities. On 7 November the revolution spread to Munich, and on 9 November to Berlin. The Emperor abdicated and the Crown Prince renounced the throne before quickly fleeing the scene. Thereupon the Social Democrat, Philipp Scheidemann, proclaimed the Republic. On 10 November a revolutionary Council of People's Delegates (*Rat der Volksbeauftragten*), comprising three members each from the SPD and USPD, took over the running of government. This Council conferred political authority on the Majority Social Democrat, Friedrich Ebert, who, thus legitimised, took charge of the government. There was, therefore, no direct line of succession from Prince Max von Baden. The history of the German Empire of 1871 had not even lasted a full forty-eight years.

8.5   *The German revolution: social democracy or conservative republic?*

What was it that set the seal on the German Empire's defeat? Was it a mutiny or a revolution? What historical options for Germany's future development existed between the end of October 1918 and the elections at the end of January 1919, when all the German princes had been overthrown but the relative open-endedness of the situation was already gone and certain lines had been drawn up for the Republic to follow? That Germany had indeed experienced a revolution, if only for a short time, cannot be doubted. Structural problems, which had built up over a long period, finally broke through the crumbling barriers holding them back in November and December 1918. The old ruling political system was swept away. Workers' and soldiers' councils assumed power, and it seemed that a realignment of social forces, together with completely new institutional arrangements, was in the offing. On 11 November the left-wing liberal journalist, Theodor Wolff, writing in the *Berliner Tageblatt*, described the radical upheaval as 'the greatest of all revolutions, because never before had such an impregnable bastion, surrounded by such solid walls, been taken in one attempt'. And Ernst Troeltsch, an academic with an acute sense for contemporary problems, wrote: 'Today, Germany has its successful revolution, just as England, America and France once had theirs', though admittedly 'at a disastrous time of a general military, economic and nervous breakdown'.[29] It was not only starvation, resulting from the blockade, military defeat and a revolt by its soldiers that produced the revolution. Profound socio-economic tensions, together with a long-concealed, but ultimately decisive, political crisis of fundamental proportions, enormously exacerbated by the loss of political authority during the war, had created a widespread desire for change, which finally produced a revolutionary explosion.

Up to the end of the 1950s most historians argued that, towards the end of the war, options still remained open for Germany's future political development. They believed that the alternative had existed between either a Bolshevik-style dictatorship based on workers' councils or a parliamentary republic in the style of Weimar. More recent discussion, which goes back to the views of a critical outsider like Arthur Rosenberg and takes as its yardstick the idea of a 'solidly based democratic republic' unlike that of Weimar, basically offers the alternative of a conservative republic or social democracy. The Bolshevik-style revolution is now regarded 'at best' as a 'fictitious, and not a real' possibility.[30] There can be no doubt that the workers' and soldiers' councils, which form a key element in both these interpretations, arose spontaneously — partly following the Russian examples of 1905–07 and 1917–18 — in their role as 'provisional fighting and governing instruments' of a mass-protest movement.[31] They formulated their aims in the political language of the Marxist workers' movement, since that, after all, was the only language they were familiar with in the 'subculture' they wished to break out of. Up until the spring of 1919, however, the vast majority of councils were anti-Bolshevik in their views. They saw themselves as an improvised, transitional system in which only a few elements lent themselves to incorporation into the new institutional structure of a parliamentary republic. In November 1917 Lenin was able to rely on the support of 250,000 party members and an absolute Bolshevik majority of 60 per cent at the Second All-Russian Congress of Soviets. Also, in the elections to the Constitutional Assembly, held at the end of November following the introduction of universal suffrage, he won 9 million votes (25 per cent) and the cooperation of the left-wing Social Revolutionaries. The Spartakists' and the German Communist Party (KPD), on the other hand, had no more than a few thousand members in January 1919. Their influence extended at most to 2.5 per cent of the delegates at the Berlin Congress of Councils. In the *Reichstag* elections of June 1920, the Communist Party won a mere 2.1 per cent of the vote. Arthur Rosenberg has estimated that, had the Communists participated in the elections to the new National Assembly in January 1919, they might have received only 1 per cent of the total vote. The majority of the Left at this time was active in the USPD, which should be seen as a broad grouping of militant Social Democrats and radical democrats. The generally shared view that it was time to make a break with the past temporarily brought into its ranks even Kautsky and Bernstein, the erstwhile opponents in the dispute over revisionism. But there were no Communist Party cadres of sufficient strength for an armed seizure of power, just as there was also a lack of deliberate planning and preparation. This was shown quite clearly by the January Uprising of 1919. Basically, the Spartakists and the German Communist Party did not have the slightest chance of success in 1918 and 1919. The threat posed by the 'red terror' was grotesquely exaggerated in the minds of the petty bourgeoisie and the propertied classes. If the primary task of the world's Communist parties over the past fifty years has been to undertake a partial modernisation of developing countries through programmes of rapid industrialisation, such a platform was no longer available to the

German Communists. This explains why, then as now, the German Communist Party has lacked a genuine functional role in German politics, and why it has generally failed to win credibility in the struggle for social and political participation and democratic controls.

While there was no serious danger from the extreme Left, the vacuum at the top of the power pyramid still had to be filled once the monarchy had collapsed and the October Reforms had failed. Moreover, it could be regarded as a major task of the revolution to bring about fundamental changes in the way that political, social and economic power had been distributed under the old order. Bethmann, however, had set forth his melancholy reflections in 1916 on 'the impossibility of changing things east of the Elbe'; concluding that 'it [the power of the land-owners] must be smashed — it must go under'. Even Troeltsch had sceptically raised the question of 'whether this socialist revolution could or could not have been avoided; whether the steps taken by Prince Max von Baden's government against the fierce opposition of the old ruling élites, including undeniably far-reaching and thorough social reforms, could have got anywhere, or whether in fact anything could have been achieved without the complete destruction of the old order'. As Gustav Mayer reflected as early as 20 October 1918, without such intervention, would not the 'German politicians of violence . . . come to power again . . . ' sooner or later?[32]

The German revolution was defeated as a result of its failure to carry out its historic tasks of a fundamental reform and democratisation of the state with its bureaucratic, social and economic institutions. Why was this? Although Friedrich Ebert, as First Chairman of the Majority Socialists (MSPD) after 1917, received his mandate to run the government from the revolution and not the imperial government, he immediately concluded an informal alliance with General Groener, who represented the army. It was, indirectly, also an alliance with the old ruling élites. This pact was intended to provide the new government with a maximum of public order during the period of transition before elections, in return for which the mass movement was to be kept in check as an essential requirement in the defence of the *status quo*. For precisely those reasons, it must be regarded as a symbol of the frustration and containment of the revolution. Leading Majority Socialists presented it as unavoidable in the circumstances. Faced with military defeat they could expect a situation of widespread disorder to follow the demobilisation of an army of millions. Against this background they also had to re-adjust from the war economy while the Allied blockade continued. In this situation, outflanked on the Left by the USPD and the councils, which above all expressed a crisis of confidence in 'existing forms of opposition' and a deep distrust of party and trade-union organisations, they feared they might suffer the same fate as had befallen Kerensky's Provisional Government in Russia: the radicalisation of the revolution to the point where it would slide into an abhorrent Bolshevik take-over. Much of this fear revolved around imaginary dangers, however, and conjuring them up led to their freedom of choice in decision-making being narrowed down far too early. As well as this, the so-called Central Working Alliance (*Zentralarbeitsgemeinschaft*), headed by the industrialist Stinnes and the trade-union leader Legien from mid-November, had the effect in this period of upheaval of keeping organised labour in its place. At about the same time the Ebert–Groener pact was being concluded, the employers and the trade unions were cooperating in order to defend their respective positions.[33]

The basically defensive posture adopted by the MSPD leaders towards the revolution cannot be understood simply in terms of the immediate events of 1917–18. It is important to realise that their historically conditioned mentality, their traditional patterns of behaviour and their specific relationship to theory and practice were the obvious overriding factors which precluded their embarking on a bold programme of reform. Yet vital decisions depended on their leadership. Both the USPD and the councils were urging change at this time and would have supported such a programme. The masses, too, including the Majority Socialist support in their midst, 'fulfilled every expectation one could have had of them'. They had risen against and toppled the old regime, thus creating the right conditions for a new departure. Now they showed their willingness to give active support to the setting up of a genuinely democratic order. However, their political leaders failed them.[34]

One would be hard put to see in Imperial Germany's SPD 'subculture' a breeding ground for revolutionaries. Its organisational activities, designed to defend and extend what had already been achieved and what they were still working towards, absorbed most of their energies. At the same time, discrimination and harassment did not become unbearable to the point where they produced a revolutionary mood. For this reason, too — and leaving the question of personal charisma aside — a German Lenin or Trotsky was unlikely to emerge among the SPD's leaders. The outcome of the debate over mass strikes in the decade before the war is just as disillusioning in this respect as the fact that before 1918 the use of the general strike as a political weapon was discussed by no more than a handful of extreme left-wingers. The revolutionary rhetoric of Kautsky's supporters covered up a trend towards practical reform policies. Nevertheless they favoured a fatalistic policy of inaction over the alternative which involved continually taking risks. For decades the SPD leadership had perceived it as their future task to bring about a reform of the monarchical state. Now, suddenly, they were expected to act from a position of political responsibility against a background of revolution and surrounded on all sides by unfamiliar tasks. And so it happened that the MSPD leaders found themselves incapable of breaking out of the mould of their traditional patterns of thought and action; even though these need not necessarily have led to inertia — as the USPD leaders, council delegates, 'revolutionary chairmen' and the mass movement demonstrated. Trapped by powerful continuities at work in German history, they perceived the liberating discontinuity of the revolution mainly as a threat. They did not see it as an opportunity for reshaping the state. They did not feel they were the revolution's plenipotentiaries, but merely custodians of the state, consciously regarding their transitional government as a brief interlude. Even now they were victims of the illusion that a consensus was necessary. They prolonged the 'civic peace' on their own initiative, rather than attempting to face the reality of conflicts. To their patient, quietist mentality the exaggerated threat from the Left appeared to be more of a danger than their vulnerability to the political Right, which was only temporarily paralysed. When the moment of truth came, no matter how seriously they took the many calls for change, they showed they were simply not up to the challenge.

Subjectively, the MSDP leaders believed they could not act any differently in the situation. In view of their past experiences this is not difficult to understand. But whoever cares to examine the objective results of their actions cannot ignore the numerous consequences (of which more later). Their syndrome of attitudes stood, at any rate, in the way of any forceful and rapid change: it prevented a reform of the army, even though this was expected, by many officers as well as by the soldiers' councils; it stood in the way of economic reforms, even though these were considered absolutely necessary, not only by the workers' councils but by broad sections of the liberal parties and the middle classes; it prevented agrarian reforms, even though these were the only way to break the economic backbone of the powerful land-owning aristocracy; finally, it blocked a reform of the judiciary and the bureaucracy, even though this was the only way to remove the power of the imperial civil service. Taken overall, it was certain that a price would have to be paid for failing to carry out reforms, even if there was no way at that time of measuring exactly what the cost might be to German society.

Not only did a petty-bourgeois mentality based on a desire for order stand in the way of those reforms, but the MSPD's fear of having to face a situation similar at least to that of civil war. The Ebert–Groener pact was not least the product of this fear. Yet it was precisely their dealings with the military which showed up the basic miscalculation of the MSPD representatives on the Council of People's Delegates. Groener promised to provide ten divisions for the task of stabilising the internal situation. In all, only 1,800 men turned up, and even they disappeared by 24 December after coming up against revolutionary sailors from the navy. The imperial army, by now in the process of complete disintegration, no longer obeyed orders from the Supreme Command. When the Spartakist Uprising began on 6 January, the government still had no troops at its disposal. But some 300,000 workers, called upon to fight, protected the Imperial Chancellery, saved the government and occupied virtually the entire capital before the *Freikorps* moved in on 11 January. While the Austrian Social Democrats managed to keep order by means of a republican People's Militia, the MSPD leadership frittered away the chance to form pro-republican militias over a whole two months, even though hundreds of thousands of its members, as well as officers and quantities of arms, were available. Instead of organising and arming the Social Democratic masses and satisfying the call of the crowds for 'Guns, guns! Give us guns!', which could be heard on 6 January, if not before, the MSPD leaders were afraid of their own supporters and refused to build up reliable forces. The Supreme Command, instead of being dismissed, remained in office, and the way was left open for the *Freikorps*.

When the elections to the National Assembly began in January 1919, it was already clear that 'the entire political and intellectual apparatus of the Empire had been preserved', including 'the administration, the judiciary, the universities, the economy and the generals'.[35] Only later, when the first bourgeois–democratic phase of the revolution was over, was there a sudden change in mood to one of disillusionment leading to a growth in radicalism. This second phase witnessed sections of the working class rise in revolt in the spring of 1919. It ended in rapid failure when it was violently crushed by the military. Two months after the start of the revolution, the old power-élites had begun to recover politically and militarily from 'the paralysis of will brought on by the period of upheaval'.[36] Nowhere had they been dealt with quickly and effectively enough. The elections and the Weimar Coalition, made up of the SPD, the Centre and those Liberals forming the German Democratic Party (DDP) produced in effect a return to the government of Prince Max von Baden. The revolution was seen, therefore, as a superfluous, disturbing interlude. Soon it was widely denied that a genuine revolution had ever taken place. The Weimar Republic, which characteristically continued to style itself officially 'the German Empire', embodied, as Troeltsch was to remark:

> . . . basically an anti-revolutionary principle devoted to the establishment of law and order in the state. Only the short-sighted could exult at this and believe that the goal of 1848 had been achieved. But no — what had been a bold step forward on the path of progress in 1848 had now become a conservative move which blocked and frustrated the revolution in order to ensure its enemies a continued legality of their actions and increasing influence.[37]

The short history of the first German Republic began, therefore, with this oppressive handicap of failure to carry out a radical reform of the state, its personnel and its institutions.

Two further problems still have to be dealt with at this point.

(1) Without a thorough reorganisation of the state apparatus, we would argue, no democracy could have emerged in Germany after 1918 which could have functioned in the long term. For this to happen, the desire for reform, of which the councils were partly an expression, would have had to have been mobilised with determination. This is not to argue the case that a system of councils could have provided a permanent institutional arrangement. Nor was this ever argued by the majority of the councils themselves. In my opinion, there are convincing objections to such a view which can be outlined only briefly here and which favoured the principle of representative democracy as opposed to that of 'direct' democracy represented by the councils.[38] A system of councils relies upon the constant participation and vigilance of its members. But the level of permanent political mobilisation it demands seems scarcely feasible given the general human need to alternate continually between spells of activity and recuperation. Similarly, the political objectivity, to which it lays claim, seems equally difficult to achieve in practice: either party-style factions begin to form immediately or

political parties are called upon to mediate in the event of disagreement. Even councils find they cannot dispense with the need for bureaucracy. The 'executive council' (*Vollzugsrat*) of the time soon had 500 officials working for it. Economic planning and economic controls in a highly complex society are, in fact, scarcely conceivable without bureaucracies of experts. Similarly, hierarchies eventually form, given the way that councils are organised. The higher levels gain an advantage in the collection of information by virtue of the place they occupy in the channels of communication. They come to have an interest in their self-perpetuation and prove difficult to abolish. Whatever problems might be caused in practice by the principle of the separation of powers, its abolition as a basis for new institutional arrangements increases the opportunity for a monopoly of power to emerge in the upper councils, thus reducing the liberties of individuals and groups. Historically speaking, councils have been traditionally established by workers and soldiers. But how, once a period of conflict is over, are minorities to be afforded protection under such a system? Are those who lose their rights expected to suffer in silence? Or, if the right of resistance is recognised as legitimate, how is it to be exercised? The ideal of self-government presupposes rational deliberation and behaviour. If these are lacking, the usurpation of power by a dictatorial minority is more difficult than ever to resist because a system of checks and balances is lacking. The theory of rule by councils rests fundamentally, moreover, on an assumed identity of the rulers and the ruled. Implicit in this system, therefore, is the romantic desire for a harmonious society which is contradicted by the plurality of interests actually obtaining in complex modern societies. Consequently, this theory also does not acknowledge social conflicts as structurally generated forces propelling social development. It therefore provides far weaker safeguards for minorities than those in a parliamentary democracy. Despite the justified criticisms of bureaucracies and oligarchies in the state and economy, then and in our own day, and despite the pressing need for more effective controls over political representatives and the decision-making processes, as a permanent institutional structure a system of councils in an industrial society would appear to be extremely problematical and inferior to representative institutions capable of reform. Nevertheless, in a situation of radical upheaval like that of 1918–19 the councils which emerged in Germany could have been used to restructure society, if the political leadership of the time had encouraged such a course with more determination than it showed. For the crucial point remains that the great majority of councils showed a desire for greater democracy throughout this time, but not in the style of a Bolshevik dictatorship of the proletariat. For anyone willing to bring about this process of democratisation — which meant removing the fundamental factors determining the political, social and economic framework up to that point — there was no other way to achieve this than with the help of the soldiers' and workers' councils.

(2) On a great many points concerning the period of transition from the Empire to the Weimar Republic one is left with hypothetical considerations regarding the different options open to Germany's future development: 'What would have happened, if . . . ?' There is no doubt something artificial in this way of thinking, and yet the historian cannot and must not avoid making judgements of the possible alternatives. In this respect the question is that of the social costs incurred in opting for the Weimar Republic — costs which became apparent all too soon. Nowadays it may be easier in Germany to discuss Weimar's kind of social costs by reference to Asia or other regions. Did China's revolutionary 'great leap forward' in the process of social and economic modernisation cost less in terms of suffering than India's evolutionary path, despite the bloody sacrifices involved? Is it not that in the meantime the Indian solution has cost far more in human lives because the feeding of sacred cows was regarded as more important than the feeding of starving human beings, i.e. than the fight against catastrophic floods and famines? Such questions are so complex and involve so many variables that no definitive answers can be found in a discussion of this kind. But a sense of intellectual honesty and confidence in our ability to learn from the past requires that the question of the political and economic costs of decisions taken, as well as those not taken, should be raised again and again. No judgement on Weimar's chances of survival can skirt round the problem that after a little more than a dozen years the downward spiral to Brüning's authoritarian regime began, only to be followed by the successful National Socialist 'seizure of power' in 1933. The latter undoubtedly represented a convergence of certain trends in German history. This convergence can only be explained if we look not merely at the many problems which came in the wake of Germany's defeat in the First World War but at the whole range of historically inherited handicaps and their long-term effects. The situation of 1918–19, which decided Germany's subsequent course of development, does not, however, lose its obvious significance. Does one not have to balance the costs that

a new departure would have incurred — namely, that of the exclusion of the old ruling élites, involving the weakness or even the temporary paralysis of the governmental system — against the sacrifices and horrors after 1933? If one approves of the solution which Weimar represented, does one not also have to accept the fact that it ended the way it did? If so, does this not make the assertion that 1933 represented a 'break' in historical continuity even more open to question? Do the rapidly felt consequences of the opportunities that were missed not force us to sharpen our awareness of the complexity of the situation in relation to the decisions taken and the problems that followed from them? Since continuity in the imperial bureaucracy and the army, in the education system and the political parties, in the economy and its pressure groups, and so on, was largely preserved, one thing at least was assured: the traditional power-élites were able to depute the stirrup-holders for Hitler. Whether the Nazi Party's own dynamism and the radicalisation of the middle classes, its winning over of the rural population and the weakening of the workers' movement — whether all these would have made the 'seizure of power' by the strongest party in the *Reichstag* at the time inevitable is an open question. In the concrete circumstances which prevailed, however, the *Führer* could never, at any rate, have climbed into the saddle without the stirrups to help him. Viewed in this light, the costs of the decisions taken in 1918–19 began, in 1933, to assume undreamt-of dimensions which were eventually to involve the whole world.

IV

A Balance Sheet

'The proud citadel of the new German Empire was built in opposition to the spirit of the age', said the liberal historian, Johannes Ziekursch, a few years after its demise; '. . . through cunning and force, in a hard struggle with its enemies at home and abroad, amid breaches of the constitution and civil war, disregarding the King's opposition and against the will of a large section of the German people who had no desire to travel down Bismarck's chosen path'.[1] That the seeds of its own destruction were, therefore, already implanted in the foundations of the new state, was indeed the view long held by outsiders who came in for severe criticism. This study has also taken the view that the configurations of forces prevailing during the years of the Empire's foundation had far-reaching ramifications, and that from this time on profound structural weaknesses were built into the Bismarckian state. But, taking a broader view of German history, this does not at all help us answer the question as to whether the Greater Prussian monarchical and authoritarian state would still have been capable of further development had the war not intervened. Would a process of social and political modernisation have proved possible, if the German Empire had not been defeated in war, given that the old order would have been legitimised as never before by a successful military outcome and even by the successful preservation of the *status quo* from before 1914? Or should we go further back in time and see the eventual collapse of the authoritarian regime in war and revolution as the result of its own policies and basic constitutional character? Can one really continue to regard 1918 as an accidental occurrence which might have been reversed, while at the same time insisting on the German Empire's capacity to reform itself, as an older generation has tended to do? Or should we not point to the deliberate use of a policy based on calculated risks and look at the configurations of forces behind it, thus focussing on the historically shaped rigidity of institutions, sectional interests and ideas? Would we not discover in their very frailty the proof of their anachronistic nature? Other monarchies have, after all, survived defeat in war. It would be foolish to deny the difficulties of undertaking a critical appraisal. Nevertheless, it is necessary to attempt one in view of the part played by Germany in unleashing two world wars, the escalation of these conflicts into total war and the emergence of a radical fascism, all of which have had huge repercussions down to the present day. It is, however, made easier by the fact that the spell of the unified German nation state and its power to impose standards on our judgements appears to have been broken. A discussion of this kind becomes possible if it can be organised around certain arguable, but nevertheless illuminating criteria.

So far as I can see, three main sets of ideas might serve as the starting-point of such a discussion, even if the questions raised often remain no more than markers and the answers remain incomplete. These questions are:

(1) To what extent was a comprehensive and permanent social and economic modernisation possible? And connected with this: how could equal rights and participation in social and political decision-making have been extended? How far were legal equality and geographical and social mobility achieved? And how were structural conflicts regulated?

(2) How were the social costs and benefits of successful or obstructed modernisation distributed? How high were the costs of this in the long and short terms for specific social classes or for the society as a whole?

(3) How effective was German society's collective capacity to adapt in the face of rapidly increasing change? Here, a legitimate interest of learning theory converges with a version of Marxism which also views history as a process of continual adaptation. The capacity to adapt to changing circumstances has to be examined with special reference to the power-élites who were responsible for the important decisions taken in the German Empire. This raises the further question of whether or not the value systems of the nation as a whole and specific classes within it encouraged the process of adaptation; and whether these also favoured particular interests and were consequently supported by specific structures.

The question immediately arises as to the ends modernisation was supposed to serve. What possible goals of learning should have been striven for within the confines of experience at the time? A guiding assumption, which has already been outlined in the Introduction, lies behind our questions on the subject: that it was necessary at the time to try to synchronise as far as possible the socio-economic change which was taking place with the development of political institutions, with a view to extending rights of political participation as well as the democratic legitimation of decisions, while also providing formal guarantees for them. Alternatively, the choice was to accept the cost of creating a dangerous growth in tensions and a precarious constitutional fragility; of lapsing into a situation of 'pathological learning', thus rendering the country's capacity for peaceful evolution even more improbable. Certainly, it is true that industrialisation and democracy do not necessarily go hand in hand, as can be seen from the histories of Germany, Japan, Russia and most developing countries. Rather, their experiences suggest that it is industrialisation and bureaucratisation which are generally linked together in a mutual functional dependency. To this extent, the process of democratisation does not automatically result from industrialisation, however much industrial and democratic revolutions may have developed in conjunction with one another since the eighteenth century. Industrialisation and democracy are the laboriously achieved product of political and social struggles to develop and then retain the political conditions which up until now have proved to be the most suitable for industrial societies. A basically democratic order best appears to afford such societies a flexibility of political institutions and a strong basis for legitimation during the process of constructing a modern state. Without this flexibility and legitimation crises of a fundamental nature occur which prove difficult to resolve. Social and political modernisation cannot, therefore, be separated from the need for a democratic political and social order; and any judgement on the extent of a society's ability to learn may take as its main criterion the extent to which, and the speed with which, the socio-economic changes of the industrial world are met with the realisation of equal rights, greater public knowledge of how decisions are taken, democratic controls on those in power, adequate provisions for all the basic necessities of life — in short, the step-by-step realisation of the democratic welfare state. This is not to assert dogmatically that no higher stage can be reached. But it does take account of the experience of history which shows that such a constitution represents, more than any other, a step in the direction of a more humane and open society, in which the possibility of revising earlier decisions is greater.

That economic progress, in the sense of a rapid expansion of industrialisation, was also possible in a state like Prusso–Germany, at first still dominated by tradition, can be seen from its economic history in the period after 1850. Indeed, it has been pointed out several times over that it was precisely the undeniable success of Germany's industrial economy that gave rise to its particular problems. Certainly, the land-owning lobby tried to sabotage the development of industry right up to the beginning of the war by, for example, having favourable tax and financial bills passed in the *Reichstag*. They also adopted economic measures which worked to their own advantage on the stock market. But since the long-term process of industrialisation had all the support it needed, institutionally, politically and intellectually, the agrarians no longer had any real chance of changing anything. The rise of the industrial economy prevailed over all attempts to resist it. Eventually, even 'organised capitalism' proved unstoppable.

The impact of social modernisation produces conflicting effects. A legal and spatial-vertical mobilisation of the population had been formally achieved even before 1871. In practice this modernisation was also able to benefit after the 1890s from the massive internal migration taking place among the rural population. But vertical social mobility encountered serious obstacles because of the 'imperial nation's' characteristic division into late-feudal estates, and later on into modern social classes as well. The possibility of rising into the higher strata or classes was never entirely ruled out. There were several astonishing success stories of careers in Germany, just as there were in post-civil war America. But social origins, religious affiliation and access to educational institutions etc., determined one's chances of social mobility at an earlier stage and more permanently in Germany compared with America. In the majority of cases it appears to have taken several generations to climb the social ladder from, for instance, a skilled worker to an elementary schoolteacher and on to the civil servant or academic. 'The separation of the classes is so strict here', wrote Walther Rathenau in 1917, 'that I have experienced only once in thirty years the case of a worker or the son of a worker rising to a high position in the middle class.'[2] As head of the AEG electrical engineering trust Rathenau's observation was based on a sound knowledge of countless career biographies. Social rights of equality had no more than a very tenuous institutional achorage, if any at all. We can see this very clearly in the case of the education system; but it could also be observed in the way that the laws governing freedom of association blatantly discriminated against the workers and, in particular, the agricultural labourers. The ruling élites in the state made no attempt to moderate the ideological and anti-egalitarian divisions in German society, let alone abolish them.

In view of the authority of government agencies and representative political bodies to make decisions affecting the whole of society, the delaying of political modernisation assumes an obvious importance. Rochau's prognosis of 1862, that with Bismarck's appointment 'the sharpest, but last bolt of reaction by the grace of God' had been shot; and that one could expect a liberal breakthrough within a short space of time,[3] had already proved unrealistic by 1871. Three wars and the founding of the Greater Prussian Empire succeeded in stabilising the old structures of power, and these efforts were subsequently continued by means of a whole range of measures designed to preserve the *status quo*. Bismarck repeatedly expressed the view in several brilliant formulations (thus leading many to assume it was his guiding maxim) that history could not be 'made', that 'certain basic issues had to work themselves out', and that one could not 'direct the flow of time'[4] into a chosen direction. Yet he did the exact opposite in regard to a number of vital domestic issues and, as the agent of the ruling groups in society, he never wavered in his fight against the spread of parliamentary influence and democracy, or equal rights and opportunities for greater political participation, i.e. against some of the basic currents of the modern age. The Wilhelmine polycracy followed his lead. This was why Burckhardt's scepticism in 1871 was so accurate when he predicted that 'we may well cry our eyes out . . . at the further domestic developments which all of this will bring'.[5]

The *Reichstag* electoral law did not, it is true, fulfil the hopes of its authors for a conservative mandate based on plebiscitary support; but its democratic character did provide them indirectly with a political buffer against liberal and democratic demands for universal suffrage. Since it did not allow for a change in government at regular intervals in the parliamentary sense until October 1918, it represented no more than a half-way solution. Worse still, it facilitated the continued denunciation of the political opposition, keeping it in a state of powerlessness. There is no doubt that the importance of the political parties, forced to operate outside the uncrossable threshold of the *arcana imperii*, did increase to some extent; but overall political responsibility was still denied them. In view of this, the regime deprived itself of the chance to secure the loyalty of dissenting groups — i.e. the opportunity of producing an integrative effect by increasing access to legitimate political positions in the decision-making process. Referring to this problem, Meinecke said in 1910 of 'the Conservatives' domestic policy' that it amounted to a 'latent civil war against the Social Democrats, fought with the weapons of the police state'.[6]

The casual manner with which the *Reichstag* was treated was underlined by the obstinate defence of the Prussian Three-Class voting system, which stipulated public balloting. To it must be added the new and often overlooked, class-based franchise which Saxony introduced in 1896. This, together with other similar electoral laws, where the value of the individual's vote was effectively determined by his membership of a particular social class (e.g. in the Hanseatic towns), was a thorn in the flesh of the great majority of the electorate whose votes were devalued in federal state elections. The ruling groups in society were able not only to resist pressure on them to adapt to changing conditions; they were even able, as in the case of industrial Saxony, to change electoral laws for the worse. The world war made this blatant class egotism all the more unbearable, though not to the point where common sense prevailed upon the Conservatives to effect a change for the better. Bethmann spoke with foreboding in 1916 'of the nightmare of a revolution after the war'. He did not look forward to the 'enormous expectations harboured by the men returning home in field-grey'. What Bethmann considered to be 'enormous' pressures were concessions which, in Max Weber's view, amounted to no more than 'than bare minimum of a sense of shame and common decency' concerning the question of voting rights. Were 'the entire mass of returning warriors to find themselves once more in the lowest voting class' after having 'defended' the property of the privileged voters 'out there with their blood'? That, according to the conservatives, whatever their shade of party, was precisely what they were expected to do. 'It should be constantly emphasised that equal suffrage means the end for Prussia, as it does for any other state', wrote Ludendorff's aide, Colonel Bauer, in April 1918. 'What is the point of all these sacrifices now, if in the end we are going to suffocate under Jews and proletarians?' But the October Reforms came too late in this respect. It was in vain, therefore, that even the loyal Prussian and patriot Schmoller had prophesied in 1910 a revolution like that in France in 1848, if the Prussian franchise were not extended and made secret and direct.[7]

The *Reichstag* electoral law was never abolished, as first the liberals and subsequently the military and advocates of a *coup d'état* had desired for different reasons. But rights of political participation were also not settled at the level where decisions affecting the federal states or the German Empire as a whole were taken. Instead, they were generally extended informally — as in Baden — or occasionally even withdrawn. The much-cited involvement of workers' representatives in the work of local health insurance offices forming part of the government's social insurance scheme certainly did not at all make up for paragraph 153 of the industrial code. In force up to May 1918, this clause declared it to be a criminal offence to force workers to join trade-union strikes, thus making it difficult to organise strikes effectively.

Nor did the workers' involvement in the system make up for the outlawing of alliances between 'political' associations, with the result that the organising of trade unions on a nation-wide basis became gradually possible only after 1899. It was also no compensation for denying trade unions the right to bring court actions against the employers before the Imperial Law on Associations was passed in 1908; nor for the refusal to allow workers' participation in industry until 1916, and even then it merely covered certain aspects of life in the work-place. In short, the constitutional monarchy of the state was not even reflected in the existence of the 'constitutional' factory. It would take some time to list all the discriminations in this area.

The creation of powerful political checks was effectively blocked in other areas, too. Who was there to keep an eye on the bureaucracy, given that the *Reichstag* and the federal state assemblies were nearly paralysed? Who was there to oppose effectively the late-absolutist privileges of the military? Who was there to help the agricultural labourers against the local squirearchies in the way that factory inspectors and trade-union officials could support the urban workers? Who could insist on greater scrutiny of the legislature's decisions in view of the political weight wielded by the producers' interests? In all, it is questionable, even if difficult to measure, whether the public discussions of decisions became more open at this time. No one should underestimate the effects of the liberal journalism of the 1860s; and yet the gradual liberalisation taking place in the years before 1914 should not be overestimated either.

Pre-industrial value systems, exerting a considerable and constant influence, contributed to the defence of the ruling élites' established positions. Through a process of mystification, the ideology of the German state continued to present the policies of vested interests as motivated by impartial, above-party considerations. It nourished unfounded reservations against Germany's political parties and shielded the bureaucracy from criticism. The social romanticism of the middle classes and the *Wandervogel* movement, neo-Thomism and extreme right-wing radicals diverted attention from Germany's social conflicts. These were denounced as 'unnatural', instead of being allowed to take place openly and be resolved by political procedures. An old-style Prussian patriotism tried to justify the excesses of Prussia's policies as the invigorating proof of the military monarchy's vitality. All of these obstructed the view of reality while favouring powerful interests, allowed to operate skilfully and energetically from the lectern and the pulpit, through textbooks and the press, in the furtherance of Germany's 'true values'. A glance at the syllabuses for those subjects intended to inculcate 'proper' attitudes and 'correct' values in the elementary and grammar schools shows just how much the dominant ideas there reflected the ideas of the dominant groups in society.

Thus, the overall impression is one of the socio-political power structure of the German Empire with its supporting ideologies remaining strong enough to impose its restrictive conditions on German society up to the autumn of 1918. This had to be paid for, however, by growing disparities in politics and society, which those in charge found themselves less and less able to cope with when it came to finding long-term solutions.

If one looks at some of the modern social science theories on developing countries, we see that these societies have to respond to essentially six crises.[8] Since the founding period of the new German state was in many ways comparable to that of a developing country, it is possible for us to establish that the expansion of and growth in complexity of the state apparatus in Germany produced a real crisis of state power in conflict with society only at the time of the *Kulturkampf* in the 1870s. From then on the influence of the state increasingly penetrated social life, but without a recurrence of similar tensions. The crisis of attempts to integrate Imperial German society witnessed the emergence of a new 'imperial patriotism', a new pride in Germany's economy and its educational and military institutions — to name but a few of the more important elements. This patriotism soon became widely accepted within certain social strata. But, despite the spread of nationalism among the workers, the chronic discrimination of the Social Democrats remained to the end the visible sign of failure to achieve full integration. This failure did not, however, produce any real crisis of identity for the German Empire. The existence of a common language of education, common cultural and political traditions, unifying experiences in the age of the emerging nation-state, prevented this from occurring. On the other hand, the failure to achieve integration did not prevent problems of uncertainty in defining the German Empire's relations with neighbouring nations and its role in the international system of states. The crisis of unequal distribution was never solved. It has not admittedly been solved anywhere, even to this day. But in Imperial Germany before 1914 people were becoming accustomed to the generally rising level of prosperity of an industrial economy whose fruits were distributed completely unequally between the social classes; and it was precisely because of this inequality that the problem grew increasingly acute. Similarly, the crises of social and political participation and of the legitimation of a system of political rule, which ignored central needs and was already to a considerable extent anachronistic, persisted.

Two things exacerbated these fundamental problems. Right up to the end, social conflicts, viewed here as motive forces in a society riddled with antagonisms, were never openly acknowledged. It was not until the war that the state first sanctioned moves towards allowing free collective bargaining in wage disputes. In the *Reichstag*, as the forum for resolving conflicts, even the majority of deputies after the 1912 elections were faced with the fact that, as before, they remained inconsequential in terms of their political importance. As late as 1913, Bethmann Hollweg was able casually to ignore two censure motions (over the expropriation of the Poles and the Zabern affair), so long as he remained sure of the Emperor's support. To combat class tensions and conflicting interests, attempts were made to create the ideal of a harmonious society. Much was made of allegedly 'national' interests and finally there was the masquerade of the 'civic peace'. All of these were quite obviously intended to negate certain ideologies and were an expression of the authoritarian state's attempts to withhold from its subjects, for as long as possible, any acknowledgement of conflicts. This prevented their institutional assimilation and resolution by agreed rational procedures. The deep-rooted historical traditions which gave rise to this fear of conflict have already been pointed out. In the end, it merely led to ever-greater disparities and became one of the factors behind the revolution. The costs involved in delaying social and political modernisation — and economic modernisation, too, if one considers large-scale agriculture east of the Elbe — were often charged formally to the account of society as a whole (e.g. through *Reichstag* legislation which increased protective tariffs and taxes). But this burden was borne to a massive extent unequally by the different social classes. A major agricultural producer could react with far more equanimity to an increase in the cost of imported basic foodstuffs caused by the agricultural tariffs he had supported than could the wage-earning masses in the industrial cities. An industrial baron from heavy industry might attack the lamentably low rates of a progressive income tax as theft without substantially feeling their effects; but high indirect taxes increased the basic cost of living in millions of already sparsely furnished households. The relative economic vulnerability of the majority of wage-earning consumers, who for decades could articulate their grievances only through a constantly ostracised party, contrasted sharply with the 'policy of generous hand-outs' towards the land-owners, the careful consideration shown for heavy industry's interests, or the preferential treatment given for political reasons to the middle classes. While artisan protection laws or insurance for white-collar workers largely satisfied the material demands of these groups and their ideological need to preserve their status, the stabilisation of the system as a whole was achieved at the expense of the majority of Germany's citizens. Generally speaking, the inequity of charging the costs to the weak in society was a reflection of the growing disparities in the distribution of wealth in favour of the strong.

Social benefits and costs were also distributed unequally in a more subtle fashion. The educationally élitist university and school systems scorned any formal methods of realising equality of opportunity. They continued to confer their privileges on a narrow section of society. At a time when specialised professional knowledge was increasingly determining a person's chances of upward social mobility beyond the advantages of birth or a favourable position in the process of production, it chained the majority of citizens to the chance circumstance of their social origin by its refusal to impart specialised knowledge and general learning (*Bildung*) to them. We can observe in the development of the SPD's and USPD's views on educational arrangements how the inhibiting effects of traditional education upon social mobility were gradually identified and a remedy prepared. But even here the political Left in Germany failed almost completely to bring about changes between 1918 and 1933. The pseudo-egalitarian promises of the National Socialist 'national community' (*Volksgemeinschaft*) seem to have been attractive precisely because of the crassly paraded and painfully felt differences in education which had persisted almost unchanged.

The nature of the education system can be viewed as symptomatic of a more general problem. The collective capacity of individuals, groups, or entire societies to learn appears to depend a great deal on the extent to which social relationships are of an 'open' or 'closed' character. Here, too, many threads of development can be traced to the fact that Germany had never experienced a successful bourgeois revolution. This resulted in a lack of questioning and opening up, or at least loosening up, of traditional structures. The unbroken tradition of government by pre-industrial power-élites, the prolongation of absolutism among the military, the weakness of liberalism and the very early appearance of deliberalising measures suggest on the surface a depoliticising of society, but one which deep down favoured a continuation of the *status quo*. The same can be said of the barriers to social mobility, the holding over of differences and various norms between separate estates, which is such a revealing aspect of Imperial Germany, and the essentially élitist character of education. Much of this resulted from the political weakness and defeats suffered by the bourgeoisie in the nineteenth century, and all these factors, which are given here only as examples, had assumed their importance during a phase of historical development which was uninterrupted by a successful revolution. They were further strengthened by the success of Bismarck's policies for legitimising the *status quo*. This achievement did not preclude a partial modernisation of the economy, since after 1848 the strategy of 'revolution from above' at first had the effect of strengthening the nascent industrial system. Nor did it rule out other achievements. Technical education was so well organised against the various efforts to resist its progress that the flow of scientific and technological innovations began relatively early on and was subsequently maintained. Many of the big cities profited from the retreat of liberalism's leading lights into local government, as well as from the bureaucratic tradition. It was not by chance that, after the 1890s, German local government, together with its communally-run public services, was regarded as a model by the American 'progressives'. While it is true that in 1895 more than 170,000 workers, punished as a result of their involvement in strikes, knew what it was to be on the receiving end of a system of class justice, the law nevertheless ensured a high degree of physical safety in the towns and rural districts. This was as true for workers and for members of national minorities, as for other social groups. Anyone who thinks highly of American party democracy should also look at the darker side of life in the United States — at, for example, the jungles of New York's immigrant quarters or the lynch justice of the South, to which for decades after the Civil War at least one Black per day fell victim. Party politics, lynch justice and life in the big cities may not appear commensurable with the above; but any comparing of systems inevitably draws upon positive or negative aspects of each, for which direct comparisons are difficult to find. In the German Empire it was not only discipline and repression which ensured social cohesion — whatever their undeniable effects, both subtle and obvious — but the conditions of everyday life. All protests to the contrary, the majority of Germany's citizens did not find these so oppressive that the crises of the Empire developed into a revolutionary situation before the war.

As regards the ruling élites' ability to adapt to changing circumstances, we must again enquire into the reasons for the system's relative stability, the traditional bases for which have been pointed out several times. We can only say, in the language of modern theory, that 'pathological learning' was in evidence in several areas. The retention or introduction of class-based electoral laws, the reaction to fundamental social conflicts and the creation of income taxes, the Zabern affair of 1913 or the belated repeal of the clauses on language in the Imperial Law of Associations in April 1917 — all reveal, even if measured solely in terms of a pure self-interest in upholding the system, such an extreme narrow-mindedness that Bethmann Hollweg's judgement would seem to be borne out. History, his associate, Riezler, recorded, would reveal 'the lack of education, the stupidity of militarism and the rottenness of the entire chauvinistically minded upper class'.[9] This is what directly paved the way for the revolutionary crisis of 1918. In other areas where the élites endeavoured to hold on to their inherited positions of power, their successes outweighed the risks involved. There is no denying that the system of connections between the nobility, the ministerial bureaucracy, the provincial authorities and the district administrators — who were a veritable pillar of stability east of the river Elbe — created political tensions. But the myth of the bureaucracy's neutrality and the patina of inherited traditions, together with the preference shown to powerful interests, kept these below the danger-mark for a considerable time. Without doubt, the combination of compulsory military service with a social militarism in everyday life, in school subjects and in various organisations, created areas of friction. But the gains made in terms of the stability which these elements helped to achieve more than made up for this friction throughout the period up to and including the first years of the war. In both cases, it was not until November 1918 that the true extent of the population's strong dislike of the bureaucracy and the military could be seen.

Most effective of all, perhaps, were those strategies which, also depending on the ruling élites' capacity to learn, combined an ability to adapt to modern forms of politics and propaganda with, at the same time, a stubborn defence of their inherited positions of power. The unholy trinity of social imperialism, social protectionism and social militarism provides more than sufficient examples of this. In the case of social imperialism, the ruling élites' reaction to industrialisation was closely linked to its usefulness in stabilising the social and political hierarchy of privilege. In the case of social protectionist measures, institutional arrangements of future import, such as state legislation on social insurance, were combined with welfare measures and rights which were not essentially liberal, but reactionary, so long as they led to an increase in the numbers of 'friends of the Empire'. In the case of social militarism, which was intensively encouraged, privileges of social status handed down from the past were defended by means of modern techniques of political campaigning pursuing carefully thought-out aims. The same is true of the early forms of state interventionism. Even a modern-style pressure group like the Agrarian League reveals quite clearly how this ability to adapt to modern methods of organisation and propaganda was entirely compatible with the continued promotion of traditional interests. All in all the entire process, which Hans Rosenberg has described as 'the pseudo-democratisation' of the old agrarian elite,[10] showed an often astonishingly flexible readiness on the part of the ruling élites to move with the times while all the more ruthlessly defending their traditional positions behind the façade.

All these strategies, measures and processes of pathological and ingenuous learning were interwoven. Together with a combination of traditionalism and partial modernisation, they were able, on the one hand, to preserve the stability of an historically outdated power structure over a surprisingly long period. Time and time again they achieved the necessary social cohesion. On the other hand, they added, especially in the long run, to an unmistakably increasing burden. The various interests and traditions thus protected became all the more difficult to reconcile with the growing demands for equality, a share of power and liberation from an increasingly intolerable legacy. Just as the economic successes of German industrialisation threw up enormous social and political problems, so the successful defence of traditional political, social and economic power relationships exacted its price. The costs were all the greater and more numerous as a result. The accumulation of unsolved problems which eventually had to be faced, the petrification of institutions which had outlived their usefulness and were in need of reform and the obstinate insistence on prerogatives which should no longer have been the sole property of the privileged few, pronounce their own judgement on the extent to which the ruling élites were prepared to adapt. So do the continual recourse to evasive strategies and attempts to divert attention from the need for internal reforms, as well as the decision to accept the risk of war rather than be forced into making concessions. In practice, the ruling élites showed themselves to be neither willing nor able to initiate the transition towards modern social and political conditions when this had become necessary. This is not a judgement based on theoretical speculation but on processes which culminated in the breakdown of the German Empire in revolution and the end of the old regime. This hiatus now belongs among the undisputed facts of history and cannot be explained away. It represented the bill that had to be paid for the inability of the German Empire to adapt positively to change.

The fact that this break with the past did not go deep enough and that the consequences of the successful preservation of outworn traditions remained everywhere visible after 1918, accounts for the acute nature of the problem of continuity in twentieth-century German history. Instead of bewailing 'the distortion of judgement caused by the category of continuity',[11] in arguments which patently seek to defend the German Empire's record, we should, in keeping with the essential requirements of an historical social science, face up to the problems of continuity and seek to analyse them further, rather than encourage an escapist attitude. This does not, of course, mean we should offer superficial explanations based on the 'great men' approach to history (from Bismarck to Hitler via Wilhelm II and Hindenburg); rather we should investigate the social, economic, political and psychic structures which, acting as matrices, were able to produce the same, or similar, configurations over a long period of time. Conversely, we should also analyse those factors which gave rise to anomalies and discontinuity. The question as to whether, in fact, certain conditions favoured the emergence of charismatic political leaders in Germany should be re-examined against the background of these structures.

In the years before 1945, and indeed in some respects beyond this, the fatal successes of Imperial Germany's ruling élites, assisted by older historical traditions and new experiences, continued to exert an influence. In the widespread susceptibility towards authoritarian policies, in the hostility towards democracy in education and political life, in the continuing influence of the pre-industrial ruling élites, there begins a long inventory of serious historical problems. To this list we must add the tenacity of the German ideology of the state, its myth of the bureaucracy, the superimposition of class differences on those between the traditional late-feudal estates and the manipulation of political antisemitism. It is because of all these factors that a knowledge of the history of the German Empire between 1871 and 1918 remains absolutely indispensable for an understanding of German history over the past decades.

Abbreviations

AA   = Auswärtiges Amt (Prussian and German Foreign Office)
AHR   = *American Historical Review*
BA   = Bundesarchiv Koblenz (West German Federal Archives)
BdL   = Bund der Landwirte (Agrarian League)
DZA   = Deutsches Zentralarchiv, I: Potsdam (East German Archives)
GW   = O. v. Bismarck, *Gesammelte Werke*, 19 vols, 1924–35
GStA   = Geheimes Staatsarchiv (Prussian Secret State Archives)
HZ   = *Historische Zeitschrift*
IESS   = *International Encyclopaedia of the Social Sciences*, 17 vols, 1968
JCH   = *Journal of Contemporary History*
Jh.   = Jahrhundert
JMH   = *Journal of Modern History*
MEW   = Marx–Engels, *Werke*, 41 vols, 1957–66
MS   = Maschinenschriftliches Manuskript
PA   = Politisches Archiv des AA Bonn (Political Archives of the West German Foreign Office)
PVS   = *Politische Vierteljahresschrift*
RB   = O. von Bismarck, *Reden*, 14 vols, 1892–1905
RT   = Stenographic reports of the proceedings of the German *Reichstag*
RV   = Reichsverfassung (Imperial Constitution)
ZfG   = *Zeitschrift für Geschichtswissenschaft*
ZGS   = *Zeitschrift für die Gesamte Staatswissenschaft*
ZdI   = Zentralverband deutscher Industrieller (Central Association of German Manufacturers)

Notes

Note: In general, references are provided only for quotations. The Bibliography gives a short overview of the most important literature consulted in the sequence in which it is utilised in the text.

Translator's Preface

1. H.-U. Wehler, *Das Deutsche Kaiserreich, 1871–1918*, Göttingen, 1973; 6th ed., 1985.
2. John A. Moses, *The Politics of Illusion*, London, 1975, is still the best account in English of the controversy surrounding Fischer's work.
3. For the influence of historicism, see G. Iggers, *The German Conception of History*, Middletown, Conn., 1968, and his subsequent *New Directions in European Historiography*, Middletown, Conn., 1975, which devotes an entire chapter to the new orientation in West German historiography.
4. See Wehler's statistics in idem, 'Historiography in Germany today', in J. Habermas (ed.), *Observations on 'The Spiritual Situation of the Age'*, Cambridge, Mass., 1984, pp. 221–59. These demonstrate the effect of the post-war expansion of German higher education in breaking down the homogeneity of the historical profession and bringing the new ideas to the fore.
5. The most notable collections being Michael Stürmer (ed.), *Das Kaiserliche Deutschland*, Düsseldorf, 1970, and H.-U. Wehler (ed.), *Moderne Deutsche Sozialgeschichte*, 6th ed., Königstein, 1981.
6. The main statement of Wehler's views is contained in his *Historische Sozialwissenschaft und Geschichtsschreibung*, Göttingen, 1980, which still awaits a translator.
7. H.-U. Wehler, *Bismarck und der Imperialismus*, 5th ed., Frankfurt, 1984.
8. See the introduction by R.J. Evans in ibid. (ed.) *Society and Politics in Wilhelmine Germany*, London, 1978, where the work of Wehler and his contemporaries is acknowledged as an 'enormous advance' on previous research, but challenged as a 'new orthodoxy'.

I

1. T. Veblen, *Imperial Germany and the Industrial Revolution* (1915), Ann Arbor, Mich., 1966; see also Marx (MEW, vol. 23, pp. 12f. — fifty years previously!); A. Gerschenkron, *Economic Backwardness in Historical Perspective*, Cambridge, Mass., 1962, 2nd imp. 1965, pp. 5–30.
2. G. Schmoller, *Charakterbilder*, Munich, 1913, p. 49.
3. G. Ipsen, 'Die preussische Bauernbefreiung als Landesausbau', in *Zeitschrift für Agrargeschichte*, vol. 2, 1954, p. 47; F. Lütge, *Geschichte der deutschen Agrarverfassung vom frühen Mittelalter bis zum 19. Jh.*, Stuttgart, 1963, 2nd imp. 1967, p. 228.
4. Foregoing quotations from H. Rosenberg, 'Die Pseudodemokratisierung der Rittergutsbesitzerklasse', in his *Probleme*, pp. 33, 12, 16f.
5. Gerschenkron, p. 62.
6. T. Hamerow, *Restoration, Revolution, Reaction: Economics and Politics in Germany, 1815–71*, Princeton, NJ, 1958, pp. 207, 210; A. Desai, *Real Wages in Germany, 1871–1913*, Oxford, 1968, pp. 108, 117; I. Äkerman, *Theory of Industrialism*, Lund, 1960, pp. 305, 307, 309, 311, 331–80. Economic and social statistical data, unless otherwise stated, from W.G. Hoffmann *et al.*, *Das Wachstum der deutschen Wirtschaft*, Heidelberg, 1965. The figures for strikes from W. Steglich, 'Eine Streiktabelle für Deutschland, 1864–80', in *Jahrbuch für Wirtschaftsgeschichte*, 1960, vol. II, pp. 235–83.
7. *Chargé* de Rumigny, 4. 4. 1829, in P. Benaerts, *Les origines de la grande industrie allemande*, Paris, 1933, p. 15.; Metternich's memorandum for the Emperor Franz, June 1833, in A. von Klinkowström (ed.), *Aus Metternichs Nachgelassenen Papieren*, vol. V, Vienna, 1882, pp. 505, 509.
8. MEW, vol. 13, pp. 639, 642. The term 'class' is understood as an analytical category throughout this section.
9. *Stenographische Berichte über die Verhandlungen des Preussischen Hauses der Abgeordneten, 1855–56*, vol. II, p. 462 (20. 2. 1856).
10. E.N. Anderson, *The Social and Political Conflict in Prussia, 1858–64*. Lincoln, Neb., 1954, p. 441; M. Messerschmidt, 'Die Armee in Staat und Gesellschaft', in *Das Kaiserliche Deutschland*, ed. M. Stürmer, Düsseldorf, 1970, p. 95.
11. O. von Bismarck, GW, vol. XV, p. 165, cf. p. 114; H. Oncken, *R. von Bennigsen*, vol. II, Stuttgart, 1910, p. 45; G. Ritter, *Die preussischen Konservativen und Bismarcks deutsche Politik, 1858–76*, Heidelberg, 1913, p. 74.
12. G.A. Craig, *Die preussisch-deutsche Armee, 1640–1954*, Düsseldorf, 1960, p. 214; F. Lassalle, *Gesammelte Reden und Schriften*, ed. E. Bernstein, vol. IV, Berlin, 1919, pp. 307f.
13. Rosenberg (*Probleme*, p. 52), following C. Schmitt, *Verfassungslehre* (1928), 2nd imp., Berlin, 1957, pp. 31f., 118.
14. H. Rothfels, 'Probleme einer Bismarck-Biographie', *Deutsche Beiträge*, 1948, vol. II, p. 170 (adapted). Typically diluted in his *Bismarck*, Stuttgart, 1970, p. 20.
15. G. Mann, *Deutsche Geschichte des 19. Jhs*, Frankfurt, 1958, p. 383.
16. Burckhardt to Preen, 12. 10. and 17. 3. 1871, in J. Burckhardt, *Briefe*, ed. M. Burckhardt, vol. V, Basle, 1963, pp. 139, 152; similarly: Scrutator

(M. McColl), *Who Is Responsible for the War?*, London, 1870, pp. 95, 102.
17. R. Stadelmann, *Moltke und der Staat*. Krefeld, 1950, p. 145; J. Becker, 'Zum Problem der Bismarckschen Politik in der spanischen Thronfrage', in HZ, no. 212, 1971, p. 603; and his 'Der Krieg mit Frankreich als Problem der kleindeutschen Einigungspolitik Bismarcks, 1866–70', in *Das Kaiserliche Deutschland*, p. 83. On Clausewitz, see Wehler, pp. 110–12.
18. W. Sauer, 'Die politische Geschichte der deutschen Armee und das Problem des Militarismus', in PVS, 6, 1965, p. 349. On the following, see also his 'Das Problem des deutschen Nationalstaats', in H.-U. Wehler, (ed.), *Moderne deutsche Sozialgeschichte*, Cologne, 4th imp., 1973, pp. 407–36.
19. GW, vol. V, pp. 514f.; Bismarck to Talleyrand, 13. 8. 1799, in P. Bailleu, *Preussen und Frankreich, 1795–1807. Diplomatische Correspondenzen*, Leipzig, 1881, p. 505; K. Schwartz, *Leben des Generals C. von Clausewitz*, vol. I, Berlin, 1878, p. 234 (21. 5. 1809); K. Griewank (ed.), *Gneisenau. Ein Leben in Briefen*, Leipzig, 1939, pp. 397f. (9., 14. 8. 1830); GW, vol. VIII, p. 459.
20. Freytag (Sept. 1871) in H. Kohn, *Wege und Irrwege. Vom Geist des deutschen Bürgertums*, Düsseldorf, 1962, p. 178; A. von Villers, *Briefe eines Unbekannten*, vol. II, Leipzig, 5th imp., 1910, pp. 44f. (to A. von Warsberg, 24. 7. 1870); G.G. Gervinus, *Hinterlassene Schriften*, Vienna, 1872, pp. 21–3 (first memorandum on the peace at the beginning of 1871); Marx, *Kritik des Gothaer Programms* (1875), MEW, vol. 19, 1962, p. 29.
21. R. Stadelmann, 'Deutschland und die westeuropäischen Revolutionen', in his *Deutschland und Westeuropa*, Laupheim, 1948, pp. 14, 27f., 31.

II

1. J. Habermas, *Technik und Wissenschaft als 'Ideologie'*, Frankfurt, 1968, p. 68.
2. R. Höhn (ed.), *Die vaterlandslosen Gesellen, 1878–1914*, vol. I, Cologne, 1964, p. 29; MEW, vol. 6, 1959, p. 405; Desai, p. 108. Exact dates up to 1914 from A.F. Burns, 'Business Cycles', in IESS, vol. 2, 1968, p. 231, Table 1. For more details: Rosenberg, *Depression*; H.-U. Wehler, *Bismarck und der Imperialismus*, pp. 39–111.
3. MEW, vol. 23, p. 28 (1873).
4. Höhn, vol. I, p. 29; W. Mommsen (ed.), *Deutsche Parteiprogramme*, Munich, 1960, p. 790.
5. Rosenberg, *Depression*, p. 187; his *Probleme*, p. 72; tariff amounts in H.-H. Herlemann, 'Vom Ursprung des deutschen Agrarprotektionismus', in *Agrarwirtschaft und Agrarpolitik*, ed. E. Gerhardt and P. Kuhlmann, Cologne, 1969, p. 189; on the motives involved, K.W. Hardach, *Die Bedeutung wirtschaftlicher Faktoren bei der Wiedereinführung der Eisen- und Getreidezölle in Deutschland 1879*, Berlin, 1967, pp. 30–49.
6. A. Gerschenkron, *Bread and Democracy in Germany* (1943), New York, 2nd imp., 1966, p. 67.

7. Statistisches Bundesamt (ed.), *Statistisches Jahrbuch 1963*, Stuttgart, 1963, p. 57.
8. J.A. Schumpeter, *Theorie der wirtschaftlichen Entwicklung* (1911), Berlin, 6th imp., 1964, p. 102.
9. F. Kleinwächter, *Die Kartelle*, Innsbruck, 1883, p. 143.
10. R. Calwer (ed.), *Handel und Wandel 1900*, Berlin, 1901, p. 27.
11. In addition to Hoffmann see P.-C. Witt, *Die Finanzpolitik des Deutschen Reiches, 1903–13*, Lübeck, 1970, pp. 382–5; A. Feiler, *Die Konjunkturperiode 1907–13*, Jena, 1914, pp. 86, 171f., tables pp. 177–204. On capital concentration, Wehler, *Krisenherde*, pp. 308f., and literature, pp. 428f.
12. F. Grumbach and H. König, 'Beschäftigung und Löhne der deutschen Industriewirtschaft, 1888–1954', in *Welwirtschaftliches Archiv*, no. 79, 1957, vol. II, p. 153; T. Orsagh, 'Löhne in Deutschland, 1871–1913', in ZGS, no. 125, 1969, pp. 476–83.
13. F. Naumann, *Demokratie und Kaisertum*, Berlin, 1900, pp. 92f; K. Kitzel, *Die Herrfurthsche Landgemeindeordnung*, Stuttgart, 1957, pp. 13–65, quotation 18; M. Weber, *Gesammelte Aufsätze zur Sozial- und Wirtschaftsgeschichte*, Tübingen, 1924, p. 503.
14. L. Bamberger, *Erinnerungen*, Berlin, 1899, pp. 501–17; *Deutscher Ökonomist* of 12. 6. 1909, p. 387f.
15. L. Bamberger, *Bismarcks Grosses Spiel. Die Geheimen Tagebücher*, Frankfurt, 1932, p. 339 (6. 6. 1887). See T. Fontane, *Briefe an Friedländer*, ed. K. Schreinert, Heidelberg, 1954, p. 305, also for firms in general, e.g. G. Briefs, *Betriebsführung und Betriebsleben in der Industrie*, Stuttgart, 1934, p. 120.
16. M. Weber, *Gesammelte Politische Schriften*, Tübingen, 2nd imp., 1958, p. 19.
17. L. Brentano, *Die deutschen Getreidezölle* (1911), Stuttgart, 3rd imp., 1925, pp. 25–32.
18. F. Beckmann, 'Die Entwicklung des deutsch-russischen Getreideverkehrs unter den Handelsverträgen von 1894 und 1904', in *Jahrbücher für Nationalökonomie und Statistik*, no. 101, 1913, pp. 145–71; G. Schmoller, 'Einige Worte zum Antrag Kanitz', in *Schmollers Jahrbuch*, vol. 19, 1895, p. 617; Gerschenkron, *Bread*, pp. 53f., 64, 69, 74f., 79f.; Rosenberg, *Probleme*, pp. 67–80.
19. H. Heller, *Staatslehre*, Leiden, 3rd imp., 1963, p. 113.
20. H. von Friedberg to Crown Prince Friedrich, 4. 5. 1879, O. von Richthofen Papers, 1–1.2, PA, AA Bonn; T.W. Adorno's introduction in his *Spätkapitalismus oder Industriegesellschaft?*, Stuttgart, 1969, pp. 23f.
21. Habermas, pp. 76f., 84, 92.
22. Cf. Hardach, pp. 70–2.
23. A. Bebel, 'Zum 1. Oktober', in *Neue Zeit*, no. 9, 1891, vol. II, p. 7.

III.1

1. A. Rosenberg, p. 15; Bismarck to Bülow, 21. 12. 1877, GW, vol. VI, p. 103.
2. Weber, *Politische Schriften*, p. 233. Bismarck quotation from R. von Friesen, *Erinnerungen aus meinem Leben*, vol. III, Dresden, 1910, pp. 11f.
3. G. Anschütz, 'Der deutsche Föderalismus', in *Veröffentlichungen der Vereinigung der Deutschen Staatsrechtslehrer*, vol. I, Berlin, 1924, pp. 14f.; T.

Hobbes, *Leviathan*, ed. I. Fetscher, Neuwied, 1966, p. 206 (Chapter II, p. 26, section 6).

4. E.R. Huber, *Deutsche Verfassungsgeschichte nach 1789*, vol. III, Stuttgart, 1963, p. 11; following quotations p. 18.

5. Marx to Ruge, 5. 3. 1842, MEW, vol. 27, p. 397.

6. K.D. Bracher, *Die Auflösung der Weimarer Republik*, Villingen, 5th imp., 1971, p. 11.

7. Lassalle, vol. II, p. 60 (1862).

8. Roggenbach to Bamberger, 11. 2. 1879, Bamberger Papers, DZA, I, 173/4–5. In W.P. Fuchs (ed., *Grossherzog Friedrich von Baden und die Reichspolitik, 1871–1907*, vol. I, Stuttgart, 1968) one can find a dozen or so statements concerning the dictatorial nature of the regime.

9. F. Meinecke, 'Reich und Nation von 1871–1914', in his *Staat und Persönlichkeit*, Berlin, 1933, p. 167.

10. L. von Schweinitz, *Denkwürdigkeiten*, vol. II, Berlin, 1927, p. 83 (18. 11. 1879), p. 270 (April 1884), cf. p. 307; also his *Briefwechsel*, Berlin, 1928, p. 214 (May 1886); Bosse quoted from J. Röhl, *Deutschland ohne Bismarck*, Tübingen, 1969, p. 26; K. Oldenburg, *Aus Bismarcks Bundesrat, 1878–85*, Berlin, 1929, pp. 10, 38, 55; J. Hansen, *G. von Mevissen*, vol. I, Berlin, 1906, p. 843 (1884); Kapp to Cohen, 23. 8. 1879 and 9. 7. 1881, in F. Kapp, *Vom radikalen Frühsozialisten des Vormärz zum liberalen Parteipolitiker des Bismarckreichs. Briefe 1848–1884*, ed. H.-U. Wehler, Frankfurt, 1969, pp. 122, 133. Ampthill to Granville, 11. 3. 1882, in P. Knaplund (ed.), *Letters from the Berlin Embassy*, Washington, DC, 1944, p. 256; Kasson to Bayard, 30. 4. 1885, in O. Stolberg-Wernigerode, *Deutschland und die Vereinigten Staaten im Zeitalter Bismarcks*, Berlin, 1933, pp. 327, 329.

11. L. Bamberger, *Bismarck Posthumus*, Berlin, 1899, p. 8; GW, vol. VIc, p. 156 (4. 2. 1879); GW, vol. VIII, p. 532.

12. *Der 18. Brumaire de Louis Bonaparte* (1852), MEW, vol. 8, pp. 115-207.

13. L. Bamberger, *Charakteristiken*, Berlin, 1894, p. 84; Engels to Marx, 13. 4. 1866, MEW, vol. 31, p. 208.

14. Bamberger, *Posthumus*, pp. 58, 25; Burckhardt to Preen, 26. 9. 1890, in Burckhardt, *Briefe*, ed. F. Kaphahn, Leipzig, 1935, p. 490; *Die Geheimen Papiere F. von Holsteins*, vol. II, Göttingen, 1957, p. 181 (17. 11. 1884).

15. H. Gollwitzer, *Der Cäserismus Napoleons III. im Widerhall der öffentlichen Meinung Deutschlands*, in HZ, no. 173, 1952, p. 65; see F. Mehring, *Weltkrach und Weltmarkt*, Berlin, 1900, p. 34; S. Hellmann, *Die grossen europäischen Revolutionen*, Munich, 2nd imp., 1919, pp. 15–17.

16. L. Bamberger, *Zum Jahrestag der Entlassung Bismarcks* (1891), in his *Gesammelte Schriften*, vol. V, Berlin, 1897, p. 340. See the complaint by Crown Princess Victoria in G. Mann, pp. 430f.

17. H. Rothfels, p. 170; similarly K. Griewank (*Das Problem des christlichen Staatsmannes bei Bismarck*, Berlin, 1953, p. 55: 'Anstoss und Vorbild für Entartungserscheinungen').

18. A. von Deines to H. Deines, 20. 3. 1890, Military Archives, Freiburg, N 32/11; Burckhardt to Preen, 13. 4. 1877, in *Briefe*, vol. VI, 1966, p. 124; Mommsen from Kohn, pp. 198, 201.

19. GW, vol. XV, p. 640.

20. Bismarck to Wilhelm I, Oct. 1879, Bismarck Papers, 13 in Schloss

Friedrichsruh; also H. Pachnike, *Führende Männer im alten und im neuen Reich*, Berlin, 1930, p. 63.

21. M. Stürmer, Introduction to his ed., *Das Kaiserliche Deutschland*, pp. 20f.
22. GW, vol. XIV, p. 1475, 27. 11. 1872. The classical interpretation of the Prussian bureaucracy's development in H. Rosenberg, *Bureaucracy, Aristocracy, Autocracy: The Prussian Experience, 1660–1815*, Cambridge, Mass. (1958), 2nd imp. 1968.
23. K. Heinig, *Das Budget*, vol. I, Tübingen, 1949, p. 388. E. Kehr, 'Das soziale System der Reaktion in Preussen unter dem Ministerium Puttkamer', in his *Der Primat der Innenpolitik*, ed. H.-U. Wehler, Berlin, 2nd imp., 1970, pp. 64–86, and the literature for III.1.4 in Bibliography.
24. C. zu Hohenlohe-Schillingsfürst, *Denkwürdigkeiten aus der Reichskanzlerzeit*, Stuttgart, 1931, p. 290; P. Molt, *Der Reichstag vor der improvisierten Revolution*, Cologne, 1963, pp. 142f.; P. Rassow and K.E. Born (eds), *Akten zur staatlichen Sozialpolitik in Deutschland, 1890–1914*, Wiesbaden, 1959, p. 146.
25. E.N. Anderson, *Political Institutions and Social Change in Continental Europe in the 19th Century*, Berkeley, Calif., 1967, pp. 167, 166–237; O. Hintze, 'Der Beamtenstand', in his *Soziologie und Geschichte*, Göttingen, 2nd imp., 1964, pp. 68, 66–125. A more detailed account of the period up to 1918 is to be found in J. Kocka, *Facing Total War: German Society, 1914–1918*, Leamington Spa 1984, Chapter 3.
26. From Max Weber, e.g. *Wirtschaft und Gesellschaft*, vol. I, Tübingen, 4th imp. 1956, pp. 125–30; vol. II, pp. 823–76; his *Politische Schriften*, pp. 294–431. For an overview see A. Lotz, *Geschichte des deutschen Beamtentums*, Berlin, 1909.
27. Anderson, p. 195; Molt, p. 143; L. Muncy, *The Junker in the Prussian Administration, 1888-1914*, Providence, RI, 1944, pp. 189f.; R. Lewinsohn, *Das Geld in der Politik*, Berlin, 1930, pp. 20f.; W. Runge, *Politik und Beamtentum im Parteienstaat*, Stuttgart, 1965, pp. 170–4, 181; R. Morsey, *Die Oberste Reichsverwaltung unter Bismarck, 1867–90*, Münster, 1957, p. 246.
28. C. Schmitt, 'H. Preuss in der deutschen Staatsrechtslehre', in *Neue Rundschau*, no. 41, 1930, p. 290; Runge, p. 173; J. Röhl, 'Beamtenpolitik im Wilhelminischen Deutschland', in *Das Kaiserliche Deutschland*, p. 295.
29. J. Kocka, 'Vorindustrielle Faktoren in der deutschen Industrialisierung', in *Das Kaiserliche Deutschland*, pp. 265–86; for more details see also his *Unternehmensverwaltung und Angestelltenschaft, Siemens 1847–1914*, Stuttgart, 1969.

III.2

1. T. Heuss, 'Das Bismarck-Bild im Wandel', in L. Gall (ed.), *Das Bismarck-Problem*, Cologne, 1971, p. 264.
2. The following observations are based on the interpretations by M.R. Lepsius, 'Parteiensystem und Sozialstruktur: Zum Problem der Demokratisierung der deutschen Gesellschaft', in *Festschrift* for F. Lütge, Stuttgart, 1966, pp. 371–93; *Extremer Nationalismus*, Stuttgart, 1966; 'Demokratie in Deutschland als historisch-soziologisches Problem', in

Spätkapitalismus?, pp. 197–213, and T. Nipperdey, 'Über einige Grundzüge der deutschen Parteigeschichte', in *Festschrift* for H.C. Nipperdey, vol. II, Munich, 1965, pp. 815–41.

3. T.H. Marshall, 'Citizenship and Social Class', in his *Class, Citizenship, and Social Development*, New York, 1965, pp. 71–134.
4. G. Mayer, 'Die Trennung der proletarischen von der bürgerlichen Demokratie in Deutschland, 1863–70' (1912), in his *Radikalismus, Sozialismus und bürgerliche Demokratie*, ed. H.-U. Wehler, Frankfurt, 2nd imp., 1969, pp. 108–78.
5. F.J. Stahl, *Die gegenwärtigen Parteien in Staat und Kirche*, Berlin, 1863, p. 73.
6. Kapp to Cohen, 5. 1. 1875, *Briefe*, pp. 107f.; Hammacher to his wife, 28. 5. 1879, Hammacher Papers, 20/36f., DZA, I.
7. Bamberger, *Erinnerungen*, p. 501.
8. Indispensable for this: H.J. Puhle, *Agrarische Interessenpolitik und preussischer Konservatismus im wilhelminischen Reich, 1893–1914*, Hanover, 1966.
9. H. Boldt, 'Deutscher Konstitutionalismus und Bismarckreich', in *Das Kaiserliche Deutschland*, p. 127.
10. Minister of the Interior, von Puttkamer, 5. 12. 1883, speech in the Prussian Lower House, in H. von Gerlach, *Die Geschichte des preussischen Wahlrechts*, Berlin, 1908, p. 37.
11. A. Schäffle, *Die Quintessenz des Sozialismus*, Gotha, 3rd imp., 1878, p. 1.
12. W. Andreas (ed.), 'Gespräche Bismarcks mit dem badischen Finanzminister M. Ellstätter', in *Zeitschrift für die Geschichte des Oberrheins*, no. 82, 1930, p. 449(1. 2. 1877); similarly, H. von Poschinger, *Stunden bei Bismarck*, Vienna, 1910, p. 98; RB, vol. VI, pp. 346f.; vol. VII, p. 287.
13. H. Rosenberg, *Depression*, pp. 82–8. On the SPD's political programme, see Mommsen, *Parteiprogramme*, pp. 294–403; on its political activities, see the literature for III. 2. 1 in Bibliography.
14. Schmoller, p. 52; Griewank, p. 47.
15. E. Bernstein (review), in *Dokumente des Sozialismus*, 1, 1902, p. 473; see also F. Naumann, *Die Politischen Parteien*, Berlin, 1910, p. 96.
16. Mommsen (*Nation*, 13. 12. 1902), from L.M. Hartmann, *T. Mommsen*, Gotha, 1908, p. 258.
17. G. Mayer, *Erinnerungen*, Munich, 1949, p. 179.
18. Rosenberg, *Probleme*, pp. 34f.
19. W. Hennis, *Verfassungsordnung und Verbandseinfluss*, PVS, vol. 2, 1961, pp. 23–35.
20. E. Kehr, 'Soziale und finanzielle Grundlagen der Tirpitzschen Flottenpropaganda', in his *Primat*, pp. 130–48; also his *Schlachtflottenbau und Parteipolitik, 1894–1901*, Berlin, 1930, 2nd imp. 1966, pp. 169f. (transl. as *Battleship Building and Party Politics in Germany*, Chicago, 1973); W. Marienfeld, *Wissenschaft und Schlachtflottenbau in Deutschland, 1897–1906*, Berlin, 1957, p. 83; H.A. Bueck, *Der Zentralverband Deutscher Industrieller*, vol. I, Berlin, 1902, pp. 291f.
21. K. von der Heydt to Hammacher, 30. 6. 1886, Hammacher Papers, 57; K. Lamprecht, *Deutsche Geschichte. Zur jüngsten deutschen Vergangenheit* (1903), vol. II/2, Berlin, 4th imp., 1921, p. 737.
22. G. Radbruch, 'Die Politischen Parteien im System des deutschen Verfassungsrechts', in G. Anschütz and R. Thoma (eds), *Handbuch des*

deutschen Staatsrechts, vol. I, Tübingen, 1930, p. 289.

23. W. Liebknecht, 9. 12. 1870, Norddt. RT, 1:2:154.

24. Sybel to Baumgarten, 27. 1. 1871, in J. Heyderhoff and P. Wentzke (eds), *Deutscher Liberalismus im Zeitalter Bismarcks*, vol. I, Osnabrück, 2nd imp., 1967, p. 494; R. Stadelmann, 'Moltke und das 19.Jh.', in HZ, no. 166, 1942, p. 309.

25. Sauer, *Problem*, pp. 428–36. — N.B. for 'neo-traditionalists': techniques of this sort need not find expression in contemporary writings (with the result that 'direct' sources may not be available). Nevertheless, they can be inferred from the rationale of what lay in the interests of the ruling groups and was incorporated into patterns of political behaviour. They can establish themselves over the heads of those involved, as a response to a challenge, but can nevertheless be retrospectively interpreted as a form of strategic need akin to deliberate actions.

26. O. Pfülf, *Bischof von Ketteler*, vol. III, Mainz, 1899, p. 166.

27. RB, vol. 12, p. 305; GW, vol. VIII, p. 419; vol. XIV/II, p. 910; H. Hofmann, *Fürst Bismarck*, vol. III, Stuttgart, 1914, p. 154; GW, vol. XIV/II, p. 955.

28. See the more detailed discussion on political antisemitism in III. 3. 3 above.

29. GW, vol. VIc, p. 350 (24. 12. 1886).

30. R. Lucius von Ballhausen, *Bismarck-Erinnerungen*, Stuttgart, 1921, p. 304 (25. 10. 1884); E. Foerster, *A. Falk*, Gotha, 1927, p. 430 (29 and 30. 8. 1878); M. Stürmer (ed.), *Bismarck und die preussisch-deutsche Politik*, Munich, 1970, pp. 131, 127; a more detailed account is given in his 'Staatsstreichgedanken im Bismarckreich', in HZ, no. 209, 1969, pp. 566–615.

31. Marx, in H.-U. Wehler, *Sozialdemokratie und Nationalstaat, Nationalitätenfragen in Deutschland, 1840–1914*, Göttingen, 2nd imp., 1971, p. 57; Burckhardt to Preen, 26. 4. 1872, *Briefe* vol. V, p. 160.

32. Bismarck to Puttkamer, 3. 3. 1883, BA, P 135/6348 (printed in Stümer (ed.), *Bismarck*, p. 195).

33. Pourtalès to Bethmann, 15. 10. 1853, in A. von Mutius (ed.), *Graf A. Pourtalès*, Berlin, 1933, p. 73; Mann, p. 443.

34. Rosenberg, *Probleme*, p. 33.

35. Schmoller, p. 41; Bismarck to Mittnacht, autumn 1878 (draft), Bismarck Papers, XLVII; GW, vol. VIII, p. 298 (18. 2. 1879); minutes of the Crown Council of 5. 6. 1878 in Stürmer (ed.), p. 125; C. von Tiedemann, *Aus 7 Jahrzehnten*, vol. II: *6 Jahre Chef der Reichskanzlei*, Leipzig, 1909, p. 258; J.M. von Radowitz, *Aufzeichnungen und Erinnerungen, 1839–90*, ed. H. Holborn, vol. II, Stuttgart, 1925; Wehler, *Bismarck und der Imperialismus*, pp. 189–91.

36. For draft, note 35; GW, vol. VIII, p. 492; H. von Bismarck to Rantzau, 29. 10. 1881, Bismarck Papers, 41 (also W. Bussmann (ed.), *Staatssekretär Graf H. von Bismarck. Aus seiner politischen Privatkorrespondenz*, Göttingen, 1964, p. 108); 30. 10. 1881, ibid., *Minutes of the meeting of ministers of state* of 8. 12. 1884 in Stürmer (ed.), p. 207; GW, vol. XV, pp. 288, 393, 398, 449, 465.

37. Hofmann, vol. I, p. 132 (see GW, vol. VIII, p. 304; RB, vol. X, p. 130); vol. II, pp. 406–8 (11. 3. 1897); D. Stegmann, *Die Erben Bismarcks*,

1897–1918, Cologne, 1970, p. 67; E. Kehr 'Englandhass und Weltpolitik', in his *Primat*, p. 164; also his *Schlachtflottenbau*, p. 265; see V. Berghahn, *Der Tirpitz-Plan*, Düsseldorf, 1979, and H.A. Winkler, *Mittelstand, Demokratie und Nationalsozialismus*, Cologne, 1972, pp. 40–64.

38. Hofmann, vol. I, p. 130, (RB, vol. X, p. 56); GW, vol. VIc, p. 121; O. Hintze, 'Das monarchische Prinzip und die konstitutionelle Verfassung', in his *Staat und Verfassung*, Göttingen, 3rd imp., 1970, p. 378.

39. Naumann, *Demokratie*, p. 139.

40. H.-G. Zmarzlik, *Bethmann Hollweg als Reichskanzler, 1909–14*, Düsseldorf, 1957, p. 50; Reichsarchiv (ed.), *Der Weltkrieg* (Kriegsrüstung und Kriegswirtschaft, Anlagen I), Berlin, 1930, pp. 122f.; Stegmann, pp. 216f., 288, 404–99.

41. W. Rathenau, *An Deutschlands Jugend*, Berlin, 1918, p. 100.

III.3

1. J. Heyderhoff (ed.), *Im Ring der Gegner Bismarcks, 1865–1896*, Leipzig, 1943, p. 223 (Roggenbach to Stosch, 7. 11. 1883).

2. L. Bamberger, *Die Nachfolge Bismarcks*, Berlin, 2nd imp., 1889, p. 41.

3. GW, vol. VIb, p. 486 (12. 9. 1870).

4. GW, vol. VIII, p. 79 (21. 4. 1873), p. 441 (12. 12. 1881, Bennigsen).

5. In R. Hilferding's *Das Finanzkapital*, 1910, Berlin, 1947, pp. 504f., and O. Bauer's *Die Nationalitätenfrage und die Sozialdemokratie*, Vienna, 2nd imp., 1924, pp. 491ff., — a splendid discussion!

6. W. Rathenau, *Gesammelte Schriften*, vol. I, Berlin, 1925, pp. 188f. (present tense in the original).

7. E. Bernstein, *Geschichte der Berliner Arbeiterbewegung*, vol. II, Berlin, 1907, p. 59.

8. T. Mommsen to anonymous recipient, 13. 8. 1882, Bamberger Papers, 151/4, DZA, I; Bamberger to Hillebrand, 17. 12. 1882, ibid., 91/72; Bleichröder (1880) from W. Frank, *Hofprediger A. Stoecker und die christlichsoziale Bewegung*, Hamburg, 2nd imp., 1935, p. 86.

9. Election statement by the German conservatives in the Goldschmidt Papers, PA.

10. Mommsen, *Parteiprogramme*, p. 84.

11. Foerster, *Falk*, p. 485 (10. 3. 1878, Lasker); Bamberger, *Posthumus*, p. 35 (Friedenthal).

12. Frank, p. 110; H. von Bismarck to Rantzau, 2. 11. 1881, Herbert von Bismarck Papers, 41.

13. W. von Bismarck to Rantzau, 23. 5. 1884, Rottenburg Papers, 4/203, GStA Berlin-Dahlem.

14. H. von Bismarck to Rottenburg, 8. 8. 1882 (Bleichröder), Rottenburg Papers, 3; 25. 9. 1887 (AA), ibid., 3; to Münster, 20. 4. 1885 (Meade), Münster Papers, 5, Schloss Derneburg.

15. Bamberger to Hillebrand, 7. 12. 1880, Bamberger Papers, 91/33; Mommsen to H. Bahr from P.W. Massing, *Vorgeschichte des politischen Antisemitismus*, Frankfurt, 1959, p. 177.

16. GW, vol. XIV/1, p. 568 (Bismarck to his sister, 26. 3. 1861).

17. Rantzau to Rottenburg, 12. 12. 1886, Rottenburg Papers, 5/237 and

O. von Bismarck Papers; Holstein to H. von Bismarck, 13. 12. 1884, Bismarck Papers, 44.

18. Wehler, *Krisenherde*, p. 188; on policies towards Poland: pp. 181–99 (with figures); Alsace-Lorraine: pp. 51–6; North Schleswig: see my *Sozialdemokratie*, pp. 86–102.

19. *Papiere Holsteins*, vol. III, 1961, p. 214 (Bülow to Holstein, 10. 12. 1887); Schieder from Wehler, *Krisenherde*, p. 194.

20. F. Meinecke, *Ausgewählter Briefwechsel*, ed. L. Dehio and P. Classen, Stuttgart, 1962, p. 59 (to Goetz, 6. 5. 1915).

21. Weber, *Wirtschaft und Gesellschaft*, vol. II, pp. 683f., 698f.

22. *Ministerialblatt für die gesamte innere Verwaltung 37. 1876*, Berlin, 1877, p. 44.

23. A. de Tocqueville, *Über die Demokratie in Amerika*, vol. I, Stuttgart, 1959, p. 343.

24. Quoted from H.-U. Wehler (ed.), *Geschichte und Psychoanalyse*, Cologne, 1971, pp. 28f. (Litt, Adorno, Hartmann).

25. Lepsius, *Demokratie*, p. 204.

26. Weber, *Politische Schriften*, pp. 235f.

27. R. Dahrendorf, *Soziale Klassen und Klassenkonflikt in der industriellen Gesellschaft*, Stuttgart, 1957, p. 64.

28. G.W.F. Hegel, *Briefe*, ed. J. Hoffmeister, vol. I, Hamburg, 1953, p. 253 (to Niethammer, 28. 10. 1808).

29. T. Nipperdey, 'Volksschule und Revolution im Vormärz', in *Festschrift* for T. Schieder, Munich, 1968, p. 117 (Frederick William IV), pp. 141f.

30. The following figures from F. Ringer, 'Higher Education in Germany in the 19th Century', in JCH, 2, 1967, pp. 123–38; W. Zorn, 'Hochschule und höhere Schule in der deutschen Sozialgeschichte der Neuzeit', in *Festschrift* for M. Braubach, Münster, 1964, pp. 321–39.

31. C. von Ferber, *Die Entwicklung des Lehrkörpers der deutschen Universitäten und Hochschulen, 1864–1954*, Göttingen, 1956, pp. 176f.

32. *Der Preussische Landtag. Handbuch für sozialdemokratische Wähler*, Berlin, 1908, p. 505.

33. R. Michels, *Umschichtungen der herrschenden Klassen nach dem Kriege*, Stuttgart, 1934, p. 68.

34. T. Eschenburg, *Ämterpatronage*, Stuttgart, 1961, p. 20, cf. pp. 33–41.

35. A personal reminiscence: even as late as 1953 the admission made during a discussion by the chairman of the previously extremely feudal Corps Borussia in Bonn, that two middle-class members had been admitted, was greeted with derision.

36. R. Schmidt, *Die Zeit*, 13. 10. 1967, p. 29.

37. E. Fraenkel, *Zur Soziologie der Klassenjustiz*, Berlin, 1927, (Darmstadt, 1968), p. 41.

38. Weber, *Wirtschaft und Gesellschaft*, vol. II, p. 660; A. Einstein in H. and M. Born, *Briefwechsel, 1916–55*, Munich, 1969, p. 39 (9. 12. 1919).

39. O. Hintze, 'Die Industrialisierungspolitik Friedrich des Grossen', in his *Historische und Politische Aufsätze*, vol. II, Berlin, 2nd imp., no year, p. 132 (and beforehand on p. 131, 'An effect of Frederician ideas in the internal administration as in foreign policy'!).

40. In H. Dietzel, *Bismarck, Handwörterbuch der Staatswissenschaften*, vol. III, Jena, 3rd imp., 1909, p. 65.

41. Motion by Stumm et al., RT, 4: 3: 3, *Anlage*, I, p. 17; H. Herzfeld, *J. von Miquel*, vol. II, Detmold, 1938, p. 33; Wehler, *Bismarck und der Imperialismus*, pp. 459–64.
42. Schmoller, *Charakterbilder*, pp. 41, 59.
43. 'Stolbergs Votum im Preussischen Staatsministerium, 11. 9. 1878', in Stürmer (ed.), p. 133; B. Croce, *Geschichte Europas im 19.Jh.*, Frankfurt, 3rd imp., 1968, p. 266.
44. RB, vol. XII, pp. 639f.
45. GW, vol. VIc, p. 230; vol. VIII, p.396; H. Rothfels, *T. Lohmann, 1871–1905*, Berlin, 1927, pp. 63f.
46. H. von Lerchenfeld-Koefering, *Erinnerungen und Denkwürdigkeiten, 1848–1925*, Berlin, 2nd imp., 1935, p. 297 (1890); *Briefe und sozialpolitische Aufsätze von Dr. Rodbertus-Jagetzow*, ed. R. Meyer, vol. I, Berlin, 1882, p. 136 (Rodbertus to Meyer, 29. 11. 1871).
47. H. Delbrück, 'Politische Korrespondenz', in *Preussische Jahrbücher*, vol. 57, 1886, p. 312; figures from *Deutsche Wirtschaftskunde*, Berlin, 1930, pp. 337–42; S. Andić and J. Veverka, 'The Growth of Government Expenditures in Germany since the Unification', in *Finanzarchiv*, 23, 1963/64, p. 247. Expenditure *per capita*:

    | 1885 | 59m | |
    | 1891 | 158m, i.e. | 5.1% of the imperial budget |
    | 1901 | 424m | 8.7% |
    | 1907 | 686m | 9.6% |
    | 1913 | 994m | 10.3% |

48. K.E. Born, *Staat und Sozialpolitik nach Bismarcks Sturz, 1890–1914*, Wiesbaden, 1957, pp. 98, 104f., 178, 183, 214, 218, 223, 101, 90, 96, 246.

III.4

1. R. Goldscheid, 'Staat, öffentlicher Haushalt und Gesellschaft', in *Handbuch der Finanzwissenschaft*, ed. W. Gerloff, vol. I, Tübingen, 1926, p. 171; and his *Staatssozialismus oder Staatskapitalismus*, Vienna, 1917.
2. W. Gerloff, *Der Staatshaushalt und das Finanzsystem Deutschlands, 1820–1927*, in his ed., vol. III, 1929, p. 9; I follow his summary (pp. 1–69) which has not yet been superseded; the next quotation: ibid., p. 10.
3. GW, vol. VI c, p. 406 (22. 1. 1889). The quotation following is from Rosenberg, *Probleme*, pp. 69, 19.
4. F. Hartung, *Deutsche Geschichte, 1871–1919*, Stuttgart, 6th imp., 1952, p. 232.
5. Gerloff, p. 28.
6. Witt, p. 275; on the development prior to this, pp. 139ff., cf. pp. 292ff.
7. *Provinzial-Korrespondenz*, 12. 10. 1881.
8. Gerloff, pp. 19f., 23, 28; A. Wagner, *Grundlegung der politischen Ökonomie*, Leipzig, 3rd imp., 1892, p. 895. See in general, Andić and Veverka, pp. 243–78.
9. Rosenberg, *Depression*, p. 45. Figures from A. Spiethoff, *Die wirtschaftlichen Wechsellagen*, vol. II, Tübingen, 1955, p. 2; H. Stuebel, *Staat und Banken im preussischen Anleihewesen, 1871–1913*, Berlin, 1935, pp. 22, 43.
10. W. Fischer and P. Czada, 'Die soziale Verteilung von mobilem Ver-

mögen in Deutschland seit dem Spätmittelalter', in *3. International Conference of Economic History*, vol. II, Paris, 1968, p. 287. Figures from W.G. Hoffmann and J.H. Müller, *Das deutsche Volkseinkommen, 1851–1955*, Tübingen, 1959; P. Jostock, 'The Long-term Growth of National Income in Germany', in *Income and Wealth*, vol. V, ed. S. Kuznets, London, 1955, pp. 79–122; Andić and Veverka, p. 241.
11. P.N. Stearns, *European Society in Upheaval: Social History since 1800*, New York, 1967, p. 206.
12. Hoffmann, *Wachstum*, pp. 86f., 95, 100.

III.5

1. GW, vol. X, p. 324 (11. 3. 1867).
2. Stürmer (ed.), p. 221 (9. 1. 1887); Lucius, p. 51.
3. Richter, in E. Eyck, *Bismarck*, vol. III, Zurich, 1944, p. 76; Mallinckrodt, in A. Wahl, *Deutsche Geschichte von der Reichsgründung bis zum Ausbruch des Weltkrieges*, vol. I, Stuttgart, 1926, p. 114; Bennigsen, in RT, 2: 1: 2: 754.
4. R. Schmidt-Bückeburg, *Das Militärkabinett der preussischen Könige und deutschen Kaiser, 1787–1918*, Berlin, 1933, p. 78.
5. Hohenlohe-Schillingsfürst, *Reichskanzlerzeit*, p. 116 (2. 11. 1895).
6. Friedrich III, *Das Kriegstagebuch von 1870/71*, ed. H.O. Meisner, Berlin, 1926, p. 325.
7. *Grossherzog* F. von Baden, p. 93 (12. 4. 1875).
8. Wehler, *Krisenherde*, pp. 174f.
9. G. Ritter, *Der Schlieffenplan*, Munich, 1956, pp. 68f.; on the following, see pp. 27, 71f., 79, 81, 35.
10. F. Meinecke, *Die deutsche Katastrophe* (1946), in his *Autobiographische Schriften*, Stuttgart, 1969, p. 367.
11. T. von Bethmann Hollweg, *Betrachtungen zum Weltkriege*, vol. II, Berlin, 1919, p. 9.
12. Ritter, *Schlieffenplan*, pp. 95, 83, 91.
13. H. Bley, *Kolonialherrschaft und Sozialstruktur in Deutsch-Südwestafrika, 1894–1914*, Hamburg, 1968, pp. 203f.
14. G. Ritter, *Staatskunst und Kriegshandwerk*, vol. I, Munich, 1954, p. 32.
15. Ibid., vol. II, 1960, p. 115.
16. MEW, vol. 17, p. 106 (Engels, 17. 9. 1870).
17. A. von Roon, *Denkwürdigkeiten*, vol. III, Berlin, 5th imp., 1905, p. 390 (4. 2. 1874).
18. Waldersee to von Gossler, 20. 2. 1897, from the Bülow Papers, 22, 85–91, BA; A. von Waldersee, *Denkwürdigkeiten*, ed. H.O. Meisner, vol. II, Stuttgart, 1923, p. 388 (to Wilhelm II, 27. 1. 1897).
19. W. Deist, 'Die Armee in Staat und Gesellschaft, 1890–1914', in *Das Kaiserliche Deutschland*, pp. 318, 329.
20. Roon, vol. I, p. 154 (24. 3. 1848).
21. Stadelmann, *Moltke*, p. 407 (6. 12. 1861).
22. Schweinitz, *Denkwürdigkeiten*, vol. I, p. 259 (26. 5. 1870).
23. Waldersee to Manteuffel, 8. 2. 1877, from Ritter, vol. II, pp. 360f.
24. *Der Weltkrieg*, II, p. 91 (no. 26, 19. 4. 1904).
25. M. Kitchen, *The German Officer Corps, 1890–1914*, Oxford, 1968, pp. 5,

22, 24; Deist, p. 322,; Kehr, *Primat*, p. 58.
26. *Der Weltkrieg*, II, p. 180 (no. 56, 20. 1. 1913); previously: H. Herzfeld, *Die deutsche Rüstungspolitik vor dem Weltkrieg*, Bonn, 1923, p. 63.
27. Kitchen, p. 148; for antisemitism, pp. 22–48; Courts of Honour: p. 51.
28. Wehler, *Krisenherde*, pp. 65–83.
29. Messerschmidt, p. 110.
30. Kitchen, pp. 132, 141f.; K. Saul, 'Der "Deutsche Kriegerbund"', in *Militärgeschichtliche Mitteilungen*, 1969/II, p. 159.
31. Berghahn, *Tirpitz-Plan*.
32. A. von Tirpitz, *Erinnerungen*, Leipzig, 2nd imp., 1920, pp. 98, 96, 52.
33. Kehr, *Schlachtflottenbau*, pp. 45, 107; A.T. Mahan, *The Influence of Sea Power upon History*, Boston, Mass., 1890; cf. his *Die weisse Rasse und die Seeherrschaft*, Leipzig, 1909.
34. T. Heuss, *F. Naumann*, Stuttgart, 1937, p. 138.
35. Bethmann to Valentini, 9. 12. 1915, in Stegmann, p. 456.
36. Beehler to the State Department, 31. 3. 1900, Record Group 59, National Archives, Washington, DC.
37. See Kehr and Berghahn on this.
38. Berghahn, p. 392.

III.6

1. Wehler, *Bismarck*, p. 41f., and *Krisenherde*, pp. 360f.
2. Nipperdey, *Grundzüge*, pp. 832f.
3. E. von Weber, *4 Jahre in Afrika*, vol. II, Leipzig, 1878, p. 564; on the following, see Wehler, *Bismarck*, pp. 112–93, especially pp. 121, 163.
4. Miquel, in H. Böhme, *Deutschlands Weg zur Grossmacht*, Cologne, 2nd imp., 1972, p. 316; Holstein to Kiderlen, 30. 4. 1897, in Kiderlen Papers (Böhme copy); similarly to Eulenburg, 4. 12. 1894, in J. Haller (ed.), *Aus dem Leben des Fürsten P. zu Eulenburg*, Berlin, 1924, p. 173.
5. In A. Kirchhoff (ed.), *Deutsche Universitätslehrer über die Flottenvorlage*, Berlin, 1900, p. 21.
6. Diary entry of 31. 12. 1895, in H. Mohs (ed.), *A. Graf von Waldersee in seinem militärischen Wirken*, vol. II, Berlin, 1929, p. 383; Bülow to Eulenburg, 26. 12. 1897, in Röhl, *Deutschland*, p. 229.
7. B. von Bülow, 'Deutsche Politik', in *Deutschland unter Kaiser Wilhelm II*, ed. S. Körte *et al.*, vol. I, Berlin, 1914, pp. 97f.
8. K.D. Bracher, *Deutschland zwischen Demokratie und Diktatur*, Munich, 1964, p. 155.
9. A.L. von Rochau, *Grundsätze der Realpolitik*, Stuttgart, 1853, p. 28 (ed. H.-U. Wehler, Berlin, 1972, p. 40).
10. MEW, vol. 30, p. 249 (18. 6. 1862); pp. 20, 565 (*Dialektik der Natur*); to Lawrow, 12/17. 11. 1875, ibid., pp. 34, 170; H. Plessner, 'Zur Soziologie der modernen Forschung', in *Versuche zu einer Soziologie des Wissens*, Munich, 1924, p. 423.
11. G. Himmelfarb, *Darwin and the Darwinian Revolution*, New York, 1959, pp. 157–61, 235f., 393–6; R.M. Young, 'Malthus and the Evolutionists: The Common Context of Biological and Social Theory', in *Past and Present*, no. 43, 1969, pp. 109–45; H.-U. Wehler, 'Sozialdarwinismus im

expandierenden Industriestaat', in *Festschrift* for F. Fischer, Düsseldorf, 1973, pp. 133–42; C. Darwin, *The Descent of Man*, vol. I, New York, 1871, pp. 154, 173f.; and his *Life and Letters*, ed. F. Darwin, vol. I, London, 1887, pp. 69, 316.
12. Hilferding, pp. 504–6; similarly Bauer, pp. 491–507.

III.7

1. From A. Hillgruber, 'Entwicklung, Wandlung und Zerstörung des deutschen Nationalstaats, 1871–1945', in *1871. Fragen an die Deutsche Geschichte*, Berlin, 1971, pp. 171–203.
2. Ranke from E. Kessel, 'Rankes Auffassung der amerikanischen Geschichte', in *Jahrbuch für Amerikastudien*, 7, 1962, p. 31, (from his posthumous papers).
3. MEW, vol. 17, 1964, pp. 268–79; see also Wehler, *Krisenherde*, pp. 22f. on this; for Wilhelm I's judgement: ibid., p. 331, note 16.
4. Bismarck to Arnim, 2. 2. 1873, GP, vol. I, no. 96; Wehler, *Bismarck*, p. 316.
5. A. von Waldersee, *Aus dem Briefwechsel*, ed. H.O. Meisner, vol. I, Berlin, 1928, pp. 36, 57, 69; K.E. Jeismann, *Das Problem des Präventivkriegs*, Freiburg, 1957, pp. 109ff.; Bismarck to Bronsart, 31. 12. 1887, GW, VIc, pp. 378f.
6. Wehler, *Krisenherde*, pp. 334f., note 31; GP, vol. XII, p. 279, (22. 1. 1897); Schlieffen: Kitchen, p. 105.
7. B. von Bülow, *Denkwürdigkeiten*, vol. I, Berlin, 1930, p. 429; Schweinitz, *Briefwechsel*, p. 193.
8. F. Ponsonby (ed.), *Briefe der Kaiserin Friederich*, Berlin, 1929, p. 471; Queen Victoria, *Letters* (2nd series), vol. III, London, 1928, pp. 505f.; Holstein, vol. II, p. 167; GW, vol. VIII, pp. 381, 383.
9. Holstein vol. I, p. 123. On the following see Wehler, *Krisenherde*, pp. 163–80.
10. R. Wittram, 'Bismarcks Russlandpolitik nach der Reichsgründung', in H. Hallmann (ed.), *Zur Geschichte und Problematik des deutsch-russischen Rückversicherungsvertrags von 1887*, Darmstadt, 1968, p. 469.
11. Bismarck to Reuss, 15. 12. 1887, GP, vol. VI, p. 1163; Stürmer (ed.), p. 245; Wehler, *Krisenherde*, p. 175.
12. H. Oncken, *Das alte und das neue Mitteleuropa*, Gotha, 1917, p. 56.

III.8

1. F. Fischer, *Griff nach der Weltmacht*, Düsseldorf, 1961 (transl. as *Germany's War Aims in the First World War*, London, 1967); and his *Krieg der Illusionen. Die deutsche Politik 1911–14*, Düsseldorf, 1969 (transl. as *War of Illusions*, London, 1975).
2. Fischer, *Krieg*, p. 366.
3. F. Meinecke, *Werke*, vol. II, Darmstadt, 1958, p. 62 (22. 5. 1912); W.J. Mommsen, *Neue Politische Literatur*, 1971, p. 485.
4. Bueck and Erzberger are quoted in Fischer, *Krieg der Illusionen*, pp. 53,

47. Cf. D. Groh, *Negative Integration und revolutionärer Attentismus, Die deutsche Sozialdemokratie, 1909–1914*, Berlin, 1973, Chapter 4; and his 'Je eher, desto besser. Innenpolitische Faktoren für die Präventivkriegsbereitschaft des Deutschen Reiches 1913/14', in PVS, no. 13, 1972, pp. 501–21; Ratibor's conversation with Cambon in *The Diary of Lord Bertie of Thame, 1914-1918*, ed. L.A.G. Lennox, vol. I, London, 1924, pp. 352, 355 (1/2. 6. 1916 from Cambon); for Lerchenfeld, see P. Dirr (ed.), *Bayerische Dokumente zum Kriegsausbruch*, Munich, 3rd imp., 1925, p. 113 (4. 6. 1914); for Heydebrand, see K. Riezler, *Tagebücher*, ed. K.D. Erdmann, Göttingen, 1972, p. 183 (7. 7. 1914).

5. Bethmann's conversation with Haussmann of 24. 1. 1918 in W. Steglich, *Die Friedenspolitik der Mittelmächte*, vol. I, Wiesbaden, 1964, p. 418 (here also 'in two years').

6. See Lerchenfeld and Riezler, note 4.

7. Mommsen, p. 493.

8. Burckhardt, *Briefe*, vol. V, p. 160; MEW, vol. 21, pp. 350f.; F.X. Kraus, *Tagebücher*, ed. H. Schiel, Cologne, 1957, p. 684 (21. 3. 1897, reported by Jolly after a visit to Friedrichsruh).

9. This and the following in F. Lütge, 'Die deutsche Kriegsfinanzierung im 1. und 2. Weltkrieg', in *Festschrift* for R. Stucken, Göttingen, 1953, pp. 243–57, quotation pp. 249f.; R. Andexel (*Imperialismus, Staatsfinanzen, Rüstung, Krieg*, Berlin, 1968, pp. 15–59) estimates 150–170 billion marks, i.e. 85–95 million per day. Cf. England: 105; France: 74; together: 485 billion marks.

10. From G. Keiser, 'Die Erschütterung der Kreditwirtschaft zu Beginn des Krieges 1914/18', in *Bankarchiv*, 39, 1939, p. 505.

11. G.D. Feldman, *Army, Industry and Labor in Germany, 1914-18*, Princeton, NJ, 1966, pp. 149–249; this is the best work on the subject which, alongside Kocka's analysis (*Facing Total War*), should be consulted throughout for Part III, Section 8.

12. Thus runs the subtitle of K.-H. Janssen's *Macht und Verblendung*, Göttingen, 1963. For the literature on Germany's war aims, see W. Schieder (ed.), *Erster Weltkrieg*, Cologne, 1969.

13. See note 4 and MEW, vol. 21, p. 351.

14. A. Hillgruber, *Deutschlands Rolle in der Vorgeschichte der beiden Weltkriege*, Göttingen, 1967, p. 58.

15. Quotations, ibid., pp. 64, 66, cf. pp. 60–7; quotation below, p. 63. For the treaties, see H. Stoecker, (ed.), *Handbuch der Verträge, 1871–1964*, Berlin, 1968, pp. 171–5.

16. Ludendorff to H. Delbrück, 29. 12. 1915, from E. Zechlin, 'Ludendorff im Jahre 1915', in HZ, no. 211, 1970, p. 352.

17. See Wehler, *Krisenherde*, pp. 98–109, on this.

18. K. Kraus, *Unsterblicher Witz*, Munich, 1961, pp. 318, 329.

19. For H. Delbrück see *Das Werk des Untersuchungsausschusses der Verfassungsgebenden Deutschen Nationalversammlung und des Deutschen Reichstags* (series IV), vol. 4, p. 156, cf. vol. 2, p. 173; vol. 7, p. 261. For Bauer, see W. Deist (ed.), *Militär und Innenpolitik im Weltkrieg, 1914-18*, vol. II. Düsseldorf, 1970, pp. 651f. (no. 246), with arguments against the thesis of a dictatorship of the Supreme Command of the Army in the introduction to vol. I; see also von Thaer (and note 23), pp. 151, 198; W.J.

Mommsen, 'Die deutsche öffentliche Meinung und der Zusammenbruch des Regierungssystems Bethmann Hollweg', in *Geschichte in Wissenschaft und Unterricht*, vol. 20, 1969, p. 657, note 4; Wehler, *Krisenherde*, p. 364, note 37.

20. From Stegmann, p. 501 (3. 8. 1918), cf. pp. 497–519.
21. Meinecke, *Werke*, vol. II, p. 251, cf. p. 222.
22. Meinecke, *Autobiographische Schriften*, p. 354 (*Die Deutsche Katastrophe*, 1946).
23. A. von Thaer, *Generalstabsdienst an der Front und in der Obersten Heeresleitung*, ed. S.A. Kaehler, Göttingen, 1958, pp. 234f. Riezler, p. 480.
24. Thaer, p. 236, W. Groener, *Lebenserinnerungen*, ed. F. Hiller von Gaertringen, Göttingen, 1957, p. 466; Stegmann, p. 515.
25. *Werk des Untersuchungsausschusses*, vol. IV, pp. 2, 401; *Illustrierte Geschichte der Deutschen Revolution*, Berlin, 1929, p. 169; Feldman, p. 516, cf. pp. 363, 502–7; Groener, p. 450.
26. E. Matthias and R. Morsey, 'Die Bildung der Regierung des Prinzen M. von Baden', in *Vom Kaiserreich zur Weimarer Republik*, ed. E. Kolb, Cologne, 1972, p. 76, note 68 (after P. Scheidemann, *Memoiren eines Sozialdemokraten*, vol. II, Dresden, 1928, p. 187); here, for example, the thesis in question.
27. A. Rosenberg, p. 218; E. Matthias and R. Morsey (eds.), *Die Regierung des Prinzen M. von Baden*, Düsseldorf, 1962, p. 216 (16. 10. 1918).
28. Deist, vol. II, p. 1316, note 8; and his 'Die Politik der Seekriegsleitung und die Rebellion der Flotte Ende Oktober 1918', in *Vierteljahrshefte für Zeitgeschichte*, vol. 14, 1966, pp. 341–68; W. Sauer, 'Das Scheitern der parlamentarischen Monarchie', in Kolb (ed.), pp. 77–99.
29. E. Troeltsch, *Spektator-Briefe*, Tübingen, 1924, p. 19 (30. 11. 1918). The following according to R. Rürup (*Probleme der Revolution in Deutschland 1918/19*, Wiesbaden, 1968), E. Kolb (ed.), and the compilation there of recent literature by Oertzen, Kolb, Tormin, among others.
30. Kolb, p. 25, and H. Grebing, ibid., pp. 386–403. For the earlier interpretation see K.D. Erdmann, *Das Zeitalter der Weltkriege* (Gebhardt vol. IV), Stuttgart, 8th imp., 1959, pp. 77–92.
31. Rürup, p. 20.
32. Riezler, p. 359 (14. 6. 1916); Troeltsch, pp. 302f.; Mayer, Erinnerungen, p. 314.
33. G.D. Feldman et al., 'Die Massenbewegungen der Arbeiterschaft in Deutschland am Ende des Ersten Weltkrieges (1917–1920); PVS, vol. 13, 1972, p. 85 (quotation); and his 'The Origins of the Stinnes–Legien Agreement', in *Festschrift* for H. Rosenberg, Berlin, 1970, pp. 312–41.
34. R.N. Hunt, 'F. Ebert und die deutsche Revolution von 1918', in Kolb (ed.), p. 135 (which I have drawn on for my remarks on military policy).
35. G. Mann, *Deutsche Geschichte des 19. und 20. Jhs.*, Frankfurt 1958, p. 670.
36. Feldman et al., p. 97.
37. Troeltsch, p. 15.
38. Following the argument of G. A. Ritter, '"Direkte Demokratie" und Rätewesen in Geschichte und Theorie', in E.K. Scheuch (ed.), *Die Widertäufer in der Wohlstandsgesellschaft*, Cologne, 1969, pp. 188–216.

IV

1. J. Ziekursch, *Politische Geschichte des Neuen Deutschen Kaiserreichs*, vol. I, Frankfurt, 1925, pp. 3f.
2. W. Rathenau, *Briefe*, vol. I, p. 250 (to E. Norlind, 1. 4. 1917).
3. *Rochau*, ed. Wehler, p. 9.
4. GW, vol. VIII, p. 340; RB, vol. 13, p. 105, cf. vol. 4, p. 192, vol. 12, p. 380, vol. 13, p. 130.
5. Burckhardt, vol. V, p. 130 (12. 10. 1871).
6. Meinecke, *Werke*, vol. II, p. 41.
7. Riezler, p. 359; Weber, *Politische Schriften*, p. 235; Stegmann, p. 502; G. Schmoller, 'Die preussische Wahlrechtsreform von 1910', in *Schmollers Jahrbuch*, vol. 33, 1910, pp. 357, 361–4.
8. Cf. Committee on Comparative Politics (ed.), *Studies in Political Development*, 7 vols, Princeton, NJ, 1963–71, in particular L. Binder (ed.), *Crises*, 1971.
9. Riezler, p. 426 (13. 4. 1917).
10. Rosenberg, *Probleme*, pp. 7–49.
11. P. Kielmansegg, 'Von den Schwierigkeiten, deutsche Geschichte zu schreiben', in *Merkur*, 276, 1971, pp. 366–79.

Bibliography

The following references represent a brief selection only which have been chosen with two criteria in mind: it was intended to include, on the one hand, monographs of general importance (possibly containing extended bibliographies), and works of a particularly stimulating and controversial character, on the other. Published sources have not been listed, because they can easily be found with the help of bibliographies, reference works and monographs. The bibliography first lists the general works (A–G). It then follows the sequence of the book's chapters which are themselves structured according to subject area.

Bibliographies of primary and secondary sources

Dahlmann-Waitz, *Quellenkunde zur deutschen Geschichte*, (ed.) H. Heimpel, Stuttgart 1969[10].
Brief: W. Baumgart (ed.), *Bücherverzeichnis zur deutschen Geschichte*, Berlin 1971 and subs.; H.-U. Wehler (ed.), *Die moderne deutsche Geschichte in der internationalen Forschung 1945–1975 = Geschichte u. Gesellschaft*, special issue 4, Göttingen 1978; idem (ed.), *Bibliographie zur modernen deutschen Sozialgeschichte, 18.–20. Jh.*, ibid., 1976; idem (ed.), *Bibliographie zur modernen deutschen Wirtschaftsgeschichte, 18.–20. Jh.*, ibid., 1976; H. Berding (ed.), *Bibliographie zur Geschichtstheorie*, ibid., 1977; H. A. Winkler and T. Schnabel (eds.), *Bibliographie zum Nationalismus*, ibid. 1979; J. Hess and E. van Steensel van der Aa (eds.), *Bibliographie zum deutschen Liberalismus*, ibid. 1981; H.-P. Ullmann (ed.), *Bibliographie zur Geschichte der deutschen Parteien u. Interessenverbände*, ibid. 1978; K. Tenfelde (ed.), *Geschichte der Arbeiterschaft u. der Arbeiterbewegung. Die internationale Forschung*, Munich, 1984; idem and G. A. Ritter (eds.), *Bibliographie zur Geschichte der deutschen Arbeiterschaft u. Arbeiterbewegung 1863–1914*, Bonn, 1981; H. J. Steinberg (ed.), *Die deutsche sozialistische Arbeiterbewegung bis 1914. Eine bibliographische Einführung*, Frankfurt, 1979; J.-P. Halstead and S. Porcari (eds.), *Modern European Imperialismus: A Bibliography of Books and Articles*, 2 vols., Boston, 1974; H.-U. Wehler (ed.), *Bibliographie zum Imperialismus*, Göttingen, 1977; G. P. Meyer (ed.), *Bibliographie zur Revolution von 1918*, ibid., 1977.

A. General and political history

T. Schieder, *Handbuch der Europäischen Geschichte*, VI, Stuttgart, 1968, XV–230; VII/1, 1979, 1–137; idem, *Staatensystem als Vormacht der Welt 1848–1918*, Berlin, 1977; H. Grundmann (ed.), *Gebhardt-Handbuch der Deutschen Geschichte*, III, Stuttgart 1970[9]; IV, 1959[8]; L. Just (ed.), *Handbuch der Deutschen Geschichte*, III/2; IV/1. Konstanz 1956/Frankfurt 1972; E. Büssem and M. Neher (eds.), *Repetitorium der deutschen Geschichte*, Neuzeit 3: 1871–1914. Edited by G. Höhler et al., Munich 1972, 1981; K. G. A. Jeserich et al. (eds.), *Deutsche Verwaltungsgeschichte*, vols. 2, 3: 1806–1918, Stuttgart, 1983–4.

B. Constitutional history

E. R. Huber, *Deutsche Verfassungsgeschichte seit 1789*, vols. III–VI, Stuttgart, 1963–81; D. Grimm, *Deutsche Verfassungsgeschichte 1806–1980*, Frankfurt, 1985; H. Boldt, *Deutsche Verfassunsgeschichte*, Munich, 1984; H. Fenske, *Deutsche Verfassungsgeschichte 1867–1980*, Berlin, 1981; E.-W. Böckenförde and R. Wahl (eds.), *Moderne Deutsche Verfassungsgeschichte 1918–1918*, Cologne, 1972/Königstein, 1981.[2]

C. Social history

G. Hohorst et al., *Sozialgeschichtliches Arbeitsbuch II: Materialien zur Statistik des Kaiserreichs 1870–1914*, Munich, 1978[2]; D. Petzina et al., *Sozialgeschichtliches Arbeitsbuch III: 1914–1945*, ibid., 1978; H.-U. Wehler (ed.), *Moderne Deutsche Sozialgeschichte*, Cologne, 1966/Königstein, 1981[6]; idem (ed.), *Klassen in der europäischen Sozialgeschichte*, Göttingen, 1979; idem (ed.), *Analyse von sozialen Strukturen = Geschichte u. Gesellschaft*, 3, 1977/4; J. Kocka, *Sozialgeschichte*, ibid., 1977; idem (ed.), *Soziale Schichtung u. Mobilität in Deutschland im 19. u. 20. Jahrhundert = Geschichte u. Gesellschaft*, 1, 1975/1; idem (ed.), *Sozialgeschichte u. Kulturanthropologie = Geschichte u. Gesellschaft*, 10, 1984/3; idem, *Unternehmensverwaltung u. Angestelltenschaft, Siemens 1847-1914*, Stuttgart, 1969; idem, *Angestellte zwischen Faschismus u. Demokratie*, Göttingen, 1977; idem, *Die Angestellten in der deutschen Geschichte 1850–1980*, ibid. 1981; idem (ed.), *Angestellte im europäischen Vergleich = Geschichte u. Gesellschaft*, special issue 7, ibid. 1981; H. Kaelble, *Industrialisation and Social Inequality. Europe in the 19th Century*, Leamington Spa 1985; idem, *Social Mobility and Equality in the 19th and 20th Centuries. An International Comparison*, Leamington Spa 1985; idem, *Historische Mobilitätsforschung*, Darmstadt, 1978; idem (ed.), *Geschichte der sozialen Mobilität seit der Industriellen Revolution*, Königstein, 1978; P. Marschalck, *Deutsche Bevölkerungsgeschichte im 19. u. 20. Jh.*, Frankfurt, 1984; W. Köllmann and P. Marschalck (eds.), *Bevölkerungsgeschichte*, Cologne, 1972; idem, *Bevölkerung in der industriellen Revolution*, Göttingen, 1974; G. Neuhaus, *Die Bewegung der Bevölkerung im Zeitalter des modernen Kapitalismus*, in *Grundriß der Sozialökonomik*, IX, 1, Tübingen, 1926, pp. 360–505; idem, *Die berufliche u. soziale Gliederung der Bevölkerung im Zeitalter des Kapitalismus*, in ibid.; F. Zahn, *Die Entwicklung der räumlichen, beruflichen u. sozialen Gliederung des deutschen Volkes seit dem Aufkommen der industriell-kapitalistischen Wirtschaftsweise*, in B.

Harms (ed.), *Volk u. Reich der Deutschen*, I, Berlin, 1929, pp. 220–89; P. Marschalck, *Deutsche Überseewanderung im 19. Jh.*, Stuttgart, 1973; K. J. Bade, *Vom Auswanderungsland zum Einwanderungsland*. *Deutschland 1880–1980*, Berlin, 1983; J. Reulecke, *Urbanisierung in Deutschland 1850–1980*, Frankfurt, 1984; E. Sagarra, *A Social History of Germany 1648-1914*, London, 1977; H. Burgelin, *La société allemande 1871-1968*, Paris, 1969; W. Conze and J. Kocka (eds.), *Bildungsbürgertum im 19. Jh.*, I, Stuttgart, 1984; K. Vondung (ed.), *Das wilhelminische Bildungsbürgertum*, Göttingen, 1976; H. Pohl (ed.), *Sozialgeschichtliche Probleme in der Zeit der Hochindustrialisierung 1800–1914*, Paderborn, 1979; G. Hardach, 'Klassen u. Schichten in Deutschland 1848-1970. Probleme einer historischen Sozialstrukturanalyse', in *Geschichte u. Gesellschaft*, 3, 1977, pp. 503–24; D. Blackbourn, 'The Mittelstand in German Society and Politics 1871–1914', in *Social History*, 4, 1977, pp. 409–33; R. Gellately, *The Politics of Economic Despair. Shopkeepers and German Politics 1890–1914*, London, 1974. Detailed references in the above bibliography by Wehler.

D. Economic history

W. G. Hoffmann et al., *Das Wachstum der deutschen Wirtschaft seit der Mitte des 19. Jh.*, Heidelberg, 1965; Statistisches Bundesamt (ed.), *Bevölkerung u. Wirtschaft 1872–1972*, Stuttgart, 1972; H.-U. Wehler, 'Probleme der modernen deutschen Wirtschaftsgeschichte', in idem, *Krisenherde des Kaiserreichs*, Göttingen, 1970, pp. 291–311, 408–30; rev. ed. in idem, *Historische Sozialwissenschaft u. Geschichtsschreibung*, ibid., 1980, pp. 106–25, 346–55; W. Zorn and H. Aubin (eds.), *Handbuch der deutschen Wirtschafts- u. Sozialgeschichte, II: 1800–1970*, Stuttgart, 1976; D. S. Landes, 'Technological Change and Development in Western Europe 1750–1914', in *Cambridge Economic History of Europe*, VI/2, 1965, pp. 943–1007; idem, *Prometheus Unbound*, London, 1969; C. Cipolla and K. Borchardt (eds.), *Europäische Wirtschaftsgeschichte*, vols. 3–5, Stuttgart, 1976–80; S. Pollard, *Peaceful Conquest. The Industrialization of Europe 1760–1980*, Oxford, 1981; idem, *Europa im Zeitalter der Industrialisierung 1750–1980*, Göttingen, 1984; K. Borchardt, *Grundriß der deutschen Wirtschaftsgeschichte.*, ibid. 1978; idem, *The Industrial Revolution in Germany 1700–1914*, London, 1972; F.-W. Henning, *Die Industrialisierung Deutschlands 1800–1914*, Paderborn, 1976[3]; idem, *Das industrialisierte Deutschland 1914–1976*, ibid., 1978[4]; H. Radandt et al. (eds.), *Handbuch Wirtschaftsgeschichte*, 2 vols., Berlin, 1981; H. Nußbaum and L. Zumpe (eds.), *Wirtschaft u. Staat in Deutschland, I: up to 1918/19*, ibid., 1978; H. Mottek et al., *Wirtschaftsgeschichte Deutschlands, III: 1871–1945*, ibid., 1974; G. Hardach, *Deutschland in der Weltwirtschaft 1870–1970. Eine Einführung in die Sozial- u. Wirtschaftsgeschichte*, Frankfurt, 1977; K. W. Hardach, *Wirtschaftsgeschichte Deutschlands im 2o. Jh.*, Göttingen, 1979[2]; V. Hentschel, *Deutsche Wirtschafts- u. Sozialpolitik 1815-1914*, Königstein, 1980; W. Fischer, *Deutsche Wirtschaftspolitik 1918-45*, Opladen, 1968[3]; W. O. Henderson, *The Rise of German Industrial Power 1834-1914*, London, 1976; C. P. Kindleberger, *A Financial History of Western Europe*, ibid., 1984. Detailed references in the above bibliography by Wehler.

E. Historiography, theory and methodological problems

G. G. Iggers, *The German Conception of History*, Middletown, Conn., 1968; idem, *Deutsche Geschichtswissenschaft*, Munich, 1976³; W. J. Mommsen, 'Gegenwärtige Tendenzen in der Geschichtsschreibung der Bundesrepublik', in *Geschichte u. Gesellschaft*, 7, 1981, pp. 149–88; H.-U. Wehler, 'Geschichtswissenschaft heute 1949-1979', in J. Habermas (ed.), *Stichworte zur geistigen Situation der Zeit*, II, Frankfurt, 1979/1980³, pp. 709–53; rev. ed. in Wehler, *Historische Sozialwissenschaft u. Geschichtsschreibung*, Göttingen, 1980, pp. 13-41; idem, *Geschichte als historische Sozialwissenschaft*, Frankfurt, 1973/1980³; idem, *Modernisierungstheorie u. Geschichte*, Göttingen, 1975; idem (ed.), *Deutsche Historiker*, 9 vols., ibid., 1971–82; J. Streisand (ed.), *Studien über die deutsche Geschichtswissenschaft*, 2 vols., Berlin, 1963, 1965; E. Schulin, *Traditionskritik u. Rekonstruktionsversuch*, Göttingen, 1979; G. Heydermann, *Geschichtswissenschaft im geteilten Deutschland*, Frankfurt, 1980. Detailed references in the above bibliography by Berding.

F. General

A selection of some works written from differing viewpoints: G. Mann, *Deutsche Geschichte des 19. u. 2o. Jh.*, Frankfurt, 1958 a subs.; G. A. Craig, *Germany 1866–1945*, Oxford, 1978; T. Nipperdey, *Deutsche Geschichte 1800–1866. Bürgerwelt u. starker Staat*, Munich, 1983; M. Stürmer, *Das ruhelose Reich 1866–1918*, Berlin, 1983; J. Ziekursch, *Politische Geschichte des Neuen Deutschen Kaiserreiches*, 3 vols., Frankfurt, 1925–30; C. Stern and H. A. Winkler (eds.), *Wendepunkte deutscher Geschichte 1848–1945*, ibid., 1979; R. Dahrendorf, *Society and Democracy in Germany*, New York, 1967; K. Buchheim, *Das Deutsche Kaiserreich 1871–1918*, ibid., 1969; E. Engelberg, *Deutschland 1871–1897*, Berlin, 1965; F. Klein, *Deutschland 1897–1917*, ibid., 1969³; V. R. Berghahn, *Modern Germany. Society, Economy, and Politics in the 20th Century*, Cambridge, 1982; F.-G. Dreyfus, *Histoire des Allemagnes*. Paris, 1972²; P. Aycoberry, *L'unité allemande 1800–1871*, ibid., 1972²; J. Droz, *La formation de l'unité allemande 1789–1871*, ibid., 1971; P. Guillen, *L'empire allemande 1871–1918*, ibid. 1970; R. Poidevin and J. Bariéty, *Deutschland u. Frankreich 1815–1975*, Munich, 1982; L. Gall, *Europa auf dem Weg in die Moderne 1850–1890*, ibid., 1984; G. Palmade (ed.), *Das bürgerliche Zeitalter 1848–1890*, Frankfurt, 1974; E. N. and P. R. Anderson, *Political Institutions and Social Change in Continental Europe in the 19th Century*, Berkeley, 1967; A. J. Mayer, *The Persistence of the Old Regime. Europe to the Great War*, New York, 1981; idem, *Dynamics of Counterrevolution in Europe 1870–1956*, ibid., 1971; M. Kolinsky, *Continuity and Change in European Society since 1870*, London, 1974; T. S. Hamerow, *The Birth of a New Europe. State and Society in the 19th Century*, Chapel Hill, 1983; E. J. Hobsbawm, *The Age of Capital 1848–1875*, London, 1975; J. A. S. Grenville, *Europe Reshaped 1848–1878*, New York, 1980²; N. Stone, *Europe Transformed 1878–1919*, Glasgow, 1983; *The New Cambridge Modern History*, XI: 1870–98, 1962; XII: 1898–1945, 1960, 1968²; G. Barraclough, *Introduction to Contemporary History*, Harmondsworth, 1967.

G. Recent reference works and anthologies

P. Flora et al., *State, Economy, and Society in Western Europe 1815–1980. A Data Handbook*, 2 vols., Frankfurt, 1983; H.-U. Wehler, *Krisenherde des Kaiserreichs* Göttingen, 1979[2]; E. Kehr, *Der Primat der Innenpolitik*, edited by H.-U. Wehler, Berlin, 1965/1976[3]; M. Stürmer (ed.), *Das Kaiserliche Deutschland*, Düsseldorf, 1970 and subs.; idem (ed.), *Bismarck u. die preußisch-deutsche Politik 1871–1890*, Munich, 1970; G. A. Ritter (ed.), *Das Kaiserreich 1871–1914. Ein historisches Lesebuch*, Göttingen, 1977[3]; idem (ed.), *Gesellschaft, Parlament u. Regierung. Zur Geschichte des Parlamentarismus in Deutschland*, Düsseldorf, 1974; H. Berding (ed.), *Wirtschaftliche u. politische Integration in Europa im 19. u. 20. Jh. = Geschichte u. Gesellschaft*, special issue 10, Göttingen, 1984; D. Blasius (ed.), *Preußen in der deutschen Geschichte*. Königstein, 1980; H.-J. Puhle and H.-U. Wehler (eds.), *Preußen im Rückblick = Geschichte u. Gesellschaft*, special issue 6, Göttingen, 1980; H. Böhme (ed.), *Probleme der Reichsgründungszeit 1848–79*, Cologne, 1968, 1973[2]; idem (ed.), *Die Reichsgründung*, Munich, 1967; H. Bartel and E. Engelberg (eds.), *Die großpreußisch-militärische Reichsgründung*, 2 vols., Berlin, 1971; O. Pflanze (ed.), *Innenpolitische Probleme des Bismarck-Reiches*, Munich, 1983; R. J. Evans (ed.), *Society and Politics in Wilhelmine Germany*, London, 1978; V. Valentin, *Von Bismarck zur Weimarer Republik*, edited by H.-U. Wehler, Cologne, 1979; H.-U. Wehler (ed.), *Geschichte u. Ökonomie*, ibid., 1973; W. Abelshauser and D. Petzina (eds.), *Deutsche Wirtschaftsgeschichte im Industriezeitalter*, Königstein, 1981; D. Petzina and G. van Roon (eds.), *Konjunktur, Krise, Gesellschaft*, Stuttgart, 1981; W. H. Schröder and R. Spree (eds.), *Historische Konjunkturforschung*, Stuttgart, 1980; K. Borchardt, *Wachstum, Krisen u. Handlungsspielräume der Wirtschaftspolitik*, Göttingen, 1982; R. H. Tilly, *Kapital, Staat u. sozialer Protest in der deutschen Industrialisierung*, ibid., 1980; H. Kellenbenz (eds.), *Wachstumsschwankungen*, Stuttgart, 1981; T. Pierenkemper and R. H. Tilly (eds.), *Historische Arbeitsmarktforschung*, Göttingen, 1982; S. Pollard (ed.), *Region u. Industrialisierung*, ibid., 1980; S. Pollard and C. Holmes (eds.), *Documents of European Economic History, III: Industrial Power and National Rivalry, 1870–1914*, London, 1972; H.-U. Wehler (ed.), *Geschichte u. Soziologie*, Cologne, 1972/Königstein, 1984[3]; G. A. Ritter and J. Kocka (eds.), *Deutsche Sozialgeschichte 1870–1914*, Munich, 1974, 1982[3]; K. Tenfelde and H. Volkmann (eds.), *Streik*, ibid. 1981; T. Nipperdey, *Gesellschaft, Kultur, Theorie*, Göttingen, 1976; W. Kröber and R. Nitsche (eds.), *Grundbuch der bürgerlichen Gesellschaft*, vols. I, II, Neuwied, 1979; H. M. Enzensberger et al. (eds.), *Klassenbuch, II: Ein Lesebuch zu den Klassenkämpfen in Deutschland 1860–1919*, Neuwied, 1972 and subs.

I.1

W. Abel, *Agrarkrisen u. Agrarkonjunktur*, Berlin, 1966[2]; S. v. Ciriacy-Wantrup, *Agrarkrisen u. Stockungsspannen*, ibid., 1936; H. W. Finck v. Finckenstein, *Die Entwicklung der Landwirtschaft 1800–1930*, Würzburg, 1960; E. Klein, *Geschichte der deutschen Landwirtschaft im Industriezeitalter*, Wiesbaden, 1973; F.-W. Henning, *Landwirtschaft u. ländliche Gesellschaft in Deutschland, II: 1750–1976*, Paderborn, 1978; J. Flemming and K. Saul, *Sozialgeschichte der Landarbeiter in*

Preußen 1800–1914, Munich, 1985; A. Gerschenkron, *Bread and Democracy in Germany*, 1943, New York, 1966²; H. Rosenberg, *Machteliten u. Wirtschaftskonjunkturen*, Göttingen, 1978; idem, *Probleme der deutschen Sozialgeschichte*, Frankfurt, 1969; H. Schissler, *Geschichte des preußischen Junkertums*, Frankfurt, 1985; idem 'Die Junker. Zur Sozialgeschichte u. historischen Bedeutung der agrarischen Elite in Preußen', in H.-J. Puhle and H.-U Wehler (eds.), *Preußen im Rückblick = Geschichte u. Gesellschaft*, special issue 6, Göttinghen, 1980, p. 122; H. Reif, 'Westfälischer Adel 1770–1860', ibid., 1979; F. Tönnies, 'Deutscher Adel im 19. Jh.', in *Neue Rundschau*, 23, 1912/II, pp. 1041–63; R. Meyer, 'Adelsstand u. Junkerklasse', in *Neue Deutsche Rundschau*, 10, 1899, pp. 1078–90; H. Preuss, *Die Junkerfrage*, Berlin, 1897.

I.2

R. Spree, *Wachstumstrends u. Konjunkturzyklen in der deutschen Wirtschaft 1820–1913*, Göttingen, 1978; idem, *Die Wachstumszyklen der deutschen Wirtschaft, 1840–1880*, Berlin, 1977; R. Spree and J. Bergmann, 'Die konjunkturelle Entwicklung der deutschen Wirtschaft 1840–1864', in *Sozialgeschichte Heute. Fs. H. Rosenberg*, H.-U. Wehler (ed.), Göttingen, 1974, pp. 289–325; W. G. Hoffmann, 'The Take-Off in Germany', in W. W. Rostow (ed.), *The Economics of Take-Off Into Sustained Growth*, London, 1968², pp. 95–118; R. H. Tilly (ed.), *Deutsche Frühindustrialisierung = Geschichte u. Gesellschaft*, 5, 1979/2; H. Rosenberg, *Die Weltwirtschaftskrise 1857–59*, Stuttgart, 1934/Göttingen 1974²; J. Kocka, 'Vorindustrielle Faktoren in der deutschen Industrialisierung', in *Das Kaiserliche Deutschland*, M. Stürmer (ed.), Düsseldorf, 1970, pp. 265–86; H. Böhme, *Deutschlands Weg zur Großmacht 1848–81*, Cologne, 1966, 1972²; T. S. Hamerow, *Restoration, Revolution, Reaction. Economics and Politics in Germany 1815–71*, Princeton, 1958 and subs.; H. Kaelble, 'Der Mythos von der rapiden Industrialisierung in Deutschland', in *Geschichte u. Gesellschaft*, 9, 1983, pp. 106–19; R. Fremdling, *Eisenbahnen u. deutsches Wirtschaftswachstum, 1840–1879*, Dortmund, 1975; T. Pierenkemper, Die westfälischen Schwerindustriellen 1851–1913, Göttingen, 1979; G. Ambrosius, *Der Staat als Unternehmer. Öffentliche Wirtschaft u. Kapitalismus seit dem 19. Jh.*, ibid., 1984.

I.3

R. Wahl, 'Der preußische Verfassungskonflikt u. das konstitutionelle System des Kaiserreichs', in E.-W. Böckenförde and idem (eds.), *Moderne Deutsche Verfassungsgeschichte*, Cologne, 1972/Königstein 1981², pp. 171–94; H. Boldt, 'Verfassungskonflikt u. Verfassungshistorie', in E.-W. Böckenförde (ed.), *Probleme des Konstitutionalismus*, Berlin, 1975, pp. 75–102; E. N. Anderson, *The Social and Political Conflict in Prussia 1858–64*, Lincoln, 1954; K. H. Dikrair, *Die Krise der preußischen Monarchie*, Berlin, 1976; G. Mayer, *Radikalismus, Sozialismus u. bürgerliche Demokratie*, edited by H.-U. Wehler, Frankfurt, 1969²; M. Gugel, *Industrieller Aufstieg u. bürgerliche Herrschaft. Sozioökonomische Interessen u. politische Ziele des liberalen Bürgertums z.Zt. des Verfassungskonflikts 1857–1867*, Cologne, 1975; T. S. Hamerow, *The Social Foundations of German Unification, 1858–71*, 2 vols., Princeton, 1969, 1972; idem, 'The Origins of

Mass Politics in Germany 1866–1867', in *Fs. F. Fischer*, Düsseldorf, 1973, pp. 105–20; K. Kluxen, *Geschichte u. Problematik des Parlamentarismus*, Frankfurt, 1983.

I.4

From the extensive literature (for a selection see Gall, below, III. 1, and in Stürmer, above, F) only three titles have been chosen: J. Becker, 'Der Krieg mit Frankreich als Problem der kleindeutschen Einigungspolitik Bismarcks 1866–1870', in *Das Kaiserliche Deutschland*, M. Stürmer (ed.), Düsseldorf, 1970, pp. 75–88; idem, 'Zum Problem der Bismarckschen Politik in der spanischen Thronfolge 1879', in HZ, 212, 1971, pp. 529–607 (where the author argues convincingly against the untenable exoneration of Prussian politics as presented by E. Kolb, *Der Kriegsausbruch 1870*, Göttingen, 1980).

II.1

P. Bairoch, 'Europe's Gross National Product 1800–1975', in *Journal of European Economic History*, 5, 1976, pp. 273–340; A. Maddison, 'A Comparison of Levels of GDP p.c. in Developed and Developing Countries 1700–1980', in *Journal of Economic History*, 43, 1983, pp. 27–41; A. Spiethoff, *Die wirtschaftlichen Wechsellagen*, 2 vols., Tübingen, 1955; D. André, *Indikatoren des technischen Fortschritts. Eine Analyse der Wirtschaftsentwicklung in Deutschland 1850–1913*, Hamburg, 1971; H. Rosenberg, *Große Depression u. Bismarckzeit*, Berlin, 1967, 1976[2]; H. Siegenthaler, 'Ansätze zu einer generalisierenden Interpretation langwelliger Wachstumsschwankungen u. ihrer sozialen Implikationen im 19. u. frühen 20. Jh.', in H. Kellenbenz (ed.), *Wachstumsschwankungen*, Stuttgart, 1981, pp. 1–45; H. Mottek, 'Die Gründerkrise', in *Jahrbuch für Wirtschaftsgeschichte 1966/I*, pp. 51–128; H. Helbig (ed.), *Führungskräfte der Wirtschaft 1790–1914*, Limburg, 1977; N. Horn and J. Kocka (eds.), *Recht u. Entwicklung der Großunternehmen im 19. u. frühen 20. Jh.*, Göttingen, 1979; J. Krengel, *Die deutsche Roheisenindustrie 1871–1913*, Berlin, 1983; W. Feldenkirchen, *Die Eisen- u. Stahlindustrie des Ruhrgebiets 1879–1914*, Wiesbaden, 1982; E. Barth, *Entwicklungslinien der deutschen Maschinenbauindustrie 1870–1914*, Berlin, 1973; G. Kirchhain, *Das Wachstum der deutschen Baumwollindustrie im 19. Jh.*, New York, 1977; H. Neuburger, *German Banks and German Economic Growth 1871–1914*, ibid. 1977; H. Stuebel, *Staat u. Banken im preußischen Anleihewesen 1871–1913*, Berlin, 1935; F. B. Tipton, *Regional Variations in the Economic Development of Germany during the 19th Century*, Middletown, Conn., 1976; G. Hohorst, *Wirtschaftswachstum u. Bevölkerungsentwicklung in Preußen 1816–1914*, New York, 1977; V. Hentschel, 'Produktion, Wachstum u. Produktivität in England, Frankreich u. Deutschland 1850–1914', in *Vierteljahrsschrift für Sozial- u. Wirtschaftsgeschichte*, 68, 1981, pp. 457–510; W. Berg, *Wirtschaft u.Gesellschaft in Deutschland u. Großbritannien im Übergang zum 'Organisierten Kapitalismus'. Unternehmer, Angestellte, Arbeiter u. Staat im Steinkohlenbergbau des Ruhrgebiets u. von Südwales 1850–1914*, Berlin, 1984; K. W. Hardach, *Die Bedeutung wirtschaftlicher Faktoren bei der Wiedereinführung der Eisen- u. Getreidezölle in Deutschland 1879*, Berlin, 1967; H.-P. Ullmann, 'Staatliche Exportförderung u. private Exportinitiative. Probleme des Staatsinterventionismus im Deutschen Kaiserreich am Beispiel der staatlichen Außenhandelsförderung (1880–1919)', in *Vierteljahrsschrift für Sozial- u. Wirtschaftsgeschichte*, 65, 1978, pp. 157–216; R. Moeller, 'Peasants and Tariffs in the Kaiserreich. How Backward Were the "Bauern"?', in *Agricultural History*, 55, 1981, pp. 370–84; S.Webb, 'Tariffs, Cartels, Technology, and Growth in the German Steel Industry 1879–1914', in *Journal of Economic History*, 40, 1980, pp. 309–29; idem 'Tariff Protection for the Iron Industry, Cotton Textiles, and Agriculture in Germany 1879–1914', in *Jahrbücher für Nationalökonomie u. Statistik*, 192, 1977, pp. 336–57; H. Reuter, 'Schutzzollpolitik u. Zolltarife für Getreide 1880–1900', in *Zeitschrift für Agrargeschichte*, 25, 1977, pp. 199–213; J. C. Hunt, 'Peasants, Grain Tariffs, and Meat Quotas: Imperial German Protectionism Reexamined', in *Central European History*, 7, 1974, pp. 311–31; D. Blackbourn, 'Peasants and Politics in Germany 1871–1914', in *European History Quarterly*, 14, 1984, pp. 47–75; F. B. Tipton, 'Farm Labor and Power Politics in Germany 1850–1914', in *Journal of Economic History*, 34, 1974, pp. 951–79.

II.2

W. Paretti and G. Bloch, 'Industrial Production in Western Europe and the United States, 1901–1955', in *Banca Nazionale del Lavoro Quarterly Review*, 9, 1956, pp. 186–234; E. W. Axe and H. M. Flinn, 'An Index of General Business Conditions for Germany, 1898–1914', in *Review of Economic Statistics*, 7, 1925, pp. 263–87; A. Feiler, *Die Konjunkturperiode 1907–13*, Jena, 1914; H. Siegrist, 'Deutsche Großunternehmen vom späten 19. Jh. bis zur Weimarer Republik', in *Geschichte u. Gesellschaft*, 6, 1980, pp. 60–120. On the beginnings of 'organised capitalism' and the rise of the interventionist state see i.a.: H. A. Winkler (ed.), *Organisierter Kapitalismus*, Göttingen, 1973; H.-U. Wehler, 'Der Aufstieg des Organisierten Kapitalismus in Deutschland', in idem, *Krisenherde des Kaiserreichs*, Göttingen, 1979², pp. 290–308; H.-J. Puhle (ed.), *Kapitalismus, Korporatismus, Keynesianismus = Geschichte u. Gesellschaft*, 10, 1984/2; idem, 'Vom Wohlfahrtsausschuß zum Wohlfahrtsstaat', in G. A. Ritter (ed.), Cologne, 1973, pp. 29–68; W. J. Mommsen and W. Mock (eds.), *Die Entstehung des Wohlfahrtsstaats in Großbritannien u. Deutschland 1850–1950*, Stuttgart, 1982; H. Daems and H. v.d. Wee (eds), *The Rise of Managerial Capitalism*, The Hague, 1974; E. Lederer, *Kapitalismus, Klassenstruktur u. Probleme der Demokratie in Deutschland 1910–1940*, edited by J. Kocka, Göttingen, 1979; G. Brüggemeier, *Entwicklung des Rechts im organisierten Kapitalismus*, I, Frankfurt, 1977; F. Neumark, *Wirtschafts u. Finanzprobleme des Interventionsstaats*, Tübingen, 1961; J. A. Schumpeter, 'Die Krise des Steuerstaats', in idem, *Aufsätze zur Soziologie*, Tübingen 1953, pp. 1–71; M. Geyer and A. Lüdtke, 'Krisenmanagement, Herrschaft u. Protest im organisierten Monopol-Kapitalismus 1890–1939', in *Sozialwissenschaftliche Informationen*, 4, 1975, pp. 12–23; H. Kaelble and H. Volkmann, 'Konjunktur u. Streik während des Übergangs zum Organisierten Kapitalismus in Deutschland', in *Zeitschrift für Wirtschafts u. Sozialwissenschaften*, 92, 1972, pp. 513–44; S. Andic and J. Veverka, 'The Growth of Government Expenditure in Germany Since the Unification', in *Finanzarchiv*, 23, 1963, pp. 169–278; J. P. Cullity, 'The Growth of Governmental Employment in Germany

1882–1950', in ZGS, 123, 1967, pp. 207–17; H. Timm, 'Das Gesetz der wachsenden Staatsausgaben', in *Finanzarchiv*, 21, 1961, pp. 201–47; F. Facius, *Wirtschaft u. Staat. Die Entwicklung der staatlichen Wirtschaftsverwaltung in Deutschland bis 1945*, Boppard, 1959.

III.1.1

L. Gall, *Bismarck*, Berlin, 1980 and subs.; F. Eyck, *Bismarck*, 3 vols. Zürich 1941/44; F. Stern, *Gold and Iron*, London, 1977; E.-W. Böckenförde, 'Der Verfassungstyp der deutschen konstitutionellen Monarchie im 19. Jh.' in *Moderne Deutsche Verfassungsgeschichte 1815–1918*, idem and R. Wahl (eds), Cologne, 1972/Königstein 1981², pp. 146–70; H. Boldt, 'Deutscher Konstitutionalismus u. Bismarckreich', in *Das Kaiserliche Deutschland*, M. Stürmer (ed.), Düsseldorf, 1970, pp. 119–42; W. J. Mommsen, 'Die Verfassung des Deutschen Reiches von 1871 als dilatorischer Herrschaftskompromiß', in O. Pflanze (ed.), *Innenpolitische Probleme des Bismarck-Reiches*, Munich, 1983, pp. 195–216; idem, 'Das Deutsche Kaiserreich als System umgangener Entscheidungen', in *2. Fs. Schieder*, Munich, 1978, pp. 239–66; M. Stürmer, *Regierung u. Reichstag im Bismarckstaat 1871-1800*, Düsseldorf, 1974; H.-W. Wetzel, *Presseinnenpolitik im Bismarckreich 1874-1890*, Frankfurt, 1975; K. Schwabe (ed.), *Die Regierungen der deutschen Mittel- u. Kleinstaaten 1815–1933*, Boppard, 1983.

III.1.2

K. Hammer and P. C. Hartmann (eds), *Der Bonapartismus*, Munich, 1977; W. Wippermann, *Die Bonapartismustheorie von Marx u. Engels*, Stuttgart, 1983; L. Gall, 'Bismarck u. der Bonapartismus', in HZ, 223, 1976, pp. 618–32; A. Mitchell, 'Der Bonapartismus als Modell der Bismarckschen Reichspolitik', in *Beihefte der Francia*, 6, 1977, pp. 56–76; A. Kuhn, 'Elemente des Bonapartismus in Bismarck-Deutschland', in *Jahrbuch des Instituts für Deutsche Geschichte Tel Aviv*, 7, 1978, pp. 277–97; H. Gollwitzer, 'Der Cäsarismus Napoleons III. im Widerhall der öffentlichen Meinung Deutschlands', in *HZ*, 173, 1952, pp. 23–75; E. Engelberg, 'Zur Entstehung u. historischen Stellung des preußisch-deutschen Bonapartismus', in *Fs. A. Meusel*, Berlin, 1956, pp. 236–51; G. Seeber, 'Preußisch-deutscher Bonapartismus u. Bourgeoisie', in *Jahrbuch für Geschichte*, 16, 1977, pp. 71–118; G. Seeber and H. Wolter, 'Die Krise der bonapartistischen Diktatur Bismarcks 1885/86', in *Fs. E. Engelberg*, II, Berlin, 1976, pp. 499–540; H. Wolter, 'Zum Verhältnis von Außenpolitik u. Bismarckschem Bonapartismus', in *Jahrbuch für Geschichte*, 16, 1977, pp. 119–37; G. Seeber et al., *Bismarcks Sturz*, Berlin, 1977; R. Griepenburg and K. H. Tjaden, 'Faschismus u. Bonapartismus', in *Das Argument*, 8, 1966 (41), pp. 461–72. A summary of critical reservations towards this type of regime may be found in: H.-U. Wehler, 'Kritik u. kritische Antikritik', in idem, *Krisenherde des Kaiserreichs*, Göttingen 1979², pp. 404–26.

III.1.3

For a purely personalistic approach which minimises structural conditions and thus totally misses the importance of non-individual processes, see J. Röhl, *Germany after Bismarck*, London, 1967. For opposing views, see J. A. Nichols, *Germany After Bismarck 1890–94*, Cambridge/Mass., 1958; E. Eyck, *Das persönliche Regiment Wilhelms II*, Zürich, 1948; W. J. Mommsen, *Max Weber u. die deutsche Politik 1890–1920*, Tübingen, 1974²; R. Weitowitz, *Deutsche Politik u. Handelspolitik unter Reichskanzler L. v. Caprivi 1890–94*, Düsseldorf, 1978; P. Leibenguth, 'Modernisierungskrisis des Kaiserreichs an der Schwelle zum Wilhelminischen Imperialismus. Politische Probleme der Ära Caprivi 1890–1894', Diss., Cologne, 1972/1975; K. Saul, *Staat, Industrie u. Arbeiterbewegung im Kaiserreich. Zur Innen- u. Sozialpolitik des Wilhelminischen Deutschland 1903–1914*, Düsseldorf, 1974; E.T. Wilke, *Political Decadence in Imperial Germany 1894–1897*, Urbana, Ill., 1976; D. Grosser, *Vom monarchischen Konstitutionalismus zur parlamentarischen Demokratie*, The Hague, 1970; M. Rauh, *Föderalismus u. Parlamentarismus im wilhelminischen Reich 1890–1909*, Düsseldorf, 1972; idem, *Die Parlamentarisierung des Deutschen Reiches*, ibid. 1977; B. Heckart, *From Bassermann to Bebel. The Grand Bloc's Quest for Reform in the Kaiserreich 1900–1914*, New Haven, 1974; C. G. Crothers, *The German Elections of 1907*, New York, 1941; D. Fricke, 'Der deutsche Imperialismus u. die Reichstagswahlen 1907', in *ZfG*, 9, 1961, pp. 538–76; J. Bertram, *Die Wahlen zum Deutschen Reichstag vom Jahre 1912*, Düsseldorf, 1964; G. U. Scheideler, 'Parlament, Parteien u. Regierung im wilhelminischen Deutschland 1890–1914', in *Aus Politik u. Zeitgeschichte*, vol. 12/71, pp. 16–24; G. Schmidt, 'Innenpolitische Blockbildungen in Deutschland am Vorabend des Ersten Weltkriegs', in *Aus Politik u. Zeitgeschichte*, vol. 20/72, pp. 3–32; idem, 'Parlamentarisierung oder "Präventive Konterrevolution"? Die deutsche Innenpolitik im Spannungsfeld konservativer Sammlungsbewegungen u. latenter Reformbestrebungen 1907–1914', in G. A. Ritter (ed.), *Gesellschaft, Parlament u. Regierung*, Düsseldorf, 1974, pp. 249–78; H.-U. Wehler, 'Der Fall Zabern von 1913/14 als Verfassungskrise des Wilhelminischen Kaiserreichs', in idem, *Krisenherde des Kaiserreichs*, Göttingen, 1979², pp. 70–88.

III.1.4

R. Morsey, *Die oberste Reichsverwaltung unter Bismarck 1867–90*, Münster, 1957; J. Röhl, 'Beamtenpolitik im Wilhelminischen Deutschland', in *Das Kaiserliche Deutschland*, edited by M. Stürmer, Düsseldorf, 1970, pp. 287–311; E. Kehr, 'Das soziale System der Reaktion in Preußen unter dem Ministerium Puttkamer', in idem, *Der Primat der Innenpolitik*, edited by H.-U. Wehler, Berlin, 1965, 1976³, pp. 64–86; M. L. Anderson and K. Barkin, 'The Myth of the Puttkamer Purge and the Reality of the Kulturkampf: Some Reflections on the Historiography of Imperial Germany', in *JMH*, 54, 1982, pp. 647–86; G. Bonham, 'State Autonomy or Class Domination: Approaches to Administrative Politics in Wilhelmine Germany', in *World Politics*, 35, 1983, pp. 631–51; L. Schücking, *Die Reaktion in der inneren Verwaltung Preußens*, Berlin, 1908; L. W. Muncy, *The Junker in the Prussian Administration*.

1888–1914, Providence, 1944/New York, 1970; idem, 'The Prussian Landräte in the Last Years of the Monarchy, 1890–1918', in *Central European History*, 6, 1973, pp. 299–338; P.-C. Witt, 'Der preußische Landrat als Steuerbeamter 1891–1918', in *Fs. F. Fischer*, Düsseldorf, 1973, pp. 205–19; P. G. Lauren, *Diplomats and Bureaucrats*. *The First Institutional Response to 20th Century Diplomacy in France and Germany*, Stanford, 1976; L. Cecil, *The German Diplomatic Service, 1871–1914*, Princeton, 1976. General: W. Schluchter, *Aspekte bürokratischer Herrschaft*, Munich, 1972/Frankfurt, 1984; R. Mayntz (ed.), *Bürokratische Organisation*, Cologne, 1968; R. K. Merton et al. (eds.), *Bureaucracy*, New York, 1952.

III.2.1

W. Mommsen (ed.), *Deutsche Parteiprogramme*, Munich, 1960; G. A. Ritter and M. Niehuss, *Wahlgeschichtliches Arbeitsbuch*. *Materialien zur Statistik des Kaiserreichs 1871–1918*, ibid., 1980; idem (eds.), *Deutsche Parteien vor 1918*, Cologne, 1973; D. Fricke (ed.), *Die bürgerlichen Parteien in Deutschland, 1830–1945*, 2 vols., Leipzig, 1968, 1970; idem (ed.), *Deutsche Demokraten 1830–1945*, 1981; L. Bergsträsser and W. Mommsen, *Geschichte der politischen Parteien in Deutschland*, Munich, 1965[11]; W. Tormin, *Geschichte der deutschen Parteien seit 1848*, Stuttgart 1970[3]; T. Nipperdey, 'Über einige Grundzüge der deutschen Parteigeschichte', in *Moderne Deutsche Verfassungsgeschichte*, E.-W. Böckenförde and R. Wahl (eds.), Cologne, 1972/Königstein 1981[2], pp. 237–57; M. R. Lepsius, 'Parteiensystem u. Sozialstruktur', in *Fs. F. Lütge*, Stuttgart 1966, pp. 371–93; idem, 'Demokratie in Deutschland als historisch-soziologisches Problem', in *Spätkapitalismus oder Industriegesellschaft?*, T. W. Adorno (ed.), Stuttgart 1969, pp. 197–213; J. J. Sheehan, 'Klasse u. Partei im Kaiserreich: Einige Gedanken zur Sozialgeschichte der deutschen Politik', in O. Pflanze (ed.), *Innenpolitische Probleme des Bismarck-Reiches*, Munich, 1983, pp. 1–24; idem 'Political Leadership in the German Reichstag, 1871–1918', in *AHR*, 74, 1968, pp. 511–28; E. Pikart, 'Die Rolle der Parteien im deutschen konstitutionellen System vor 1914', in *Moderne Deutsche Verfassungsgeschichte*, E.-W. Böckenförde and R. Wahl (eds.), Cologne, 1972/Königstein, 1981[2], pp. 258–81; N. Diederich et al. (eds.), *Wahlstatistik in Deutschland. Bibliographie 1848–1975*, Munich, 1976; B. Vogel et al., *Wahlen in Deutschland 1848–1970*, Berlin, 1971; O. Büsch et al. (eds.), *Wählerbewegungen in der deutschen Geschichte 1871–1933*, ibid. 1978; idem, 'Parteien u. Wahlen in Deutschland bis zum Ersten Weltkrieg', in *Abhandlungen aus der Pädagogischen Hochschule Berlin*, I, Berlin, 1974, pp. 178–264. For the Liberals: J. J. Sheehan, *German Liberalism in the 19th Century*, Chicago, 1978; H. A. Winkler, *Liberalismus u. Antiliberalismus*, Göttingen, 1979; L. Gall (ed.), *Liberalismus*, Cologne, 1976/Königstein 1980[2]; idem and R. Koch (eds.), *Der europäische Liberalismus im 19. Jh.*, 4 vols., Frankfurt, 1981; W. J. Mommsen (ed.), *Liberalismus im aufsteigenden Industriestaat* = *Geschichte u. Gesellschaft*, 4, 1978/1; G. Seeber, *Zwischen Bebel u. Bismarck. Zur Geschichte des Linksliberalismus in Deutschland 1871–1893*, Berlin, 1965; J. S. Lorenz, *E. Richter 1871–1906*, Husum, 1981; A. Milatz, 'Die linksliberalen Parteien u. Gruppen in den Reichstagswahlen 1871–1912', in *Archiv für Sozialgeschichte*, 12, 1972, pp. 273–93; J. C. Hunt, *The People's Party in Württemberg and Southern*

Germany 1890–1914, Stuttgart, 1975; L. Elm, *Zwischen Fortschritt u. Reaktion. Geschichte der Parteien der liberalen Bourgeoisie in Deutschland 1893–1918*, Berlin, 1968; G. Schmidt, 'Die Nationalliberalen — eine regierungsfähige Partei? Zur Problematik der inneren Reichsgründung 1870–1878', in G. A. Ritter (ed.), *Deutsche Parteien vor 1918*, Cologne, 1973, pp. 208–23; D. S. White, *The Splintered Party: National Liberalism in Hessen and the Reich 1867–1918*, Cambridge, Mass., 1976; J. Thiel, *Die Großblockpolitik der Nationalliberalen Partei Badens 1905–1914*, Stuttgart 1976; G. R. Mork, 'Bismarck and the "Capitulation" of German Liberalism', in *JMH*, 43, 1971, pp. 59–75; S. Zucker, *L. Bamberger, 1823–1899*, Pittsburgh, 1975; J. J. Sheehan, 'Liberalism and the City in 19th Century Germany', in *Past & Present*, 51, 1971, pp. 116–37; K. Holl and G. List (eds.), *Liberalismus u. imperialistischer Staat. Der Imperialismus als Problem liberaler Parteien 1890–1914*, Göttingen, 1975.

For the Centre Party: K.-E. Loenne, *Politischer Katholizismus*, Frankfurt, 1985; J. Schauff, *Das Wahlverhalten der deutschen Katholiken im Kaiserreich u. in der Weimarer Republik, 1871–1928*, Mainz, 1975²; E. L. Evans, *The German Center Party 1870–1933*, Carbondale, Ill., 1981; R. J. Ross, *Beleaguered Tower: The Dilemma of Political Catholicism in Wilhelmian Germany*, Notre Dame, 1976; J. K. Zeender, *The German Center Party 1880–1906*, Philadelphia, 1976; M. L. Anderson, *Windthorst*, New York, 1981; W. Loth, *Katholiken im Kaiserreich. Der politische Katholizismus in der Krise des wilhelminischen Deutschland*, Düsseldorf, 1984; U. Mittmann, *Fraktion und Partei. Ein Vergleich von Zentrum und Sozialdemokratie im Kaiserreich*, Düsseldorf, 1976; K. Bachem, *Vorgeschichte, Geschichte u. Politik der deutschen Zentrumspartei 1814–1914*, 8 vols., Cologne, 1927/32/Aalen 1965²; D. Blackbourn, *Class, Religion and Local Politics in Wilhelmine Germany. The Centre Party in Württemberg Before 1914*, Wiesbaden, 1980; idem, 'The Problem of Democratisation: German Catholics and the Role of the Centre Party', in *Society and Politics in Wilhelmine Germany*, R. J. Evans (ed.), London 1978, pp. 160–85; idem, 'The Political Alignment of the Centre Party in Wilhelmine Germany', in *Historical Journal*, 18, 1975, pp. 821–50; idem, 'Class and Politics in Wilhelmine Germany: The Centre Party and the Social Democrats in Württemberg', in *Central European History*, 9, 1976, pp. 220–49; idem, 'Die Zentrumspartei u. die deutschen Katholiken während des Kulturkampfes u. danach', in O. Pflanze (ed.), *Innenpolitische Probleme des Bismarck-Reiches*, Munich, 1983; idem, 'Roman Catholics, the Centre Party and Anti-Semitism in Imperial Germany', in P. Kennedy and A. Nicholls (eds.), *Nationalist and Racialist Movements in Britain and Germany before 1914*, London, 1981, pp. 106–29; R. Morsey, 'Die deutschen Katholiken u. der Nationalstaat zwischen Kulturkampf u. dem Ersten Weltkrieg', in *Historisches Jahrbuch*, 90, 1970, pp. 31–64; H. Meier, 'Katholizismus, nationale Bewegung u. nationale Demokratie in Deutschland', in *Hochland*, 57, 1976, pp. 318–33.

For the Conservatives: J. Flemming, *Deutscher Konservativismus 1780–1980*, Frankfurt, 1985; H.-J. Puhle, *Deutscher Konservativismus*, Göttingen, 1985; idem, *Von der Agrarkrise zum Präfaschismus*, Wiesbaden, 1972; H. G. Schumann (ed.), *Konservativismus*, Cologne, 1974; S. Neumann, *Die Stufen des preußischen Konservativismus*, Berlin, 1930; H. Booms, *Die Deutsch-Konservative Partei*, Düsseldorf, 1954; G. Eley, *Reshaping the German Right*, New Haven, 1980; idem, 'Reshaping the Right', in *Historical Journal*, 21, 1978, pp. 327–54; idem, 'The Wilhelmine Right: How It Changed', in *Society and*

Politics in Wilhelmine Germany, R. J. Evans (ed.), London, 1978, pp. 112–35; D. Stegmann, 'Between Economic Interests and Radical Nationalism. Attempts to Found a New Right Wing Party in Imperial Germany 1887-97', in *Fs. O. Pflanze*, New York, 1984; idem, 'Vom Neokonservativismus zum Proto-Faschismus. Konservative Partei, Vereine u. Verbände 1893–1920', in *3. Fs. F. Fischer*, Bonn, 1983, 199–230; R. M. Berdahl, 'Conservative Politics and Aristocratic Landholders in Bismarckian Germany', in *JMH*, 44, 1972, pp. 1–20; A. J. Peck, *Radicals and Reactionaries: The Crisis of Conservativism in Wilhelmine Germany*, Washington, D.C., 1978. For the Social Democrats: J. Kocka, *Lohnarbeit u. Klassenbildung. Arbeiter u. Arbeiterbewegung in Deutschland 1800–1875*, Bonn, 1983; idem (ed.), *Europäische Arbeiterbewegungen im 19. Jh.*, Göttingen, 1983; G.A. Ritter, *Staat, Arbeiterschaft u. Arbeiterbewegung in Deutschland 1840–1933*, Berlin, 1980; D. Lehnert, *Deutsche Sozialdemokratie 1863–1983*, Frankfurt, 1983; J. Mooser, *Arbeiterleben in Deutschland. Klassenlage, Kultur u. Politik 1900–1970*, Frankfurt, 1984; H. Wachenheim, *Die deutsche Arbeiterbewegung 1844–1914*, ibid., 1971[2]; W. L. Guttsman, *The German Social Democractic Party 1875–1933*, London, 1981; D. Fricke, *Die deutsche Arbeiterbewegung 1869–1914*, Berlin, 1976; G. A. Ritter, *Die Arbeiterbewegung im wilhelminischen Reich 1890–1900*, ibid., 1963[2]; G. Roth, *Social Democrats in Imperial Germany*, Totowa, 1963; C. E. Schorske, *German Social Democracy 1905–1917*, Cambridge, Mass., 1955; D. Groh, *Negative Integration u. revolutionärer Attentismus, 1909–14*, ibid., 1973; I. Costas, *Auswirkungen der Konzentration des Kapitals auf die Arbeiterklasse in Deutschland 1880–1914*, Frankfurt, 1981; H. J. Steinberg, *Sozialismus u. deutsche Sozialdemokratie*, ibid., 1979[5]; W. H. Maehl, *A. Bebel: Shadow Emperor of the German Workers*, Philadelphia, 1980; H.-U. Wehler, *Sozialdemokratie u. Nationalstaat 1840–1914*, Würzburg, 1962/Göttingen, 1971[2]; H. Grebing, *Der Revisionismus*, Munich, 1977; V. L. Lidtke, *The Outlawed Party 1878–1890*, Princeton, 1966; R. J. Evans (ed.), *The German Working Class 1888–1933*, London, 1982; H. Mommsen, *Arbeiterbewegung u. Nationale Frage*, Göttingen, 1979; G. A. Ritter, *Arbeiterbewegung, Parteien u. Parlamentarismus*, ibid., 1976; G. Mayer, *Arbeiterbewegung u. Obrigkeitsstaat*, edited by H.-U. Wehler, Bonn, 1972; D. Geary, *European Labour Protest 1848–1939*, London, 1981/1984; G. A. Ritter (ed.), *Arbeiterkultur*, Königstein, 1979; J. Kocka (ed.), *Arbeiterkultur im 19. Jh.* = *Geschichte u. Gesellschaft*, 5, 1979/1; D. Langewiesche and K. Schönhoven (eds.), *Arbeiter in Deutschland*, Paderborn, 1981; K. Saul et al. (eds.), *Arbeiterfamilien im Kaiserreich 1871–1914*, Düsseldorf, 1982.

III.2.2

F. Blaich, *Staat u. Verbände in Deutschland 1871–1945*, Wiesbaden, 1979; H. J. Varain (ed.), *Interessenverbände in Deutschland*, Cologne, 1973; H.-P. Ullmann, 'Zur Rolle industrieller Interessenorganisationen in Preußen u. Deutschland bis zum Ersten Weltkrieg', in H.-J. Puhle and H.-U. Wehler (eds.), *Preußen im Rückblick = Geschichte u. Gesellschaft*, special issue 4, Göttingen, 1980, pp. 300–23; H.-J. Puhle, 'Parlament, Parteien u. Interessenverbände, 1890–1914', in *Das Kaiserliche Deutschland*, M. Stürmer (ed.), Düsseldorf, 1970, pp. 340–77; H. A. Winkler, 'Pluralismus oder Protektionismus? Verfassungspolitische Probleme des Verbandwesens im Deutschen Kaiserreich', in idem, *Liberalismus u. Antiliberalismus*, Göttingen, 1979, pp. 163–74; T. Nipperdey, 'Interessenverbände u. Parteien in Deutschland vor dem Ersten Weltkrieg', in H.-U. Wehler (ed.), *Moderne Deutsche Sozialgeschichte*, Cologne, 1966/Königstein 1981[6], pp. 369–88; W. Fischer, 'Staatsverwaltung u. Interessenverbände im Deutschen Reich 1871–1914', in idem, *Wirtschaft u. Gesellschaft im Zeitalter der Industrialisierung*, Göttingen, 1972, pp. 194–213; H. Kaelble, *Industrielle Interessenpolitik in der wilhelminischen Gesellschaft. Centralverband Deutscher Industrieller 1894-1914*, Berlin, 1967; idem, 'Industrielle Interessenverbände vor 1914', in W. Ruegg and O. Neuloh (eds.), *Zur soziologischen Theorie und Analyse des 19. Jahrhunderts*, Göttingen, 1971, pp. 180–92; P. Ullmann, *Der Bund der Industriellen*, ibid., 1976; S. Mielke, *Der Hansa-Bund für Gewerbe, Handel u. Industrie 1909-1914*, ibid., 1976; H. A. Winkler, 'Der rückversicherte Mittelstand: Die Interessenverbände von Handwerk u. Kleinhandel im Deutschen Kaiserreich', in idem, *Liberalismus u. Antiliberalismus*, ibid., 1979, pp. 83–98; H.-J. Puhle, *Politische Agrarbewegungen in kapitalistischen Industriegesellschaften*, ibid. 1976; idem, *Agrarische Interessenpolitik u. preußischer Konservativismus im wilhelminischen Reich 1893-1914*, Hanover, 1966, 1974[2]; idem, 'Der "Bund der Landwirte" im wilhelminischen Reich', in W. Ruegg and O. Neuloh (eds.), *Zur soziologischen Theorie u. Analyse des 19. Jh*, Göttingen, 1971, pp. 145-62; J. C. Hunt, 'The "Egalitarianism" of the Right. The Agrarian League in Southwest Germany 1893–1914', in *JCH*, 10, 1975, pp. 513–30. On the nationalist propaganda organisations, see below III, 3.2, 5.2, 6.3, as well as H.-U. Wehler, 'Historische Verbandsforschung. Zur Funktion u. Struktur nationaler Kampfverbände im Kaiserreich', in idem, *Historische Sozialawissenschaft u. Geschichtsschreibung*, Göttingen, 1980, pp. 151–60. For literature on the trade unions see under III.2.1 above, in particular: J. A. Moses, *German Trade Unionism from Bismarck to Hitler*, 2 vols., London, 1981; K. Saul, 'Gewerkschaften zwischen Repression u. Integration. Staat u. Arbeitskampf im Kaiserreich 1884–1914', in W. J. Mommsen and H.-G. Husung (eds.), *Auf dem Wege zur Massengewerkschaft, 1880-1914*, Stuttgart, 1984, pp. 433–53; G. A. Ritter and K. Tenfelde, 'Der Durchbruch der Freien Gewerkschaften zur Massenbewegung im letzten Viertel des 19. Jh.', in idem, *Arbeiterbewegung. Parteien u. Parlamentarismus*, Göttingen, 1976, pp. 55–101.

III.2.3

W. Sauer, 'Das Problem des Deutschen Nationalstaats', in H.-U. Wehler (ed.), *Moderne Deutsche Sozialgeschichte*, Cologne, 1966/Königstein, 1981[6], pp. 407–36; O. Pflanze, 'Bismarcks Herrschaftstechnik als Problem der gegenwärtigen Historiographie', in *HZ*, 234, 1982, pp. 561–99.

III.2.4

D. Stegmann, *Die Erben Bismarcks, Parteien u. Verbände in der Spätphase des wilhelminischen Deutschlands. Sammlungspolitik 1897–1918*, Cologne, 1970; idem, 'Wirtschaft u. Politik nach Bismarcks Sturz. Zur Genesis der Miquelschen Sammlungspolitik 1890–1897', in *1. Fs. F. Fischer*, Düsseldorf, 1974[2], pp. 161–84; O. Pflanze, ' "Sammlungspolitik" 1875–1886', in idem (ed.), *Innenpolitische Probleme des Bismarck-Reiches*, Munich, 1983, pp. 155–93. See also the general literature on political history above, III.1.1.

III.3.1

L. Krieger, *The German Idea of Freedom*, Boston, 1957/Chicago, 1972 and subs.; H. Plessner, *Die verspätete Nation*, Stuttgart, 1959[3]; K. D. Bracher, *Das Deutsche Dilemma*, Munich, 1971; F. Stern, *The Failure of Illiberalism*, N.Y. 1972; W. Struwe, *Elites against Democracy. Leadership Ideals in Bourgeois Political Thought in Germany 1890–1933*, Princeton, 1973; B. Loewenstein, 'Zur Problematik des deutschen Antidemokratismus', in *Historica*, 11, 1965, pp. 121–76; H. Lübbe, *Politische Philosophie in Deutschland*, Stuttgart, 1963; W. Gottschalch et al., *Geschichte der sozialen Ideen in Deutschland*, Munich, 1969; L. R. Pye and S. Verba (eds.), *Political Culture and Political Development*, Princeton, 1965.

III.3.2

P. Alter, *Nationalismus*, Frankfurt, 1985; H. A. Winkler (ed.), *Nationalismus*, Königstein, 1978; K. W. Deutsch, *Nationalism and Social Communication*, Cambridge, Mass., 1966[2]; H. Kohn, *Die Idee des Nationalismus*, Heidelberg, 1950 and subs.; G. L. Mosse, *Die Nationalisierung der Massen*, Berlin, 1976; T. Schieder, *Das deutsche Kaiserreich von 1871 als Nationalstaat*, Cologne, 1961; idem and O. Dann (eds.), *Nationale Bewegung u. soziale Organisation*, I, Munich, 1978; idem and P. Alter (eds.), *Staatsgründung u. Nationalitätenprinzip*, ibid., 1974; idem and P. Burian (eds.), *Sozialstruktur u. Organisation europäischer Nationalbewegungen*, ibid., 1971; H. A. Winkler, 'Vom linken zum rechten Nationalismus. Der deutsche Liberalismus in der Krise von 1878/79', in *Geschichte u. Gesellschaft*, 4, 1978, pp. 5–28; R. M. Berdahl, 'New Thoughts on German Nationalism', in *AHR*, 77, 1972, pp. 65–80; M. R. Lepsius, *Extremer Nationalismus*, Stuttgart, 1966; E. Kehr, 'Englandhaß u. Weltpolitik', in idem, *Der Primat der Innenpolitik*, edited by H.-U. Wehler, Berlin, 1965/1976[3], pp. 149–76; P. R. Anderson, *The Background of Anti-English Feeling in Germany 1890–1902*, New York, 1969[2].

III.3.3

R. Rürup and T. Nipperdey, 'Antisemitismus', in O. Brunner et al. (eds.), *Geschichtliche Grundbegriffe*, I, Stuttgart, 1972, pp. 129–53; A. A. Rogow, 'Anti-Semitism', in *IESS*, 1, 1968, pp. 345–49; H. Berding, *Deutscher Antisemitismus 1870–1980*, Frankfurt, 1984; B. Martin and E. Schulin (eds.), *Die Juden als Minderheit in der Geschichte*, Munich, 1981; M. Richarz (ed.), *Jüdisches Leben in Deutschland, II: 1871–1918*, Stuttgart, 1979; P. von zur Mühlen, *Rassenideologien*, Berlin 1979[2]; G. L. Mosse, *The Crisis of German Ideology*, London, 1966; R. Rürup, *Emanzipation u. Antisemitismus. Studien zur Judenfrage der bürgerlichen Gesellschaft*, Göttingen, 1975; idem (ed.), *Antisemitismus u. Judentum = Geschichte u. Gesellschaft*, 5, 1979/4; idem, 'Emanzipation u.

Krise. Zur Geschichte der "Judenfrage" in Deutschland vor 1890', in *Juden im wilhelminischen Deutschland 1890–1914*, Tübingen, 1976, pp. 1–56; U. Tal, *Christians and Jews in Germany 1870–1914*, Ithaca, 1974; P. Pulzer, *The Rise of Political Antisemitism in Austria and Germany*, New York, 1964; P. W. Massing, *Rehearsal for Destruction*, New York, 1967; A. Bein, 'Die Judenfrage in der Literatur des modernen Antisemitismus', in *Bulletin L. Baeck Institute*, 6, 1963, pp. 4–51; W. Boehlich (ed.), *Der Berliner Antisemitismus-Streit*, Frankfurt, 1965; R. Lill, 'Zu den Anfängen des Antisemitismus im Bismarck-Reich', in *Saeculum*, 26, 1975, pp. 214–31; H. M. Klinkenberg, 'Zwischen Liberalismus u. Nationalismus im deutschen Kaiserreich (1870-1918)', in *Monumenta Judaica*, Cologne, 1963, pp. 309–84; W. Mosse (ed.), *Die Juden im wilhelminischen Deutschland*, Tübingen, 1976; S. Volkov, 'Jüdische Assimilation u. jüdische Eigenart im Deutschen Kaiserreich', in *Geschichte u. Gesellschaft*, 9, 1983, pp. 331–48; R. S. Levy, *The Downfall of the Anti-Semitic Political Parties in Imperial Germany*, New Haven, 1975; R. Gutteridge, *The German Evangelical Church and the Jews 1879–1950*, New York, 1976; W. T. Angress, 'Prussia's Army and the Jewish Reserve Officer Controversy Before World War One', in J. J. Sheehan (ed.), *Imperial Germany*, New York, 1975, pp. 93–128. On the Poles, Alsatians and Danes and the nationalities question within the German Empire see also: M. Broszat, *200 Jahre deutsche Polenpolitik*, Frankfurt, 1972²; W. W. Hagen, *Germans, Poles, and Jews. The Nationality Conflict in the Prussian East 1772–1914*, Chicago, 1980; R. Blanke, *Prussian Poland in the German Empire 1871–1900*, New York, 1981; H. K. Rosenthal, *German and Pole. National Conflict and Modern Myth*, Gainesville, 1975; R. Baier, *Der deutsche Osten als soziale Frage. Eine Studie zur preußischen u. deutschen Siedlungs- u. Polenpolitik in den Ostprovinzen 1871–1933*, Cologne, 1980; A. Galos et al., *Die Hakatisten. Der Deutsche Ostmarkenverein 1894–1934*, Berlin, 1966; H.-U. Wehler, 'Polenpolitik im Deutschen Kaiserreich 1871–1918', in idem, *Krisenherde des Kaiserreichs*, Göttingen, 1979², pp. 184–202; W. Conze, 'Nationsbildung durch Trennung. Deutsche u. Polen im preußischen Osten', in O. Pflanze (ed.), *Innenpolitische Probleme des Bismarck-Reichs*, Munich, 1983, pp. 95–119; O. Hauser, 'Polen u. Dänen im Deutschen Reich', in *Reichsgründung 1870/71*, Stuttgart, 1970, pp. 291–318; D. P. Silverman, *Reluctant Union. Alsace-Lorraine and Imperial Germany 1871–1918*, London 1972; H.-U. Wehler, 'Das "Reichsland" Elsaß-Lothringen 1870–1918', in idem, *Krisenherde des Kaiserreichs*, Göttingen, 1979², pp. 23–69.

III.3.4

On the problems in general, see reference works such as *Religion in Geschichte und Gegenwart*, the *Staatslexikon* or the general bibliography above. More particularly: G. Brakelmann, *Kirche, Soziale Frage u. Sozialismus 1871–1914*, Gütersloh, 1977; K. Hammer, *Deutsche Kriegstheologie 1870–1918*, Munich, 1971/1974²; idem, 'Der deutsche Protestantismus u. der Erste Weltkrieg', in *Francia*, 2, 1975, pp. 398–414; W. Pressel, *Die Kriegspredigt 1914–18 in der evangelischen Kirche Deutschlands*, Göttingen, 1967; H. Missalla, *'Gott mit uns'. Die deutsche katholische Kriegspredigt 1914–18*, Munich, 1968; R. van Dülmen, 'Der deutsche Katholizismus u. der Erste Weltkrieg', in *Francia*, 2, 1975, pp. 347–76.

III.3.5

M. Horkheimer (ed.), *Studien über Autorität u. Familie*, Paris, 1936; U. Oevermann, *Sprache u. soziale Herkunft*, Frankfurt, 1972; M. Mitterauer and R. Sieder (eds.), *Historische Familienforschung*, ibid., 1982; idem, *Vom Patriarchat zur Partnerschaft*. *Zum Strukturwandel der Familie*, Munich, 1977/1980[2]; H. Reif (ed.), *Die Familie in der Geschichte*, Göttingen, 1982; H. Rosenbaum, *Formen der Familie (in der deutschen Gesellschaft des 19. Jh.)*, Frankfurt, 1982; N. Bulst et al. (eds.), *Familie zwischen Tradition u. Moderne*, Göttingen, 1981; W. Conze (ed.), *Sozialgeschichte der Familie in der Neuzeit Europas*, Stuttgart, 1976; H.-U. Wehler (ed.), *Historische Familienforschung = Geschichte u. Gesellschaft*, 1, 1975/ 2, 3; idem (ed.), *Frauen in der Geschichte des 19. u. 20. Jh. = Geschichte u. Gesellschaft*, 7, 1981/ 3, 4; B. Greven-Aschoff, *Die bürgerliche Frauenbewegung in Deutschland 1894–1933*, Göttingen, 1981; R. J. Evans, *The Feminist Movement in Germany 1894–1933*, London, 1976; J. Hardach-Pinke, *Kinderalltag 1700–1900*, Frankfurt, 1981; idem and G. Hardach (eds.), *Deutsche Kindheiten 1700–1900*, Kronberg, 1978; E.M. Johansen, *Betrogene Kinder*. *Eine Sozialgeschichte der Kindheit*, Frankfurt 1978; J. R. Gillis, *Youth and History 1770 to the Present*, New York, 1974.

Generally, on problems of education and the school system: F. Ringer, *Education and Society in Modern Europe*, Bloomington, 1979; idem, 'Bildung, Wirtschaft u. Gesellschaft in Deutschland 1800–1960', in *Geschichte u. Gesellschaft*, 6, 1980, pp. 5–35; H. G. Herrlitz et al., *Deutsche Schulgeschichte 1800–1980*, Königstein, 1981; P. Lundgreen, *Sozialgeschichte der deutschen Schule im Überblick. I: 1770–1918*, Göttingen, 1980; D. K. Müller, *Sozialstruktur u. Schulsystem*, ibid., 1977; F. Meyer, *Schule der Untertanen, Preußen 1848–1900*, Hamburg, 1976; W. Lexis (ed.), *Das Unterrichtswesen im Deutschen Reich*. 4 vols., Berlin, 1904; K. L. Hartmann et al. (eds.), *Schule u. Staat im 18. u. 19. Jh.*, Frankfurt, 1974; K.-H. Günther et al. *Geschichte der Erziehung*, Berlin, 1966[7]; H. König, *Imperialistische u. militaristische Erziehung in den Hörsälen u. Schulstuben Deutschlands 1870–1960*, ibid., 1962; R. Bölling, *Sozialgeschichte der deutschen Lehrer*, Göttingen, 1983; U. Walz, *Sozialgeschichte des Lehrers*, Heidelberg, 1981; H. Schallenberger, *Untersuchungen zum Geschichtsbild der Wilhelminischen Ära u. der Weimarer Republik*, Ratingen, 1964; D. Hoffmann, *Politische Bildung 1890–1933*, Hanover, 1971; P. Baumgart (ed.), *Bildungspolitik in Preußen zur Zeit des Kaiserreichs*, Stuttgart, 1980; U. Bendele, *Sozialdemokratische Schulpolitik u. Pädagogik im wilhelminischen Deutschland 1890–1914*, Frankfurt, 1979. See also especially: E. N. Anderson, 'The Prussian Volksschule in the 19th Century', in G. A. Ritter (ed.), *Fs. H. Rosenberg*, Berlin, 1970, pp. 261–79; W. C. Langsam, 'Nationalism and History in the Prussian Elementary Schools', in *Fs. C. Hayes*, New York, 1950, pp. 241–60.

For the grammar schools: M. Kraul, *Das deutsche Gymnasium 1780–1980*, Frankfurt, 1984; F. Paulsen, *Geschichte des gelehrten Unterrichts*, 2 vols., Berlin, 1919/21[3]; H. Romberg, *Staat u. höhere Schule 1800–1914*, Frankfurt, 1979; J. S. Albisetti, *Secondary School Reform in Imperial Germany*, Princeton, 1983; F. Ringer, 'Higher Education in Germany in the 19th Century', in *JCH*, 2, 1967, pp. 123–38. On the youth protest movement of the *Wandervogel* (which largely consisted of grammar school pupils) see: O. Neuloh and W. Zietus,

Die Wandervögel, Göttingen, 1982; U. Aufmuth, *Die deutsche Wandervogelbewegung*, ibid., 1979; J. Müller, *Die Jugendbewegung als deutsche Hauptrichtung neukonservativer Reform*, Zürich, 1971; W. Kindt (ed.), *Die Wandervogelzeit 1896–1919*, Düsseldorf, 1968; H. Pross, *Jugend, Eros, Politik*, Berne, 1964; W. Z. Laqueur, *Young Germany*, New York, 1962. For the universities: R. vom Bruch, *Deutsche Universitäten 1734–1980*, Frankfurt, 1985; C. E. McClelland, *State, Society, and University in Germany 1700–1914*, Cambridge, 1980; H.-W. Prahl, *Sozialgeschichte des Hochschulwesens*, Munich, 1978; H. Berding (ed.), *Universität u. Gesellschaft = Geschichte u. Gesellschaft*, 10, 1984/1; R. v. Westphalen, *Akademisches Privileg u. demokratischer Staat*, Stuttgart, 1979; W. Zorn, 'Hochschule u. höhere Schule in der deutschen Sozialgeschichte der Neuzeit', in *Fs. M. Braubach*, Münster, 1964, pp. 312–39; K. Jarausch, *Deutsche Studenten 1800–1980*, Frankfurt, 1984; idem, *Students, Society, and Politics in Imperial Germany. The Rise of Academic Illiberalism*, Princeton, 1982; idem (ed.), *The Transformation of Higher Learning 1860–1930*, Stuttgart, 1982; F. Ringer, *The Decline of the German Mandarins 1890–1933*, Cambridge, Mass., 1969; F. Pfetsch, *Zur Entwicklung der Wissenschaftspolitik in Deutschland 1750–1914*, Berlin, 1974; L. Burchardt, *Wissenschaftspolitik im wilhelminischen Deutschland*, Göttingen, 1975; R. Riese, *Die Hochschule auf dem Weg zum wissenschaftlichen Großbetrieb (Heidelberg 1860–1914)*, Stuttgart, 1977; P. Borscheid, *Entwicklung der Naturwissenschaften u. wissenchaftlich-technischen Revolution (Baden 1848–1913)*, Stuttgart, 1976; R. vom Bruch, *Wissenschaft, Politik u. öffentliche Meinung. Gelehrtenpolitik im wilhelminischen Deutschland 1890–1914*, Husum, 1980; D. Krüger, *Nationalökonomen im wilhelminischen Deutschland*, Göttingen, 1983; D. Fricke, 'Zur Militarisierung des deutschen Geisteslebens im wilhelminischen Kaiserreich. Der Fall L. Arons', in *ZfG*, 8, 1960, pp. 1069–1107. On student fraternities, see also Jarausch's works, as well as D. Grieswelle, 'Zur Soziologie des Kösener Corps 1870–1914', in C. Helfer and M. Rassem (eds.), *Student u. Hochschule im 19. Jh.*, Göttingen, 1975, pp. 346–65; H. John, *Das Reserveoffizierkorps im deutschen Kaiserreich 1890–1914*, Frankfurt, 1981; E. Kehr, 'Zur Genesis des Kgl. Preuß. Reserveoffiziers', in idem, *Der Primat der Innenpolitik*, edited by H.-U. Wehler, Berlin, 1965/1976[3], pp. 53–63.

III.3.6

E. Fraenkel, *Zur Soziologie der Klassenjustiz*, Berlin, 1927/Darmstadt 1968[2]; E. Kuttner, *Klassenjustiz*, Berlin, 1980; J. Wagner, *Politischer Terrorismus. Strafrecht im Deutschen Kaiserreich von 1871*, Heidelberg, 1981; D. Blasius, *Geschichte der politischen Kriminalität in Deutschland 1800–1980*, Frankfurt, 1983; L. Cecil, 'The Creation of Nobles in Prussia 1871–1918', in *AHR*, 75, 1970, pp. 757–95.

III.3.7

F. Tennstedt, *Sozialgeschichte der Sozialpolitik in Deutschland*, Göttingen, 1981; idem, 'Sozialgeschichte der Sozialversicherung', in *Handbuch der Sozialmedizin*, M. Blohmke et al. (eds.), III, Stuttgart, 1976, pp. 385–492; C. Sachße and F. Tennstedt, *Geschichte der Armenfürsorge in Deutschland bis 1914*, ibid., 1980; V. Hentschel, *Deutsche Sozialpolitik 1880–1980*, Frankfurt, 1983; idem, 'Das System der sozialen Sicherung in historischer Sicht 1800–1975', in *Archiv für Sozialgeschichte*, 18, 1978, pp. 307–52; A. Gladen, *Geschichte der deutschen Sozialpolitik bis zur Gegenwart*, Wiesbaden, 1974; W. Vogel, *Bismarcks Arbeiterversicherung*, Braunschweig, 1951; M. Stolleis, 'Die Sozialversicherung Bismarcks', in *H. F. Zacher* (ed.), *Bedingungen für die Entstehung u. Entwicklung von Sozialversicherung*, Berlin 1979, pp. 387–410; idem, '100 Jahre Sozialversicherung in Deutschland', in *Zeitschrift für die Ges. Versicherungswissenschaft*, 69, 1980, pp. 155–224; K. Saul, '100 Jahre Sozialversicherung in Deutschland. Wirtschafts- u. sozialpolitische Grundlagen. Industrialisierung, "Systemstabilisierung" u. Sozialversicherung', in ibid., pp. 155–224; F. Syrup and O. Neuloh, *100 Jahre staatliche Sozialpolitik 1839–1939*, Stuttgart, 1957; W. Junius and O. Neuloh, 'Soziale Innovation als Folge sozialer Konflikte: die Bismarckche Sozialgesetzgebung (Unfallversicherung)', in O. Neuloh (ed.), *Soziale Innovation u. sozialer Konflikt*, Göttingen, 1977, pp. 146–66; H.-P. Ullmann, 'Industrielle Interessen u. die Entstehung der deutschen Sozialversicherung 1880–89', in *HZ* 229, 1979, pp. 574–610; M. Breges, *Die Haltung der industriellen Unternehmer zur staatl. Sozialpolitik 1878–1891*, Frankfurt, 1982; J. Umlauf, *Die deutsche Arbeiterschutzgesetzgebung 1880–1980*, Berlin, 1980; K. E. Born, *Staat u. Sozialpolitik seit Bismarcks Sturz, 1890–1914*, Wiesbaden, 1957; G. A. Ritter, *Sozialversicherung in Deutschland u. England*, Munich, 1982; U. Frevert, *Krankheit als politisches Problem 1770–1880*, Göttingen, 1984; A. Berger-Thimme, *Wohnungsfrage u. Sozialstaat 1873–1918*, Frankfurt, 1976.

III.4.1

J. v. Kruedener, *Deutsche Finanzpolitik 1871–1980*, Frankfurt 1985; F. Terhalle, 'Geschichte der deutschen öffentlichen Finanzwirtschaft 1800–1945', in W. Gerloff (ed.), *Handbuch der Finanzwissenschaft*, I, Tübingen, 1952[2], pp. 274–326; W. Gerloff, 'Der Staatshaushalt u. das Finanzsystem Deutschlands 1820–1927', in idem (ed.), *Handbuch der Finanzwissenschaft*, III, ibid. 1929, pp. 1–69; idem, *Die Finanz- u. Zollpolitik des Deutschen Reiches 1867–1913*, Jena, 1913; P.-C. Witt, 'Finanzpolitik u. sozialer Wandel. Wachstum u. Funktionswandel der Staatsausgaben in Deutschland, 1871–1933', in *Sozialgeschichte Heute. Fs. H. Rosenberg*, H.-U. Wehler (ed.), Göttingen, 1974, pp. 565–74; idem, *Die Finanzpolitik des Deutschen Reiches 1903–13*, Lübeck, 1970.

III.4.2–3

A. Jeck, *Wachstum u. Verteilung des Volkseinkommens in Deutschland 1870–1913*, Tübingen, 1970, H.-J. Müller and S. Geisenberger, *Die Einkommensstruktur in verschiedenen deutschen Ländern 1874–1913*, Berlin, 1972; W. G. Hoffmann et al., *Das deutsche Volkseinkommen 1851–1955*, Tübingen, 1959; W. Fischer and P. Czada, 'Die soziale Verteilung von mobilem Vermögen in Deutschland seit dem Spätmittelalter', in *Third International Conference of Economic History*, Paris, 1968, pp. 253–304; T. Orsagh, 'Löhne in Deutschland 1871–1913', in *ZGS*, 125, 1969, pp. 476–83; A. Desai, *Real Wages in Germany 1871–1913*, Oxford, 1968; F. Grumbach and H. König, 'Beschäftigung u. Löhne der deutschen Industriewirtschaft 1888–1954', in *Weltwirtschaftliches Archiv*, 79, 1957/II, pp. 125–55.

III.5.1

G. A. Craig, *The Politics of the Prussian Army, 1640–1945*, Oxford, 1956; M. Geyer, *Deutsche Rüstungspolitik 1860–1980*, Frankfurt, 1983; *Handbuch der deutschen Militärgeschichte*, IV/1, 2: *1814–1890*, Munich, 1975, 1976; M. Kitchen, *A Military History of Germany From the 18th Century to the Present*, Bloomington, 1975; D. Bald, *Der deutsche Generalstab 1859–1939*, Munich, 1977; M. Messerschmidt, 'Preußens Militär in seinem gesellschaftlichen Umfeld', in H.-J. Puhle and H.-U. Wehler (eds.), *Preußen im Rückblick*, Göttingen, 1980, pp. 43–88; idem, *Militär u. Politik in der Bismarckzeit u. im wilhelminischen Deutschland*, Darmstadt, 1975; idem, 'Die Armee in Staat u. Gesellschaft', in *Das Kaiserliche Deutschland*, M. Stürmer (ed.), Düsseldorf, 1970 and subs., pp. 89–118; M. Stürmer, 'Militärkonflikt u. Bismarckstaat. Zur Bedeutung der Reichsmilitärgesetze 1874–1890', in *Gesellschaft, Parlament u. Regierung*, G. A. Ritter (ed.), ibid. 1974, pp. 225–48; W. Deist, 'Die Armee in Staat u. Gesellschaft 1890–1914', in *Das Kaiserliche Deutschland*, M. Stürmer (ed.), 1970 and subs., pp. 312–30; G. Ritter, *Staatskunst u. Kriegshandwerk*, vols. I, II, Munich, 1954, 1960; B.-F. Schulte, *Die Deutsche Armee 1900–1914*, Düsseldorf, 1977; E. Kehr, 'Klassenkämpfe u. Rüstungspolitik im kaiserlichen Deutschland', in idem, *Der Primat der Innenpolitik*, edited by H.-U. Wehler, Berlin, 1965/1976³, pp. 87–110; E. Höhn, *Sozialismus u. Heer*, 3 vols. ibid., 1959/69; W. Deist, 'Armee u. Arbeiterschaft 1905–1918', in *Francia*, 2, 1975, pp. 458–81; P.-C. Witt, 'Reichsfinanzen u. Rüstungspolitik 1898–1914', in *Marine u. Marinepolitik im kaiserlichen Deutschland 1871–1914*, H. Schottelius and W. Deist (eds.), Düsseldorf, 1972, pp. 146–77; K. E. Jeismann, *Das Problem des Präventivkriegs*, Freiburg, 1957; G. Ritter, *Der Schlieffenplan*, Munich, 1956; H.-U. Wehler, 'Vom "Absoluten" zum "Totalen" Krieg oder: Von Clausewitz zu Ludendorff', in idem, *Krisenherde des Kaiserreichs*, Göttingen, 1979², pp. 89–116; H. H. Hofmann (ed.), *Das deutsche Offizierkorps 1860–1960*, Boppard, 1980; M. Kitchen, *The German Officer Corps 1890–1914*, Oxford, 1968; K. Demeter, *Das Deutsche Offizierkorps in Gesellschaft u. Staat 1650–1945*, Frankfurt, 1965⁴; D. Bald, 'Sozialgeschichte der Rekrutierung des deutschen Offizierkorps von der Reichsgründung bis zur Gegenwart', in idem et al., *Zur sozialen Herkunft des Offiziers*, Munich, 1977, pp. 17–47; H. Rumschöttel, *Das bayerische Offizierkorps 1868–1914*, Berlin, 1973; G. Martin, *Die bürgerlichen Exzellenzen. Zur Sozialgeschichte der preußischen Generalität 1812–1918*, Düsseldorf, 1978; D. J. Hughes, 'Occupational Origins of Prussia's Generals 1871–1914', in *Central European History*, 13, 1980, pp. 3–33; J.-K. Zabel, *Das preußische Kadettenkorps*, Frankfurt, 1978.

III.5.2

J. Erickson and H. Mommsen, 'Militarismus', in *Sowjetsystem u. Demokratische Gesellschaft*, 4, 1971, pp. 528–68; V. R. Berghahn, *Militarism 1861–1979*, Leamington Spa, 1982; idem (ed.), *Militarismus*, Cologne, 1975; A. Vagts, *A History of Militarism*, New York, 1967³; K. Buchheim, *Militarismus u. ziviler Geist*, Munich, 1964; L. Quidde, 'Der Militarismus im heutigen deutschen Reich (1893)', in idem, *Caligula. Schriften über Militarismus u. Pazifismus*, edited by H.-U. Wehler, Frankfurt, 1977, pp. 81–130; H. Wiedner, 'Soldatenmißhandlungen im Wilhelminischen Kaiserreich 1890–1914', in *Archiv für Sozialgeschichte*, 22, 1982, pp. 159–200; K. Saul, 'Der "Deutsche Kriegerbund"', in *Militärgeschichtl. Mitteilungen*, 1969/II, pp. 95–130.

III.5.3

Following the pioneering studies by Kehr (E. Kehr, *Schlachtflottenbau u. Parteipolitik 1894–1901*, Berlin, 1930/Vaduz, 1965; idem, 'Soziale u. finanzielle Grundlagen der Tirpitzschen Flottenpropaganda', in idem, *Der Primat der Innenpolitik*, edited by H.-U. Wehler, Berlin, 1965/1976³, pp. 130–48; idem, 'Die deutsche Flotte in den 9oer Jahren u. der politisch-militärische Dualismus des Kaiserreichs', in idem, *Der Primat der Innenpolitik*, edited by H.-U. Wehler, Berlin, 1965/1976³, pp. 111–29) the apologias of Hubatsch have at last been disproved by critical analyses. See: V. Berghahn, *Der Tirpitz-Plan*, Düsseldorf, 1971; idem, 'Flottenrüstung u. Machtgefüge', in *Das Kaiserliche Deutschland*, M. Stürmer (ed.), ibid. 1970, pp. 378–96; idem, 'Zu den Zielen des deutschen Flottenbaus unter Wilhelm II.', in *HZ*, 210, 1970, pp. 34–100; H. Herwig, *'Luxury' Fleet. The Imperial German Navy 1888–1918*, London, 1980; idem, *The German Naval Officer Corps. 1890–1981*, Oxford, 1973; H. Schottelius and W. Deist (eds.), *Marine u. Marinepolitik im kaiserlichen Deutschland 1871–1914*, Düsseldorf, 1972; W. Deist, *Flottenpolitik und Flottenpropaganda. Das Nachrichtenbureau des Reichsmarineamtes 1897–1914*, Stuttgart, 1976; G. Eley, 'Sammlungspolitik, Social Imperialism and the Navy Law of 1898', in *Militärgeschichtl. Mitteilungen*, 1974/I, pp. 29–63; W. Marienfeld, *Wissenschaft u. Schlachtflottenbau in Deutschland 1897–1906*, Berlin, 1957; C. A. Gemzell, *Organization, Conflict, and Innovation. A Study of German Naval Strategic Planning 1888–1940*, Lund, 1974; J. Steinberg, *Yesterday's Deterrent. Tirpitz and the Birth of the German Battle Fleet*, London, 1965; H. Ehlert, 'Marine- u. Heeresetat im deutschen Rüstungsbudget 1898–1912', in *Marine Rundschau*, 75, 1978, pp. 311–23.

III.6.1–2

Comprehensive references to be found in both the above mentioned specialised bibliographies. Particularly recommended are: H.-U. Wehler (ed.), *Imperialismus*, Cologne, 1970/Königstein, 1979⁴; W. J. Mommsen (ed.), *Imperialismus*, Hamburg, 1977; idem (ed.), *Der Moderne Imperialismus*, Stuttgart, 1971; K. J. Bade, *Europäischer Imperialismus im Vergleich*, Frankfurt, 1985; R. v.Albertini and A. Wirz, *Europäische Kolonialherrschaft 1880–1940*,

Zürich, 1976; R. F. Betts, *The False Dawn. European Imperialism in the 19th Century*, Minneapolis, 1976; W. D. Smith, *European Imperialism in the 19th and 20th Centuries*, Chicago, 1982; V. G. Kiernan, *From Conquest to Collapse. European Empires 1815–1960*, New York, 1982; W. J. Mommsen, *Der europäische Imperialismus*, Göttingen, 1979; idem (ed.), *Imperialismus im Nahen u. Mittleren Osten = Geschichte u. Gesellschaft*, I, 1975/4; idem, *Imperialismustheorien*, Göttingen, 1980²; P. Hampe, *Die ökonomische Imperialismustheorie*, Munich, 1976; W. D. Smith, *The German Colonial Empire*, New York, 1978; H.-U. Wehler, *Bismarck u. der Imperialismus*, Cologne, 1969/Frankfurt, 1984⁵; H.-U. Wehler, 'Probleme des Imperialismus', in idem, *Krisenherde des Kaiserreichs*, Göttingen, 1979², pp. 117–38; idem, 'Bismarcks Imperialismus', in idem, *Krisenherde des Kaiserreichs*, ibid. pp. 139–65; idem, 'Deutscher Imperialismus in der Bismarckzeit', in ibid. pp. 309–36, 518–25; A. Wirz, 'Die deutschen Kolonien in Afrika', in idem and R. v.Albertini, *Europäische Kolonialherrschaft 1880–1940*, Zürich, 1976, pp. 302–27; K. J. Bade, 'Das Kaiserreich als Kolonialmacht: Ideologische Projektionen u. histor. Erfahrungen', in J. Becker and A. Hillgruber (eds.), *Die Deutsche Frage im 19. u. 20. Jh.*, Munich, 1983, pp. 91–108; idem, *F. Fabri u. der Imperialismus in der Bismarckzeit*, Zürich, 1975; J. L. D. Forbes, 'Social Imperialism and Wilhelmine Germany', in *Historical Journal*, 22, 1979, pp. 331–49; G. Eley, 'Social Imperialism in Germany', in *Fs. G. W. F. Hallgarten*, I. Geiss and J. Radkau (eds.), Munich, 1976 pp. 71–86; G. Eley, 'Defining Social Imperialism: Use and Abuse of an Idea', in *Social History*, 1, 1976, pp. 265–90; H.-C. Schröder, *Sozialismus u. Imperialismus*, Hanover, 1968/1975²; P. Winzen, *Bülows Weltmachtkonzept 1897–1901*, Boppard, 1977; G. Ziebura, 'Sozialökonomische Grundfragen des deutschen Imperialismus 1914', in *Sozialgeschichte Heute. Fs. H. Rosenberg*, H.-U. Wehler (ed.), Göttingen, 1974, pp. 495–524.

III.6.3

H.-U. Wehler, 'Sozialdarwinismus im expandierenden Industriestaat', in idem, *Krisenherde des Kaiserreichs*, Göttingen, 1979², pp. 281–89; H. W. Koch, *Der Sozialdarwinismus*, Munich, 1973; R. Chickering, *We Men Who Feel Most German. A Cultural Study of the Pan-German League 1886–1914*, London 1984; A. Kruck, *Geschichte des Alldeutschen Verbandes 1890–1939*, Wiesbaden, 1954; P. Kennedy and A. Nicholls (eds.), *Nationalist and Racialist Movements in Britain and Germany Before 1914*, London, 1982, pp. 1–20; E. Hartwig, 'Zur Politik u. Entwicklung des Alldeutschen Verbandes, 1891–1914', Diss., Jena, 1966, ms.; K. Schilling, 'Beiträge zu einer Geschichte des radikalen Nationalismus 1890–1909', Diss., Cologne, 1968.

III.7.1

A. Hillgruber, *Die gescheiterte Großmacht 1871–1945*, Düsseldorf, 1980; idem, 'Entwicklung, Wandlung u. Zerstörung des deutschen Nationalstaats 1871–1945', in *1871 — Fragen an die deutsche Geschichte*, Berlin, 1971 and subs., pp. 171–203; I. Geiss, *German Foreign Policy 1871–1914*, London, 1976; L. L. Farrar, *Arrogance and Anxiety. The Ambivalence of German Power 1848–1914*,

Iowa City, 1981; A. Mayer, 'Internal Crisis and War Since 1870', in C. L. Bertrand (ed.), *Situations Révolutionaires en Europe 1917–1922*, Quebec, 1977, pp. 201–38; A. Hillgruber, *Bismarcks Außenpolitik*, Freiburg, 1972; idem, 'Die "Krieg-in-Sicht"-Krise 1875', in *Fs. M. Göring*, Wiesbaden, 1968, pp. 239–53; H. Wolter, *Bismarcks Außenpolitik 1871–81*, Berlin, 1983; W. J. Mommsen, *Die latente Krise des Deutschen Reiches 1909–14*, Frankfurt, 1972; A Vagts, *Bilanzen u. Balancen. Aufsätze zur internationalen Finanz u. internationalen Politik*, edited by H.-U. Wehler, ibid. 1979; H.-U. Wehler, 'Moderne Politikgeschichte oder "Große Politik der Kabinette"?', in idem, *Krisenherde des Kaiserreichs*, Göttingen, 1979², pp. 383–403, 532–37.

III.7.2

H. Müller-Link, *Industrialisierung u. Außenpolitik. Preußen-Deutschland u. das Zarenreich 1860–1890*, Göttingen, 1977; H.-U. Wehler, 'Bismarcks späte Rußlandpolitik', in idem, *Krisenherde des Kaiserreichs*, ibid. 1979², pp. 166–83; C. Wegner-Korfes, 'Zur Geschichte des Bismarckschen Lombardverbots für russische Wertpapiere 1887-94', in *Jahrbuch für Wirtschaftsgeschichte*, 1982/III, pp. 55–78; H. Deininger, *Frankreich — Rußland — Deutschland 1871–1891*, Munich, 1982; G. F. Kennan, *The Decline of Bismarck's European Order 1875–1890*, Princeton, 1980²; A. Hillgruber, 'Deutsche Rußlandpolitik 1871-1918', in *Saeculum*, 27, 1976, pp. 94–108; idem, 'Die deutsch-russischen politischen Beziehungen 1887–1917', in *Deutschland u. Rußland im Zeitalter des Kapitalismus 1861–1914*, K. O. v.Aretin and W. Conze (eds.), Wiesbaden, 1977, pp. 207–20; P. M. Kennedy, *The Rise of the Anglo-German Antagonism 1860–1914*, London, 1980; E. Kehr, 'Deutsch-englische Bündnisprobleme der Jahrhundert wende', in idem, *Der Primat der Innenpolitik*, edited by H.-U. Wehler, Berlin 1965/1976³, pp. 176–83.

III.8.1

From among the many titles which continue to proliferate since the publication of Fritz Fischer's *Germany's War Aims in the First World War*, London 1967, see: idem, *War of Illusions*, London 1974. The new Fischer argument that the German Government purposefully pursued the unleashing of a major war from December 1912 onwards is unconvincing: F. Fischer, *Juli 1914: Wir sind nicht hineingeschlittert*, Reinbek, 1983. See also: V. R. Berghahn, *Germany and the Approach of War in 1914*, London, 1973; B. F. Schulte, *Vor dem Kriegsausbruch 1914*, Düsseldorf, 1980; idem, *Europäische Krise u. Erster Weltkrieg*, Frankfurt, 1983; D. Groh, ' "Je eher, desto besser". Innenpolitische Faktoren für die Präventivkriegsbereitschaft des Deutschen Reiches 1913/14', in *PVS*, 13, 1972, pp. 501–21; A. Gasser, 'Deutschlands Entschluß zum Präventivkrieg 1913/14', in *Fs. E. Bonjour*, I, Basle, 1968, pp. 173–224; W. Schieder (ed.), *Erster Weltkrieg*, Cologne, 1969; I. Geiss (ed.), *Juli 1914*, Munich, 1965; idem, *Das Deutsche Reich u. die Vorgeschichte des Ersten Weltkriegs*, ibid. 1978; idem, *Das Deutsche Reich u. der Erste Weltkrieg*, ibid., 1978; A. Hillgruber, *Deutschlands Rolle in der Vorgeschichte der beiden Weltkriege*, Göttingen, 1967/1979²; E. Zechlin, *Krieg u. Kriegsrisiko 1914–1918*,

Düsseldorf, 1979; J. Joll, *1914 — The Unspoken Assumptions*, London, 1968; F. Stern, 'Bethmann Hollweg and the War', in L. Krieger (ed.), *The Responsibility of Power*, London, 1968; K. Jarausch, *The Enigmatic Chancellor: Bethmann Hollweg and the Hubris of Imperial Germany*, New Haven, 1972; W. C. Thompson, *In the Eye of the Storm: K. Riezler and the Crisis of Modern Germany*, Iowa City, 1980; D. E. Kaiser, 'Germany and the Origins of the First World War', in *JMH*, 55, 1983, pp. 442–74; M. R. Gordon, 'Domestic Conflict and the Origins of the First World War. The British and the German Cases', in *JMH*, 46, 1974, pp. 191–226; K. v. See, *Die Ideen von 1789 u. 1914. Völkisches Denken in Deutschland*, Frankfurt, 1975; L. Burchardt, *Friedenswirtschaft u. Kriegsvorsorge. Deutschlands wirtschaftliche Rüstungsbestrebungen vor 1914*, Boppard, 1968; T. Wolff, *Tagebücher, 1914–1919*, 2 vols., edited by B. Sösemann, ibid. 1984; P. Kielsmansegg, *Deutschland u. der Erste Weltkrieg*, Frankfurt, 1968/Stuttgart, 1982²; F. Klein et al., *Deutschland im Ersten Weltkrieg*, 3 vols., Berlin, 1968/70; W. Deist (ed.), *Militär u. Innenpolitik im Weltkrieg*, 2 vols., Düsseldorf, 1970; A. Marwick, *War and Social Change in the 20th Century. A Comparative Study of Britain, France, Germany, Russia, and the United States*, London, 1974.

III.8.2

G. Hardach, *Der Erste Weltkrieg*, Munich, 1973; F. Lütge, 'Die deutsche Kriegsfinanzierung im Ersten u. Zweiten Weltkrieg', in *Fs. R. Stucken*, Göttingen, 1953, pp. 243–57; M. Lanter, *Die Finanzierung des Krieges*, Lucerne, 1950; G. F. Feldman, *Army, Industry, and Labor in Germany 1914–18*, Princeton, 1966; idem and H. Homburg, *Industrie u. Inflation 1916–1923*, Hamburg, 1977; idem, *Iron and Steel in the German Inflation 1916–1923*, Princeton, 1977; R. Andexel, *Imperialismus — Staatsfinanzen — Rüstung — Krieg*, Berlin, 1968; J. T. Shotwell (ed.), *Wirtschafts- u. Sozialgeschichte des Weltkriegs*, 11 vols. Stuttgart 1927/32.

III.8.3

Apart from the books by Fischer mentioned under III.8.1 on the war aims question, see in particular: W. J. Mommsen, 'Die deutsche Kriegszielpolitik 1914–18', in *Kriegsausbruch 1914*, Munich, 1967, pp. 60–100; K. H. Janssen, *Macht u. Verblendung. Kriegszielpolitik der deutschen Bundesstaaten 1914–18*, Göttingen, 1963; M. L. Edwards, *Stresemann and the Greater Germany 1914–18*, New York, 1963; J. Kocka, *Facing Total War. German Society 1914–1918*, Leamington Spa, 1984; H. Lebovics, *Social Conservatism and the Middle Classes in Germany 1914–33*, Princeton, 1969; F. Zunkel, *Industrie u. Staatssozialismus. Der Kampf um die Wirtschaftsordnung in Deutschland 1914–1918*, Tübingen, 1974; G. Schramm, 'Militarisierung u. Demokratisierung: Typen der Massenintegration im Ersten Weltkrieg', in *Francia*, 3, 1976, pp. 475–97; K. Schwabe, *Wissenschaft u. Kriegsmoral 1914–18*, Göttingen, 1969; F. Klein, 'Die deutschen Historiker im Ersten Weltkrieg', in J. Streisand (ed.), *Studien über die deutsche Geschichtswissenschaft*, II, Berlin, 1965, pp. 227–48; K. Saul, 'Jugend im Schatten des Krieges 1914–1918', in *Militärgeschichtl. Mitteilungen*,

1983/2, pp. 91–184; E. Johann, *Innenansicht eines Krieges 1914–18*, Frankfurt, 1968; M. Weber, *Ges. Politische Schriften*, Tübingen 1971³.

III.8.4–5

Excellent bibliographies in Kolb's volumes: *Vom Kaiserreich zur Weimarer Republik*, Cologne, 1972 (see above all the contributions by Sauer, Hunt, Kolb, Rürup, Grebing); idem, *Die Weimarer Republik*, Munich, 1984; U. Kluge, *Die Deutsche Revolution 1918/19*, Frankfurt, 1985. See, apart from *PVS*, special issue 2, 1970: F. L. Carsten, *Revolution in Mitteleuropa 1918–1919*, Cologne, 1973; H. A. Winkler, *Von der Revolution zur Stabilisierung. Arbeiter u. Arbeiterbewegung 1918–1924*, Berlin, 1984; idem, *Die Sozialdemokratie u. die Revolution von 1918/19*, ibid. 1980²; idem (ed.), *Sozialgeschichtliche Aspekte europäischer Revolutionen = Geschichte u. Gesellschaft*, 4, 1978/3; G. D. Feldman et al., *Die Massenbewegungen der Arbeiterschaft in Deutschland am Ende des Ersten Weltkriegs, 1917–20*, in *PVS*, 13, 1972, pp. 84–105; idem, *Vom Weltkrieg zur Weltwirtschaftskrise*, Göttingen, 1984; R. Rürup, *Probleme der Revolution in Deutschland 1918/19*, Wiesbaden, 1968; idem, 'Demokratische Revolution u. "dritter Weg". Die deutsche Revolution von 1918/19', in *Geschichte u. Gesellschaft*, 9, 1983, pp. 278–301; idem (ed.), *Arbeiter- u. Soldatenräte im rheinisch-westfälischen Industriegebiet. Studien zur Geschichte der Revolution 1918/19*, Wuppertal, 1975; E. Kolb, *Die Arbeiterräte in der deutschen Innenpolitik 1918/19*, Düsseldorf, 1962/Berlin, 1978; P. v.Oertzen, *Betriebsräte in der Novemberrevolution*, Düsseldorf, 1963/Berlin, 1976²; U. Kluge, *Soldatenräte u. Revolution 1918/19*, Göttingen, 1975; H.-J. Bieber, *Gewerkschaften in Krieg u. Revolution 1914–1920*, 2 vols., Hamburg, 1982; S. Miller, *Burgfrieden u. Klassenkampf. Die deutsche Sozialdemokratie im Ersten Weltkrieg*, Düsseldorf, 1974; idem, *Die Bürde der Macht. Die deutsche Sozialdemokratie 1918/20*, ibid., 1978; D. Lehnert, *Sozialdemokratie u. Novemberrevolution 1918/19*, Frankfurt, 1983; J. W. Mishark, *The Road to Revolution, German Marxism and World War I*, Detroit, 1967; C. Geyer, *Die revolutionäre Illusion*, W. Benz and H. Graml (eds.), Stuttgart, 1976; K. R. Calkins, *H. Haase*, Berlin, 1976; C. Bertrand (ed.), *Revolutionary Situations in Europe 1917–1922*, Quebec, 1977; V. Rittberger, 'Revolution and Pseudo-Democratization: The Foundation of the Weimar Republic', in G. Almond et al. (eds.), *Crisis, Choice, and Change*, Boston, 1973, pp. 285–391; W. Elben, *Das Problem der Kontinuität in der deutschen Revolution*, Düsseldorf, 1965; L. Haupts, *Deutsche Friedenspolitik 1918/19*, Düsseldorf, 1976; A. Rosenberg, *Entstehung u. Geschichte der Weimarer Republik*, Frankfurt, 1955 and subs.; H. Schulze, *Weimar. Deutschland 1917–1933*, Berlin, 1982; A. Decker, 'Die Novemberrevolution u. die Geschichtswissenschaft in der DDR', in *Internationale Wissenschaftliche Korrespondenz zur Geschichte der deutschen Arbeiterbewegung*, 10, 1974, pp. 269–94.

IV

On the problem of continuity from the Empire to 1945 see, above all: F. Fischer, *Bündnis der Eliten. Zur Kontinuität der Machtstrukturen in Deutschland 1871–1945*, Düsseldorf, 1979; idem, 'Zum Problem der Kontinuität in der

deutschen Geschichte von Bismarck zu Hitler', in *Studia Historica Slavo-Germanica*, 1, Posen, 1973, pp. 115–27; idem, 'Zur Problematik der Kontinuität in der deutschen Geschichte', in O. Franz (ed.), *Am Wendepunkt der europäischen Geschichte*, Göttingen, 1981, pp. 41–71; K.-H. Jarausch, 'From Second to Third Reich: The Problem of Continuity in German Foreign Policy', in *Central European History*, 12, 1979, pp. 68–82; A. Hillgruber, 'Kontinuität u. Diskontinuität in der deutschen Außenpolitik von Bismarck bis Hitler', in idem, *Großmacht u. Militarismus im 20. Jh.*, Düsseldorf, 1974, pp. 11–36; T. Nipperdey, '1933 u. die Kontinuität der deutschen Geschichte', in *HZ*, 227, 1978, pp. 86–111; idem, 'Probleme der Modernisierung in Deutschland', in *Saeculum*, 30, 1979, pp. 292–303; W. Alff, *Materialien zum Kontinuitätsproblem der deutschen Geschichte*, Frankfurt 1976. Surveys of the so-called 'Fischer controversy' (war aims and problems of continuity) since 1961 are to be found in W. Jäger, *Historische Forschung u. politische Kultur in Deutschland. Die Debatte 1914–1980 über den Ausbruch des Ersten Weltkriegs*, Göttingen, 1984; V. R. Berghahn, 'Die Fischer-Kontroverse — 15 Jahre danach', in *Geschichte u. Gesellschaft*, 6, 1980, pp. 403–19; idem, 'F. Fischer u. seine Schüler', in *Neue Politische Literatur*, 19, 1974, pp. 143–54; A. Sywottek, 'Die Fischer-Kontroverse', in *1. Fs. F. Fischer*, Düsseldorf, 1974², pp. 19–47; H. Wereszycki, 'From Bismarck to Hitler. The Problems of Continuity', in *Polish Western Affairs*, 14, 1973, pp. 19–32; I. Geiss, 'Die Fischer-Kontroverse', in idem, *Studien über Geschichte u. Geschichtswissenschaft*, Frankfurt, 1972, pp. 108–98; J. A. Moses, *The Politics of Illusion. The Fischer-Controversy in German Historiography*, London, 1975.
Criticism of this book may be found in: T. Nipperdey, 'Wehlers "Kaiserreich". Eine kritische Auseinandersetzung', in *Geschichte u. Gesellschaft*, 1, 1975, pp. 539–60; more comprehensive in: idem, *Gesellschaft, Kultur, Theorie*, Göttingen, 1976, pp. 360–89; H.-G. Zmarzlik, 'Das Kaiserreich in neuer Sicht?', in *HZ*, 222, 1976, pp. 105–26; idem, 'Das Kaiserreich als Einbahnstraße?', in K. Holl and G. List (eds.), *Liberalismus u. imperialistischer Staat*, Göttingen, 1975, pp. 62–71; E. Nolte, 'Deutscher Scheinkonstitutionalismus?', in idem, *Was ist bürgerlich?*, Stuttgart, 1979, pp. 179–208; D. Langewiesche, 'Das Deutsche Kaiserreich — Bemerkungen zur Diskussion über Parlamentarisierung u. Demokratisierung Deutschlands', in *Archiv für Sozialgeschichte*, 19, 1979, pp. 628–42; V. Hentschel, *Wirtschaft u. Wirtschaftspolitik im wilhelminischen Deutschland. Organisierter Kapitalismus u. Interventionsstaat?*, Stuttgart, 1978.
My reply, for the time being: H.-U. Wehler, 'Kritik u. Kritische Antikritik', in idem, *Krisenherde des Kaiserreichs*, Göttingen, 1979², pp. 404–26.

Index

Napoleon III, Louis Bonaparte, 26f.
57, 92, 132, 150
Naumann, Friedrich, 44, 75, 98, 167,
176, 196
Nietzsche, Friedrich, 179
Noske, Gustav, 158

von Oldenburg-Januschau, Elard, 56
Oncken, Hermann, 24

Peter the Great, Tsar, 211
Peters, Carl, 87, 175
Plessner, Helmuth, 180
von Posadowsky, Arthur, 135
von Puttkamer, Robert, 61, 66, 69,
80, 89, 108, 128f.

von Radowitz, Joseph M., 95
von Ranke, Leopold, 184
von Ratibor, Herzog, 199
Rathenau, Walther, 99, 106, 160,
203, 235
von Raumer, Karl O., 121
von Rechberg, Johann B., 20
Rehm, Hermann, 177
Renouvin, Pierre, 192
Richter, Eugen, 75, 147
Ridder, Helmut, 146
Riezler, Kurt, 218
Ritter, Gerhard, 155
von Rochau, Ludwig A., 179, 236
Rodbertus, Carl, 131
Röchling, Louis, 217
Roetger, Max, 217
von Roggenbach, Franz, 101
Rohrbach, Paul, 181
von Roon, Albrecht, 21, 24, 147,
157f.
Rosenberg, Arthur, 53, 220, 222
Rosenberg, Hans, 12, 174, 244
Rothfels, Hans, 61

von Scharnhorst, Gerhard, 22
Scheidemann, Philipp, 221
Schieder, Theodor, 112
von Schlieffen, Alfred, 150–4, 160,
169, 187, 198
von Schmoller, Gustav, 28, 47, 81,
95, 125, 132, 136, 237
von Scholz, Adolf H. W., 156
Schulze-Gävernitz, Gerhard, 41
Schumpeter, Joseph A., 41, 138

von Schwarzenberg, Felix, 20
von Schweinitz, Lothar, 56, 158, 188
von Siemens, Werner, 70, 217
Smith, Adam, 42
Spengler, Oswald, 179
Stahl, Friedrich J., 74
von Stauffenberg, Franz, 75
Stegmann, Dirk, 96
von Stein, Lorenz, 28
Stiehl, Anton W. F., 121
Stinnes, Hugo, 217, 225
Stoecker, Adolf, 79, 106
von Stolberg, Udo, 132
Stresemann, Gustav, 85, 218
von Struënsee, Karl G., 28
von Stumm, Carl F., 131
von Sybel, Heinrich, 90

von Tiedemann, Christoph, 87
von Tirpitz, Alfred, 63, 87, 97,
165–70, 176, 189, 196, 216F.
de Tocqueville, Alexis, 115
von Treitschke, Heinrich, 72, 106
Troeltsch, Ernst, 222, 224, 228
Trotsky, Leo, 225

von Unruh, Hans V., 19

St. Vallier, M., 56
Veblen, Thorstein, 9
Victoria, Crown Princess, 188
von Villers, Alexander, 29
Virchow, Rudolf, 125

Wagener, Hermann, 21, 131
Wagner, Adolph, 143
von Waldersee, Alfred, 151, 157f.,
177
Wallace, Alfred R., 180
Weber, Max, 41, 46, 53, 62, 67f., 120,
129, 176, 196, 237
von Wegerer, Alfred, 192
Wilhelm I, Kaiser, 56, 187
Wilhelm II, Kaiser, 62f., 64, 121, 135,
164f., 176, 245
Wilson, Woodrow, 218, 221
Windthorst, Ludwig, 116
Wolff, Theodor, 222

Ziekursch, Johannes, 232
Zöberlein, Ernst, 204